WEB-BASED LEARNING

THEORY, RESEARCH, AND PRACTICE

WEB-BASED LEARNING

THEORY, RESEARCH, AND PRACTICE

Edited by

Harold F. O'Neil
University of Southern California/CRESST

Ray S. Perez
Office of Naval Research

2006

LAWRENCE ERLBAUM ASSOCIATES, PUBLISHERS
Mahwah, New Jersey   London

Copyright © 2006 by Lawrence Erlbaum Associates, Inc.
All rights reserved. No part of this book may be reproduced in
any form, by photostat, microform, retrieval system, or any
other means, without prior written permission of the
publisher.

Lawrence Erlbaum Associates, Inc., Publishers
10 Industrial Avenue
Mahwah, New Jersey 07430
www.erlbaum.com

Cover design by Tomai Maridou

Library of Congress Cataloging-in-Publication Data

Web-based learning : theory, research, and practice / edited by
Harold F. O'Neil, Ray S. Perez.
    p. cm.
Includes bibliographical references and index.
ISBN 0-8058-5100-3 (alk. paper)
1. Web-based instruction. 2. Education—Computer network
resources. I. O'Neil, Harold F., 1943– II. Perez, Ray S.
LB1044.87.W436 2006
371.33'44678—dc22
                                                2005052310
                                                        CIP

Books published by Lawrence Erlbaum Associates are printed on
acid-free paper, and their bindings are chosen for strength and
durability.

Printed in the United States of America
10 9 8 7 6 5 4 3 2 1

To our wives
Eva L. Baker and Dorothy A. Lange
who by their support have made this book a reality

Contents

Preface:
Web-Based Learning: Theory, Research, and Practice[1]

Edited by

Harold F. O'Neil
University of Southern California/CRESST

and

Ray S. Perez
Office of Naval Research

Web-based learning: Theory, research, and practice is designed for professionals and graduate students in the educational technology, human performance, assessment and evaluation, vocational/technical, and educational psychology communities. It explores the state of the art in the research and use of technology in education and training from a learning perspective. Theoretical, research, and practice issues are explored.

An Office of Naval Research/National Science Foundation conference on this topic was held in Redondo Beach, California, and chaired by the editors. The purpose of the conference was to assess the state of the art in learning and technology and its implications for Web-based learning. The initial

[1]The work reported herein was supported in part by the Office of Naval Research, under Award No. N00014-04-1-0209 and Award No. N00014-02-1-0179, and in part by the National Science Foundation, under Grant No. 0307027. Any opinions, findings, and conclusions or recommendations expressed in this material are those of the author(s) and do not necessarily reflect the views of the Office of Naval Research or the National Science Foundation.

assessment was accomplished in the conference setting and involved many of the leading thinkers in technology and education. The experts were from government (both Department of Defense and civilian sectors) and academia. Technology (both hard and soft) was characterized from a series of different theoretical and empirical viewpoints. The major issue was learning, not hardware/software per se. To reflect insights from the conference on their work, following the conference, authors wrote the chapters that comprise this book.

The book addresses several important issues. These are (a) the primacy of learning as a focus for technology; (b) the need to integrate technology with high standards and content expectations; (c) the paucity of and need to support the development of technology-based curriculum and tools; (d) the need to integrate assessment in technology and improve assessment through the use of technology; and (e) the need for theory-driven research and evaluation studies to increase our knowledge and efficacy.

This edited book is divided into three major sections: (a) Policy, Practice, and Implementation Issues, (b) Theory and Research Issues, and (c) Summary and Conclusions. The Policy, Practice, and Implementation section includes an overview of policy issues informed by an evidence-based focus as well as tools and designs to facilitate implementation of Web-based learning. The Theory and Research Issues section provides different "takes" on possible theoretical foundations of current and future Web-based learning. The section also includes empirical studies of Web-based learning. This is followed by the Summary and Conclusions section, which attempts to highlight key issues in each chapter and outlines a research and development agenda in this area.

This book could not have come into existence without the help and encouragement of many people. Our thanks to our Lawrence Erlbaum Associates editors, Lane Akers and Lori Kelly, for their support and guidance in the publication process. We thank Ms. Joanne Michiuye and Ms. Katharine Fry for their excellent assistance in preparing the manuscript.

—*Harold F. O'Neil*
Los Angeles
—*Ray S. Perez*
Arlington, Virginia

Part I

POLICY, PRACTICE, AND IMPLEMENTATION ISSUES

Chapter 1

Evaluating Web-Based Learning Environments

Eva L. Baker
UCLA/National Center for Research on Evaluation, Standards, and Student Testing (CRESST)

Harold F. O'Neil
University of Southern California/CRESST

Despite best efforts, technology-based innovations seem to have persistently avoided significant, innovative evaluation. Standard approaches, perhaps spiced with a Web-site survey of satisfaction (Kirkpatrick, 1994; Sugrue & Kim, 2004), dominate evaluation for those cases where evaluation rises to attention. Why is this so? Part of the problem is the speed of technology development, and the difficulty of conducting evaluations of learning as deadlines loom. But there may be other reasons, related to tradition, novelty, unrealized claims, or the obviousness of a good idea, that inhibit evaluation of Web-based learning environments. Web systems have not yet been caught up in the wave of results-based activity that has hit hard the schools, business, and the military, in spite of the availability of several versions of evaluation or accountability standards (e.g., Baker & Linn, 2004; Joint Committee on Standards for Educational Evaluation, 1981; Stufflebeam, 2004). This chapter is intended to describe Web-based evaluation, how it could work, and at what points of entry the process may begin. Two preliminaries are required: First, we delimit the realm of Web-based learning so it is sensible to describe its evaluation approaches; second, we clarify the meanings we ascribe (but which vary by community) to common evaluation terms.

WHAT COUNTS AS WEB-BASED LEARNING?

When "Web-based learning" is used, a range of environments may come to mind. In Table 1.1, we list nine somewhat overlapping conceptions of Web-based learning, varying from "traditional" or more formal uses to environments where learning is incidental to achieving other goals. One frequent type of Web-based learning is that focused on formal courses. In this case, the term is sometimes used synonymously with distance learning, where a course (either academic or professional development) is wholly or significantly resident on a Web site, and where particular course objectives are partially or entirely intended to be met by sequenced instructional interventions. A second variation is blended courses, any of which may have varying degrees of instruction provided online with a significant component of personal, teacher, classroom, or peer support. A third form of Web-

TABLE 1.1
Nine Types of Web-Based Learning Experiences

1. Formal course or module of distance learning—goal focused and wholly delivered through a distributed network. Place and time of instruction partially unconstrained.

2. Blended course—goal focused, core instructional delivery and interaction is shared by live and computer-supported instruction. Some synchronous instruction required.

3. Technology-supported courses—course materials, assignments, chat and other features are available to augment a traditional live teacher, but the balance is on live instruction

4. Technology-enriched environments—practice opportunities or simulations particularly for subtasks are provided by the Web. Most instruction is live.

5. Discretionary Web activity—enrichment or other activities supporting computer literacy skills.

6. Tool use—learning that occurs related to the use of interactive tools involving search, document preparation, and spreadsheet and database design and collaborative work.

7. Focused games and simulations—goal focused or goal emergent with a set of learning expectations including content, strategy, and persistence.

8. Exploratory games and simulations—goal-focused, emergent, and unpredictable learnings occur; processes outcomes with opportunities to investigate relationships among procedures, constraints, and processes.

9. Domain specific incidental learning—relevant to learning rules and rewards of using (usually) commercial sites.

based learning involves the provision of course support materials, feedback, and opportunities for interaction by distance, but with the majority of instruction taking place in face-to-face, unmediated environments. Such is the case, for instance, in many university courses. A fourth form involves isolated units of instruction, where the majority of the course is offered in its traditional live form, but there is a particular component intended for practice or enrichment that is available on the Web. These four types of distance learning are used in business, in the military, and at postsecondary as well as in elementary or secondary schools. A fifth type (Web-based experiences, in contrast to more formal, purpose-driven uses) may also take place in formal school-like settings, but possesses more diffuse goals. For example, permitting children to play with drawing programs, matching games, or voluntary choices of software may have the consequence of meeting general goals of computer literacy (using a mouse, starting, stopping, finding one's folders), as well as supporting incidental learning inherent in the program.

A sixth variation of Web-based learning occurs with the use of tools that may serve both formal and informal goals. Students' use of word processing, browsers, spreadsheets, and the like may be motivated by particular assignments but may also provide practice in fluency of use of computer software. Strategies for search, planning, and feedback in addition to the content addressed are often supported by tools.

A seventh, important Web-based approach falls under the growing use of games and simulations to provide complex practice environments or to teach specific planned goals. These games, developed for commercial distribution, may involve role playing, strategy planning and execution, and collaboration (or conflict) with other users. Games, which are highly motivational, often include competitive components and almost unlimited paths, and require significant inferences to be made about the environment. The simulation component creates lifelike stimuli and complexity for learning. The eighth approach involves less goal-oriented games and simulations, where the lesson is to acquire particular processes so that the learner has complex understanding of the processes needed for success. Frequently the learner is encouraged to explore the effects of modifying variables, or the simulation gives the learner even greater opportunity to design the circumstances in which he is involved.

A ninth type of Web-based learning occurs in the process of using systems intended to accomplish ends other than learning. Informal or instrumental learning follows from an eBay user's experiences (learning when to bid, how to check the seller's credentials, the social expectations of that community), and learners may be rewarded or punished by the consequences (forgetting to ask if "new" meant "seconds" or to check the cost of the shipping). The myriad opportunities for e-commerce or e-information bring with them the fluency with particular procedures, driven by desires to accomplish specific ends (e.g., buy a computer). Evaluation here is through self-assessment—Did I get what I thought? and did I pay more than the others?

Terms Used in the Domain

Within a particular community, it is assumed that technical terms have similar meaning. For example, in the education world, for almost 40 years, summative evaluation (Scriven, 1967) has signified judgments made as a basis for comparative decisions, to choose a course of action for competitive interventions. The term "formative evaluation" has a slightly broader interpretation, including reviews of data related to interim or desired outcomes, arrangements of settings and instructional sequences, and achievement of different groups. Nonetheless, the core meaning remains that coined by Susan Meyer Markle, also many years ago (1967), that is, developmental testing, (i.e., testing in the process of developing a program, system, or intervention), whose purpose is to improve the functioning and impact of instruction.

Formative testing, or formative assessment, is a more recent entry (Black & Wiliam, 1998; Pellegrino, Chudowsky, & Glaser, 2001) and refers to the use of interactions of teacher and student to make judgments about student understanding and the next useful learning experience. In technical systems, Mislevy, Steinberg, Breyer, Almond, and Johnson (1999), following on the work of artificial intelligence-supported tutors (Anderson, 1983; Corbett, Koedinger, & Anderson, 1997), described the updating of a student model as formative. Student models are the sum of inferences made about an individual's learning, based on his or her responses to tasks, tests, and other program-based information. These models may be based on theoretical progress toward an expert's level of attainment, documented paths that have led to different levels of success (Vendlinski & Stevens, 2000), or probability estimates related to a network of student responses (Mislevy et al., 1999).

Variations also involve the use of terms intended to mean the measurement of achievement. Testing and assessment are almost synonymous in education, with the nuance that testing has a harder edge and a sometimes more standardized connotation. Similarly, achievement and performance are used interchangeably in education, with the nuance that performance may connote constructed or demonstrated learning, including physical skill. Evaluation in education is used to describe judgments of status about programs, institutions, and individuals for the purpose of improvement (formative) or decisions (summative). The notion of research—randomized field trials of interventions—is one notion of evaluation (Cook & Campbell, 1979; Freeman & Sherwood, 1970). Although randomized field trials are the gold standard of "research" design (as has been true at least since the days of R. A. Fisher—see Fisher, 1951), current usage focuses on decisions to be made, rather than on conclusions to be drawn, a distinction made in a landmark volume by Cronbach and Suppes (1969), and on interventions rather than on operationalized variables, much like the early days of evaluation (Freeman & Sherwood). In practice, differences in usage of terms can create confusion. For instance, the term "performance" in some military settings not only signals the "doing" of tasks, but also specifies their setting—on-the-job. It would follow, to a military trainer, that performance tests or assessments could never occur in school-like venues, but only in ongoing job settings.

To further confuse the issue, the military and some business enterprises frequently use the term "assessment" to mean the evaluation of programs, policies, or interventions, as in technology assessment (Baker & O'Neil, 1994; O'Neil & Baker, 1994). So to assess training does not necessarily include or exclude the measurement of individual or team achievement or performance. It might mean review the status or content of a program. In addition, computer scientists have their own spin on these topics, with assessment and performance sometimes focusing on questions of preferences and performance as it refers to computer software systems rather than to individuals (O'Neil & Baker).

All of that said, it would be desirable to standardize language across groups, both to facilitate interactive communication and to allow appropriate inferences to be drawn from research and development in adjacent fields. The best we can do is to specify how we use terms here:

Formative evaluation is information obtained during the developmental stages of a product or system, used to revise the system with the intention of making it more effective and/or less costly. Minimally, formative evaluation should address interim and targeted learner outcomes.

Summative evaluation is comparative study, typically of contending programs, usually requiring strong research designs (experimental), criterion measures that span goals of contending interventions, verification of treatment or program implementation, and results used to make choices of programs for goals, groups, or settings. Cost is usually an important factor.

Performance refers to a product that is created or a process that is available for observation. Constructed response(s), usually multistep, are made by the learner.

Assessment is measuring through systematic approaches the achievement, affective states, or performance of individuals or groups.

EVALUATING WEB INTERVENTIONS: GOALS

What should evaluation of Web-based learning try to achieve? One clear directive is that it should authenticate claims that the provided interactions result in planned outcomes; that is, allegations that students learn something are supported.

Moreover, in considering different types of evaluation practice, we link them to the nine types of evaluation in Table 1.1.

Systematic Studies

The first class of studies are those that are tightly designed; they have identified goals, measures, and often instrumentation to gather process findings. For the most part, they are implemented as other evaluations, pretests, interim measures, posttests, measures of satisfaction [these correspond to Kirkpatrick's (1994) first two levels of evaluation—reaction vs. attitude and learning]. Web-based evaluation can make this a simpler task (for instance, learners can easily be placed in variations of treatment without much trouble, and their responses to exercises or tests unobtrusively tabulated). These evaluations, however, can be troublesome to administer, with some problem in finding comparable control groups (particularly for technically demanding tasks), problems of persistence, too few students to infer much about patterns of engagement, and so on. We have been successful in using temporary employment agencies to select groups to which we could administer, modify or withhold treatment. Such an approach is partially successful but never mirrors the exact characteristics of the desired learner (in a job setting or voluntarily taking a course—in fact, paying for it) Also, because using "temps" costs money, replicating efforts of an entire term's costs is enormously expensive. For that reason, many studies of courses— the first three types of Web-based learning—are more typically evaluated by having individuals work through components. The most frequent option is post hoc designs.

Post Hoc Evaluation

Evaluations conducted without much scientific flavor, and after the fact correspond to Cook and Campbell's (1979) most flawed design. People are asked how they reacted to course components and may be given a posttest related to information thought to be important. They may be followed up in the future to see on-the-job activities presumably influenced by the intervention. These approaches correspond vaguely to Kirkpatrick's (1994) formulation of evaluation. But they need three conditions to be met: (a) The comparison of observed performance has to be calibrated against something—weakest is prior performance of trainees, nonequivalent control groups come next, and a real randomized experiment (using the unit of randomization as the one in the analysis) would be helpful; (b) Clear statement of the intended outcomes (this is a hard one for many Web-based interventions); and (c) Developed measures of performance would count as making significant progress toward expertise envisioned.

Summative Approaches to Evaluation

Many Web-based evaluations are conducted in a post hoc manner, that is, a completed system or course is tested, sometimes in a comparative way, sometimes just as a simple post hoc study. Why? The system takes time and energy to be created. Bugs have to be discovered and fixed. The priority often is getting a course up and running by the time students are to be there. As a result, there may be little time for the niceties of good evaluation. Sometimes the course examination that has been used for non-Web-supported instruction becomes the examination for the posttest. The consequences of this decision reduce pressure on the evaluator and provide for a basis of comparison that is widely used (but deeply flawed)—that is, the comparison between Web-based and regular instruction. Most seriously, however, such examinations may miss the specific benefits thought to accrue by the Web environment, for instance, looking at student productions in terms of increased use of external resources, and the like. Most of these types of evaluations are summative in orientation, and focus on what was intended and what was learned.

Formative Approaches to Evaluation

Formative evaluation can be thought to comprise a number of different processes and is useful for all types of evaluation in Table 1.1. First there is opinion of experts, invoked at the design and development phases. Most Web interventions are evaluated by review and opinion. Experts may review content, technology specialists may review functionality and ease of operations, adopters will review effectiveness criteria, and potential users or administrators will review based on opinion. Formative evaluation has been difficult to carry out because many Web interventions do not have specific goals associated with them. They support exploration (a valuable part of education), but may operate under the assumption that they are a *de facto* good, and that their existence, without crashing excessively, is tantamount to success. It is also true that it may be impossible to forecast the full range of uses that learners or participants may develop. They may find new, creative approaches to individual, interactive, or group participation.

Formative evaluation may mean evaluation intended to help the developer revise instruction or the structure of the intervention. It may focus on directing the student to go through various pathways to reach desired levels of competence. Even when we are unable to identify the full range of potential outcomes, the evaluator is not incapacitated. There may be valuable skills and propensities of known or probable importance, independent of whether people learn particular content or strategies. These might include search strategies (Klein, Yarnall, & Glaubke, 2003), help dependencies (Tobias, in press), interaction with others, metacognitive skills (O'Neil, 1999), and the like. Some researchers have developed multiple approaches for capturing patterns of performance, key strokes, and attentional measures, for a few, that could be studied on-the-fly with an eye toward making changes (Chung & Baker, 2003; Vendlinski et al., 2004) A simple and frequently used strategy in the game world is to observe play and then debrief or question players to determine not only the game features that assist or impede performance, but also the strategic and fun elements. Game developers frequently enlist their selected subjects (often sophisticated with games) to suggest options that might make a game work better or be more fun to play.

Three things impede evaluation of Web-based interventions. The first is timing, for example, competitive or commercial, the need to be first (and then fix up bugs that are noticed). The second is the developers' potential need to control evaluation outcomes, where the scientific goals and commercial goals may come directly into conflict. The third is that evaluations, even those with the most benign intentions, invariably turn up some information that is regarded as "damaging" to the claims made, and may add time to fix. It is possible that not only the developer wishes to avoid these problems, but also the funders, particularly if the Web-based intervention makes its case on its production values rather than on its demonstrated instructional effectiveness. Of course, it is inevitable—or at least highly possible—that visible interventions lacking objective evaluation may later be shown to be ineffective; those concerns often do not carry much weight. Thus, the next set of precepts are experiential or clinically based on an experience and are offered to help increase the credibility and utility of serious evaluation in a Web-based world.

Avoiding Damaging Studies

How to avoid studies that damage interventions or innovations, and poison the well for new settings or users of technology of learning? Other than not doing such studies, there are a few key precepts.

1. Do not evaluate the outcomes of unstable systems.
   - Content yourself with assessing interim goals, quality of instructional science underlying the implementation, appropriateness for the setting. Otherwise the report will be sodden with comments about inability to replicate, unreliable recognition engines, and frustrating interfaces (Baker & Herman, 2003).

2. When the system is medium-mature (it works for more than 10 people), be judicious in your selection of outcome measures.
   - Select, or more likely design, outcome measures that are consistent with realistic expectations of the Web-based system (rather than relying on its rhetorical claims).
   - Avoid standardized measures at early stages of development, because despite the allure of normed comparison data, they are unlikely to measure the effects of your Web-based system and more likely to give you a measure of who your learners are (e.g., their prior knowledge or socioeconomic status).
3. Become colleagues of the program developer because improvement is a shared goal.
   - This is a tough one. Evaluators will have to show that they can add value (within the time period allocated) to program developers, should the developers be interested in formative improvement. Evaluators have to be friendly, learn as much as possible about the intervention, but avoid being coopted so that the study they do is ultimately discredited as or seen as biased.
   - In reports, however, the evaluator must provide a balance of rhetoric for the developer and use words to modify descriptions of negative or absent functions such as "as yet," "not that we could find," and "apparently" to illustrate both the temporality of the evaluation—that is, things can be fixed—as well as the inherent fallibility of evaluators, to avoid a did–didn't confrontation with the developer. In particular, such language choice encourages the developer to improve rather than to present a hardened positive but unrealistic view of the system.
   - Try to focus on *why* outcomes, positive and negative, are likely to have occurred.

DESIGN ARCHITECTURES FOR EVALUATION

To create an architecture for the evaluation of Web environments, key principles must be represented (however they are actually operationalized in observations and evaluation designs and inferences). The evaluation architecture represents the key structural arrangement of inferences about degrees of effectiveness. We present three architectures to represent somewhat separable units of the evaluation.

The typical flow chart for evaluation involves description of tasks from a high-level general perspective, where the goals, design, implementation, evaluation, and revision are presented as large blocks of action within a generally clockwise loop. This approach typically assumes a clean, progressive plan, where goals are fixed before instruction is designed, measures are developed, learners are engaged, data are collected, and inferences are drawn. It seems to us, however, that architectures for evaluation are best developed from the perspective of particular actors within the environment. These actors could be the user, the designer, or the funder, with deep layers depicting certain functions within the development, for instance, graphics design.

As an exploration, we present architectures from each of these perspectives and describe constructs that may be salient to each of the key actors. It should be obvious, however, that if one quickly, creatively, and efficiently develops a course or other Web-based implementation that attracts learners and leads to documented learning, the architectures may be superfluous. However, we believe that they are worth considering in the case of implementations that do not instantly reach success.

What should an architecture do? The evaluation architectures should allow evaluators and commissioners of evaluation to clarify the attributes of evaluation of greatest importance to them. The architecture serves three functions; first, it is a graphical display of functional relationships suggesting order of action. Second, it is a representation of priority concerns from different perspectives, for instance the salience of schedule versus the salience of effectiveness. Third, it represents the structural relationship of tasks, including their hierarchy within the evaluation process. Although it may be argued that these general attributes apply to evaluation of Web-based programs, school-based systems, or technical training components, the resistance in general to evaluation in Web environments (so far) and the dual confounds of the speed of technological change and the competitive, commercial options make this evaluation context somewhat more challenging.

User-Centered Evaluation Architecture

The first microarchitecture, user-centered evaluation (Fig. 1.1), focuses on evaluation from the perspective of the user. Each node specifies desirable information for the evaluation. The user domain specifies the motivation and the background of the user. It leads to information about how user access is stimulated or acquired, and who the main types of users are (or their experience, cognitive, and motivational backgrounds). It also describes the degree or degrees of control over the user (are they required to do this to complete a qualification, as part of a course, as part of the expectations for employees?). The user background also helps specify the nature of the learner goals from the perspective of the user's benefit.

Note that there is no specification of learning conditions in themselves, but rather the evaluation looks to determine the extent to which the "black box" allowed learners to attain their qualifications, under what condition,

FIG. 1.1.   User-centered evaluation architecture.

and documents acquisition of goals through process and outcome measures. Learner satisfaction and learning are measured and feed into user benefit. This microarchitecture focuses its priorities on the characteristics, features, and reactions of users as they attain their goals.

Designer-Centered Evaluation Architecture

Designer-centered evaluation (Fig. 1.2) posits some level of success by users, but the attention here is from the viewpoint of the designer confronted with a project, with real time, real or limited staff capacities, and a budget. In this environment, the evaluator is interested in determining whether the project is organized in such a way to take advantage of extant expertise, whether it is able to capture compatible techniques that may offer advantages, how the developer manages cycle time (that is, versions), and whether strategies are used to improve decisions about cost of modifying core designs, interfaces, or content. What might have been added here has been the publicity-seeking behavior of some developers as they create small com-

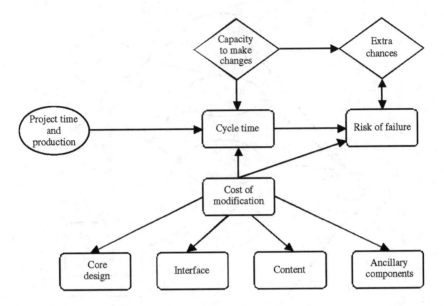

FIG. 1.2.   Designer-centered evaluation architecture.

ponents. The press releases and demonstrations to important others also create an interesting momentum, one that may draw attention away from the desired learner outcomes, and toward the degree to which a Web-based system can develop a particularly difficult sort of voice recognition or other technology application. The goal of evaluation of this sort is to understand the developer's or project manager's behavior so that guidelines or recommendations may be provided. Of particular interest to an evaluator is what happens for those projects that fail, either because they are very high risk, circumstances change, or the project is unable to map its capacities adequately to needs.

Funder-Centered Evaluation Architecture

The third microarchitecture (shown in Fig. 1.3) is that of funder-centered evaluation. This type of evaluation has been used to describe whether it is feasible to evaluate a proposed intervention. This architecture is most useful to funders or decision makers.

From the funder's perspective, it first focuses on the potential audiences for the system and for reports about the system given the intended utility. It is concerned about whether there is sufficient access and knowledge to

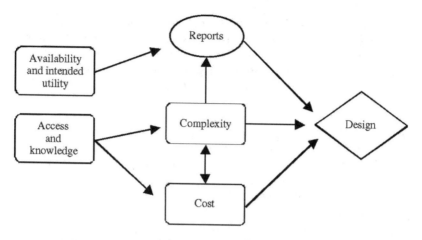

FIG. 1.3.   Funder-centered evaluation architecture.

build, trial, and revise the system. These important decisions are influenced by the complexity of the intervention and the cost of accomplishing the outcomes. The decision here is not whether students have learned or reached their qualification, but rather whether the project should be continued, expanded, or dropped.

The challenge for evaluators of Web-based environments is that their customer is nominally the developer, ultimately the funder, and tacitly the learner, and the timeline for all decisions proceeds at a far more rapid pace than educational or social evaluations in the past.

The operational struggle is how to address with appropriate attention, with limited time and financial resources, the elements of evaluation so that good short-term decisions will be made about the intervention under study, and knowledge about project management, funder's needs, and long-term evaluation improvement will also occur.

Certainly there are not enough interesting examples of Web-based evaluations with a range of viewpoints to allow a compendium of guidance. Instead, we meld together some recommendations that from our collective experience seem to hold promise, but we do not claim that we can offer either logical or empirical proofs in their support. To that end, we include two examples from *What Works in Distance Learning: Guidelines* (O'Neil, 2005) to show the more empirical perspective in this area. Then we offer our clinical perspective.

As the research community often knows more (i.e., the state of the art) than the practice community (i.e., the state of the practice), it is useful to capture the state of the art in terms of evaluation guidelines. O'Neil (2005) has edited a set of guidelines on what works in distance learning. A subset of these guidelines regarding formative and summative evaluation is shown in Figs. 1.4 and 1.5. A consistent format is followed—that is, the text of the guideline itself; whether the guideline was based on theory or research; the guideline author's degree of confidence (high vs. medium vs. low) in the

Strategies Based on Formative Evaluation
(Baker, Aguirre-Muñoz, Wang, & Niemi, v.11, 4/29/04)

1. Guideline:	Formative evaluation provides information that focuses on improvement of an innovation and is designed to assist the developer.
2. Guideline based on:	Theory and research
3. Degree of confidence:	High
4. Comments:	Formative evaluation is a method that was created to assist in the development of instructional (training) programs. While the evaluation team maintains quasi objectivity, they typically interact with and understand program goals, processes, and constraints at a deeper level than evaluation teams focused exclusively on bottom-line assessments of success or failure (i.e., outcomes-only, summative evaluation). Their intent is to assist their client (either funding agency or project staff) in using systematic data collection to promote the improvement of the effort.
	Formative evaluation efforts are instituted at the outset of the development of an innovation and have a different purpose than summative evaluation. Formative evaluation addresses the effectiveness of the development procedures used, in order to predict whether the application of similar approaches is likely to have effective and efficient results. In that function, formative evaluation seeks to improve both the technology at large and the specific instances, addressed one at a time. The formative evaluation approach is designed so that its principal outputs are identification of the degree of success and failure of segments, components, and details of programs, rather than a simple, overall estimate of project success. This approach requires that data be developed to permit the isolation of elements for improvement and, ideally, the generation of remedial options to assure that subsequent revisions have a higher probability of success.
	Formative evaluation is strong in identifying what to do if the new system is not an immediate, unqualified success. Given that this state is most common in early stages of development, comparative, summative-type evaluations are usually mis-timed and may create an unduly negative environment for productivity. Furthermore, because summative evaluation is typically not designed to pinpoint weaknesses and explore potential remedies, it provides almost no help in the development/improvement cycle that characterizes the systematic creation of new methods.
5. References:	Baker, E. L. (1974). Beyond objectives: Domain-referenced tests for evaluation and instructional improvement. In W. Hively (Ed.), *Domain-referenced testing* (pp. 16-30). Englewood Cliffs, NJ: Educational Technology Publications.
	Baker, E. L. (1988). Evaluating new technology: Formative evaluation of intelligent computer-assisted instruction. In R. J. Seidel & P. D. Weddle (Eds.), *Computer-based instruction in military environments* (pp. 155-162). New York: Plenum Publishing.
	Baker, E. L., & Herman, J. L. (in press). Technology and evaluation. In G. Haertel & B. Means (Eds.), *Approaches to evaluating the impact of educational technology*. New York: Teachers College Press.
6. Glossary:	*Formative evaluation:* Begins and ends in the developmental stage of the program evaluation. It improves the program by providing information on implementation and progress (Baker, 1974).
	Summative evaluation: Evaluation designed to present conclusions about the merit or worth of an object and recommendations about whether it should be retained, altered, or eliminated (see *Glossary of evaluation terms.* Kalamazoo: Western Michigan University, Evaluation Center. Retrieved July 26, 2002, from http://ec.wmich.edu/glossary). The final evaluation that determines whether the program has succeeded in reaching its goals and whether it should be implemented.
7. User:	Program manager, assessment designer

FIG. 1.4.   Strategies based on formative evaluation.

Strategies Based on Summative Evaluation
(Baker, Aguirre-Muñoz, Wang, & Niemi, v.12, 2/18/04)

1. Guideline:	Summative evaluation should assist decision makers in their decisions on whether they should select, continue, modify, or drop a program.
2. Guideline based on:	Theory and research
3. Degree of confidence:	High
4. Comments:	Test performance should be used in decisions judging the utility, appropriateness, implementation, and quality of the outcome of a program, usually in a comparative research design, contrasting performance of trainees under different training experiences, and evaluating them using common measures. Evaluate distance learning efforts using measures of implementation, outcomes, efficiencies, satisfaction, and long-term impact.
	The issue of the effect of learning via distance using technology is still problematic, with one of the problems being that current research is not providing sufficiently robust data. A majority of articles on distance education are opinion pieces and how-to-do-it articles. Mixed results of actual research may be explained by the fact that the research is based on individual case studies, qualitative data, or self-report studies. Many studies in distance learning indicate that teaching and learning at a distance is as effective as traditional classroom instruction and results in high satisfaction when compared to traditional approaches. There is the call to incorporate evaluation models, such as Kirkpatrick's (1994) four-level approach.
	After deciding on the purposes or goals of the evaluation, the decision makers should narrow the assessment search, define the target population, the program participants, what should be evaluated, and the population to which the results are to be generalized. The cost and credibility of adopting an existing test meeting program purposes or goals should be compared with the cost of designing, administering, and reporting a new test. Summative evaluation can be supplemented with formative evaluation.
5. References:	American Educational Research Association, American Psychological Association, & National Council on Measurement in Education. (1999). *Standards for educational and psychological testing.* Washington, DC: American Educational Research Association. Baker, E. L. (1974). Beyond objectives: Domain-referenced tests for evaluation and instructional improvement. In W. Hively (Ed.), *Domain-referenced testing* (pp. 16-30). Englewood Cliffs, NJ: Educational Technology Publications. Berge, Z. L., & Mrozowski, S. (2001). Review of research in distance education, 1990-1999. *American Journal of Distance Education, 13*(3), 5-19. Kirkpatrick, D. L. (1994). *Evaluating training programs: The four levels.* San Francisco: Berrett-Koehler.
6. Glossary:	*Formative evaluation:* Begins and ends in the developmental stage of the program evaluation. It improves the program by providing information on implementation and progress (Baker, 1974).
	Kirkpatrick's four levels: A four-level model consisting of (1) reaction, (2) learning, (3) transfer, and (4) results. According to this model, evaluation should always begin with level one and then, as time and budget allow, should move sequentially through levels two, three, and four. [Hoffman, B. (Ed.). (2004). *Encyclopedia of educational technology.* San Diego, CA: San Diego State University, Department of Educational Technology. Retrieved July 26, 2002, from http://ccoe.sdsu.edu/eet]
	Summative evaluation: Evaluation designed to present conclusions about the merit or worth of an object and recommendations about whether it should be retained, altered, or eliminated (see *Glossary of evaluation terms.* Kalamazoo: Western Michigan University, Evaluation Center. Retrieved July 26, 2002, from http://ec.wmich.edu/glossary). The final evaluation that determines whether the program has succeeded in reaching its goals and whether it should be implemented.
7. User:	Program manager, assessment designer

FIG. 1.5.   Strategies based on summative evaluation.

guideline; seminal or recent references to provide empirical evidence for the guideline and comments on it; a glossary, provided for jargon used in the guideline or comments; and finally a specification of the intended user(s) of the guideline.

CLINICALLY BASED GUIDELINES FOR EVALUATION

Clinically based guidelines for evaluation are the same for many targets, including distance learning. For example, be honest, justify conclusions or recommendations with data.

Participating in a Formative Evaluation of a Web-Based System

Design
- Size evaluation structure to available cost.
- Assume a supportive rather than a skeptical position.
- Begin early so that you can influence design and goals.
- Get early agreement on levels of effort and contingencies for program delays, especially those that might require you to retain staff through periods of development.
- Conduct studies with long and shorter intervals of engagement.
- Vary subjects to match claimed target users.

Measure
- Help, if possible, in the design of measures of effectiveness, at both the process and the product level.
- Use dependent measures with strict and relaxed standards.
- Use more than one measure for any key area.
- Avoid one-item scales ("I liked this exercise").
- Assist developers to monitor engagement through instrumented and qualitative approaches.

Reporting
- Verify your conclusions by having one or more independent reviewers, ideally representing the development community, the funding community, and evaluators.
- Give the developer a chance to respond to drafts if at all possible.

SUMMARY

In this chapter, we first describe overlapping conceptions of Web-based learning and then offer some clarification (we hope) of terms used in the Web-based learning domain. Using these conceptions and terms, we offer goals for the evaluation of Web-based instruction that result in either systematic studies or post hoc evaluations. Both formative and summative approaches to the evaluation of Web-based learning are described in both empirical and clinical terms. Finally, we suggest several kinds of design architecture (i.e., user centered, designer centered, or funder centered).

ACKNOWLEDGMENTS

Eva L. Baker, UCLA National Center for Research on Evaluation, Standards, and Student Testing (CRESST); Harold F. O'Neil, Rossier School of Education, University of Southern California, and CRESST.

The work reported herein was supported in part under Office of Naval Research Award Number N00014-04-1-0209 to the National Center for Research on Evaluation, Standards, and Student Testing (CRESST), as administered by the Office of Naval Research, and in part under the Educational Research and Development Centers Program, PR/Award Number R305B960002, as administered by the Institute of Education Sciences (IES), U.S. Department of Education. The findings and opinions expressed in this publication do not reflect the positions or policies of the Office of Naval Research, the National Center for Education Research, the Institute of Education Sciences, or the U.S. Department of Education.

REFERENCES

Anderson, J. (1983). *The architecture of cognition.* Cambridge, MA: Harvard University Press.

Baker, E. L., & Herman, J. L. (2003). A distributed evaluation model. In G. Haertel & B. Means (Eds.), *Evaluating educational technology: Effective research designs for improving learning* (pp. 95–119). New York: Teachers College Press.

Baker, E. L., & Linn, R. L. (2004). Validity issues for accountability systems. In S. Fuhrman & R. Elmore (Eds.), *Redesigning accountability systems for education* (pp. 47–72). New York: Teachers College Press.

Baker, E. L., & O'Neil, H. F., Jr. (Eds.). (1994). *Technology assessment in education and training.* Hillsdale, NJ: Lawrence Erlbaum Associates.

Black, P., & Wiliam, D. (1998). Assessment and classroom learning. *Assessment in Education, 5,* 7–74.

Chung, G. K. W. K., & Baker, E. L. (2003). An exploratory study to examine the feasibility of measuring problem-solving processes using a click-through interface. *Journal of Technology, Learning, and Assessment, 2*(2). Retrieved August 14, 2005, from http://jtla.org

Cook, T. D., & Campbell, D. T. (1979). *Quasi-experimentation: Design and analysis issues for field settings.* Boston: Houghton Mifflin.

Corbett, A. T., Koedinger, K. R., & Anderson, J. R. (1997). Intelligent tutoring systems. In M. G. Helander, T. K. Landauer, & P. V. Prabhu (Eds.), *Handbook of human–computer interaction* (pp. 849–874). Amsterdam, The Netherlands: Elsevier.

Cronbach, L. J., & Suppes, P. (Eds.). (1969). *Research for tomorrow's schools: Disciplined inquiry for education* (Report of the National Academy of Education, Committee on Educational Research). New York: Macmillan.

Fisher, R. A., Sir. (1951). *The designs of experiments* (6th ed.). Edinburgh, UK: Oliver and Boyd.

Freeman, H. E., & Sherwood, C. C. (1970). *Social research and social policy.* Englewood Cliffs, NJ: Prentice-Hall.

Joint Committee on Standards for Educational Evaluation. (1981). *Standards for evaluations of educational programs, projects, and materials*. New York: McGraw-Hill Book Co.

Kirkpatrick, D. L. (1994). *Evaluation training programs. The four levels*. San Francisco, CA: Berrett-Koehler Publishers.

Klein, D. C. D., Yarnall, L., & Glaubke, C. (2003). Using technology to assess students' Web expertise. In H. F. O'Neil, Jr. & R. S. Perez (Eds.), *Technology applications in education: A learning view* (pp. 305–320). Mahwah, NJ: Lawrence Erlbaum Associates.

Markle, S. M. (1967). Empirical testing of programs. In P. C. Lange (Ed.), *Programmed instruction: Sixty-sixth yearbook of the National Society for the Study of Education, Part II* (pp. 104–140). Chicago: National Society for the Study of Education.

Mislevy, R. J., Steinberg, L. S., Breyer, F. J., Almond, R. G., & Johnson, L. (1999). A cognitive task analysis with implications for designing simulation-based performance assessment. *Computers in Human Behavior, 15*, 335–374.

O'Neil, H. F., Jr. (1999). Perspectives on computer-based performance assessment of problem solving: Editor's introduction. *Computers in Human Behavior, 15*, 255–268.

O'Neil, H. F., Jr. (Ed.). (2005). *What works in distance learning: Guidelines*. Greenwich, CT: Information Age Publishing Inc.

O'Neil, H. F., Jr., & Baker, E. L. (Eds.). (1994). *Technology assessment in software applications*. Hillsdale, NJ: Lawrence Erlbaum Associates.

Pellegrino, J., Chudowsky, N., & Glaser, R. (Eds.). (2001). *Knowing what students know: The science and design of educational assessments* (Committee on the Foundations of Assessment; Board on Testing and Assessment, Center for Education. Division on Behavioral and Social Sciences and Education, National Research Council). Washington, DC: National Academy Press.

Scriven, M. (1967). The methodology of evaluation. In R. W. Tyler, R. M. Gagné, & M. Scriven (Eds.), *Perspectives of curriculum evaluation* (American Educational Research Association Monograph Series on Curriculum Evaluation, No. 1, pp. 39–83). Chicago: Rand McNally.

Stufflebeam, D. L. (2004). A note on the purposes, development, and applicability of the Joint Committee evaluation standards. *American Journal of Evaluation, 25*(1), 99–102.

Sugrue, B., & Kim, K.-H. (2004). *ASTD 2004 state of the industry report*. Alexandria, VA: American Association for Training and Development.

Tobias, S. (in press). The importance of motivation, metacognition, and help seeking in web-based learning. In H. F. O'Neil, Jr. & R. Perez (Eds.), *Web-based learning: Theory, research, and practice*. Mahwah, NJ: Lawrence Erlbaum Associates.

Vendlinski, T. P. J. F., Munro, A., Pizzini, Q. A., Bewley, W. L., Chung, G. K. W. K., Stuart, G., et al. (2004). Learning complex cognitive skills with an interactive job aid. *Proceedings of the I/ITSEC, 26*, Orlando, FL.

Vendlinski, T., & Stevens, R. (2000). The use of artificial neural nets (ANN) to help evaluate student problem solving strategies. In B. Fishman & S. O'Conner-Divelbliss (Eds.), *Proceedings of the fourth international conference of the learning sciences* (pp. 108–114). Mahwah, NJ: Lawrence Erlbaum Associates.

Chapter 2

Infrastructure
for Web-Based Learning

Kenneth E. Lane
California State University, San Bernardino

Stephen Hull
California State University, San Bernardino

The introduction of the World Wide Web several years ago presented many exciting opportunities and challenges for learning institutions. In the dot-com heyday, some described scenarios where all training would occur online and brick-and-mortar institutions would at best consolidate to a best of breed. Just as e-Toys did not replace Toys-R-Us in the commercial world, e-learning has not replaced traditional delivery methods. However, just as commercial retail stores offer Web-based access to their products and services, many institutions have moved to the Web for delivering courses at varying levels because it offers convenience, lower cost, and the ability to deliver to nontraditional learners. Web-based learning options now range from assisting traditional courses (gradebook, discussion forums, etc.) to delivering complete, online degree programs with minimal or no same-place student–instructor interactions.

To support these types of learning environments, several in-house and commercial products have emerged as part of the complete Web-based learning solution. Some vendors strive to provide a complete integrated solution whereas others are established as leaders in niche markets like content management, portal systems, and back-end student records systems. However, the market has yet to consolidate to a small handful of vendors with complete, best-of-breed solutions and there is no indication that it is moving in that direction yet. The fact that there are no quality single vendor solutions requires institutions to take components of functionality and "glue" them together to meet the institution's specific needs. These solutions commonly include a variety of commercial products, open-source solutions, and in-house development. Because there are no single-vendor, one-size-fits-all solutions, organizations must mix and match commercially available and homegrown components to satisfy their requirements.

This process constitutes what the National Center for Excellence in Distance Learning (NCEDL) has done and is presented here as a case study including our requirements analysis, our survey of available components, decision factors used in making the build or buy decision, our system design, and lessons learned. NCEDL is located at California State University, San Bernardino, and works in consultation with the University's Academic Affairs and Information Resources Technology Divisions and collaborates with faculty, staff, and administration in the identification and development of credit and noncredit distance learning projects for primary delivery to the civilian workforce of the U.S. Navy with future delivery to other Department of Defense and corporate clients. NCEDL delivers distance learning through a range of available and appropriate delivery systems—specifically, compressed video, Internet, and online systems. NCEDL enables the University to develop the capacity to deliver a combination of training and degree programs on the use of enterprise systems that are central to the challenge of ensuring that the civilian populations of the U.S. Navy and future clients are proficient in the knowledge and application of the technologies employed.

The approach presented in this chapter offers a solution that strives to offer users a personalized, engaging, Web-based environment for learning. The approach is personalized because it allows each user to modify their view through portal technology, providing access from anywhere through multiple device interfaces, and delivering content based on the learner's profile and knowledge of their historical performance data. The approach is engaging because it delivers content and information in a customizable, simple manner that intelligently interacts with the user. Finally, the approach is Web based because it leverages Web technologies, standards, and open-source resources to manage and deliver information to users. We begin by discussing the requirements for the proposed system and then present a model for the solution space composed of four layers; user experience, content architecture, tools and technology, and organization and operations. We then discuss issues and solutions for each of those areas.

REQUIREMENTS FOR WEB-BASED LEARNING SYSTEM

This section presents a set of requirements for the Web-based learning system. The requirements revolve around the need to service a variety of learning models—instructor-led with Web assistance, Web-based with instructor assistance, as well as completely online material with no instructor support. Users of the system include learners, teachers, authors, graphics designers, and so forth. These requirements are detailed later.

The *end-user portal* serves as the primary interface for end users to access all learning resources including content, collaborations, and certifications. Portal technology offers the ability for personalization and learner-directed experience based on their role type (job responsibilities) and individual information (historical information).

The *learning management system* (LMS) manages and tracks learning activities of all learner job profiles and individuals. It contains the master catalog of all learning solutions, allowing learners to find learning solutions and to launch them. It tracks learner history and certifications/qualifications. The LMS tracks all learning activities including traditional (classroom) and alternative offerings (self-paced, Web-based). The LMS also provides virtual classroom/collaboration tools such as learner directory information, chat, discussion forums, calendars, gradebooks, and so forth. Finally, the LMS in cooperation with the LCMS needs to manage e-commerce requirements for all learning activities.

The *learning content management system* (LCMS) manages and categorizes content (learning objects) accessible through the portal either individually or as a sequence in a course. The LCMS also provides metatagging information for search as well as access rights for individuals or groups of individuals who can read, update, and so forth, content perhaps based on e-commerce decisions. The backend for this system could be a commercial content repository that may already be populated with material or federated with other content repositories across institutional boundaries.

The *delivery* delivers content to the learner. Content delivery should be highly flexible so as to deliver to different types of learners running different platforms (e.g., PDA, cellular phone) as well as highly scalable because this part of the Web-based learning system will be by far the most exercised. Delivery assembles learning objects and delivers them based on the learner's needs and tracks learner's progress to report to the LMS. The Web-based learning system must embrace digital media and address the bandwidth costs, security issues, and performance/scalability challenges associated with such a distribution system. Content delivery network (CDN) exists to help bridge this problem, which incorporates the idea of bandwidth harvesting and caching content at the outer edge of the network.

The *content authoring tools* are commercial products used to author learning and assessment content. These tools would be selected to best fit the developer's needs and would comply with content standards such as AICC (Aviation Industry CBT Committee, 2004) and SCORM (Sharable Content Object Reference Model) Level 2 from Advanced Distributed Learning Initiative (2004) and loaded into a compliant delivery system for delivery to learners. Delivery must also return assessment results to an LMS for reporting.

The *performance management system*, although not technically a part of the learning system, could be the central "system of record" for the client. This system would be used to support the skills and on-the-job performance objective, identifying high-performance contractor employees and facilitating their further career development and growth.

The *competency management system* allows for the identification of competencies needed to perform a given job role and links these competencies to learning solutions that can be used to remove any skill gaps and to facilitate growth into more advanced job roles. The system provides the means of managing competency and skill dictionaries. It supports assessment of learners against identified competencies. Given the overlap of commercial products, all or part of the functionality found in a competency management system may reside within the LMS.

Because this project is in its initial stages, we are first emphasizing requirements. Our long-term goal is to produce a test bed to enable research and establish programs for outreach that will disseminate the research results required to understand and enhance the user experience in distance learning. The requirements as detailed earlier form the outline for the rest of this chapter and partition the requirements into competencies that underlie the infrastructure. These layers can be labeled as the user experience, content architecture, technology architecture, and organization and operations architecture. This identification of tasks and activities helps identify ownership of the underlying processes.

User Experience Layer

One of the principal challenges facing distance learning (and other flavors of technology-based learning) is how to create an engaging user experience that approximates more traditional learning experiences. Straightforward technology-based learning approaches focus on marshaling existing content into a format suitable for Web-based distribution, such as static HTML. A "more engaging experience" has initially been limited to supplemental audio, video, and animation (Flash, Shockwave) files embedded in the HTML. Only recently has the distance-learning community realized that content and learning activities need to be integrated in new ways to provide a more comprehensive and enriching experience. Distance-learning research in these areas has been lacking. The proposed test bed will enable research on the impact of variables such as interactivity, feedback, multimedia strategies, and the effect of SCORM. Additionally, establishing programs for outreach will disseminate the research results required to understand, and designed to enhance, the user experience in distance learning.

From a technology-based perspective, we feel that the best approach to comprehensive, integrated, and personalized learning is provided by technologies such as the Academus eLearning suite. The portal-based universal interface (UI) provides a single comprehensive navigational and management interface—a one-stop shop for instructor and learning resources. Users go to their portal learning page to access personalized learning objects (LOs), learning activities, auxiliary content, and task-oriented information to maximize their learning experience. Another positive aspect of the portal is the ability to securely deliver this information in a variety of ways to a variety of devices. In this way learners get the support they need when and how they need it.

The Academus suite also includes support for engaging delivery of personalized content with integrated assessment-based feedback via the Virtuoso Delivery engine. Virtuoso provides dynamic delivery capabilities for personalized content, with support for sophisticated distribution networks (see content architecture layer). One way this capability is featured is via personalized feedback—the ability to remediate a learner back to LOs that support objectives for which the learner has not gained a desired level of expertise. Another powerful capability is MoreInfo—the ability to dynamically deliver per the learner requests.

Content Architecture Layer

Dynamic content is essential to the infrastructure framework of this project. There is a critical need to have learners take ownership of their education process and develop critical outcome assessments of their progress. The tool that can make this happen is one in which "interactive conversation," perhaps embedded in game settings, will create the feeling that a human being is behind the information being taught. The goal is to develop content so users feel the medium is responding to them in a human way. The current vernacular has coined this process as Interactive Conversation Interface (iCi). This type of software causes the learner to exercise a phenomenon commonly referred to as "the suspension of disbelief." This software is an off-the-shelf component that will be incorporated into all content development, provided appropriate test bed parameters can be developed to measure the effectiveness of the idea.

The Web-based learning system proposed intends to fully embrace digital media. Use of this media-rich environment comes with bandwidth costs, lack of security, and poor-performing distribution systems. To overcome these issues, this project's infrastructure embraces the concept of a Global Learning Network (GLN), which will incorporate the idea of bandwidth harvesting and caching content at the outer edge of the network.

The next step in this layer of content architecture is to forecast the program's needs for the next 5 years. This step is essential if this project is to be established as and to remain a leader in Web-based learning. We must plan for our content to evolve. We begin with media-rich interactive content through virtual classroom delivery. This environment has stretched and will continue to stretch the ability of the Web. The very architecture of the Web's HTTP protocol makes it cumbersome as a highly interactive, media-rich content delivery platform. The architecture of the GLN helps to mitigate the Web's shortcomings in this area by pushing content and capabilities closer to the end user. The GLN seamlessly integrates curriculum, learning applications, services, and content delivery. The GLN is based on a Cisco AVVID (Architecture for Voice, Video, and Integrated Data; 2004) e-learning architecture that extends end-to-end from the main distribution and management network to the local institution. This architecture provides a networked, tested, and fully documented set of technologies and support services. With the GLN as the foundation, we can begin plugging components into this architecture to achieve our test bed objectives, but this alone will not be sufficient. Our technology will have to evolve with the continuing rapid evolution of the Web. As the availability of bandwidth, advanced routing protocols, and richer client-side capabilities such as plug-ins and Extensible Markup Language/Extensible Stylesheet Language Transformations (Microsoft, 2004) within browsers become pervasive, we will have to quickly migrate to richer platforms to utilize these technologies.

Technology and Tools Layer

Apart from the usual needs for file servers, routers, switches, platforms, and very private networks, the real workings of this project's infrastructure revolve and evolve through the software that will support the content developed. The key software elements that have been identified for this program are Content Management System (CMS) and Learning Management System (LMS). These two systems will eventually transition into a Learning Content Management System (LCMS).

There is little problem understanding the purpose of a CMS, but a distinction needs to be drawn between the purpose of an LMS and an LCMS for purposes of clarity. The LMS primarily focuses on organizational and individual skill competencies, blended learning activities, and the logistics of delivering instructor-led or online learning activities. It does not focus on creation, reusability, management, or improvement of subject matter content itself. The LCMS in contrast helps create, locate, deliver, manage, and improve learning content. Content is typically maintained in a centralized content repository in the form of small, self-describing, uniquely identifiable objects, or learning objects, each of which satisfies one or more well-defined learning objectives. Each learning object may have been created from scratch or by repurposing existing knowledge documents in other formats. An LCMS may locate and deliver a learning object to the end user as an individual unit to satisfy a job-specific need, or it could deliver the learning object as part of a larger course, curriculum, or learning activity defined in an LMS.

An advanced LCMS tracks the user's interactions with each learning object and uses this detailed information to deliver highly personalized future learning experiences. This ability also provides content developers with rich reports for analyzing the clarity, relevance, and effectiveness of content, so it can be improved on an ongoing basis. Some LCMS products are also beginning to enable powerful "real-time" collaboration and knowledge exchange to enable remote subject-matter experts to collaborate on specific learning objects with full version control. These collaborative exchanges are captured, archived, and made easily available to future users to expand and supplement the knowledge encapsulated by that learning object.

An LCMS essentially focuses on creating, reusing, locating, delivering, managing, and improving content. With certain products, the focus also extends to fostering knowledge communities and capturing the unstructured knowledge around the learning object in a tangible form. An LCMS does not manage the logistics of a learning event or the creation of curricula; it handles the instructional design and development cycles, whereas the LMS handles instructional delivery.

Both systems play a phased and complementary role in the infrastructure with the same organizational goal; to accelerate knowledge and skill transfer. Both systems monitor the delivery of content but at different levels of granularity. An LMS concentrates on course-level tracking, particularly completion status and roll-up scores. In contrast, an LCMS employs detailed tracking at the learning-object level not only to trace user performance and interactions at a finer granularity, but also to provide the metrics that help authors analyze the learning object's clarity, relevance, and effectiveness to learners.

The integration between LMS and LCMS products enables advanced personalization capabilities that are not achieved through either product alone. The overall granularity of the tracking in a combined LMS–LCMS ecosystem helps organizational subject-matter experts (SMEs) gain insight into the effectiveness of their reusable learning objects (RLOs). The amount of peer collaboration that the LCMS enables across the organization ensures that individual learning objects are more accurate and up-to-date throughout the combined learning system.

Our current test bed development utilizes Academus as the LMS, Virtuoso as the LCMS, and Virtuoso and GLN as the delivery mechanism. Academus provides a rich set of LMS functionality directly within a portal solution, resulting in a consistent user experience. Virtuoso dynamically renders personalized content, and when integrated with the GLN, provides the ability to deliver content via a globally scalable infrastructure for managing deployed resources. It is our belief that these platforms will allow us to achieve our stated goals of developing a test bed to enable research on the effects of personalized, engaging content and learner interactions on learner outcomes in distance learning.

Organization and Operations Layer

So far we have presented the various layers of technologies that assist in providing services for the distance-learning suite. User experience focuses on usability of the distance learning site to support engaging learning; content architecture addresses how rich content may be delivered and how this content plays a strategic role in learner engagement; and tools and technology describes prevailing system-level architectures for managing the learning experience. Organization and operations focuses on the organization's value-on-investment (VOI; Dictionary.com, 2004) for distance learning.

To maximize the VOI for an organization, that organization's strategic goals and tactical plans for achieving those goals must be understood. Strategically, an organization must align the expected benefits of utilizing distance learning with their strategic direction. If the two are not aligned directionally, then despite how engaging the technology is, learners are left with a "why did I just learn that?" experience, and organizations do not receive a high VOI because the knowledge and skills gained do not support where the organization is going.

We also argue that maximizing the value on investment for distance learning requires an understanding of an organization's tactical plans for achieving strategic objectives. In fact, we believe that distance learning is a key tactical element of the tactical plan, and therefore requires tight integration into the plan. Knowledge and skill training is often considered a luxury, or an add-on that one undertakes when "convenient"; instead we contend that it is a necessary component for effectively participating in the organization's business processes (which are the foundation of its tactical plans). Therefore, learning objects should be delivered to learners that are personalized to not only learner skill level but also to tactical objectives, so learners will understand not only what they are learning but why they are learning it.

Finally, a key aspect of achieving a high VOI is the ability to measure VOI. As discussed under tools and technology, facilities may exist within the technology suite to track learner events and include scoring and reporting capabilities. This collected data must be mapped to the organization's expected VOI, requiring that a VOI model be defined. We feel the development and codification of such models is an important area of research for the direction of this program and the distance-learning field in general.

Lessons Learned

Large organizations are reluctant to implement this type of Web-based learning due to security issues that have surfaced since the events of September 11, 2001, in New York. State institutions such as universities tend not to implement such a system due to the resistance to change and the acceptance of Web-based learning as a viable method of teaching by faculty and the lack of advocacy by those in leadership positions within the university. The lack of advocacy may well be due to the hesitancy to expend time challenging collective bargaining and union positions. However, unless there is a change in the infrastructure, the current system will collapse on itself and private entrepreneurial organizations will fill the void.

SUMMARY

This chapter presents our requirements for a Web-based learning environment and discusses technical infrastructures to realize solutions. We trimmed our requirements to focus on creating a personalized and engaging user experience. These requirements manifest themselves in all layers discussed earlier, user experience, content architecture, tools and technology, and organization and operations.

Personalizing the user's experience is realized by a flexible portal that spans the entire organization. It is realized by delivering content appropriate to the user's learning style and by delivering rich, bandwidth-intensive content at the content architecture layer. It is realized by the LMS managing a rich set of user profile information and historical learning information to deliver the right content to the user at the tools and technology layer.

Engaging users is realized by flexible portal systems and dynamic and interactive content types at the User Experience layer. It is realized by flexible content delivery that utilizes Content Delivery Networks to optimally provide high-bandwidth media at the content architecture layer. It is realized by richness at the tools and technology layer as the LCMS must manage rich content types and the LMS must manage rich historical user information to deliver the right content at the right time. Finally, the need to engage learners is the large win for the organization and operations layer to invest in Web-based learning.

Finally, one output of this effort will be to develop a handbook describing the steps for creating a virtual learning environment between two or more sites connected with broadband technology. Our end goal is to produce a project methodology that relates to technology planning, equipment selection, acquisition, installation, testing, and integration; formulates an instructional design plan focusing on learning objectives, and Web-based delivery in content development; develops user guidelines for instructors, learners, managers, production, and technical staff; documents problems encountered and their solutions; and develops case studies to demonstrate examples of how the learning environment may be used.

REFERENCES

Advanced Distributed Learning Initiative. (2004, August). *SCORM Overview*. Retrieved August 30, 2004, from http://www.adlnet.org/index.cfm?fuseaction=scormabt

Aviation Industry CBL Committee. (2004, August). *Welcome to the AICC Web Site*. Retrieved August 30, 2004, from http://www.aicc.org

Cisco Systems. (2004, August). *Cisco AVVID: Introduction*. Retrieved August 30, 2004, from http://www.cisco.com/en/US/netsol/ns340/ns19/networking_solutions_ market_segment_solutions_home.html

Dictionary.com. (2004, August). *Acronyms & Abbreviations*. Retrieved August 30, 2004, from http://www.acronymfinder.com/af-query.asp?p=dict&String=exact& Acronym=VOI

Microsoft Corporation. (2004). *MSDN XML Standards Reference*. Retrieved August 30, 2004, from http://msdn.microsoft.com/library/default.asp?url=/library/ en-us/xmlsdk/html/oriXMLStandards.asp

Chapter 3

The ADL Vision
and Getting from Here to There

J. D. Fletcher
Institute for Defense Analyses

The Advanced Distributed Learning (ADL) initiative was undertaken by the Department of Defense (DoD) at the request of the White House Office of Science and Technology Policy and in cooperation with the other federal agencies. It is intended to provide a model for all federal agencies to use in making education, training, and performance-aiding readily accessible anytime, anywhere. It is being developed through intense, frequent collaboration among industry, government, and academic participants. Its specifications are being adopted across Europe, Asia, the Pacific Rim, and the Americas.

ADL is expected to deliver both training, which, as a means to an end, prepares individuals to perform specific tasks and jobs, and education, which prepares individuals for life and is an end in itself. The knowledge representations and user interactions underlying these instructional applications are effectively identical to those needed to assist users in decision making, planning, problem solving, maintaining and operating equipment, and other performance-aiding functions. For these reasons, along with the costs to be saved by providing such functions (e.g., Fletcher & Johnston, 2002), performance aiding as well as instruction is a significant objective of the ADL initiative (Dodds & Fletcher, 2004; Wisher & Fletcher, 2004). However, performance aiding is a substantial topic by itself, and space limits discussion of its possibilities, promise, and implications here.

The implications of the ADL initiative are not limited to federal agencies. It presents opportunities and challenges in many other settings—including classroom instruction, especially as it is organized for K–16 education. ADL is not antithetical to such instruction. Its anytime, anywhere instructional goals include classrooms as well as workplaces, conference rooms, job sites, and homes. Nonetheless, the wide access to instruction that ADL will provide to students outside traditional instructional institutions and venues challenges instructors, administrators, and policymakers, as well as K–12 students and their parents, to assume new and unaccustomed roles with new and unaccustomed responsibilities.

With or without ADL, fully accessible anytime, anywhere education (and training and performance-aiding) is likely to become a reality. If nothing else, ADL is a harbinger of future learning processes, capabilities, and opportunities. Sooner or later, our instructional institutions must deal with them. If they do so successfully, their efforts will benefit everyone concerned with human learning and performance.

THE ADL VISION

The ADL initiative is based on the view of future education, training, and performance-aiding illustrated in Fig. 3.1. As the figure suggests, this view, or "vision," keys on three main components: (1) a global information grid—currently the World Wide Web—shown as the cloud on the left side of the figure, which provides an infrastructure populated by reusable instructional objects; (2) a server, shown in the middle of the figure, which locates and then assembles instructional objects into education, training, and/or performance-aiding materials tailored to user needs; and (3) devices, shown on the right side of the figure, which may be carried or worn and serve as personal learning associates that deliver education, training, and performance-aiding to users anywhere, anytime.

From an instructional point of view, the critical element in this vision is the server. It will assemble material needed to support interactions with learners and users on demand and in real time. These interactions will be tailored to the needs, capabilities, intentions, and learning state of each individual or group of individuals. The long-term vision of ADL is to establish instruction and performance-aiding interactions between technology and (human) users that consist of goal-directed *conversations* tailored to each learner's or user's needs, skills, knowledge, abilities, and interests.

Such conversations must draw on effective instructional strategies, accurate representations of the user, and comprehensive representations of relevant subject matter. Generative systems of this sort have been the objective of research and development investment by the DoD since the mid-1960s

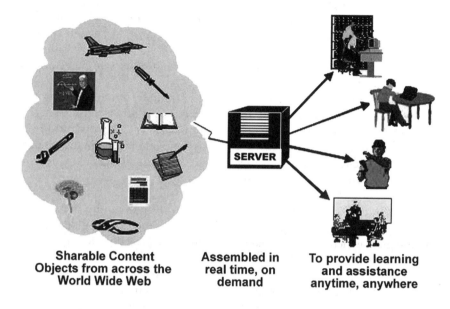

Sharable Content Objects from across the World Wide Web   **Assembled in real time, on demand**   **To provide learning and assistance anytime, anywhere**

FIG. 3.1.   An advanced distributed learning future.

(Carbonell, 1970; Fletcher, 1988; Fletcher & Rockway, 1986). They are the original goal of what today are called Intelligent Tutoring Systems (ITS). Generative capabilities were supported by the DoD, not so much as a clever application of artificial intelligence, but as a way to reduce the costs of instructional materials preparation by substituting the capital of technology and automation for human labor (Fletcher & Rockway, 1986). They remain essential to achieving the long-term goals of ADL.

The Basis for ADL

ADL goals arise from four main technical opportunities; advances in electronics, the pervasive accessibility of the World Wide Web, capabilities developed for Intelligent Tutoring Systems (ITS), and emerging specifications for reusable, sharable instructional objects.

Electronics.   The first and most obvious opportunity keys on the rapid development of digital electronics spurred on by the operation of Moore's Law (Mann, 2000; Service, 1996). As readers may recall, Gordon Moore is a semiconductor pioneer and cofounder of the Intel Corporation. In 1965,

Moore noted that engineers were doubling the number of electronic devices (basically transistors) on chips every year. In 1975, he revised his prediction to say that the doubling would occur every 2 years. If we split the difference and predict that it will occur every 18 months, our expectations fit reality quite closely.

A consequence of Moore's Law is that computers initially selling for $3,000 may cost about half that 18 months later. Another consequence is that the delivery devices shown on the right side of Fig. 3.1, will continue to decrease as much in physical size and cost as they will increase in functionality—not unlike today's cellular telephones, which themselves may provide ubiquitous platforms for ADL delivery.

World Wide Web. The second technological opportunity underlying ADL arises from the development and implementation of the global information grid, which currently takes the form of the World Wide Web. It was the Web that made feasible the DoD goal of accessible education, training, and performance-aiding available anytime and anywhere. Development of the Semantic Web will contribute substantially to achieving the long-term interactive instructional goals of ADL by providing the semantic linkages needed to create comprehensive representations of subject matter, expertise, learners, and users.

Intelligent Tutoring Systems. The third technological opportunity is presented by the generative capabilities of Intelligent Tutoring Systems (ITS). ADL development assumes that to be successful, its functionalities must be tailored to the specific needs, abilities, goals, and interests of the individual student or user (Dodds & Fletcher, 2004; Fletcher, 2003; Wisher & Fletcher, 2004). This tailoring, or individualization, is as critical for performance-aiding as it is for education and training. ADL functions are expected to provide what Brown, Burton, and DeKleer (1982) called articulate expertise. Not only must these functions provide helpful and relevant guidance, they must do so in a way that learners and users with varying levels of knowledge and skill can understand. ADL will, therefore, need to be "intelligent," building on capabilities that have been the developmental province of ITS.

At this point, it may be worth emphasizing the capabilities provided by "nonintelligent" computer-based instruction programs since the 1950s. They have been able to:

- Accommodate individual students' rate of progress, allowing as much or as little time as each student needs to reach instructional objectives;
- Tailor both the content and the sequence of instructional content to each student's needs;

- Make the instruction as easy or difficult, specific or abstract, applied or theoretical as necessary; and
- Adjust to students' most efficient learning styles (collaborative or individual, verbal or visual, etc.).

These capabilities have been described, discussed, and reviewed by Galanter (1959), Atkinson and Wilson (1969), Suppes and Morningstar (1972), Fletcher and Rockway (1986), and many others. To one degree or another, they have been implemented and available in computer-based instruction from its inception.

Intelligence in Intelligent Tutoring Systems is a different matter and more than a marketing term. When it was first introduced into computer-based instruction, it concerned quite specific goals. The distinction between ITS and other computer-based instruction was keyed to specific capabilities that were first targeted in the 1960s (Carbonell, 1970; Sleeman & Brown, 1982). Two of these defining capabilities are that ITS:

- Allow either the system or the student to ask open-ended questions and initiate instructional, "mixed-initiative" dialogue as needed or desired, and
- Generate instructional material and interactions on demand rather than require developers to foresee and prestore all materials and interactions needed to meet all possible eventualities.

Mixed-initiative dialogue requires a language for information retrieval, decision aiding, and instruction that is shared by both the system and the student/user. Natural language has been a frequent choice for this capability (e.g., Brown, Burton, & DeKleer, 1982; Graesser, Person, & Magliano, 1995), but the language of mathematics, mathematical logic, electronics, and other well-structured communication systems have also been used (Barr, Beard, & Atkinson, 1975; Psotka, Massey, & Mutter, 1988; Sleeman & Brown, 1982; Suppes, 1981; Woolf & Regian, 2000).

Generative capability requires the system to devise on demand—not draw from predicted and prestored formats—interactions with students. This capability involves not just generating problems tailored to each student's needs, but also coaching, hints, critiques of completed solutions, appropriate and effective teaching strategies, and, overall, the interactions and presentations needed for one-on-one tutorial instruction. These interactions must be generated from information primitives using an "instructional grammar" that is analogous to the deep structure grammar of linguistics.

Motivations for these two capabilities can be found in the perennial desire for cost containment accomplished by generating rather than anticipating and prestoring responses to all possible student states and actions. But they also arise from basic research on human learning, memory, perception, and cognition. In the 1960s–1970s, as documented by Neisser (1967), among others, the emphasis in basic research and understanding of human behavior shifted from the strict logical positivism of behavioral psychology, which focused on directly observable actions, to consideration of the internal, cognitive processes that were needed to explain empirically observed behavioral phenomena and are assumed to mediate and enable human learning.

The hallmark of this approach is the understanding that seeing, hearing, and remembering are all acts of *construction,* making more or less use of the limited stimulus information provided by our perceptual capabilities. Constructivist approaches are the subject of much current and relevant discussion in instructional research circles (e.g., Duffy & Jonassen, 1992; Tobias & Frase, 2000), but they are firmly grounded in the primordial foundations of scientific psychology. For instance, William James (1890/1950) stated his General Law of Perception as the following: "Whilst part of what we perceive comes through our senses from the object before us, another part (and it may be the larger part) always comes out of our mind" (p. 747).

In this sense, the generative capability sought by ADL and ITS developers is not merely something nice to have, but essential if we are to advance beyond the constraints of prescribed, prebranched, programmed learning, and ad hoc principles commonly used to design computer-based instruction. We need an interactive, generative capability if we are to deal successfully with the extent, variety, and mutability of human cognition.

As stated, the ADL vision is that training, education, and performance-aiding will take the form of human–computer conversations. This capability has been realized in systems that could converse in a formal language such as computer programming, e.g., BIP (Barr et al., 1975), or propositional calculus, e.g., EXCHECK (Suppes, 1981), or could base the conversation on determinate technical phenomena using clearly defined and well-understood terms, e.g., SOPHIE, (Brown et al., 1982). More recent research such as that discussed by Chipman (2003), Graesser, Gernsbacher, and Goldman (2003), and others suggests that significant natural language dialogue capabilities are achievable. Currently, however, they remain closer to the "bleeding edge" of technology than the mainstream. Although the ability to assemble reusable objects in real time and on demand into meaningful instructional or performance-aiding conversations has yet to be conclusively demonstrated, progress in the development of intelligent tutoring systems suggests that it is not an unreasonable goal.

Instructional Objects. Finally, ADL keys on technological opportunities offered by instructional objects. ADL development is presently focused on packaging instructional objects in anticipation of what has been called by Spohrer, Sumner, and Shum (1998) the "educational object economy." In such an economy, the emphasis in preparing materials for technology-based instruction (or performance-aiding) will shift from the current concern with developing instructional objects themselves to one of integrating already available objects into meaningful, relevant, and effective interactions.

The recent evolution of instructional objects has not escaped the attention of researchers. In assessing the educational value of objects, Roschelle and Kaput (1995) emphasized the ability to combine many kinds of interactive content in multiple display formats and obtain for education the benefits now being realized in business from the use of integrated office software. Roschelle et al. (1999) described software technologies underlying the development of five object-based education projects and reviewed their relative effectiveness. Gibbons, Nelson, and Richards (2000) reviewed in detail the nature and value of instructional objects for educational applications and concluded, along with Wiley (2000), that they are the technology of choice in supporting the evolution of technology-based instruction, because of their potential for reusability, adaptability, and scalability. Wiley (2000) provided the first scholarly, book-length treatment of instructional objects, and others may be expected to follow. However, beyond the economies, capabilities, and other benefits discussed by these researchers, is the possibility that the development of sharable instructional objects opens the door to genuinely generative instruction.

Instructional objects may then supply the primitives from which instructional interactions can be created on demand and in real time, and serve as reusable instructional components that reduce the costs of developing basic instructional materials—including graphics, simulations, and simulation scenarios (e.g., Towne, 1998, 2003). An economically viable, generative capability for instruction, in turn, depends on specifications for the development of sharable instructional objects. Developing these specifications has become a significant activity of the ADL initiative. The specifications are intended to separate objects from context-specific, run-time constraints, and proprietary systems so that the objects can be incorporated into other applications. They prescribe common interfaces and data interchange procedures so instructional objects can be aggregated into assemblies that guide and assist learners and users. Instructional objects so specified must be:

- *Accessible:* It should be possible to identify, locate, and access objects in one remote location and deliver them to many other locations when and where they are needed.
- *Interoperable:* Objects developed in one location with one set of tools or platform should be accessible and usable in other locations with dif-

ferent tools operating in different environments on different platforms.

- *Durable:* Objects should withstand technology changes (including version changes and upgrades) without redesign, reconfiguration, or recoding.
- *Reusable:* Objects should be sufficiently flexible to be independent of and used in multiple applications and contexts.

These criteria underlie SCORM, the Sharable Content Object Reference Model, which is an evolving specification for creating instructional objects that meet these criteria (Dodds, 2002; Dodds & Fletcher, 2004; Wisher & Fletcher, 2004). The SCORM specification is by no means the totality of ADL, but it provides a basis for populating the World Wide Web, or whatever form the global information grid takes in the future, with a ready supply of accessible, useable instructional objects. Once these objects exist, they must be identified, assessed, selected, and aggregated in real time and then handed to devices that deliver instruction and/or performance-aiding. As stated, this is the job of the server shown in the middle of Fig. 3.1. By importing "logic" or instructional strategy objects, as well as "content" objects, the server may also acquire expert tutoring capabilities.

This vision and view of instruction and performance-aiding conducted through human/computer conversations seem inevitable—sooner or later computer and instructional technology will produce personal learning associates with the functionalities envisioned by ADL. In its pursuit of instructional efficiency and knowledge accessibility, the ADL initiative seeks to bring it about sooner rather than later. Although difficult issues remain to be resolved, the most intransigent barriers to this future may be those arising from the current institutions, organizational structures, instructional practices, and administrative policies that are now vested in instruction conducted as lessons for students gathered together in one place and at one time. That is to say instruction conducted in classrooms, and not as tutorial conversations available to individuals anytime, anywhere. Although ADL technologies can be used as easily in classrooms as not, their impact will be to shift the emphasis in instructional practice, organizations, and approaches away from classrooms and onto individual users (Fletcher & Tobias, 2003).

Instructional Design

With SCORM, ADL has begun a process to populate the cloud on the left side of Fig. 3.1. The process assumes continued development of sharable instructional objects, continued development, expansion, and use of the

World Wide Web, continued influence of Moore's Law on the cost and capabilities of electronics, and increasingly powerful, portable, and affordable electronic devices, which are depicted on the right side of Fig. 3.1. How might the server (in the middle of Fig. 3.1) operate to assemble instructional objects into effective instructional (and performance-aiding) interactions? How might it design these interactions?

At present, there is a gap between the one-of-a-kind, monolithic products of computer-based instruction development and Intelligent Tutoring Systems on one hand and the object-based development targeted by ADL on the other. The SCORM specifications are intended to make instructional components sharable and reusable by either computers and/or the human designers who assemble these components into instructional (and performance-aiding) interactions. These specifications attempt to bridge the gap between ADL goals and current instructional design by providing a foundation for object-based assembly that begins with relatively small, reusable learning resources, which are then aggregated to form units of instruction (or performance-aiding). By themselves, the objects may have no specific context. When they are combined with other objects, the resulting aggregation provides context and enables interactions with users in a sustained instructional or problem-solving conversation.

Working forward from SCORM we might well ask how its specifications and operating principles for instructional objects affect and shape the process of instructional design. SCORM has evolved through a series of versions, each intended to build on previous versions, rather than replace them. Its organizational structure may be described as a set of semi-independent functions. The SCORM specifications (currently available at www.adlnet.org) integrate and harmonize application details and requirements drawn from various standards and other specifications. They may be summarized as the following:

- *SCORM Content Aggregation Model* describes how to develop sharable instructional objects, package them for exchange from system to system, and describe them for search and discovery.
- *SCORM Run-Time Environment* describes the Learning Management System (or server) requirements needed to manage the ADL run-time environment, covering such matters as materials launch, communication between materials and server, and data model elements for sharing information about the learner's progress and needs.
- *SCORM Sequencing and Navigation* describes how SCORM materials may be sequenced through a set of learner-initiated or system-initiated navigation events. Branching and flow may be described by a predefined set of activities, determined at design time, or generated as needed on demand.

Although the SCORM Content Aggregation and Run–Time Environment specifications present functions that are essential to ADL, it is SCORM Sequencing and Navigation that most affects the process of instructional design. With "sequencing" we find software engineers discussing what instructional designers might call "branching," and with "navigation" we find them addressing issues that instructional designers might call "learner control." The SCORM specifications ensure that sequencing and navigation implemented in any conformant development environment using any conformant tools will operate successfully and as required by the developer(s) in any conformant run-time environment.

The SCORM Sequencing and Navigation specifications are based on "use cases" drawn from already delivered and currently used technology-based instruction. These examples and the Sequencing and Navigation specifications developed for them key on techniques that are the base of what instructional designers may recognize as Keller's Personalized System of Instruction (PSI) and Crowder's intrinsic programming.

Keller's PSI involves a process of breaking up a course of instruction into an ordered series of modules and then pretesting students for their mastery of each module's content before beginning work in it (Keller, 1968). Students who pass the pretest skip the module and proceed to a pretest for the next module in the series. Students who do not pass the pretest are required to complete the module and then be retested. They repeat this process until they pass the test, in practice one of several parallel tests, and only then proceed on to the next module.

Various studies found PSI to be effective. A meta-analysis of 75 empirical comparisons of PSI with standard classroom practices was reported by Kulik, Kulik, and Cohen (1979). They found that the PSI programs they reviewed raised final examination scores by about 0.50 standard deviations, roughly an increase in the performance of 50th percentile students to that of 69th percentile students. They also found that PSI produced less variation in achievement, higher student ratings, and fewer course withdrawals. Despite these favorable results, Keller (1985) grew pessimistic about the use of PSI because of the substantial amount of instructor time required to set up PSI courses and the lack of support (mostly in the form of release time) from administrators.

Crowder's intrinsic programming (e.g., 1959) is interesting because it and not Skinner's approach (e.g., 1954) is the one almost exclusively found in practice—even though Skinner's extrinsic programming is most frequently cited as the backbone of programmed instruction. Crowder's approach will be familiar to most instructional developers. An example is the following:

In the multiplication $3 \times 4 = 12$, the number 12 is called a _____

A: Factor	{Branch to remedial X1}
B: Quotient	{Branch to remedial X2}
C: Product	{Reinforce, go to the next item}
D: Power	{Branch to remedial X3}

In this item, the system, the computer instructor, assumes that a student responding "A" misunderstands the meaning of "Factor," or lacks an understanding of "Product," or both. The student is branched to instructional items intended to correct one and/or the other of these cognitive states and then is returned to this or a similar item to try again. A similar remedial approach is applied to responses of "B" and "D." A student responding with "C" is usually rewarded, "reinforced," with encouraging, positive feedback and then sent on to whatever item best continues his or her progress through the instruction, an action that by itself may constitute positive reinforcement.

These two approaches for sequencing between modules (PSI) and within modules (intrinsic programming) provide the basis for much computer-based instruction delivered today and, either consciously or not, for the use cases that the SCORM Sequencing and Navigation specifications were intended to accommodate. A comparison between computer-based instruction branching and SCORM sequencing is shown in Fig. 3.2. The typical computer-based instruction branching structure on the left would be implemented as shown on the right by using SCORM Sequencing and Navigation. Both sides of the figure depict typical Keller PSI branching, although it is not difficult to see how the same schemes might be extended to within-module Crowder intrinsic programming. Boxes A, B, and C may all be instructional objects (even if one or more of them is an assessment module), or they may be assembled from more granular objects by the server.

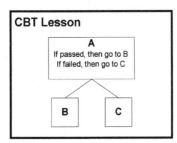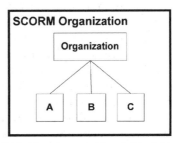

FIG. 3.2.   Comparison of Computer-based Instruction Branching and SCORM Navigation.

The elements shown in Fig. 3.2 can be used as a basis for an entire course by repeating and extending them into a comprehensive tree structure that starts with a single entry point and branches out to as many modules as are needed. In this way, SCORM Sequencing and Navigation accommodate Keller's and Crowder's approaches and others as well. Learners proceed through the tree from module to module until they run out of modules and can proceed no further. At that point they are done with the course, unit, or lesson.[1]

The SCORM Sequencing and Navigation specifications assume that most learning design strategies can be represented as a tree of learning modules and that instructional designers will be able to map their instructional designs and strategies into this structure. SCORM allows access to global variables that can be used to communicate data from one module or object in the tree to another. It also allows modules to be invisible to learners thereby permitting use of specialized computations to implement more elaborate instructional approaches such as those involving Bayesian networks (e.g., Conati, Gertner, VanLehn, & Druzdzel, 1997; Corbett, Koedinger, & Anderson, 1997). These approaches should be able to function in the SCORM tree structure, determining if users are on the right track, shaping the scope and sequence of instruction they receive, and guiding their progress. Hidden Markov Models such as those used by Soller and Lesgold (2003) to facilitate collaboration among physically distributed participants may also be incorporated in a similar fashion to help learners collaborate in solving problems.

SCORM Sequencing and Navigation specifications are new and await empirical validation to determine the extent to which they support these and other approaches. The question naturally arises as to how much farther SCORM Sequencing and Navigation can be pushed toward the ADL vision in which instruction consists less of predefined lessons, testing, and screening and becomes more of a conversation between the learner/user and the technology.

Empirical demonstrations to answer this question may be showcased through "Designfests" that are analogs of the current ADL/SCORM "Plugfests." The ADL initiative uses Plugfests to assess and demonstrate how well servers, objects, and authoring tools conform to SCORM specifications and, in turn, how satisfactory the specifications are in meeting users' needs. In a similar fashion, Designfests will demonstrate how and to what extent SCORM specifications can be used to implement the instructional designs intentions of developers. Designfests will help identify gaps be-

---

[1]Fig. 3.2 is adapted from *SCORM Best Practices Guide for Content Developers* (2003), prepared by the Carnegie Mellon Learning Systems Architecture Lab to assist instructional developers. Readers who seek more information about implementing instructional strategies under SCORM Sequencing and Navigation are encouraged to consult the *Guide*.

tween what developers want to do and what is practicable under SCORM Sequencing and Navigation specification. They will also set priorities for further development of SCORM specifications.

TOWARD MORE ADAPTIVE, INTELLIGENT LEARNING SYSTEMS

Mainstream learning systems often rely on predetermined and fixed-path delivery of content. Such systems lack agility in adapting to learners' mastery states, and are thereby limited in their ability to tailor learning experiences to individual learners. As specified long ago (e.g., Fletcher, 1975), an adaptive, "intelligent" learning system needs an accurate model of the learner, a model of the knowledge domain, and a capability that can evaluate the differences between the two. It can then identify and/or devise, on demand and in real time, instructional strategies that produce desired instructional outcomes.

SCORM provides globally accessible records that can store the learner's degree of mastery. A hook was included in the records that permits them to reference externally defined competencies. As the learner is sequenced through the content objects, the learning system builds up a representation of the learner's mastery and progress. Records of this sort comprise a simple, accumulative model of the learner's level of competency in the area of instructional interest.

IMS Reusable Definition of Competency or Educational Objective (2002) adds to this capability by defining a taxonomy of competencies required to meet specific learning objectives. This taxonomy may be organized hierarchically to represent dependencies, supporting skills, or prerequisites. Each competency definition includes a text description of the competency and a unique identifier that may be referenced externally. The organization of a competency definition may represent specific skills or knowledge to be acquired for a specific task or subject domain. By referencing competency model identifiers, SCORM records can be used to compare the state of the learner with the generic IMS Global Learning Consortium competencies. This capability provides a generalizable, system-based means to perform knowledge and skills gap analyses leading to more sophisticated and adaptive strategies that use such information (Wiley, 2000).

As learning system specifications become more robust, they will also become more adaptive. Improved assessment methods and results are emerging that will continuously and unobtrusively extract information from instructional interactions and better represent the state of the learner. The strategies developed by learning systems will further be informed by learner profile information, which can "preload" the learner model with mastery information from outside sources, thereby reducing the need for additional testing to determine the learner's state. This process enhances the capabilities of technology-based instructional systems to bypass relevant content of already mastered material and concentrate on relevant material yet to be learned—a process that has long been advocated by researchers (e.g., Fletcher, 1975; Tobias, 1989).

Basically we seek an engineering of instruction (e.g., Woolf & Regian, 2000) with well-articulated principles for adjusting and modulating learning experiences. Such engineering would ensure that outcomes such as retention of skills and knowledge, application and transfer of learning, motivation to continue study, speed of response, accuracy of response, and so forth are reliably achieved by each learner to the maximum extent possible within the constraints imposed by instructional time and resources. This instructional engineering would automatically identify and devise learning strategies, and locate and assemble precisely appropriate objects into successive interactions with the learner. Each interaction would be tailored, on demand and in real time, to the outcome being sought, the learner's level of knowledge, skill, and style of learning, and the instructional strategy that was indicated by instructional principles. This is a significant challenge for instructional objects, Web-based services, and the state of the art in general, but current progress suggests that they may eventually rise to meet it, yielding technology that ensures reliable achievement of targeted instructional outcomes.

The Impact of Web and Web Services on this Evolution

One way the current and near-term capabilities of learning systems may evolve is through the Semantic Web, which will provide powerful new technologies for both knowledge representation and the ontologies needed to connect them (Berners-Lee, Hendler, & Lassila, 2001). These technologies will provide ways not only to relate but also to reason about information from widely different domains.

The Semantic Web is intended to imbue information available on the Web with sufficient meaning to significantly improve the cooperation between computers and human beings. Dealing with the semantic content of Web pages and information will enhance the process of discovery needed to access relevant information and objects from the Web. Access to this semantic content will key on the development, implementation, and use of ontologies, which make it possible to identify and expose semantic linkages between highly disparate bodies of information (Chandrasekaran, Josephson, & Benjamins, 1999).

Roughly, an ontology consists of a taxonomy and a set of inference rules that formally define operations and relations among the classes defined by the taxonomy. More specifically, ontologies consist of consensual, shared, formal descriptions that identify classes of objects, each member of which possesses all the qualities that all other members of the class have in common. The classes are organized in hierarchies, and classes of classes can be developed to any necessary depth. Relationships between a member of any class defined by an ontology can not only be quickly linked to many other classes and class members but the semantic quality that forms the link can also be exposed. Ontologies thereby identify semantic links between what may appear to be quite disparate classes and class members. Web services are being devised and implemented to identify and exploit these semantic linkages, and, in general, increase the "behavioral intelligence" of Web-based applications—as Bryson, Martin, McIlraith, and Stein (2002) have suggested.

These Web services are being built on top of existing and emerging Web standards, such as Hyper-Text Transfer Protocol (HTTP), Extensible Markup Language (XML), Universal Description, Discovery, and Integration (UDDI), and Simple Object Access Protocol (SOAP). In this way, emerging services are being made language, platform, and object model independent. They enable different applications running on different operating systems developed with different object models using different programming languages and programming environments to cooperate, communicate, and interoperate. They can express complex relationships using inference rules like those of intelligent tutoring systems to perform specific tasks such as profiling learners, representing their skills, knowledge, and abilities, linking these representations to instructional objects, and managing their progress toward instructional objectives and competencies.

If successful, the Semantic Web will integrate real-world knowledge and skills acquired through simulation, education, training, performance-aiding, and experience. It will provide a foundation for building more comprehensive and substantive models of subject matter domains and learners' levels of mastery than we now have and will combine them with more precise discovery of the instructional objects learners and other users need to develop desired human competencies. Building on the already available functionalities of intelligent tutoring systems, sharable objects, and existing standards, the Semantic Web and its services will contribute substantially to the next generation of learning environments.

Content Object Discovery and Retrieval

Given these considerations, it is not surprising to find that the development of Web services used to identify and retrieve contextually relevant instructional content is becoming a major topic. The success of Google and other Web search engines has demonstrated the value and utility of content discovery and whetted everyone's appetite for rapid, accurate search and retrieval. Presently, Google may be the single most important, effective, and widely used source of Web-based education. However, Google's location of content by text crawling, indexing, and retrieving everything that is remotely relevant to a search limits its use as a discovery system for focused content assembly. Its operation could be substantially improved if it were to cooperate with content and retrieve only what is intentionally prepared and published for discovery.

More precise identification of content objects is being addressed through the use of Uniform Resource Names (URN; http://www.faqs.org/rfcs/rfc1737.html), which serve as persistent, location-independent resource identifiers. The Corporation for National Research Initiatives (CNRI) has created a URN implementation called "The Handle System" (Kahn & Wilensky, 1995; http://www.handle.net/introduction.html). This system allows digital objects to obtain a unique identifier and to link each object to its location—wherever that might be—through the use of a Handle Resolution Service (similar to domain names resolving to Internet protocol addresses through the Domain Name System). CNRI hosts a global root server that can be queried to resolve requests.

Also, the Common Indexing Protocol (CIP; http://www.faqs.org/rfcs/rfc2651.html) allows the owner of content to create its index metadata while also allowing this indexing information to be shared among different servers, thereby enabling the development of new search and discovery services. New learning and performance-aiding specifications are emerging that permit the identification of skills, competencies, and knowledge so that logical relations among them that are relevant to specific but quite different communities of practices can be identified and then represented. As suggested earlier, not only will such logical relations be discovered, but the semantic nature of these relationships, insofar as they are reflected in metadata definitions, will be exposed.

These developments, among others, may produce Web services that provide accurate, precisely focused, and contextually correct discovery and retrieval of instructional objects on an easily scalable basis. Their combination of agility and accuracy enables considerable flexibility in dealing with the idiosyncratic prior knowledge elements and associations built up by individual users. They will allow instructional programs to continuously and unobtrusively assemble models of each user's state of knowledge, style of learning, and progress toward instructional objectives. These models will in turn support the precise tailoring of instructional interactions to each student that is a characteristic and unique strength of one-on-one tutoring— they will provide an Aristotle for every Alexander and a Mark Hopkins for the rest of us.

Where Might These Capabilities Take Us?

The emphasis on instructional technology brings us to revolutions in instruction. The first of these may have occurred with the development of written language about 7,000 years ago. It allowed the content of advanced ideas and teaching to transcend time and place. The second revolution in instruction began with the technology of books. Books made the content of high-quality instruction available anywhere and anytime, but also inexpensive and thereby accessible to many more people. A third revolution in instruction appears to be accompanying the introduction of computer technology. The capability of this technology for real-time adjustment of instructional content, sequence, scope, difficulty, and style to meet the needs of individuals suggests a third pervasive and significant revolution in instruction. It makes both the content *and* the interactions of high-quality instruction widely and inexpensively accessible—again anytime, anywhere.

Building on this possibility, ADL, SCORM, intelligent tutoring, and the Semantic Web in some combination may provide a foundation for generative education, training, and performance-aiding capabilities that are available anytime, anywhere. These developments can capitalize on the growth of electronic commerce and the World Wide Web. They can build on this worldwide, almost irresistible activity, accelerate it, and apply it to a full spectrum of education, training, and performance-aiding needs. But to realize all this promise, we must also learn to combine the software engineering features offered by SCORM with the best we have to offer in the form of instructional design.

The long-term, anytime, anywhere vision for ADL differs substantially from classroom learning and the many organizational structures we have in place to support it. But ADL is not at odds with classroom practice. Anytime, anywhere includes classrooms, and ADL capabilities are as accessible in classrooms as elsewhere. The instructional and performance-aiding, human–computer conversations that are the eventual goal of ADL will access the comprehensive spectrum of human knowledge becoming available from the World Wide Web and tailor it to the user's needs. These conversations will initially be designed to mimic those that are established by human tutors, but sooner or later this guiding metaphor must evolve and these conversations will take on forms, capabilities, and infrastructure of their own. The "Columbus Effect" will take over just as it did for wireless telegraph, horseless carriages, and a host of other technological innovations that led us into territory not envisioned in the original enabling metaphor.

At least three capabilities may evolve from the ADL teaching–learning environment:

• Less predefined sequencing—An instruction (or performance-aiding) conversation will presumably take whatever direction is needed by participants in the conversation. How to develop and provide a capability that allows sequences to adjust and evolve continually—perhaps a meta-sequencing capability—is a significant challenge for instructional designers. The notion of instructional design as a process of prespecifying and predefining a sequence of activities within a lesson module will need to evolve substantially if the ADL vision of a conversation sustained on an interaction-to-interaction basis is to be fully realized.

• More assessment and fewer tests—Assessment will become more continuous and unobtrusive as the capability for developing a model of the learner/user from interactions evolves. Such assessment may be accomplished by taking account of the learner's vocabulary, use of technical information, level of abstraction, clustering (chunking) of concepts, inferred hypothesis formation, and the like. These capabilities have yet to be fully explored and verified, but enough research on their application has been completed to suggest their promise for the continuous and unobtrusive assessment of user knowledge and abilities needed to tailor instruction and performance-aiding to their needs. Some explicit testing and explicit probing may still be used to assess learner progress efficiently. What sort of probes are needed, how they are to be implemented, and what principles will guide their psychometric properties is another challenge for instructional designers—a challenge that should not be left to evaluators and the testing community as a separate, "stove-piped" activity but one that integrates evaluation with instructional design.

• No lessons—The notion of monolithic instructional modules intended to achieve instructional objectives will also need to evolve if instruction and performance-aiding conversations are to be supported. Objectives may need to be more finely specified by a more comprehensive hierarchical decomposition than called for by current instructional design. As suggested, a capability is needed to treat instruction not as an art or science, but as engineering where specific outcomes, based on detailed knowledge of the learner/user matched with comprehensive representations of the subject matter, can reliably be achieved by all learners—even when the targeted outcomes themselves are modified on the fly.

Other challenges may well occur to the reader. Issues of privacy and security, integration with our current instructional practices, certification at a distance, and the balance between individual learning and the need for social interaction all remain as topics for research, development, and implementation, but they do not seem as peculiar to the ADL vision for distributed learning as these three.

Are These Learning Environments Worthwhile

Hundreds of evaluations have been performed to assess the interactive instructional capabilities incorporated in ADL. As reviewed in more detail by Fletcher (2003), the case, based on empirical data, for using these technology-mediated learning environments may be roughly summarized as the following:

1. Tailoring instruction (education and training) to the needs of individual students has been found to be both an instructional imperative and an economic impossibility.
2. Technology can, in many cases, make this instructional imperative affordable. Under any appreciable student load, it is less expensive to provide instruction with digital technology than to hire a tutor for each student.
3. Technology-based instruction has been found to be more effective than current classroom instructional approaches in many settings across many subject matters.
4. Technology-based instruction is generally less costly than current instructional approaches, especially when many students are to be trained or when instructional objectives concern operating or maintaining costly equipment.
5. Technology-based instruction has been found to decrease the time needed to reach targeted instructional objectives.

Overall, a rule of "thirds" emerges from assessments of computer-based instruction. Findings suggest that use of interactive instructional technologies reduces the cost of instruction by about one-third, and it either reduces time of instruction by about one-third or it increases the amount of skills and knowledge acquired by about one-third. Similar, if not enhanced, results can reasonably be expected with the instructional capabilities that ADL adds to basic technology-based instruction. These results, combined with anywhere, anytime accessibility also provided by technology-based instruction, suggest the value of achieving the ADL vision.

Distance Learning and ADL

ADL approaches contrast with less interactive, less agile, and less flexible technologies such as video teletraining, video conferencing, instructional radio, paper-based correspondence instruction, and instructional telephone, all of which have been used to provide distance-learning. In general, distance learning studies using these less interactive technologies find that they provide instruction that is about as effective as residential classroom instruction, less preferred by students, but notably less costly. For instance, Russell (1999) identified 355 studies reporting no significant differences between distance education and other instructional approaches. His findings are confirmed by other researchers (Bernard, Lou, & Abrami, 2003; Lockee, Burton, & Cross, 1999; Phipps & Merisotis, 1999). Bernard et al. (2004) reported a meta-analytic review of 232 studies comparing distance education with classroom instruction. Among other things, they found superior results for classroom instruction when synchronous approaches to distance education were used and superior results for distance education when asynchronous approaches were used. In a meta-analytic review of 105 empirical studies comparing Web-based learning with classroom approaches, Sitzmann and Wisher (2005) found Web-based instruction to be more effective for teaching declarative knowledge, but they found virtually no difference in the effectiveness of the two forms of instruction for teaching procedural knowledge. In any case, it may be worth emphasizing that lower costs and enhanced accessibility suggest superior cost-effectiveness for distance education even when research finds it to be no more than equally as effective as classroom instruction.

FINAL WORD

Much remains to be done. The vision or view of the future presented in this chapter is not likely to accomplished soon, but it also seems likely, given our progress in such areas as electronics, computer technology, computer communications, and knowledge representation. Serious issues remain in the development of instructional strategies that reliably lead from the learner's (or user's) present state of knowledge, skill, and performance to one that is targeted and desired. We need a capability that is neither art nor science, but instead is most analogous to engineering where known principles are applied to achieved specified outcomes in, if we are fortunate, a cost-effective manner.

The anytime, anywhere objectives of ADL are not contrary to classroom instruction, but very different. They will require changes in roles and responsibilities of students, instructors, and administrators. The budgeting practices and organizational structures now focused on classroom settings will also require major modifications. Like all changes, these are likely to be painful and most certainly difficult to achieve. The prize, however, may be worth it. Enabling the totality of human knowledge to be affordable and available to every individual who seeks it seems a worthy goal. We may well wish that both the technical and administrative difficulties encountered in realizing this vision can and will be surmounted.

REFERENCES

Atkinson, R. C., & Wilson, H. A. (1969). *Computer-assisted instruction; A book of readings.* New York: Academic Press.

Barr, A., Beard, M., & Atkinson, R. C. (1975). A rationale and description of a CAI program to teach the BASIC programming language. *Instructional Science, 4,* 1–31.

Bernard, R. M., Abrami, P. C., Lou, Y., Borokhovski, E., Wade, A., Wozney, L., Wallet, P. A., Fiset, M., & Huang, B. (2004). How does distance education compare with classroom instruction? A meta-analysis of the empirical literature. *Review of Educational Research, 74,* 379–439.

Bernard, R. M., Lou, Y., & Abrami, P. C. (2003). *Is distance education equivalent to classroom instruction? A meta-analysis of the empirical literature.* Paper delivered at the annual convention of the American Educational Research Association, Chicago, IL.

Berners-Lee, T., Hendler, J., & Lassila, O. (2001). The semantic web. *Scientific American, 284,* 34–43.

Brown, J. S., Burton, R. R., & DeKleer, J. (1982). Pedagogical, natural language and knowledge engineering in SOPHIE I, II, and III. In D. Sleeman & J. S. Brown (Eds.), *Intelligent tutoring systems* (pp. 227–282). New York: Academic Press.

Bryson, J. J., Martin, D. L., McIlraith, S. A., & Stein, L. A. (2002). Toward behavioral intelligence in the semantic web. *Computer, 35,* 48–54.

Carbonell, J. R. (1970). AI in CAI: An artificial intelligence approach to computer-assisted instruction. *IEEE Transactions on Man-Machine Systems, 11,* 190–202.

Chandrasekaran, B., Josephson, J. R., & Benjamins, V. R. (1999). Ontologies: What are they? Why do we need them? *IEEE Intelligent Systems and their applications, 14,* 20–26.

Chipman, S. F. (2003). Gazing yet again into the silicon chip: The future of computers in education. In H. F. O'Neil, Jr. & R. Perez (Eds.), *Technology applications in education: A learning view* (pp. 31–54). Hillsdale, NJ: Lawrence Erlbaum Associates.

Conati, C., Gertner, A., VanLehn, K., & Druzdzel, M. (1997). On-line student modeling for coached problem solving using Bayesian Networks. In A. Jameson, C. Paris, & C. Tasso (Eds.), *Proceedings of UM-97, Sixth International Conference on user modeling.* New York: Springer Wien.

Corbett, A. T., Koedinger, K. R., & Anderson, J. R. (1997). Intelligent tutoring systems. In M. G. Helander, T. K. Landauer, & P. V. Prabhu (Eds.), *Handbook of human-computer interaction* (pp. 849–874). Amsterdam, The Netherlands: Elsevier.

Crowder, N. A. (1959). Automatic teaching by means of intrinsic programming. In E. Galanter (Ed.), *Automatic teaching: The state of the art* (pp. 109–116). New York: Wiley.

Dodds, P. V. W. (Ed.). (2002). *Sharable courseware object reference model (SCORM) version 1.2* (IDA Document D-2677). Alexandria, VA: Institute for Defense Analyses. [Evolving versions of SCORM are posted on line at http://www.idanet.org]

Dodds, P. V. W., & Fletcher, J. D. (2004). Opportunities for new "smart" learning environments enabled by next generation web capabilities. *Journal of Education Multimedia and Hypermedia, 13*(4), 391–404.

Duffy, T. M., & Jonassen, D. H. (Eds.). (1992). *Constructivism and the technology of instruction: A conversation.* Hillsdale, NJ: Lawrence Erlbaum Associates.

Fletcher, J. D. (1975). Models of the learner in computer-assisted instruction. *Journal of Computer-Based Instruction, 3,* 118–126.

Fletcher, J. D. (1988). Intelligent training systems in the military. In S. J. Andriole & G. W. Hopple (Eds.), *Defense applications of artificial intelligence: Progress and prospects* (pp. 33–59). Lexington, MA: Lexington Books.

Fletcher, J. D. (2003). Evidence for learning from technology-assisted instruction. In H. F. O'Neil, Jr. & R. Perez (Eds.), *Technology applications in education: A learning view* (pp. 79–99). Hillsdale, NJ: Lawrence Erlbaum Associates.

Fletcher, J. D., & Johnston, R. (2002). Effectiveness and cost benefits of computer-based aids for maintenance operations. *Computers in Human Behavior, 18*, 717–728.

Fletcher, J. D., & Rockway, M. R. (1986). Computer-based training in the military. In J. A. Ellis (Ed.), *Military contributions to instructional technology* (pp. 171–222). New York: Praeger.

Fletcher, J. D., & Tobias, S. (2003). *Implications of advanced distributed learning for education* (Urban Diversity Series). New York: ERIC Clearinghouse on Urban Education, Teachers College, Columbia University. Retrieved March 17, 2005, from http://iume.tc.columbia.edu/eric_archive/mono/UDS118.pdf

Galanter, E. (Ed.). (1959). *Automatic teaching: The state of the art.* New York: Wiley.

Gibbons, A. S., Nelson, J., & Richards, R. (2000). The nature and origin of instructional objects. In D. Wiley (Ed.), *The instructional use of learning objects.* Retrieved June 22, 2004, from http//:www.reusability.org/read

Graesser, A. C., Gernsbacher, M. A., & Goldman, S. (Eds.). (2003). *Handbook of discourse processes.* Mahwah, NJ: Lawrence Erlbaum Associates.

Graesser, A. C., Person, N. K., & Magliano, J. P. (1995). Collaborative dialogue patterns in naturalistic one-on-one tutoring. *Applied Cognitive Psychology, 9*, 495–522.

IMS reusable definition of competency or educational objective—information model: version 1.0 final specification. (2002). IMS Global Learning Consortium, Inc. Retrieved September 3, 2002, from http://www.imsglobal.org/competencies/rdceov1p0/imsrdceo_infov1p0.html

James, W. (1890/1950). *Principles of psychology: Volume I.* New York: Dover Press.

Kahn, R., & Wilensky, R. (1995). *A framework for distributed digital object services.* Retrieved March 9, 2005, from http://www.cnri.reston.va.us/k-w.html

Keller, F. S. (1968). Goodbye, teacher .... *Journal of Applied Behavior Analysis, 1*, 79–89.

Keller, F. S. (1985). Lightning strikes twice. *Teaching of Psychology, 12*, 4–8.

Kulik, J. A., Kulik, C-L. C., & Cohen, P. A. (1979). A meta-analysis of outcome studies of Keller's personalized system of instruction. *American Psychologist, 38*, 307–318.

Lockee, B. B., Burton, J. K., & Cross, L. H. (1999). No comparison: Distance education finds a new use for "no significant difference". *Educational Technology Research and Development, 47*, 33–42.

Mann, C. C. (2000). The end of Moore's Law? *Technology Review.* Retrieved December 2, 2004, from http://www.techreview.com/articles/may00/mann.htm

Neisser, U. (1967). *Cognitive psychology.* New York: Appleton, Century, Crofts.

Phipps, R. A., & Merisotis, J. O. (1999). *What's the difference? A review of contemporary research on the effectiveness of distance learning in higher education.* Washington, DC: The Institute of Higher Education Policy.

Psotka, J., Massey, L. D., & Mutter, S. A. (Eds.). (1988). *Intelligent tutoring systems: Lessons learned.* Hillsdale, NJ: Lawrence Erlbaum Associates.

Roschelle, J., & Kaput, J. (1995). Educational software architecture and systemic impact: The promise of component software. *Journal of Educational Computing Research, 14*, 217–228.

Russell, T. L. (1999). *The no significant differences phenomenon.* Chapel Hill, NC: Office of Instructional Telecommunications, North Carolina State University.

SCORM best practices guide for content developers. (2003). Pittsburgh, PA: Learning Systems Architecture Lab, Carnegie Mellon University. Retrieved November 1, 2003, from http://www.lsal.cmu.edu

Service, R. E. (1996). Can chip devices keep shrinking? *Science, 274*, 1834–1836.

Sitzmann, T. M., & Wisher, R. (2005). The effectiveness of Web-based training compared to classroom: A meta-analysis. In S. Carliner & B. Sugrue (Eds.), *ASTD research practice conference proceedings* (pp. 181–187). Alexandria, VA: American Society of Training and Development.

Sleeman, D., & Brown, J. S. (Eds.). (1982). *Intelligent tutoring systems.* New York: Academic Press.

Skinner, B. F. (1954). The science of learning and the art of teaching. *Harvard Education Review, 24*, 86–97.

Soller, A., & Lesgold, A. (2003). A computational approach to analyzing online knowledge sharing interaction. *Proceedings of Artificial Intelligence in Education 2003* (pp. 253–260). Sydney, Australia.

Spohrer, J., Sumner, T., & Shum, S. B. (1998). Educational authoring tools and the educational object economy: Introduction to the special issue from the East/West group. *Journal of Interactive Media in Education.* Retrieved January 20, 2004, from http://www-jime.open.ac.uk/98/10/spohrer-98-10-paper.html

Suppes, P. (Ed.). (1981). *University-level computer assisted instruction at Stanford: 1968–1980.* Stanford, CA: Institute for Mathematical Studies in the Social Sciences.

Suppes, P., & Morningstar, M. (1972). *Computer-assisted instruction at Stanford 1966–1968: Data, models, and evaluation of the arithmetic programs.* New York: Academic Press.

Tobias, S. (1989). Another look at research on the adaptation of instruction to student characteristics. *Educational Psychologist, 24*, 213–227.

Tobias, S., & Frase, L. T. (2000). Educational psychology and training. In S. Tobias & J. D. Fletcher (Eds.), *Training and retraining: A handbook for business, industry, government, and the military* (pp. 3–24). New York: Macmillan Library Reference.

Towne, D. M. (1998). *Development of scenario tutors in a generalized authoring environment: Feasibility study* (ONR Final Rep. No. 119). Los Angeles: Behavioral Technology Laboratories, University of Southern California.

Towne, D. M. (2003). Automated knowledge acquisition for intelligent support of diagnostic reasoning. In T. Murray, S. Blessing, & S. Ainsworth (Eds.), *Authoring tools for advanced technology learning environments* (pp. 121–147). Norwell, MA: Kluwer Academic Publishers.

Wiley, D. (2000). *The instructional use of learning objects.* Retrieved June 28, 2001, from http://www.reusability.org/read

Wisher, R. A., & Fletcher, J. D. (2004). The case for advanced distributed learning. *Information & Security: An International Journal, 14*, 17–25.

Woolf, B. P., & Regian, J. W. (2000). Knowledge-based training systems and the engineering of instruction. In S. Tobias & J. D. Fletcher (Eds.), *Training and retraining: A handbook for business, industry, government, and the military* (pp. 339–356). New York: Macmillan Library Reference.

Chapter 4

An Open Learning Model for Web-Based Learning Architecture

Ruimin Shen
Fan Yang
Peng Han
Shanghai Jiaotong University

As distance learning becomes one of the hotspots in network research and applications, many Web-based education systems have been established. Several good examples are Virtual-U (Groeneboer, Stockley, & Calvert, 1997), WebCT (WebCT, 2004), and Blackboard (Blackboard, 2004). To cover the entire spectrum of the learning process, these systems have implemented a number of fundamental components such as synchronous and asynchronous teaching systems, course-content delivery tools, polling and quiz modules, virtual workspaces for sharing resources, whiteboards, grade reporting systems, and assignment submission components. These research and commercial e-learning systems enable many more students to have access to a distance-learning environment, providing students and teachers with unprecedented flexibility and convenience.

At the same time, the Web-based learning framework also begets many problems. One of them is that traditional teachers may find it hard to put the course material online. Furthermore, to satisfy the requirements of multimedia-based courses, teachers need to spend a lot of time learning course-creation tools. This turns out to be difficult for the senior teachers who are accustomed to the traditional teaching methodology.

Another one is that both the number of students using the Web-based learning environment and the flow of e-learning materials grow very fast. This creates a problem of information overload for both students and teachers.

Demands for personalized services increase. We note that the existing Web-based systems often fail to provide sufficient support in such aspects as giving personalized services to each individual and helping them find their desired courses for study and answers to their questions. This problem has a great impact on the quality of Web-based education and has largely contributed to the decrease of students.

This chapter presents an open learning model for Web-based learning architecture, which was developed and is used at the School of Network Education of Shanghai Jiao Tong University, where we are motivated to build a new E-Learning system, enabling students to conduct online studies easily according to their own educational backgrounds, study habits, and paces. We are particularly interested in developing ways to handle both the information overload and personalized service. In short, our efforts are dedicated to making teachers feel that "everything is easy" and to making students feel that "everything is available" and "everyone is unique."

PANORAMA OF THE SYSTEM ARCHITECTURE

Figure 4.1 shows the architecture of the open learning system. It is composed of a real-time classroom, an EOD (education on demand) course center, a CBIR (content based indexing and retrieval) search interface, an ALC (aiding learning center), and a DAC (data analysis center). During the class, all the data needed by the lecturer and the students, including the video, audio, handwriting material, and screen operation, are transferred synchronously to each student's desktop. At the same time, all interactions are recorded and public materials are published on the Web. Therefore, several minutes after each class, those students who have no time to attend class can view the same content on the Web site. The CBIR search interface enables the students to find their desired materials conveniently and quickly. The ALC includes an assignment subsystem, an examination subsystem, and a system, namely, the answer machine subsystem, which helps the student complete the assignments on the network and answers their questions automatically.

All the didactical and user access information are collected in log files and analyzed by the DAC. Depending on the analysis results, the system can provide personalized service to the users. In particular, it allows students to interact with an automatic question-answering system to get their answers, and the teachers to analyze students' learning patterns and organize the Web-based contents efficiently. The open and personalized e-learning plat-

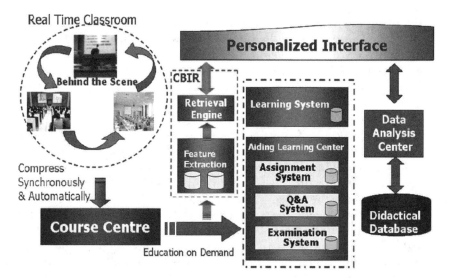

FIG. 4.1.   The architecture of the open learning system.

form is both intelligent through data mining and case-based reasoning features and user-friendly through personalized services to both teachers and students. The details of these components are discussed in the following sections.

The "Everything is Easy" Teaching Environment

Although multimedia tools have been built to help teachers create online courseware, some teachers still prefer to use blackboards, especially teachers teaching mathematics and chemistry, who feel it is difficult to write complex symbols and formulas on computer screens. To make "everything easy" for these teachers, we have developed a courseware compression system as shown in Fig. 4.2. The teachers can write anything on a computerized whiteboard and the content is transferred simultaneously to the students' desktops and integrated with the teachers' video and audio teaching materials. The students can write notes on the teachers' handwriting window. The combined information is stored in the network so the students can review it anytime. We call such content *personalized notes*. The teachers can also load their preprepared PowerPoint and Word documents into the transfer system, and then both the teachers and students can navigate these documents synchronously. Using this subsystem, the teacher can focus on teaching content instead of formats.

All the useful data from a class session are stored and published on the Web. The students missing the class session can learn themselves anytime after the class. We also convert these contents to CDS for the students who are unable to view the active online lessons due to limited bandwidth.

In such an environment, the teachers and students can always find a time to communicate that suits both parties. This conforms to our philosophy of "everything is easy."

Figures 4.3 and 4.4 show the equipment and scenario of a real classroom. We can see that there are three boards in the front of the classroom. The middle one is the video conference whiteboard, in which teachers can write everything as they wish, such as the complex mathematic formula, the chemical symbols, the maps, and so on. In front of the teacher, we can see that there is various equipment that can record all the teaching process and data during the whole class and then compress it into courseware synchronously and automatically. We also can see the two screens beside the whiteboard, which show the screen of the teacher and of the courseware separately.

In addition to the real-time learning mode, we also provide Web courses and stream courses for education on demand.

FIG. 4.3.   The equipment of a real classroom.

FIG. 4.4.   The scenario of a real classroom.

The "Everything is Available" Assistance Tool

The Content-based Indexing and Retrieval System.   A distance-learning environment often contains too many materials for students to choose. It is important to provide a tool for students to find the right materials they need. A lot of work has been done in the past on this aspect. However, many efforts have been made on standardizing the courseware with a unified data specification such as XML so that they can be indexed into the Web (Simon, 2002; Zhuang, Wu, Wu, & Liu, 2004). We believe that it is even more important to design an interface for the students to decide whether the knowledge they are searching for is inside the courseware and locate it. For example, if a student wants to review "probability," he/she can input the phrase through a textbox or microphone, and then the computer can locate the relevant materials in the courseware automatically.

In our system, we use a content-based information retrieval technology to implement this function. As we described earlier, the courseware includes such information as the teacher's video, audio, and tutorials. We consider the audio and tutorial information to be the most important materials and index them. The students can see both the teacher's video and the didactical materials such as the PowerPoint slides, as shown in Fig. 4.5.

They can also hear the teacher's voice. In addition, the system can support the courseware on demand with the index keyword input.

Question-and-Answer System Based on Case-Based Reasoning.   Because of the large number of students, usually 10 times or more than a conventional teaching class, a lot of teaching tasks have to be supported by the computer. Let's take the question and answer (Q&A) system as an example. If there are 200 students online and each student asks only one question, then it will take a teacher several hours to answer all these questions. From our experience, many questions, although put differently, usually have the same or similar meanings. The solution to this problem is to share the answers among the students and let a computer recognize similar questions and answer them automatically. If the computer cannot find an answer, it transfers the question to a teacher. After the teacher answers the question, the answer is added to the Q&A database and shared among students. Therefore, as the Q&A database accumulates questions and answers, the hit rate grows over time.

There are already some existing question-answering systems in use (IBM FAQs, 2004; Open Uni., 2004). However, most of their development was based on email-solution, keyword-matching, or word-segmentation techniques. In comparison, our system emphasizes efficiency rather than comprehension of the language. We have observed that only a limited number of questions are asked in each course and the questions are usually very simple. Therefore, we adopt an improved keyword-matching algorithm to find the answer (Han, Shen, Yang, & Yang, 2002). After a period of accumula-

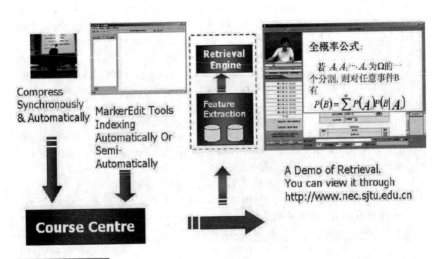

FIG. 4.5.   The workflow of the Content-based Indexing and Retrieval System.

tion, the hit rate of our Q&A system has risen to 90% and the corresponding time to answer each question is reduced to 2 s.

In order to validate the system, we are supposed to gather more data from the students. The data should not only reflect the submitted questions, as in the search engine query logs, but also how they rank the returned results. Given these question-answer log files, we can apply the above learning algorithm and keep the question-to-answer mapping always current.

When a student connects to our home page (http://www.nec.sjtu.edu.cn), he or she can select which chapter or section to study. Our system provides multimedia study materials for students, including video, audio, images, and text documents. The learning resources are well organized for study convenience. During the learning session, the student may have a question to ask. Our system provides a functional button in every study page to help the student link to the answer machine at any time. After clicking the "answer center" button, the student can access the ask question page and submit the question in natural language.

After receiving this initial query, the system shows a list of similar questions to the student. The student can choose the most similar one to see the answer. If all listed questions are not relevant, the student can submit the question to a teacher. Beyond these functions, the answer center also provides other services, such as the hot spot of lesson, the hot spot of chapter, search answer, and so on. For example, the hot spot of chapter consists of the heated discussions on certain subjects in every chapter, which is likely to help students to find out what questions other students have asked and what the correct answers are.

To be clearer, let's have a look at the case study of the Q&A system. The user can see the distribution of questions of a chapter or section in the selected time span. The results can be shown in graphs, pie charts, histograms, and so on. The user may choose different forms he likes and look into details by clicking each part of the diagram.

In addition, the relation of knowledge points can be shown in 2D or 3D graphs. According to the precedence and subsequence of a knowledge point, the system is to recommend the imperative knowledge to learn or to prepare.

The "Everyone is Different" Personalized Service

In a traditional education system, the course content is static and the teacher's assignments given to different students are the same. In reality, students have different backgrounds with the dynamic knowledge structure. Given such diversity, how do we analyze students' learning behaviors, characteristics, and knowledge structures? Furthermore, how do we send feedback of learning states to teachers? In addition, how do we visualize the analysis results to teachers and students intelligibly? In order to answer these questions, we propose a subsystem—the data analysis center, which includes an analysis tool to support the student study behavior analysis. Figure 4.6 gives the framework of the subsystem.

The function of the uniform data specification is to define a standard learning data specification based on the analysis of the learner attributes and learning behaviors (Shen, Yang, & Han, 2002). The task of the data pretreatment module is to clean and generate the learning data according to the uniform data specification. After processing, we may get some useful and clean tables. Because we organize our source with knowledge point and have relation tables of source and knowledge point, we can assess the knowledge point in two aspects. Here the knowledge point means the keyword or concept included in the courseware (Tang, Shen, Han, & Yang, 2002). The first is to use a classification algorithm to classify students into different classes based on their learning actions. The second is to find association rules among different knowledge points, the support and confidence values. What's more, it is likely to visualize the analysis results, which can help the teacher to organize different course contents and to assign homework at different difficulty levels to each student or group. The details are to be given in the following sections.

Data Pretreatment Module. As a result of the organization of data sources according to knowledge points and the building of relation tables of sources and knowledge points, the knowledge points can be assessed from two perspectives; the general information—to calculate the interest mea-

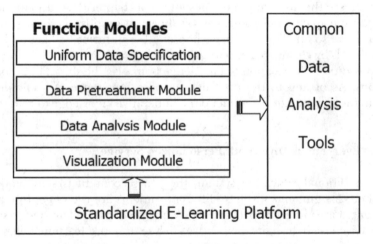

FIG. 4.6.   Framework of data analysis center.

sure and the mastery measure of each chapter point and knowledge point based on the statistical data, and the personalized information—to assign the interest measure and the mastery measure to each student. In this subsystem, the resource database is composed of two kinds of data; the log files with specification of W3C (World Wide Web Consortium) and the attribute tables in the subfunction database. The data pretreatment module will deal with the original data to clean them up. The first task is to transfer the log files into database files with DTS (data transformation services) tools. The second task is to create the corresponding tables of User_ID and IP. The transformation also solves the problem of the one-to-many relation between student's User_ID and IP attributes. The third task is to calculate the click-time and browse-span of one URL, which is very important to mine the data structure of students. The last task is to create new tables and views for further analyses. Figure 4.7 illustrates the workflow of real-time data pretreatment process.

Self-Organizing Learning Communities. In this chapter, a self-organization model is presented that relies on earlier work by Wang Fang (Wang, 2002). Around this model we have implemented our own self-organization method to cluster learners automatically and quickly, which can also help learners share their learning experiences and insights and exchange learning materials during the learning process.

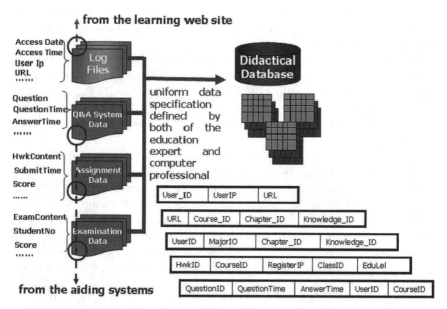

FIG. 4.7. Real-time data clean and integration.

Here, the concept "e-learner community" can be considered as a group of learners who share common preferences and mutually satisfy each other's requirements in terms of relevant knowledge resources. We constructed a two-layer multi agent mechanism to manage the learners, which consisted of learner agent (LA) and group agent (GA).

Learner agent is generated on behalf of a real learner. It has four main functions, that is, generating a learner profile for each learner and taking charge of the storage and updating of learning resources, monitoring the dynamic learning behaviors of real learner, and handling the requests of a learner.

To avoid traffic overload and to increase the efficiency of searches as well, another kind of agent, called group agent, is created. It serves as the broker for requests from a smaller community of learner agents. A group agent also has four main functions, that is, store and update local learner agents and resources, manage the association of learners to communities, interact with both the local learner agents in its management domains and the other group agents, and locate providers of resources. We also provide the formal definitions of this conceptual model (Yang, Han, Shen, Kraemer, & Fan, 2003).

As is well known, the learning behaviors are very complex. During the learning process, learners will browse online courses, query the course materials, submit questions, perform examinations, and so on. All of these behaviors represent the learning interest and intent of the learners. Generally, we view all of them as different knowledge resource requests. So we will focus on how to self-organize e-learners into communities based on the dynamic resource requests.

Based on the analysis of the dynamic learning behaviors, learners are to be asked to submit an investigation form when they register at the beginning. It can help us to collect the basic information, such as age, gender, subject, interest, and so on. Meanwhile, some special information may be collected, such as the learning preferences and resources that can be shared.

After the registration, the self-organizing engine will generate a learner agent for each learner and maintain the learner profile. Then, it will generate several group agents according to the original configuration. And every LA will choose a GA at random and register with the summarized information.

During the learning process, when a learner takes any learning action, the LA will listen to it and translate it into one kind of resource request. Here, a resource request is a keyword, such as "stack" or "queue." The GA of the requester will send this request and search through the whole community based on the search schema.

If there is an information provider matching the request, the self-organizing engine will implement the award schema, that is, the award of the requester and provider LA is increased by one. This is because both the requester and provider have made a good contribution to the system. If the provider and requester are not in the same group, the self-organizing engine will implement the exchange schema, and the exchanging rule is to move the LA with lower award toward the GA managing the LA with higher award. This hypothesis is based on the belief that a learner with high award usually means that it has either requested or provided useful information to other users. According to the clustering of the learners, the typical attributes of each group can be generated.

In order to evaluate the effectiveness and scalability of this system, we simulated the self-organizing process with increased number of learners. For simplicity in the experimental system, we made two hypotheses:

> Hypothesis 1: The resources owned by learners are documents, which can be a Web page, a slide, a session of a video. These documents can be classified into certain categories according to their context; business, education, computer science, sport, and so on.
>
> Hypothesis 2: Every learner only has one preference or interest and owns zero or more documents of relevant category.

In the experimental setting, 1,500 users were chosen, and the number of owned documents were 1,000 (one document can be owned by one or more learners); the preference category was 10.

Figure 4.8 illustrates the main test platform of this system. In the top panel, we can define the number of group agents (Gnum) and the request times per learner (maxRequestTime). The left graph at the bottom shows the learner distribution in every group, while the right one shows the statistic analysis of the request success rate.

When the experiments started, the system generated 1,500 learner agents on behalf of the real learners and 15 group agents. Learner agents randomly registered with one GA together with the summarized registration information. The GAs kept all information of learners in this group. In the learner distribution graph (the left graph at the bottom), every column represents a group, and the different colors of the rectangles represent different preferences. The height of each rectangle illustrates the number of learners with special preferences in the corresponding group. As shown in Fig. 4.8, the colors of every column are mixed and the distribution is almost average.

After the initial agent generation and registration, the LAs began to generate queries continuously in a certain period. The GAs try to cluster the learners with similar interest into one group. Figure 4.8 shows the system situation after 50 requests per learner. From the request success rate (the right graph at the bottom), we can see that the success rate increased quickly from 75% to 91% after 20 requests per learner. From the learner distribution graph (the left graph at the bottom), we find that the trend is toward fewer colors per column after 50 requests per learner. Also, we can see that some columns become shorter and some even disappeared. That means, some GAs lost all of their users during community formation. This result is consistent with the scenario of this experiment because we only have 10 categories while we generated 15 GAs. As shown in Fig. 4.9, it is the obvious trend that learners will migrate to the authority GA and some GAs were finally shifted out of the communities, such as GAs 10, 11, 12, 14.

From the request success rate graph, it can be seen that when users are not well organized, it is very unlikely for them to succeed. This is because GAs often fail to find available resources locally and need to send requests to other GAs. Because the number of searched GAs is limited, the success rate is lower during the first 10 requests per learner. Once learner communities have started forming, however, the system exhibits an obviously improved success rate and greater efficiency. Because learners who have matching requests and results are gradually grouped together, GAs can more easily find correct answers in their own groups. As a result, there is an increase in the success rate of search results. Figures 4.8 and 4.9 show that the system's ability to find correct answers to requests was obviously improving, as more and more requests were initiated in the system. And the success

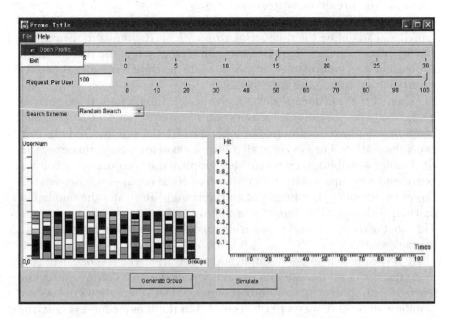

FIG. 4.8. Introduction of the test platform and system initialization.

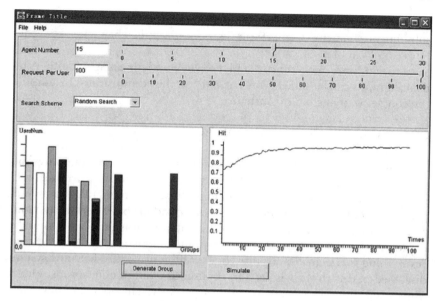

FIG. 4.9. System situation after 100 requests per learner.

rate approached 1 after the learner communities were set up. Meanwhile, the average search time for a request was greatly decreased.

The experiments have been executed using varying numbers of learners with different kinds of learners. The formation of learner communities was always quite successful and can be effectively scaled with the increased number of learners.

Visualization Module. Based on the above analysis results, we gave a visualized analysis tool for the user to view the result. At the teacher's side, we provided statistical graphs on this information; assignment complement, admitted question, exam score, and so on. As a monitor, the analysis center also can show the online study status of students, which can help the teachers to know the number of online learners, the maximum learning times, the minimum learning times, and the average learning times. According to this knowledge, the teacher can know parts of the learning status of his students and can email to the students which learning speed is too slow. The information can help teachers to reorganize the course and adapt it to better fit the needs of each group or an individual.

At the student's end, we gave the knowledge structure map of every student and signed the learning process. At each point in the knowledge map, it showed the corresponding course content and quick link of reference materials. In this part, the student can receive hints from the system on what subsequence activity to perform based on similar behavior by other "successful" students.

At the administrator's end, the high-level knowledge map and other statistical graphs can be shown, which can direct the administrator to adapt to the course content's logical structure.

CONCLUSIONS AND FUTURE WORK

This chapter presented an overall intelligent distance-learning environment, which enabled the user to do everything easily and to learn freely according to his educational background and habit. It particularly aimed at providing solutions for the information overload problem and the personalized service problem. In short, the contribution was dedicated to make the teacher feel that "everything is easy," and to make the student feel that "everything is available" and "everyone is different." The e-learning system discussed in this chapter is used by thousands of adult education students who use our distance learning networks regularly. The open and personalized e-learning platform is both intelligent through data mining and case-based reasoning features, and user friendly through personalized services to both teachers and students. In the future, we will try to extend the platform to fit wireless e-learning and try to research how to provide more personalized learning recommendations automatically.

ACKNOWLEDGMENT

This work was carried out as part of the "Research on E-Learning Collaborative Learning and Personalized Predictive Model" project (No. 60372078), supporting by NNSFC (National Nature Science Foundation of China).

REFERENCES

Blackboard. (2004). Retrieved February 12, 2003, from http://www. blackboard.com
Groeneboer, C., Stockley, D., & Calvert, T. (1997). Virtual-U: A collaborative model for online learning environments. *Proceedings of the Second International Conference on Computer support for collaborative learning*, Toronto, Ontario, 122–130.
Han, P., Shen, R. M., Yang, F., & Yang, Q. (2002). The application of case based reasoning on Q&A system. *Proceedings of Artificial Intelligence AI2002*, Canberra, Australia, 704–713.
IBM FAQs. (2004). Retrieved May 8, 2002, from http://www.ibm.com/FAQs
Open Uni. (2004). Retrieved June 20, 2003, from http://www.open.ac.uk/
Shen, R. M., Yang, F., & Han, P. (2002). Data analysis center based on E-learning platform. *Proceedings of 5th International Workshop on Internet Challenge—technology and applications*, 19–28.

Simon, S. (2002). Web-based video indexing and retrieval for teaching and learning. *Proceedings of First International Conference of Web-based learning*, Hong Kong, China, 377–385.

Tang, Y. Y, Shen, R. M., Han, P., &Yang, F. (2002). Intelligent content modifier based on concept map theory. *Journal of Shanghai Jiaotong University, 36*(5), 698–701.

Wang, F. (2002). Self-organizing communities formed by middle agents. *Proceedings of the first International conference on autonomous agents and multi-agent systems*, Bologna, Italy, 1333–1339.

WebCT. (2004). Retrieved August 7, 2002, from http://www.webct.com

Yang, F., Han, P., Shen, R. M., Kraemer, B. J., & Fan, X. W. (2003). Cooperative learning in self-organizing e-learner communities based on a multi-agents mechanism, *Proceedings of AI2003*, Perth, Australia, 490–500.

Zhuang, Y., Wu, C. M., Wu, F., & Liu, X. (2004). Improving Web-based learning: Automatic annotation of multimedia semantics and cross-media indexing. *Proceedings of the third International Conference of Web-based learning*, Beijing, China, 255–262.

Chapter 5

A Framework for Studying the Process of Implementing Web-Based Learning Systems

Ann Majchrzak
University of Southern California

Cynthia Mathis Beath
The University of Texas at Austin

The technologies of distance learning (DL) are varied. They include multimedia technology such as audio video encoding and decoding algorithms, compression and decompression techniques, computer representation of sound, and the optimization of network bandwidth efficiency (Zhang & Nunamaker, 2003). DL also utilizes knowledge management technologies such as the efficient storage, manipulation, cataloguing, searching, and retrieval of explicit knowledge in knowledgebases. In addition, ways to identify, tag, and share tacit knowledge is a key component of both knowledge management and distance learning. Collaboration technologies such as electronic bulletin boards, online chat rooms, newsgroups, and groupware are often-used components of DL technologies (Alavi, Marakas, & Yoo, 2002).

There has been a rapid growth in interest in DL technologies. For example, the market for Web-based corporate learning in the United States was expected to grow from $3 billion per annum in 1999 to $11.4 billion per annum by the mid-2000s, an annual growth rate of 40% (Zhang & Nunamaker, 2003).

Despite the emphasis and growth projections and despite some research indicating the value of technology-mediated learning environments (e.g., see several chapters in this book), current DL systems have many limitations, as reviewed by Piccoli, Ahmad, & Ivos (2001). Some students are reluctant to enroll; both students and instructors are intimidated by the technology and experience frustration and confusion; the level of engagement in the learning process can be low; and satisfaction with the learning process is lower than in traditional classroom environments. Some studies have found that simple email conversations create more effective learning environments than more sophisticated e-learning group-based systems (Alavi et al., 2002). There has been little research that would build theoretical guidance for the implementation of effective DL systems (Zhang & Nunamaker, 2003). By implementation, we encompass the many tasks related to putting a new information system into operation, usually requiring the involvement of technical information systems experts. These tasks include requirements analysis, package selection, parameterization of packages, integration of packages with other existing information systems, writing any needed customization code, training, installation, and maintenance of the system.

In this chapter, we take as our starting point that the implementation of a DL system is a more specific case of the broader class of activities referred to in the information systems literature as information systems development. As such, DL system implementation should benefit from the latest research and theorizing in information systems development. This research suggests that the traditional orientation among information systems developers to ask users to specify upfront their requirements for the content and delivery expected for the system does not apply to systems in which users' needs emerge over time (Markus, Majchrzak, & Glasser, 2002). We suggest that the needs of users (students, teachers, support) of DL systems emerge over time as they learn more about how to exploit software systems for distance learning, and more about what type of system works best for them. Therefore, a new way of managing the implementation process is needed in which requirements are allowed to develop over time and systems are designed to allow this level of flexibility. Theories and frameworks are needed to understand how to effectively manage such a complex emergent information systems implementation process. In this chapter, we describe such a framework.

THE IMPORTANCE OF KNOWLEDGE SYNTHESIS IN TODAY'S SOFTWARE DEVELOPMENT

"Knowledge acquisition, knowledge sharing, and knowledge integration" have always been the most significant activities of a software design team (Walz, Elam, & Curtis, 1993, p. 63). However, recent trends in software projects have made the need for knowledge synthesis more complex than ever before. These trends include software development projects that; 1) integrate across functions, not just within one organization but across organizations as well, 2) depend on an increasingly complex set of stakeholders throughout the development lifecycle, and 3) require that the system be designed not just for operational value, but for lasting strategic and innovative value as well. These trends suggest that software projects today require the synthesis of knowledge from a complex array of stakeholders to proceed effectively.

Integration Within and Across Organizations

Gone are the days of local systems—islands of automation—for which a small group of users could share their knowledge with a small group of programmers to obtain the system of their choice. Today's software projects seek to integrate these islands, both within and across organizations, requiring knowledge about the entire organization or organizations (Pucciarelli, Claps, Morello, & Magee, 1999). This integration often occurs by introducing shared applications and shared infrastructure, requiring knowledge about alternative packaged solution providers and infrastructure requirements (Rosser & Natis, 2000). Today's software efforts are further complicated by a need to accommodate localized customization within these integrated systems. For example, successful Web-based training delivery systems offer a wide variety of features and formats for delivering training so that parameters can be customized at the local level. Web-based initiatives have a lower cost of ownership if they rely on a standardized infrastructure of Web-related technologies and policies, yet allow individual businesses or customers to generate customized Web sites. Therefore, today's software project requires a synthesis of knowledge about infrastructure options and standards, as well as the intimate details of how different types of training needs can be met.

Dependence on a Complex Array of Stakeholders

Cross-functional or intraorganizational scope is just one factor that increases the need to synthesize diverse sources of knowledge in today's software projects. The number and diversity of stakeholders[1] is another

---

[1]We use the term "stakeholder" to refer to any group or individual who will be affected in some way by the design, development, implementation, or use of the information system, its infrastructure, or components. Stakeholders in a software project might include current or future users, clients, suppliers, consultants, sponsors, developers, trainers, students, and so forth. Ideally, all those who have a stake in decisions made during the software project are also participants when those decisions are made. Practically speaking, participation is often delegated. We use the term "participants" to refer to the group of delegates to the project who represent the interests of the stakeholders.

factor. For example, for a DL system, stakeholders may include the vendor of a packaged solution, the consultant customizing the package to the organization's needs, the consultant integrating across different packages, the platform providers, the set of business units dispersed across the company's global organization, corporate IT tasked with maintaining corporate IT standards, functional or decentralized IT staff, content experts, and different profiles of students with different needs. Gartner projects that by 2004, 90% of the multienterprise projects will involve at least 10 vendors and business partners (Phelan, 2000). Not only is there a large set of diverse actors in the process, but they all may play a role in controlling the information systems project (Kirsch, 1997). These stakeholders must collectively make a large number of decisions or design trade-off choices. Most of these stakeholders must share knowledge with each other about their technologies, businesses, requirements, and constraints in order to collectively and individually make decisions for the project as well as for their own organization.

Design for Both Strategic and Innovative Uses

Software projects in the information age are increasingly focused on achieving a strategic competitive advantage, not simply meeting an efficiency goal (Pucciarelli et al., 1999). To achieve a strategic advantage from an information system often requires solutions that uniquely integrate the organization's business products, people, processes, and information systems—not just for today, but also into the foreseeable future. Sampler (2000) argued that companies today are using the Internet to "re-invent their firms, expect the unexpected, and compete when the future is not forecastable" (p. 212)—a set of expectations that demands continuous innovation. For such innovation to occur, stakeholders must integrate knowledge not only about current facts and trends (such as technology options and specific business requirements), but also about abstractions and generalizable principles that will stimulate future ideas about how to solve emergent problems. This focus on innovation has another implication as well; how project success is defined. Traditionally, project success is defined as the delivery of an information system that meets specifications on time and within budget, and that is used to improve the effectiveness or efficiency of the business process. A focus on innovation suggests that information systems may never be "delivered" in the sense that they are finalized and the development project is ended; reinvention may continue far into the future. Moreover, a focus on innovation suggests that specifications may not be known in advance; thus, successful projects may be those that are able to identify and offer innovative solutions (Rosser, 2000). Finally, successful projects are those that teach others how to avoid mistakes in the future. Therefore, this focus on innovation introduces a broad definition of project success—a broad definition to which we subscribe in this chapter.

In sum, today's software projects require stakeholders to accumulate and synthesize knowledge about the present and future, about local and global solutions, and about differing and often conflicting needs and purposes, as viewed from a variety of different stakeholder perspectives. Therefore, broad stakeholder participation is more important than ever. Although stakeholder participation has long been viewed as an important factor in successful development and implementation of systems, the issue that has not been resolved is how stakeholders should most efficiently and effectively participate to synthesize across such a complex array of knowledge perspectives, that is, how to manage an emergent process (Markus et al., 2002).

There has been a healthy stream of research on how to manage stakeholder participation (Barki & Hartwick, 1994; Hartwick & Barki, 1994; Hunton & Beeler, 1997; Robey, 1994, to name a few post-1990). Common across this research is the recognition of the need for learning, but there is little specific, empirically validated advice on how to most efficiently and effectively engender learning during the development process (e.g., Gasson, 1999; Kirsch & Beath, 1996). For example, Browne and Rogich (2001) lamented that structured interviews are often recommended for requirements elicitation but there is surprisingly little guidance offered regarding the content of such interviews.

Therefore, research and theory are needed on how to manage encounters among stakeholders in a way that stakeholders learn from each other and develop mutual understanding and insight over time. In the next section, we draw on existing theories in cognitive and educational psychology as well as on the negotiation literature to present a theoretical framework for managing stakeholder encounters in software development projects to enhance learning. The purpose of presenting such a framework is to draw future research attention to this issue.

FRAMEWORK FOR ENHANCING LEARNING AMONG PROJECT STAKEHOLDERS

Figure 5.1 presents a framework, which we call the "path to mutual learning in information systems development efforts." This path has five elements:

1. Mutual learning is an important mediator between stakeholder participation and information systems development project success.
2. How the dialogue among stakeholders is managed during a stakeholder encounter will affect the efficiency with which mutual learning is encouraged within the team.

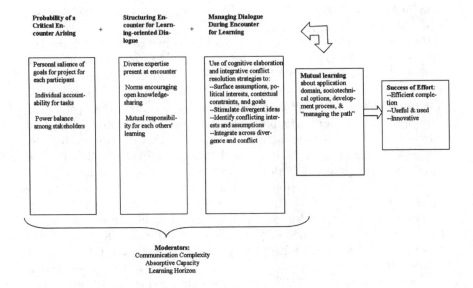

FIG. 5.1.   Path to mutual learning in information systems development efforts.

3. How a stakeholder encounter is structured will affect the efficiency and effectiveness of the dialogue for fostering mutual learning.
4. How a project is structured will affect the probability that a stakeholder encounter efficiently and effectively fosters mutual learning.
5. The "path to mutual learning" is affected by moderators.

Simply stated, we argue that mutual learning among stakeholders is important to the success of an information systems project and that this mutual learning is more likely when the probability of having critical encounters is high, and when encounters are structured and stakeholder dialogues are managed to facilitate learning from each other. This relationship between encounters, structures, dialogue, and learning is made more complicated by three moderators. In the following subsections, we discuss each of these elements of the framework, and the implications for future research that each element raises.

Element #1: Mutual Learning

Mutual learning is defined as mutual appreciation and knowledge of each other's expertise, assumptions, interests, contexts, and constraints as they contribute to the project (Nelson & Cooprider, 1996). Our model suggests that mutual learning is a key mediator between participation and successful project outcomes. That is, stakeholder participation is of value only when it leads to mutual learning. Therefore, a criterion for evaluating which participative behaviors stakeholders should engage in should be the learning that is likely to be fostered by the behavior. Learning should thus become the focus of research on how users participate, not the participation behavior per se.

Element #2: Dialogue During an Encounter Must be Managed to Engender Mutual Learning

Across the research on information systems development, the most commonly suggested method for managing stakeholder dialogue is for the developer to use good communication skills (e.g., Byrd, Cossick, & Zmud, 1992; McKeen, Guimaraes, & Wetherbe, 1994). However, this is because the learning focus is often limited to the accurate transfer of knowledge from user to analyst, rather than the building of mutual understanding and insight or the surfacing of emergent requirements. In contrast, the cognitive learning and negotiation literatures provide more specific theory-based guidance on managing dialogue to facilitate mutual learning for which empirical validation in the information systems development domain has only just begun (Lim & Majchrzak, 2002; Majchrzak, Beath, Lim, & Chin, 2004; Zhong & Majchrzak, 2004). According to these literatures, one strategy for facilitating mutual learning among interdependent and interactive learners has been referred to as "elaborative interrogation" (Willoughby, Wood, McDermott, & McLaren, 2000), "self-explanations" (Webb & Palincsar, 1996), and cognitive elaboration (O'Donnell & O'Kelly, 1994). We use the term "collaborative elaboration" (CE) to emphasize two points; the group context in which learning occurs and the elaboration process that stimulates the learning.

The notion underlying CE is that people learn not by listening to others, but by explaining what little they already know—their own assumptions, goals, language, and inferences—to others. By explaining (i.e., elaborating) their own perspectives and observing others' reactions, participants begin to see the inconsistencies between their own knowledge and that of others. Elaborating also helps learners to generalize their knowledge for use in new contexts. As all participants in the social setting explain their *own* knowledge, eventually abstracted principles can be identified and the principles can be recontextualized to the shared project at hand. In addition, explaining material to someone else leads to more differentiated, complex, and organized cognitive structures than merely learning the material by oneself. Moreover, by explicating their own knowledge, participants are able to more rapidly determine how to accommodate to new knowledge. Research has repeatedly shown that cognitive elaboration leads to a deeper understanding of new concepts and metacognitive skills compared to control conditions of nonelaborated help, being lectured to, and the use of good communication techniques (e.g., see reviews by Webb & Palincsar, 1996).

The research on cognitive elaboration has been based primarily on research conducted in school settings, in which students elaborate on their own understanding—no matter how limited—in the presence of others. Later, we suggest an operationalization of this CE strategy for managing dialogue among stakeholders in an information systems development effort, contrasting the strategy with common practice.

- Have stakeholders describe the part of the development effort they know the least about (rather than the common practice of designers giving minilectures during meetings on technology issues and clients giving minilectures during meetings on application domain issues). Therefore, clients describe technology options to the degree possible, using their accumulated knowledge (e.g., from what they have seen others do in a benchmarking visit or via public media summaries). Developers and other stakeholders then reflect on or respond to the assumptions made by the clients about the technology, and how these assumptions are the same or different from theirs. To save time, this could be done at the same time that technical options are first presented. Similarly, developers would then describe the client's work practices and organizational options, to the best of their ability, and the clients and other stakeholders would respond to the assumptions made by developers. Users from one department could be asked to describe another department's work practices with members of the other department. Clients or developers could be asked to describe the development processes to be followed by the vendors involved in the development effort. To save time, work process descriptions would be presented only in sufficient detail to elicit assumptions, not to create a data flow diagram or process flowchart. Discussions of development processes could be done at a project planning meeting, when an integrated development process is devised.

- Ask stakeholders to describe a range of concrete scenarios in order to elicit their assumptions about their practices (instead of the common procedure of asking clients for descriptions of their "normal" work practice). Role-plays, walk-throughs of real activity sequences, and reports of observations made by stakeholders during their work under various conditions are example tactics To save time, this elicitation of concrete scenarios could be done as part of other activities such as design meetings, requirements analysis, and project planning.

- Promote divergent problem definitions, interpretations of information, sources for information, as well as solutions (instead of rapidly seeking consensus among different stakeholders, as is often done in joint application development sessions; Davidson, 1999). This suggests that encounters should be managed to encourage each individual stakeholder to share his or her own divergent ideas (by using what-ifs, metaphors, scenario planning, out-of-the-box exercises, brainstorming, etc.) without any immediate requirement for convergence. These divergent ideas should be publicly captured and displayed, and their differences, in particular, should be constructively explored in some depth. To save time, brainstorming techniques and group support systems could be used. Therefore, multiple alternative sociotechnical designs, prototypes, information interpretations, and problem definitions would be considered and referenced throughout the discussion. The norm of an "agreement to allow disagreements" would be promoted.

- Make extensive use of demonstrations but have those least knowledgeable take the hands-on role during the demonstrations (instead of the common practice of developers demonstrating prototypes). For example, have clients (not developers) demonstrate the use of the prototype so that implicit assumptions about how they would use the prototype are surfaced. Similarly, have clients (rather than vendors) demonstrate commercial application domain software packages so that assumptions about the technical quality of the package can be surfaced. Or have developers (rather than vendors) demonstrate how to link the package to the existing infrastructure. To save time, these could be done as part of the normal package demonstration process; the difference from common practice is who is giving the demonstration.

- Use changes in requirements and developer reactions to proposed changes as opportunities to help learn about the business process, context, technology, and design process that invoked the need for the change (instead of treated as failures that invoke defensive strategies). Therefore, for example, a request for a requirement change is met by stakeholders as a time for everyone to reexamine their assumptions about work practices, context, or technology, rather than as a time to approve or prohibit a specific change.

- Design and present alternative prototypes to surface cognitive conflicts between prototypes and underlying assumptions (instead of converging quickly on a single prototype). The purpose in generating multiple alternative prototypes is not to garner a vote amongst them but to closely observe how people's reactions differ, so that assumptions underlying these reactions can be surfaced. By eliciting distinct reactions to multiple different prototypes, insights into the accuracy of assumptions about work processes or technologies can be gained, especially as those insights change over time as part of the emergent design process (Markus et al., 2004). To save time in generating multiple alternative prototypes, rapid application development tools and automated integration tools should be used in developing prototypes.

The practical result of using CE strategies for managing a dialogue will be extensive cognitive conflict (Barki & Hartwick, 2001). This cognitive conflict must be effectively resolved for mutual learning to be enhanced. Negotiation theory addresses conflict resolution directly. According to Smith and McKeen (1992), goal conflict—where the interests of the stakeholders are at odds and will remain at odds after the conflict is resolved— is expected in new system development projects. These conflicts do not "go away" but are continuous and recurring parts of the development project. To manage this conflict, negotiation theory suggests that resistance points (the point at which a stakeholder would walk away from a negotiation), target points (a stakeholder's fondest hopes for outcomes), and fallback options must be uncovered in a creative discovery of an attractive compromise solution (e.g., Pinkley, Neale, & Bennett, 1994). In this creative discovery and compromise process, stakeholders search for integrative solutions, that is, solutions that expand the set of rewards (the "larger pie") to satisfy more of each stakeholder's target goals (although perhaps not every one of them) than would any distributive solution (Bazerman, 1994). The negotiation literature has identified techniques to help with the search for integrative solutions, many of which are similar to cognitive elaboration. In addition, integrative dialogue emphasizes identifying resistance points so as to bracket the range of plausible alternatives from ideal to unacceptable. Managing prototype presentations for the express purpose of identifying resistance points—focusing on what is *not* acceptable, not just what is acceptable—is an example of how negotiation theory can be applied to a stakeholder dialogue. Finally, negotiation theory suggests that alternatives and resistance points come in bundles and therefore, presenting multiple prototypes explicitly to understand relationships among wants, practices, and assumptions is a way to manage the dialogue.

Element #3: Structuring the Encounter for Mutual Learning

Even though a dialogue may use cognitive elaboration and integrative conflict resolution strategies, the dialogue may not yield mutual learning if the encounter itself is not structured to support learning. Webb and Palincsar (1996) suggested that a dialogue will yield deeper understanding when a diverse mix of expertise is present during the encounter, norms for open knowledge sharing and trustworthy use of information have been established, and incentives exist for participants to take responsibility for mutual learning.

Software projects that include a diverse mix of expertise are rarely a challenge, as the implementation process includes many review checkpoints, project meetings, and opportunities for a diverse mix of experts to evaluate change requests. The more joint activities and shared tasks there are, the more learning encounters one might expect. Norms need to be established in which all stakeholders are expected and encouraged to openly share information. A DL vendor, for example, would be expected to inform other stakeholders when problems arise in preparing the software to meet the clients' needs; similarly, the client would be expected to inform the vendor when problems arise about budgeting. The norms would need to be explicitly espoused and reinforced by leaders of each and every stakeholder group. Finally, mutual responsibility for learning can be achieved by structuring the learning encounter such that individuals can only attain their personal goals if the group is successful (Johnson & Johnson, 1998). For software projects, encounters could be structured to support mutual responsibility and learning by asking or expecting stakeholders to:

- Begin a development effort by identifying crucial, project-threatening knowledge gaps (such as about the work-in-practice, software development process and tools, technology options, strategic vision, future work practice alternatives, and organizational constraints);
- Define the job of each stakeholder not to be limited to problem solving but to closing the identified knowledge gaps; and
- Periodically assess each other's knowledge to ensure that fewer knowledge gaps persist over time.

In sum, encounters that are likely to lead to learning need to be planned and utilized as opportunities for learning.

Element #4: Structuring a Project to Increase the Probability of a Critical Encounter Arising

Stakeholder encounters will arise frequently throughout a development effort. Every hallway conversation, every email, every telephone discussion between two stakeholders is an encounter. However, not all encounters are critical. Newman and Robey (1992) suggested that the way to view software development is as a process. This process is one that is punctuated by "relatively brief events ... that offer opportunities for an established equilibrium to change" (p. 255). Newman and Robey (1992) referred to these brief events as "critical encounters." Therefore, to engender mutual learning, the project manager must structure the project to increase the probability that sufficient critical encounters will arise, that is, that stakeholders will be put into situations where they will willingly share their assumptions and ideas about the design. Therefore, it is important that stakeholders participating in the project are strongly motivated (ideally by means of *both* extrinsic and intrinsic incentives) to see the project succeed. Moreover, each stakeholder must be held individually accountable for certain tasks. Finally, the CE behaviors that results in mutual learning will be difficult to engender if there are strong power differentials among the stakeholders (Kirsch, 1997). Stakeholders who stand to lose face when their ignorance is revealed will find the self-elaboration process emotionally challenging. Stakeholders who have power over other participants may also be reluctant to correct their assumptions or to give honest and open feedback. And, finally, norms of open and trusting information sharing will be difficult to establish if power differentials are too great.

Element #5: The Role of Moderators

We suggest three moderators of particular importance in our path to mutual learning; (a) communication complexity, (b) absorptive capacity, and (c) learning horizon. Communication complexity has three dimensions; cognitive complexity (intensity of information exchanged, multiplicity of views, and need to translate information before it can be used), dynamic complexity (effect of time constraints and changes on understanding), and affective complexity (sensitivity of communication to attitudes; Te'eni, 2001). Under high degrees of communication complexity, there is a greater need for learning-oriented encounters structured for mutual learning.

The second moderator, absorptive capacity of stakeholders, refers to the requirement that stakeholders have the ability to integrate cross-disciplinary perspectives of a problem (Gasson, 1999). Stakeholders with greater absorptive capacity will be able to gain greater learning benefits from the encounters.

Finally, an organization's learning horizon may be short or long, depending on its view of the period over which the learning achieved in a project will generate returns. If the project is seen as an initiative to address a temporary problem, the learning horizon may be very short. If the project is seen as one in which technical or intellectual infrastructure is being developed, then the learning horizon might be quite long. If the organization anticipates follow-on initiatives, it is likely to value learning not just about how to implement the focal system, but about developing the organization's capability to manage projects, design more effective business processes, and use information technology more effectively in future initiatives (Ross, Beath, & Goodhue, 1996). In particular, if an organization conceives of the project as simply the first step in the emergence of radically redefined and reengineered work processes, they are more likely to invest in the development of mutual learning.

IMPLICATIONS FOR DISTANCE LEARNING RESEARCH

There are many implications of our framework for distance learning systems implementation. First, DL involves many stakeholders; content developers, content deliverers, students with varying levels of background knowledge, motivation, and technology experience, technology infrastructure vendors, support staff, project managers, and business unit managers who derive benefit from well-trained employees. Each of these stakeholders has a different role to play in the development process, representing different, often conflicting needs. Each stakeholder will respond differently to each other, as they constantly renegotiate and reprioritize their emergent needs relative to others. Changes in the context will arise (e.g., organizational, technological, human, and strategic) in this rapidly growing area of distance learning. Vendors will improve their packages. In particular, students and teachers will adapt to DL, in both functional and dysfunctional ways. As such, any negotiated consensus on DL system requirements is likely to be only temporary.

A second implication of our framework for DL systems implementation is that it suggests how systems can be implemented to allow, expect, and accommodate the emergence of newly understood requirements. Drawing on the collaborative learning literature, we argue that instead of soliciting supposedly established requirements, or forcing a temporary consensus on requirements, DL systems implementers should structure the implementation process to allow for a continuous collaborative learning process. Such a process would put an emphasis on self-elaboration, learning about the domains of other stakeholders, and having stakeholders identify and coperform tasks that underscore the expected long-term interdependence among the stakeholders. Therefore, instead of having "requirements meetings," stakeholders would repeatedly engage in the coproduction and use of exemplar systems, treating each coproduction and use as an opportunity for learning about the emergent DL process.

A final implication of our framework is that the technology infrastructure underlying a DL system needs to be exceedingly flexible to accommodate to these different and evolving systems and needs. A DL system should be considered to be more of a platform containing a variety of specific content-enriched tools than a software application specifically designed for a particular DL need. Technologically, such a platform would include the range of tools available in many knowledge management, e-learning, and collaboration platforms, such as calendars, grade managers, discussion threads, interactive video, file sharing, intelligent search, data mining, simulation, as well as presentation. As important, though, the DL implementation team would need to convert these separate content-independent tools into a platform enriched with shared content. For example, calendars could be "seeded" with key events for the organization so that DL instructors would begin their customization of the calendaring feature with events that may impact the DL course scheduling. Discussion threads for a course could be seeded with suggested topics to facilitate learning so that DL instructors could easily customize the topics. Ways to represent the evolving learning of the student (e.g., through hyperbolic trees or other pattern-matching tools) could be offered as they pertain to the course content so that instructors and students could identify learning patterns. As the various stakeholders experiment with these content-enriched tools, this collective learning can be used to provide further enhancement to the DL system offerings.

In conclusion, we suggest that successful DL systems will be those that are allowed to evolve over time. Just as the students will be learning from the system, so should the developers.

REFERENCES

Alavi, M., Marakas, G. M., & Yoo, Y. (2002). A comparative study of distributed learning environments on learning outcomes. *Information Systems Research, 13*(4), 404–415.

Barki, H., & Hartwick, J. (1994). Measuring user participation, user involvement, and user attitude. *MIS Quarterly, 18*(1), 59–79.

Barki, H., & Hartwick, J. (2001). Interpersonal conflict and its management in information systems development. *MIS Quarterly, 25*(2), 195–228.

Bazerman, M. (1994). *Judgment in managerial decision making* (3rd ed.). New York: Wiley.

Browne, G. J., & Rogich, M. B. (2001). An empirical investigation of user requirements elicitation: Comparing the effectiveness of prompting techniques. *Journal of Management Information Systems, 17*(4), 223–249.

Byrd, T. A., Cossick, K. L., & Zmud, R. W. (1992). A synthesis of research on requirements analysis and knowledge acquisition techniques. *MIS Quarterly, 16*(1), 117–138.

Davidson, E. J. (1999). Joint application design (JAD) in practice. *The Journal of Systems and Software, 45*(3), 215–224.

Gasson, S. (1999). The reality of user-centered design. *Journal of End User Computing, 11*(4), 3–12.

Hartwick, J., & Barki, H. (1994). Explaining the role of user participation in information system use. *Management Science, 40*(4), 440–465.

Hunton, J. E., & Beeler, J. D. (1997). Effects of user participation in systems development: A longitudinal field experiment. *MIS Quarterly, 21*(4), 359–388.

Johnson, D. W., & Johnson, R. T. (1998). Cooperative learning and social interdependence theory. In R. S. Tindale (Ed.), *Theory and research on small groups* (pp. 9–35). New York: Plenum.

Kirsch, L. J. (1997). Portfolios of control modes in IS project management. *Information Systems Research, 8*(3), 214–239.

Kirsch, L. J., & Beath, C. M. (1996). The enactments and consequences of token, shared and compliant participation in information systems development. *Accounting, Management and Information Technology, 6*(4), 221–254.

Lim, R., & Majchrzak, A. (2002). *Patterns of cognitive conflict in ISD teams: A process view.* Paper presented at the meeting of the Academy of Management 2002 Meetings, Denver, Co.

Majchrzak, A., Beath, C. M., Lim, R., & Chin, W. (2005). Managing client dialogues during information systems design to facilitate client learning. *MIS Quarterly, 29*(4), forthcoming.

Markus, M. L., Majchrzak, A., & Gasser, L. (2002). A design theory for systems that support emergent knowledge processes. *MIS Quarterly, 26*(3), 179–212.

McKeen, J. D., Guimaraes, T., & Wetherbe, J. C. (1994). The relationship between user participation and user satisfaction: An investigation of four contingency factors. *MIS Quarterly, 18*(4), 427–451.

Nelson, K., & Cooprider, J. (1996). The contribution of shared knowledge to IS group performance. *MIS Quarterly, 20*(4), 409–432.

Newman, M., & Robey, D. (1992). A social process model of user-analyst relationships. *Information Systems Research, 16*(2), 249–266.

O'Donnell, A. M., & O'Kelly, J. (1994). Learning from peers: Beyond the rhetoric of positive results. *Educational Psychology Review, 6,* 321–349.

Phelan, P. (2000). Preparing the project manager for multi-enterprise projects. *Gartner Research Note* (No. QA-11-4853). Stamford, CT: Gartner Research.

Piccoli, G., Ahmad, R., & Ives, B. (2001). Web-based virtual learning environments: A research framework and a preliminary assessment of effectives in basic IT skills training. *MIS Quarterly, 25*(4), 401–426.

Pinkley, R. L., Neale, M. A., & Bennett, R. (1994). The impact of alternatives to settlement in a dyadic negotiation. *Organizational Behavior and Human Decision Processes, 37,* 97–116.

Pucciarelli, J., Claps, C., Morello, D. T., & Magee, F. (1999). IT management scenario: Navigating uncertainty. *Gartner Strategic Analysis Report* (No. R-08-6153). Stamford, CT: Gartner Research.

Robey, D. (1994). Modeling interpersonal processes during system development: Further thoughts and suggestions. *Information Systems Research, 5*(4), 439–445.

Ross, J. W., Beath, C. M., & Goodhue, D. L. (1996). Develop long-term competitiveness through IT assets. *Sloan Management Review, 38*(1), 31–45.

Rosser, B. (2000). Strategic planning in internet time. *Gartner Research Note* (No. TG-11-4993). Stamford, CT: Gartner Research.

Rosser, B., & Natis, Y. (2000). E-business is driving a new IT architecture. *Gartner Research Note* (No. T-10-6864). Stamford, CT: Gartner Research.

Sampler, J. (2000). The ICE (Internet Changes Everything) age. In R. W. Zmud (Ed.), *Framing the domains of IT research: Glimpsing the future through the past* (pp. 209–220). Cincinnati, OH: Pinnaflex Educational Resources Inc.

Smith, H. A., & McKeen, J. D. (1992). Computerization and management: A study of conflict and change. *Information and Management, 22*(1), 53–64.

Te'eni, D. (2001). Review: A cognitive-affective model of organizational communication for designing IT. *MIS Quarterly, 25*(2), 251–312.

Walz, D. B., Elam, J. J., & Curtis, B. (1993). Inside a software design team: Knowledge acquisition, sharing, and integration. *Communications of the ACM, 36*(10), 63–77.

Webb, N. M., & Palincsar, A. S. (1996). Group processes in the classroom. In D. Berliner & R. Calfee (Eds.), *Handbook of research in educational psychology* (pp. 841–873). London: Prentice Hall.

Willoughby, T., Wood, E., McDermott, C., & McLaren, J. (2000). Enhancing learning through strategy instruction and group interaction: Is active generation of elaborations critical? *Applied Cognitive Psychology, 14*, 19–30.

Zhang, D., & Nunamaker, J. F. (2003). Powering e-learning in the new millennium: An overview of e-learning and enabling technology. *Information Systems Frontiers, 5*(2), 207–218.

Zhong, J., & Majchrzak, A. (2004). An exploration of impact of cognitive elaboration on learning in ISD projects. *Information and Technology Management, 5*(½), 143–160.

Chapter 6

Issues in Synchronous Versus Asynchronous E-learning Platforms

Eric Hamilton
US Air Force Academy

John Cherniavsky
National Science Foundation

Learning platforms and the communications they involve can be characterized along several dimensions. We present six here and a seventh (synchronicity) in the next section:

1. The control of learning activities: *Who or what is in charge of the learning activities?* (These include traditional answers of teacher or student, but also include underlying software platforms and agent systems and social structures that emerge through the systems interactivity.)
2. The communication bandwidth (electronic or otherwise). *How much information can be transmitted and/or retained and in what time frame?* (We also propose in the final section a pedagogical variant of this dimension, *interactional bandwidth.*)
3. The granularity at which information can be shared. *The content level— symbols, information, knowledge—of the shared information.*
4. The representational forms used to share knowledge. *How is knowledge represented—text, graphics, animation, sound, video, or other means?*

5. The persistence of knowledge representations in the learning environment. *How readily available are artifacts produced by a teacher or student to the participants in the learning environment?*

6. The pedagogical frameworks that characterize the learning environment. *Is knowledge delivered, constructed individually, constructed socially? Does it scaffold and build procedural knowledge forms or higher order forms?*

These dimensions apply to both WBL and F2F classroom settings, and to their blended hybrids. For example, a typical classroom-learning platform involves a blackboard and a teacher. In a lecture mode, the locus of control generally resides with the teacher, although shared single user (student use) or simultaneous users (multiple students at the blackboard) are possible. The representation persistency is transient (blackboards are erased; discussions are not recorded). The bandwidth is adequate for text/symbols and simple graphics. The granularity level is low because little information can be captured and shared beyond what can be written on the blackboard; the communication modalities are writing and speech; and the pedagogical framework is predominantly one of knowledge delivery rather than knowledge construction.

A more modern learning platform might consist of a large whiteboard display (the whiteboard), and individual appliances that students or teachers use to communicate with the whiteboard. The locus of control can now be the teacher, shared single user, or simultaneous users; the representations are persistent assuming a database captures the whiteboard's information; the bandwidth depends on the network bandwidth and the display capabilities of the whiteboard and the appliances; the granularity may be high because all information sent to or from the blackboard can be captured and summarized or presented in a variety of forms; and the communication modalities are multimedia—writing, speech, video, sound, and graphics, all of which are fully capable of capture and persistence.

SYNCHRONICITY

One other very important dimension for characterizing learning platforms is synchronicity. F2F education settings are inherently synchronous: The teacher and learners are in the same space at the same time. WBL forms, in contrast, that provide "anytime, anyplace" flexibility to learners are asynchronous, in that they do not require learners to be online or connected to a teacher at a specific time for specific purposes. Asynchronous environments can be relatively low bandwidth, text based, and inexpensive. They can allow the learner to determine if he or she is ready to log in or participate in course activities independent of whether other learners or the course teacher or facilitator are available or present in the virtual learning space. An obvious consequence is that pure asynchronous learning, by definition, does not permit real-time interaction between students, or between a teacher and students. This does not mean that there is no interaction—a threaded discussion is a simple example of interaction-intensive but asynchronous communication form.

A typical distance learning (Simonson, Smaldino, Albright, & Zvacek, 2002) asynchronous learning session begins with a student logging into the system. Depending on the variables discussed earlier, course material may be presented to the student in the form of text or richer multimedia (e.g., simulations and models of physical phenomenon, animations, video, etc.), and the student may be asked to recite information to solve problems through an explicit problem–solution interaction or through directed interaction in a virtual world. Typical sessions may often include threaded interactions with other learners. Asynchronous distance education does not rely on students listening to or observing live, remote lectures, nor on real-time interactions between learners and other learners or the teacher. Private online universities in the United States, such as Phoenix University and Capella University, at the time of this writing, furnish a tightly formatted asynchronous environment for coursework.

In contrast to asynchronous learning platforms, synchronous platforms do not have "anytime/anyplace" flexibility; instead, they take a "same time/anyplace" approach. They may permit real-time interactions, although some synchronous learning forms, such as satellite or netcast lectures or slide presentations may actually involve considerably less interactivity than asynchronous settings. Significantly different social dynamics are obviously induced when interactive versus unidirectional.

Hybrid or blended synchronicity has been in currency for some time. In the early 1990s, for example, MIT's Sloan School of Management provided (synchronous) live video feeds for some courses to Asia while running (asynchronous) email and Internet communications for other course components (Feller, 1995). More recently, the Network College of Shanghai Jiao Tong University (SJTU) gives students the choice of sitting in classrooms to listen to live lecture feeds or accessing them later. The lecture feeds are unidirectional in one sense—students cannot interact with the lecturer—but synchronously interactive in another sense, because students can interact with each other and with teaching assistants onsite at the remote locations. Further, software agents interact with learners as they pose questions and establish ability levels by grouping learners (Yang, Han, Shen, Kraemer, & Fan, 2003).

Learning Effects

As in the case of almost any taxonomy or categorization of educational designs, one approach (e.g., synchronicity v. asynchronicity) is not inherently better than the other in terms of impact on learning. Although most distance education occurs asynchronously (Marjanovic, 1999) evidence suggests that learners express preferences for blended approaches, when possible, that include both forms and, where possible, include F2F sessions (Gregory, 2003). As in the case of just-in-time-teaching (JiTT) discussed later in this chapter, or other examples of networked and Web-active classrooms, some platforms consist of dynamic composites of F2F and WBL experiences. Learning effects research, that is, research that is able to determine an effect size using F2F vs WBL (including the large body of work that has been summed up on the "no significant difference" finding comparing distance and F2F learning; Cavanaugh, 2001), will not arrive at simplistic answers to "what works" types of questions. Questions about what works, under what conditions, and with what students are more difficult to address but ultimately are more meaningful.

Research on WBL learning effects poses challenges that can be quite different from research in other education platforms. One of the most interesting is that neither the researcher nor teachers in WBL typical investigations are advantaged (or encumbered) by having spent many years in the milieu under investigation, building their own store of observations, insights, and biases. For the first time in education research history, a domain in question has not produced the researchers investigating it. From the practitioner side, at least for the foreseeable future, this also means that the authentic craft knowledge that develops in distance education settings will likely take a different character or quality than that which has been increasingly recognized as important in effectively researching classroom practice. The divergence of WBL from F2F learning forms is a matter of gradation, and thus might be considered in terms of degrees of proximity.

Degrees of Proximity to Traditional F2F Learning

For example, a first degree of proximity is incremental and would involve WBL forms that are merely intended to mimic F2F instructional design but add distance as a variable. Satellite or netcast lecture feeds to distributed listeners closely mimics classroom lecture pedagogies. The goal of this synchronous education form is simply to extend the reach of the lecture; the skills the teachers develop are primarily translational (Kanuka, Collett, & Caswell, 2002) to recreate electronically the F2F experience of the classroom. Similarly, college courses offered online and asynchronously often are also designed only to reproduce the in-class experience for remote students. The virtual learning space may include a video media file of each of the professor's lectures; synchronized presentation slides or other visuals to accompany the lecture, and syllabus and readings. These materials may be viewed at the learner's discretion and choice of timing. The incremental advantages include anytime and anyplace flexibility for the student (including lecture and slide show replay), and more immediate access to hyperlinked resources.

A second degree removed from F2F environments are WBL settings by which the medium fundamentally alters traditional F2F classroom dynamics rather than mimic or extend them over distances. Two examples are discussions and assessments.

F2F classroom discussions provide an interactional richness, by which gestures, facial expressions or other cues, voice modulation, and the spoken word all "wrap around" or contribute to semantic content of oral discussions. In contrast, threaded discussion forms bottleneck messages in highly constraining ways. There are no facial gestures, no spoken language or auditory components, no classroom semiotics or other visual cues that become part of the discussion context. Discussions become serialized over multiple online sessions for each learner; numerous contributions can be seen at every login, but generally it is not until a subsequent login at the earliest that a participant can observe a response to a contribution. At first approximation, this may seem to inhibit or suppress the interactional richness of content-based discussions. But the very effort of reducing a message to a written form with no other scaffolding fundamentally alters the construction, lending it greater focus and clarity (Pilkington & Walker, 2003). On a technical level, asynchronous discussion threads allow time to frame or focus interactions; they can include hyperlinks, graphics, or simulations that enrich or amplify content exchanges. Disclosure of life details and personal schedules is often elicited in asynchronously linked study groups that need to plan group project activities. Additionally, as Molinari (2004) suggests, threads often include social devices such as self-revelation that individuals exercise to create community in asynchronous settings. The medium (and asynchronicity) change the message in discussions and thus F2F and WBL discourse differ in fundamental ways.

The Internet medium and asynchronicity also change the character of educational assessment. Asynchronicity requires storage of artifacts, including discussion threads. All information is collected and used to update the system's model of the student. Asynchronous interactions with the student's peers and/or instructor are logged and become a defined part of a continuous assessment of the learner. These threaded discussions can be a significant source of data for assessment (Tanimoto & Carlson, 2002). Further, the student can review progress toward learning objectives at any time.

How far away from or close to an F2F baseline that a WBL process may be is a matter of interpretation, but there are classes or processes or approaches that are spawned by mediating technologies and simply are not available without connectivity. These are especially resistant to comparative research on learning effects because they stimulate processes that do not have analogs in more traditional settings. Participatory simulations, for example, are synchronous learning events over wireless networks. In them, individual learners effectively becoming connected agents in complex systems, enacting dynamic and emergent phenomena such as the formation of traffic jams (Resnick, 1996) the mathematics of variation (Kaput, Noss, & Hoyles, 2001) or the behavior of gas molecules (Wilensky & Resnick, 1999). Participatory simulations may easily be considered at a third degree of proximity—they do not reproduce any type of phenomena that are accessible without connectivity. The netcast lecture mimics classroom lectures but leaves them largely unchanged. WBL discussions and assessments have similar characteristics to F2F forms, but alter them significantly over the Web and asynchronous translations. Participatory simulations are simply a new form altogether.

They exemplify a class of wirelessly connected Web-based learning forms referred to by Pea and Roschelle (2002) as wireless Internet learning devices (WILD).

WILD Examples

Current WILD devices include graphing calculators or handhelds connected by a wireless network. The critical WILD capabilities are ubiquity (all students have their own), mobility (they can be easily carried), and connectivity (the devices interconnect arbitrarily). Less important are their compute capabilities and such attributes as screen size. Newer technologies, such as wearable computers, have a different, larger, set of capabilities of which WILD devices are a subset.

Pea and Roschelle (2002) identified application-level capabilities around which WILD-based cooperative learning occurs. These are:

1. Augmenting physical space,
2. Leveraging topological space—e.g., using the locations, distances, and connections of objects as essential components of learning (Lemke, 1999),
3. Aggregating coherently across all students,

4. Conducting the class, and
5. Act becomes artifact.

The WILD construct focuses on Web-based collaboration over relatively small areas, but also on individual learning. The cooperative learning is designed to support individual learning. The systems used as examples of WILD cooperative learning and illustrating the previous list included:

1. Participatory simulations, as discussed earlier, use handhelds to simulate interacting physical phenomenon such as simulations of the spread of epidemic(s) (the handheld devices convey simulations of disease epidemics spreading based on entered input from participants) through handheld proximity. After experiencing a simulation, participants work together to analyze data, create hypotheses, and conduct experiments to infer underlying rules for their simulation. This is an example of leveraging topological space.

2. Classtalk is a networked classroom communication system in which questions can be asked and transmitted to handhelds with the answers aggregated for classroom discussion or guidance to the teacher (Abrahamson, 1998; Dufresne, Gerace, Leonard, Meste, & Wenk, 1996). This is an example of coherent aggregation, now emerging as what is referred to as the CATAALYST framework (Classroom Aggregation Technology for Activating and Assessing Learning and Your Students' Thinking; Roschelle & Penuel, 2003).

3. Probeware is a project that has built interfaces for inexpensive probes and sensors that can then be used to display real-time measurement data (Tinker & Krajcik, 2001). This is an example of augmenting physical space.

4. The Exploratorium, a hands-on science museum in San Francisco, is using a wireless network and handheld computers to provide information and scaffolding for museum visitors as they explore exhibits. At the end of the visit, a Web page is created for the visitor with the information they accessed when visiting the exhibit. These Web pages can be accessed by the visitor and additional information or links can be added to make a science lesson compelling. This is an example of act becoming artifact as the act of visiting the museum is captured in an artifact—the Web page.

WILD systems are typically used in a simultaneous, synchronous, nonpersistent, low bandwidth, low granularity, limited communication modalities. The learning research associated with WILD devices centers around measuring learning outcomes in using these devices. Such questions are, theoretically, amenable to careful experimental design. In practice, such experiments cannot be performed because not only are WILD devices being used but the learning environment is being radically changed. Thus most research in using WILD devices is design research (Kelly, 2003). Computer science research in WILD devices should focus on the usability of the devices—that is, the affordances that the devices provide.

LEARNER ENGAGEMENT

Across any analysis of communication variables discussed at the beginning of the chapter or how proximate a WBL platform may be to F2F platforms, a question of critical interest is how to create the feedback systems in the learning experience to sustain a high level of engagement in disciplinary content. Complex factors determine how deeply engaged a student is in a learning activity. These factors include motivation, perception of personal control in a task setting, and cognitive processing constructs such as self-regulation and strategy use (Miller, Greene, Montalvo, Ravindran, & Nichols, 1996). Asynchronous settings generally enhance personal control in the learning space and opportunities to concentrate. One especially useful factor, drawing in part both on flow theory (Csikszentmihalyi & Csikszentmihalyi, 1988, LeFevre, 1988; Massimi & Carli, 1988) and the Vygotskian (1978) proximal development zone concept, is the balance or goodness of fit between a student's skills and the tasks presented to the student in a learning environment. Goodness of fit is an oftentimes delicate balance or equilibrium between skills and task, although "skills" may more broadly include problem-solving abilities or evolving conceptual models, and "tasks" may refer more broadly to online or F2F exercises, labs, problem-solving activities, or learning from a lecture—any situation in which a learner can take action. A good fit is achieved if a task's difficulty is at the outer reaches but not beyond a learner's ability level, and learning occurs as both task levels and ability levels progressively expand.

The equilibrium between task difficulty and student ability levels is often tenuous or fragile in instructional settings, as any professor knows. It is often hard for an instructor, remotely or on site, to find that balance for even a fraction of learners. When the balance is found, it usually fluctuates throughout an F2F or distributed session and is often at risk of being lost if the instructor cannot reliably assess whether students are "staying with" new material or conditions and then adjust accordingly. An instructor can most reliably adjust course content to help a student maintain this equilibrium *if* the student is able to accurately reveal cognitive processing, and do so as a part of a learning episode rather than as a separate activity. Discussion threads in asynchronous WBL environments are especially useful in providing artifacts of thought that can be subsequently analyzed and acted on.

Theoretical Entrée to Engagement

Discussion threads in asynchronous environments enable one form of such continuous, embedded assessments. We argue that an important theoretical entrée to engagement involves embedded assessment and feedback systems more generally to maintain equilibrium of skill level, scaffolding (help by the instructor or other learners or materials), and task difficulty in a learning setting. Again, this equilibrium is hard to personalize for individual students and certainly difficult to establish for all students in both F2F and distance learning environments, with each type of environment posing unique challenges. When the equilibrium between task and skill is lost, and learning tasks either exceed the student's skill level or are too trivial for it, disengagement sets in; flow theory, discussed later, characterizes the spectrum of disengagement as anxiety (task is too difficult) to boredom and apathy (task is too easy). The assessment and feedback systems needed to preserve this equilibrium may involve dozens, hundreds, or even thousands of discrete sampling and feedback events over an instructional sequence.

Flow

While engagement is a multivariate construct, its apex—full and unbroken immersion in demanding activities—may be characterized as the state of flow. Introduced as a psychological construct by Csikszentmihalyi (1975) it has been widely researched—it is often characterized as intrinsic enjoyment or satisfaction while engaged in work or play, fully concentrated absorption in an activity whereby an individual loses a sense of time, or optimal or heroic performance in highly challenging or desperate circumstances. Because flow refers to such a broad range of intense human experience, it is not surprising that definitions and descriptions abound; a recent review reported 16 different operational definitions (Novak, Hoffman, & Yung, 1998), although usually only subtle variations separate these definitions. Csikszentmihalyi and collaborators continue to refine the concept (e.g., Nakamura & Csikszentmihalyi, 2002). Only a small fraction of the literature focuses on flow in formal educational environments, and little or none on flow in WBL settings. Shernoff, Csikszentmihalyi, and Schneider (2003) conceptualized flow in formal F2F classroom settings as simultaneously involving high levels of concentration, interest, and enjoyment in a learning task, none of which are possible without maintaining an equilibrium of challenge and ability. Both this study and that by Uekawa, Borman, & Lee (2004) examined flow experiences of high school students.

We argue that understanding the conditions for high engagement in learning is essential for building effective WBL platforms of the future. Further, we argue that WBL research should investigate whether the experience of flow while learning is a routinely inducible phenomenon. *That is, WBL platforms should seek to structure high engagement learning environments that routinely immerse learners in disciplinary content and systematically maintain a high-motivation environment with challenging tasks matching learner skills.* Our conjecture is that as the frequency of those high engagement experiences climbs for a learner, so will occurrences of flow states.

We look at two relatively new platforms (a blended asynchronous, F2F form in increasingly widespread practice and a synchronous form now emerging with the advent of tablet computing). These are chosen to illustrate WBL environments in both asynchronous and synchronous modes that are organized around the rich teacher–learner feedback and embedded assessment systems to sustain the task–skill equilibrium necessary for high engagement learning.

Just in Time Teaching (JiTT)

Just-in-time teaching (Novak, et al., 1999) is a feedback-intensive teaching and learning strategy. It is especially useful in the study of synchronicity because it is a hybrid of asynchronous WBL instruction and traditional F2F instruction, and it derives its instructional value from the features that are close to but definitely not synchronous. Students in JiTT courses respond electronically to carefully constructed Web-based assignments due shortly before an F2F class, and the instructor reviews the student submissions "just-in-time" to adjust the classroom lesson to suit the students' needs. The heart of JiTT is this "feedback loop" formed by the students' just-before-class work that fundamentally affects what happens during the subsequent in-class time together. Thus, the JiTT classroom session is intimately linked to the Web-based preparatory assignments the students complete. Exactly how the classroom time is spent depends on a variety of issues such as class size, classroom facilities, and student and instructor personalities. Minilectures (10 min maximum) are often interspersed with demonstrations, classroom discussion, worksheet exercises, and even hands-on minilabs. The common key across these variations is that the classroom component, whether interactive lecture or student activities, is informed by an analysis immediately prior to the classroom of various student responses.

In a JiTT classroom, students may be exposed to the same content as in a passive lecture, but with two important added design features. First, having completed the Web assignment very recently, the intent is that learners enter the classroom ready to actively engage in the course content. Second, they are expected to maintain a sense of ownership because the interactive lesson is based on their own wording and understanding of the relevant issues that are the focus of the class. Although the questions over the Web are short, when fully discussed, they often have complex answers. The students are expected to develop solutions as far as they can on their own as a way to "set the table" for the F2F phase, where the job is finished. The instructor uses the responses to form the framework for the classroom activities that follow. Typically, the instructor duplicates sample responses on transparencies and takes them to class. *This feedback-rich interactive classroom session, built around these responses, replaces the traditional lecture.*

JiTT practitioners are now developing a digital library of activities under NSF's National STEM digital library program (Patterson & Novak, 2003) and the agency has issued six other awards related to expanding JiTT practice, including a year-long effort to engage the national JiTT community in the formulation of research agendas to determine conditions of optimal use of the strategy (Hamilton, Patterson, 2004). The Web site http:// www.jitt.org has more information about this Web-based learning approach, which now involves several hundred faculty at over 100 institutions around the world. The institutions include high schools, 2-year colleges, 4-year colleges, professional schools, and universities, large and small, rural and urban, private and public. The 22 disciplines known to use JiTT are predominantly STEM-based (e.g., astronomy, chemistry, economics, mathematics, physics, biochemistry) but also include areas such as history, philosophy, and journalism.

The 1999 NSF-funded Project Kaleidoscope publication entitled "Then, now, and in the next decade: A commentary on strengthening undergraduate science, mathematics, engineering, and technology education" (Rothman & Narum, 1999) featured JiTT as a success story—one of the successful innovations of the decade.

Shared Workspaces (SWs)

The second platform is a fully synchronous Web-based approach to the use of shared workspaces (SW) in both remote and F2F classes. For the purposes of this discussion, an example of a workspace is a simple writing pad and pencil. This platform uses digital writing pads (using tablet computers) that can be networked and shared by different users in a classroom. Whiteboarding over a network of classroom computers is a form of a shared electronic workspace. A user at one station in a whiteboard network can use freehand writing, drawing, or annotation tools on a document, with markups or annotations appearing at the stations of other users. Whiteboarding is currently more common in corporate collaboration software than in educational settings (using commercial packages from firms such as Microsoft, Centra, and Webtex), but the advents of both wireless networking and tablet computing have created intriguing new conditions for educational tool development and research. (Tablet computing refers in this chapter to note-book computers that use the Microsoft TabletPC XP operating system and that allow freehand writing input on a display screen.)

Early pen-based SW collaboration platforms in education were originally developed by Hamilton (1993); since then, others have developed platforms with similar features (Greenberg, Hayne, & Rada, 1995; Hamilton, 1999; Walters et al., 2000) using hardware and operating system technologies that do not provide the human computer interaction (HCI) advantages that wire-lessly connected tablets now present. One version of a shared workspace plat-form is currently under prototype development in partnership with the Research Assistance Program of a Canadian multinational firm extensively involved in educational and corporate collaboration tools, Smart Technolo-gies. This platform, under development with support from the National Sci-ence Foundation (Hamilton, Patterson, et al., 2004) is a hybrid of earlier systems with more recently developed Web-based conferencing tools, and in-tegrates digital libraries and pedagogical agents within it. The platform Agent and Library Augmented Shared Knowledge Areas (ALASKA), capital-izes on the natural handwriting/typing flexibility of tablet devices and places a software design premium on giving the teacher the ability to "periscope" into and participate with unimpeded access in the workspace of students (in-dividually and in groups), and for students to do the same with each other.

Platform Structure

Leaving aside for the purposes of this discussion, the role of pedagogical agents and digital libraries in the ALASKA platform, the affordances of syn-chronous (F2F and remote) interactions in shared workspaces still loom large and exemplify potentially significant pedagogical possibilities. Prob-lems can be written on the tablet during a learning session using a pen, or teachers can prepare them in advance. The teacher may distribute a prob-lem to any student or node of students, to an entire class, or to selected groups of students. The teacher may elect to annotate the problem (or use a blank screen) to provide notes in real-time that appear at each student's sta-tion. The teacher can also provide "blackboard" notes to students in real time. Although still not in common use, these features have been available (at least with nontablet devices) since the mid-1990s.

More recently, though, the pen and tablet interface allows learners to use both a paper and pencil problem-solving mode and one conducive to physi-cal or soft keyboard input. The notebook metaphor advanced now in the Windows TabletPC operating system is appropriate—the student may save or discard sheets, retrieve them, have several sheets out at a time, use an electronic eraser, and so forth. Additionally, the student may switch in and out of keyboard input, can use drawing tools, can use a calculator that appears in the screen by pressing the appropriate icon, or can press an icon to change the ink color, and so forth.

In some synchronous SW systems, the teacher may define collaborative work groups, based on the individuals or groups who are in the learning environment at the time. Different versions of collaborative workspace environments will allow the teacher to share a work space, enabling simultaneous writing, erasing, or typing by the teacher, student (or work group members). With such a feature, the teacher can observe a student's or group's work, or actually interact or participate in the shared work space. As embedded in the ALASKA platform, for example, *the design intent is for the teacher to rapidly and repeatedly assess student conceptual frameworks and strategies and provide real-time feedback to students as they engage in substantive problem solving and knowledge construction.* All the students' efforts—as represented on this tablet—are disclosed in real-time to the teacher, and all of the students know the teacher can interact with them in their problem solving.

Additionally, within the ALASKA platform (and earlier predecessors that have contributed to its development), the teacher may view the work of many students at once, by using what are called hot boxes. When the teacher enters hot box mode, a portion of the work space of each student or student group becomes a shared work space with a corresponding window appearing in the teacher's screen. The boxes may be resized, enabling up to 20 windows to appear on the teacher's screen at one time. The teacher is in a shared work space with each student's or group's window, and can see all of the work appearing in each window at the same time. *That is, the teacher can watch all the students simultaneously as they progress through a problem or other workspace activity, and work with any one in particular by writing in their workspace, simultaneous to the student or group workspace effort.*

Sample Scenario. Consider a scenario familiar to almost any F2F teacher and to teachers of its online and distributed education analogs. An instructor poses a question and elicits responses through the time-honored method of hand raising or its electronic equivalent for remote students. This is very little information on which to make judgments about whom to call on for a response, whether electronically or physically cued. In an F2F classroom, the dynamics can become very troubling, but in both distance and F2F settings over a network, determining whom to call on in response to a question is generally a matter of guesswork.

In contrast, a shared work space system, such as the ALASKA platform, allows the instructor to concurrently see multiple (up to 20) responses—and the underlying processing, at least as the student "works" the problem—simultaneously. The design intent is for the platform to provide a dramatically bigger "pipe" to see what students are thinking, and provide a much richer information base for the rapid assessment or judgment of student understandings. The instructor can make judgments either about the aggregate online or physical classes, or on the individuals therein—but in either case, can be sufficiently informed to give specialized feedback either on a whole class or individual basis, either orally or electronically, and in the latter case with applets or annotations. *We do not suggest at all that the teacher can process 20 times as much information in a shared work space;* we do suggest that with an electronic overview of what all of the students are doing, the professor can use professional discrimination and judgment to scan and select student work spaces for deeper probing and interaction, and can "move" from student to student much more freely and judiciously with a better knowledge of ongoing cognitive load and processing. *This type of wirelessly shared work space system is intended to replace information deficits with information abundance, in order to give teachers flexibility and opportunity to interact on a deep content level with learners.* The same time frame in the dilemma discussed is now populated not with judgments and guesses based on visual cues of electronic or physical hand raising but the instructor spends the time scanning, examining, and responding to "thought-revealing" representations in the work space.

Complementarity of the JiTT and SW Platforms

Both settings (JiTT as an asynchronous blend and shared work spaces as a synchronous tool) possess specific strengths relative to the quest to engage learners deeply in challenging disciplinary content. Each sheds complementary light on the mechanisms for eliciting rich, actionable information from students for the purposes of providing feedback that will maintain challenge/skill equilibrium and that will sustain cognitive engagement.

For example, JiTT builds feedback loops in class on exercises completed immediately before class. The instructor generally views only the Web-submitted answers to the exercises, with process-oriented interactions and discussions taking place in class. Student thinking may be complex but the artifacts—Web submissions prior to class—are structured for efficiency (simple answers), with more complex representations reserved for class discussion. JiTT is a firmly established and readily adoptable practice.

The wirelessly connected tablets in the shared work space (SW) distance and F2F synchronous settings provide feedback loops on instructor observation of students working problem sets synchronously, and the instructor can see and interact with the written processing in real-time. The written process-artifacts for each individual student are much richer representations of individual cognitive processing than the Web-submitted answers, but not as amenable to generalizations that can be made across the class. Each provides rapidly actionable information to guide pedagogical decisions about both individuals and the whole class, but one (JiTT) provides information more efficiently about the class and the other (SW) provides richer real-time artifacts about individual processing. The SW environment is more sensitive than the JiTT environment to advances in the computing technology and human–computer-interface (HCI) developments, and the advent of wirelessly networked tablets accelerates the possibility for synchronous shared work spaces to become a viable instructional tool. The ALASKA platform's integration of pedagogical agents (Cole, Vuuren, et al., 2003) and digital libraries (Roschelle, Kaput, Stroup, & Kahn, 1998) creates a new set of possibilities for synchronous instruction whereby agents become real-time teaching assistants and real-time peer-to-peer collaboration brokers (Hamilton, 2004). Advances such as this expand the interactional promise of synchronous SW platforms.

Measuring Engagement

One looming research area is the measurement of engagement in learning settings such as the collaborative WILD devices, the just-in-time asynchronous setting, or platforms where the instructor can periscope into the real-time work space of online or F2F students. Each of these can make specific claims that the mediating technology and the nature of their synchronicity renders special advantages and opportunities to keep learners deeply engaged in disciplinary content, within their proximal development zone.

Uekawa et al. (2004) undertook a study of learner engagement patterns in science and mathematics classrooms in eight high schools, using a social organization framework to explore racial and ethnic contrasts in those patterns. Their study has policy implications for K-12 education, but also marks important progress in conceptualizing and measuring engagement at postsecondary and distributed settings. They reviewed key advances and shortcomings of several methods of engagement measurement, including video analysis, interaction event counts, observer protocols, discourse analysis, and use of the experience sampling method (ESM) devices—electronic paging devices Csikszentmihalyi (1975) developed in the 1970s to periodically prompt learners to self-report engagement levels during activities (such as classroom participation). They opted to use the first and last of these approaches—unobtrusive and qualitative classroom observations coupled with intrusive but more quantifiable ESM datapoints. They developed a series of quick-response questions that probed interest, engagement, and activity levels that students answered on each side of a survey form when paged two times in a 50-minute class. Adopting this methodology to online settings can yield important insights on whether specific learning platforms more readily and deeply engage learners, and can reframe research on learning effects.

RESEARCH ISSUES AND QUESTIONS

This chapter identifies selected variables useful in analyzing learning platforms in general, including synchronicity as a critical variable in Web-based
learning (WBL). We propose a simple, "three-degree" schema for examining the proximity of WBL forms to baseline and traditional face-to-face
(F2F) educational settings, focusing interest on synchronous WBL platforms that could not readily exist in F2F settings. Synchronicity is an interesting variable in structuring WBL environments relative to the study of
learner engagement and whether WBL enablements can stimulate learner
flow. Two examples, an asynchronous and F2F blended platform, and a
synchronous platform, are suggested to illustrate a series of research questions related to learner engagement.

These questions involve whether it is possible to use the affordances of
synchronous platforms to help teachers continuously assess learners and to
accurately scaffold learners in their proximal development zone. Can the
learning environment be sufficiently adaptive, in other words, to "form fit"
the learner continuously? The shared work space WBL platform discussed
here is organized around the metaphor of making thinking visible (Lesh,
Hoover, Hole, Kelly, & Post, 2000) in ways that are not readily possible in
classroom F2F settings. Equipped with far more moment-to-moment information about learner cognition, will the professor or teacher be able to rapidly forge and act on instructional judgments? This, like other technology
advances, requires more sophisticated technical and pedagogical
proficiencies of teachers. Will the increased feedback that synchronous systems allow improve the motivational climate of learners? Is it possible to
routinely induce high performance learning, or what might be called
learning flow?

Although only alluded to briefly, the role of pedagogical agents (animated or text-based or invisible to the user) in WBL environments is an
emerging area of work that is central to questions of synchronicity and
learning effectiveness. For example, software agents can perform complex
community-building and pedagogical tasks in distributed learning settings,
amplifying the real-time abilities of a teacher in a synchronous environment. The integration of effective agent systems into WBL platforms is an
increasingly important research domain. It involves questions such as
whether agents can stimulate effective learning communities in WBL settings (Yang et al., 2003) or whether they can simplify a teacher's work load
to free him or her to concentrate on more cognitively complex challenges of
the learning environment (Hamilton, 2004).

Another important area relative to synchronicity goes to the heart of
learning and teaching. The spectrum from synchronous to asynchronous and the intermediate blends all offer different content delivery func-

tionality. Shute and Towle (2003) argue that this spectrum produces highly adaptive "anywhere, anyplace, any pace" content delivery. But content delivery may be a narrow prism for analyzing WBL platforms. At their best, as we have tried to outline, they involve interactivity between learners and learners and their teachers. "Interactional bandwidth"—a way to conceptualize the richness and speed of content-based exchanges over WBL settings, may be another analytic lens for WBL platform research, and may lead to greater insights into disciplinary and social knowledge construction.

REFERENCES

Abrahamson, A. L. (1998, June). *An overview of teaching and learning research with classroom communication systems.* Paper presented at the International Conference of the Teaching of Mathematics. Village of Pythagorian, Samos, Greece.

Cole, R. S., Vuuren, V., et al. (2003). Perceptive animated interfaces: First steps for a new paradigm for human computer interaction. *Proceedings of the IEEE, special issue: Multimodal human computer interfaces* (pp. 1391–1405).

Csikszentmihalyi, M. (1975). *Beyond boredom and anxiety.* San Francisco: Jossey-Bass.

Csikszentmihalyi, M. & Csikszentmihalyi, I. (1988). *Optimal experience: Psychological studies of flow in consciousness.* Cambridge, England: Cambridge University Press.

Dufresne, R. J., Gerace, W. J., Leonard, W. J., Mestre, J. P., & Wenk, L. (1996). Classtalk: A classroom communication system for active learning. *Journal of Computing in Higher Education, 7,* 3–47.

Feller, G. (1995). East meets west—online. *Internet World, 6,* 48–50.

Greenberg, S., Hayne, S., & Rada, R., (Eds.). (1995). *Groupware for real-time drawing: A designer's guide.* Berkshire, England: McGraw-Hill.

Gregory, V. L. (2003). Student perceptions of the effectiveness of Web-based distance education. *New Library World, 104,* 426–431.

Hamilton, E. (1993). Computer-assisted instructional delivery system. *US Office Patent 5176520.*

Hamilton, E. (1999). Pen-based and multimedia shared network spaces that increase learning flow and generative learning. In G. Cumming, T. Okamoto, & L. Gomez (Eds.), *Advanced research in computers and communications in education: New human abilities for the networked society* (pp. 491–498). Tokyo: IOS Press.

Hamilton, E. (2004). Agent and library augmented shared knowledge areas (ALASKA). *Proceedings of the International Conference on Multimodal interfaces (ICMI'04)* (pp. 318–319).

Hamilton, E., & Cole, R. (2004). *Agent and library augmented shared knowledge areas* (ALASKA; National Science Award 0420310).

Hamilton, E., Patterson, E., et al. (2004). *Building an Evaluative Research Foundation for Just-in-Time Teaching,* National Science Award 0424031.

Kanuka, H., Collett, D., & Caswell, C. (2002). University instructor perceptions of the use of asynchronous text-based discussion in distance courses. *The American Journal of Distance Education, 16*(3), 151–167.

Kaput, J., Noss, R., & Hoyles, C. (2001). Developing new notations for a learnable mathematics in the computational era. In L. D. English (Ed.), *The handbook of international research in mathematics* (pp. 51–73). London, England: Kluwer.

Kelly, A. (2003). Research as design. *Educational Researcher, 32*, 3–4.

LeFevre, J. (1988). Flow and the quality of experience during work and leisure. In M. Csikszentmihalyi & I. Csikszentmihalyi (Eds.), *Optimal experience: Psychological studies of flow in consciousness* (pp. 307–318). Cambridge, England: Cambridge University Press.

Lemke, J. L. (1999). The long and the short of it: Comments on multiple timescale studies of human activity. *The Journal of the Learning Sciences, 10*(1), 17–26.

Lesh, R., Hoover, M., Hole, B., Kelly, A., & Post, T. (2000). Principles for developing thought revealing activities for students and teachers. In A. Kelly & R. Lesh (Eds.), *The handbook of research design in mathematics and science education* (pp. 591–646). Mahwah, NJ: Lawrence Erlbaum Associates.

Marjanovic, O. (1999). Learning and teaching in a synchronous collaborative environment. *Journal of Computer Assisted Learning, 15*(2), 129–138.

Massimi, F., & Carli, M. (1988). The systematic assessment of flow in daily experience. In M. Csikszentmihalyi & I. Csikszentmihalyi (Eds.), *Optimal experience: Psychological studies of flow in consciousness* (pp. 266–287). Cambridge, England: Cambridge University Press.

Miller, R. B., Greene, B. A., Montalvo, G. P., Ravindran, B., & Nichols, I. D. (1996). Engagement in academic work: The role of learning goals, future consequences, pleasing others, and perceived ability. *Contemporary Educational Psychology, 21*(4), 388–422.

Molinari, D. L. (2004). The role of social comments in problem-solving groups in an online class. *American Journal of Distance Education, 18*(2), 89–101.

Nakamura, J., & Czikszentmihalyi, M. (2002). The concept of flow. In C. R. Snyder & S. J. Lopez (Eds.), *Handbook of positive psychology* (pp. 89–105). Oxford: Oxford University Press.

Novak, G., Patterson, E., Garvin, A., & Christian, W. (1999). *Just-in-time teaching: Blending active learning with Web technology*. Englewood Cliffs, NJ: Prentice-Hall.

Novak, T. P., Hoffman, D. L., & Yung, Y. F. (2000, Winter). Measuring the customer experience in online environments: A structural modeling approach. *Marketing Science, 19*(1), 22–44.

Patterson, E., & Novak, G. (2003). JiTTDL: The just-in-time teaching digital library. *National Science Foundation Award 0333646*, United States Air Force Academy.

Pea, R., & Roschelle, J. (2002). A walk on the WILD side: How wireless handhelds may change CSCL. *Proceedings of the CSCL 2002* (pp. 51–60). Mahwah, NJ: Lawrence Erlbaum Associates.

Pilkington, R. M., & Walker, S. A. (2003). Facilitating debate in networked learning: Reflecting on online synchronous discussion in higher education. *Instructional Science, 31*(2), 41–63.

Resnick, M. (1996). Beyond the centralized mindset. *The Journal of the Learning Sciences, 5*(1), 1–22.

Roschelle, J., Kaput, J., Stroup, W., & Kahn, T. (1998). Scalable integration of educational software: Exploring the promise of component architectures. *Journal of Interactive Media in Education, NFS, Grant # 0333646*.

Roschelle, J. & Penuel, W. R. (2003). *The CATAALYST—Planning a rigorous study.* (National Science Foundation Award 0337793).Arlington, VA.

Rothman, F. & Narum, J. (1999). *Then, now, and in the next decade: A commentary on strengthening undergraduate science, mathematics, engineering, and technology education* (Project Kaleidoscope). Washington, DC.

Shernoff, D. J., Csikszentmihalyi, M., & Schneider, B. (2003). Student engagement in high school classrooms from the perspective of flow theory. *School Psychology Quarterly, 18*(2), 158–176.

Shute, V. J. & Towle, B. (2003). Adaptive E-learning. *Educational Psychologist, 38*(2), 105–114.

Simonson, M., Smaldino, S., Albright, M., & Zvacek, S. (2002). *Teaching and learning at a distance: Foundations of distance education.* Englewood Cliffs, NJ: Prentice-Hall.

Tanimoto, S., & Carlson, A. A. (2002). *Text forum features for small group discussions with facet-based pedagogy.* Proceedings of the CSCL. Mahwah, NJ: Lawrence Erlbaum Associates.

Tinker, R., & Krajcik, J. (Eds.). (2001). *Portable technologies: Science learning in context.* New York: Kluwer Academic/Plenum.

Uekawa, K., Borman, K., & Lee, R. (2004). Student engagement in America's urban high school mathematics and science classrooms. Manuscript submitted for publication.

Vygotsky, L. (1978). *Mind in society: The development of the higher psychological processes.* Cambridge, MA: Harvard University Press.

Walters, R. F., Douglas, B. B., Blake, R. J., & Fahy, D. W. (2000). Interactive tools and language acquisition. *Multilingual Computing, 11*(1), 35–39.

Wilensky, U., & Resnick, M. (1999). Thinking in levels: A dynamic systems approach to making sense of the world. *Journal of Science Education and Technology, 8*(1), 3–19.

Yang, F., Han, P., Shen, R., Kraemer, B. J., & Fan, X. (2003, December). *Cooperative learning in self-organizing E-learner communities based on a multi-agents mechanism.* 16th Australian Joint Conference on Artificial Intelligence, Perth, Australia.

Chapter 7

Virtual Reality and Simulators: Implications for Web-Based Education and Training

Ray S. Perez
Office of Naval Research

Wayne Gray
Rensselaer Polytechnic Institute

Tom Reynolds
Serco North American

The development of effective learning environments is of great importance to K–16 education, military, and industry. The goal is to provide the most effective learning environment that allows learners to acquire the knowledge and skills necessary to perform tasks in educational and real-world settings. Virtual reality simulations and games offer the potential for providing an effective Web-based learning environment.

"Virtual reality (VR) is the popular term for an interactive experience in which an individual perceives and engages a synthetic (i.e., simulated via computer) environment by means of a particular set of multisensory human-computer interface devices and interacts with synthetic objects in that environments as if they were real" (Thurman & Russo, 2000, p. 85). The development of high-fidelity simulations and games has been an area of interest to educators and training developers since the early days of computer-based instruction. The DOD over the last decade has invested a significant amount of resources to provide the infrastructure and technical base to design and deliver simulation-based training anywhere, anytime, and anyplace using the Internet. Likewise the growth of the Internet and access to it will provide K–16 education with the capability to deliver simulation-based instructional approaches over the Internet anytime and anyplace whether it is a traditional or a virtual classroom.

HIGH-FIDELITY WEB-BASED SIMULATIONS

There are two types of high-fidelity Web-based simulations (e.g., virtual reality) that will be discussed in this chapter, that is, model-based or game-based simulations. Model-based simulations are designed to and have the capability to emulate various dynamic properties of systems such as biological, physical, economic, and social phenomena that are executable on computers and that can be used to teach students about the dynamics and content of these systems. Examples of model-based simulations are microworlds or device models. These simulations that characterize the operation of dynamic systems (e.g., supersonic aircraft) have been used in the military to train technicians and operators not only how to maintain and operate complex and sophisticated equipment but to have a deeper understanding (form a mental model of the equipment) of how these systems work (see Munro, Surman, & Pizzini, chap. 15 in this volume for a detailed description of these simulations). Evidence for the efficacy of simulations comes from researchers both in education and the military. Specifically, the positive impact on motivational effects of simulations-based learning activities has long been recognized by educational researchers (Jonassen & Tennyson, 1997; Tennyson & Breuer, 2002). Earlier research by military researchers have demonstrated the efficacy of these simulations in the areas of operation and maintenance training (see Fletcher, 2003; Jones & Hennessy, 1985).

Game-based simulations offer a potentially promising medium of instruction not only for the military but for K–16 education as well. The early work of Malone and Lepper (1987) characterized the appeal of video games as highly motivating because they encouraged engagement in repetitive practice, learning through exploration, and players striving for mastery of more difficult goals. These attributes and the rapid technical advances supporting high-fidelity simulations and commercial games offer a significant potential for improving educational activities for K–16.

Emerging research on instructional games has produced some promising results in military training (Garris et al., 2001; Ricci, Salas, & Cannon-Bowers, 1996). However, the empirically based evidence on the effectiveness of such games is limited to adults.

With the addition of Web-based simulations, it is possible to provide education/training at a distance. Currently, most prerequisite knowledge and skills can be taught over the Internet except for specialized motor skills such as applying a precise twisting force during an assembly procedure (Munro, 2003). Many of the skills taught by these simulations can be characterized as higher order thinking skills and complex problem solving skills (e.g., troubleshooting).

For K–16 education, military, and industry, the creation of learning environments is critical when training on real equipment is hampered by availability, feasibility, and/or risk of injury. Further, the actual equipment may not provide an optimal learning environment to foster the acquisition of declarative and procedural knowledge and complex skills. Actual equipment may provide too complex and difficult an environment for trainees to initially learn to perform complex and difficult operational and maintenance tasks. The use of simulations (physical mock-ups) and simulated environments has a long history of use in the military and industry (Jones, Hennessy, & Deutsch, 1985). Using actual equipment for initial training may put personnel at risk and lead to devastating outcomes. For example, the airline industry has estimated that operator error (operator error has been attributed to the lack of adequate or outdated training) has been linked to over 1,789 deaths since 1959 (Jones, Hennessy, & Deutsch, 1985). Providing training on actual equipment can be very expensive. For example, in 1985, Jones, Hennessy, & Deutsch estimated that training on Boeing's 767 passenger jet costs $7,000 to $8,000 per hour, as compared to the average cost for flight simulators of $400 per hour. Training using fragile and complex equipment can lead to equipment being damaged by inexperienced personnel.

Physical Mock-ups Versus High-fidelity Simulators

Physical mock-ups and simulators have been proven to be successful training devices but the cost and time needed to build, run, and maintain these devices are often prohibitive. For example, the Navy's two-cockpit Naval air combat simulator, Device 2E6, costs over $25 million and the B-1 simulator over $75 million (Burpee, 1981). Advances in technology of the actual equipment require costly adaptations to physical mock-ups or the development of new physical mock-ups. Recent developments in the field of virtual reality (VR) technology offer the promise of providing high-fidelity, realistic cost-effective training environments. VR can be defined as interface technology that can employ a wide range of displays, interaction devices, position monitors, and feedback devices. The need for these high-quality training environments will continue to grow as technological advances lead to more complex equipment and environments. The development of training environments that can circumvent these constraints is of much interest to training developers and their clients who are dependent on adequate training scenarios.

Recent studies have elucidated the training and learning benefits of virtual reality environments as providing potentially viable learning and training experiences. Witmer, Sadowski, and Finkelstein (2002) have pointed out the benefits of VR for training. These are: (1) Multiple modes of locomotion are available, movement speed can be much faster or slower than in the real world, and participants can be transported from one location to another instantly; (2) they have the capability to permit viewing of multiple perspectives and can be augmented easily with visual and auditory features/cues that aid learning; and (3) they have the flexibility because they are driven by software models to adapt engineering changes to the actual equipment at a far lower level of effort and cost than physical mock-ups that require "bending of metal."

Several studies have shown positive transfer between experiences in virtual and analogous environments in the military (Waller, Hunt, & Knapp, 1998, 1998b; Wilson, Foreman, & Tlauka, 1997; Witmer, Bailey, & Knerr, 1995; Witmer et al., 2002). For example, Bliss, Tidwell, and Guest (1997) demonstrated the benefits of VR training with firefighters. In education, there is emerging research demonstrating the effectiveness of VR (Johnson et al., 1999; Moher, Johnson, Ohlsson, & Gillingham, 1999; Ohlsson et al., 2000) in a series of studies called the Round Earth experiments that demonstrated the power of VR to bring about conceptual change in elementary school children. Perhaps the most important point of these research studies was to identify and classify the components or features of virtual reality training environments that promote learning. A different way of asking this question is which features or components of a VR environment are responsible for bringing about learning.

Prior to the task of reviewing potentially viable education and training applications of existing virtual reality environments and their attributes, it is necessary to revisit an earlier argument proposed by Richard Clark (1983, 1985) with regard to examining the value of new technology/media.

Media are Mere Vehicles Argument

Clark (1983, 1985; Clark, Bewley, & O'Neil, this volume), in a series of papers, reviewed the literature comparing computer-based instruction to traditional classroom practice including meta-analytic and other studies that examined the influence of media (e.g., computer-based instruction) on learning. He concluded that there is consistent evidence that when one controls for instructional method and novelty, there are no learning benefits from employing any specific medium (e.g., computers) to deliver instruction. He argued that media are mere vehicles that deliver instruction/training but do not influence student learning any more than the truck that delivers groceries can cause changes in our nutrition. It is the structure and organization of the subject matter content of the vehicle, the proper mix of medium, and the learning task that can influence learning (Clark, 2001).

However, proponents of virtual reality training environments argue that this technology is clearly different from prior training technologies. This is because it enables the learning developer to create an environment that models and represents the essential features of the real-world setting (e.g., three-dimensional computer graphics) thereby fostering the transfer of skills from the training environment to the operational environment. They further argue that virtual reality environments are driven by the unique characteristics and demands of the content/tasks to be learned. Are there essential features of VR technology that distinguish it from other media? Thus, the task that lies ahead is to identify, characterize, and classify those design components and features of virtual reality environments that are unique to this media and that may or may not foster the acquisition of knowledge and skills necessary to perform tasks in real-world settings. It is important to identify learner characteristics that may or may not lead to enhanced learning in virtual environments. These identified features or components would then have to be validated with empirical research.

The method used in this chapter for selecting education and training VR components and features was threefold; (a) reviewing the extant literature, (b) reviewing of Web sites of various VR laboratories and projects, and (c) conducting site visits to a representative sample of VR laboratories. The end goal was to describe a representative sample of VR applications that provide a relatively comprehensive picture of the state-of-the-art of VR research and development efforts. The site visits to VR laboratories was guided by whether they had education or training as a research goal. Thus, only those VR laboratories were visited that had an explicit education or training component.

LITERATURE REVIEW METHODOLOGY

The literature review began with an initial examination of a series of relevant journal (e.g., *Presence*) articles on VR environments and Internet searches using search engines such as Google. The following search terms used for this search were; virtual reality, virtual environments, and simulations, and years searched were 1990 to 2002. A recent search (2004) of Psyc INFO revealed 16 references to VR. Of the 16, only one had education as its subject; the rest were either reports on the use of VR in psychotherapy, for example, to treat phobias like "fear of flying" or to enhance social dynamics among groups such as collaboration. Journals articles and Web sites were selected based on abstracts that dealt with K–16 education, training, and psychological applications and usability, technological, and research issues with VR. This chapter is limited to a discussion of K–16 education and training applications. Abstracts that did not seem to match the purpose of the literature review were discarded. As a result of these searches, 103 articles were identified and reviewed. Of these 103 articles, less than 10 had either qualitative or quantitative data as to the effectiveness of VR in K–16 education. The purpose of the search in addition to the previous characteristics was twofold; (1) to determine the current state-of the-art in VR research/technology, and (2) to identify laboratories performing representative work.

Supplemental information was provided by the senior author's visits to VR labs around the country. Sites to be visited were based on descriptions provided in articles and from these descriptions, a sample was selected that was representative. The visit usually lasted from a half to a full day.

Prior to the visit, the laboratory's principal investigator was contacted by phone and asked a series of questions. These were: (a) Describe the laboratory's content area of application of VR; (b) What are your research goals; (c) Is the laboratory using VR technologies for education and training if so how; and, (d) What types of technology are being used (e.g., head-mounted displays, magnetic tracking devices, caves and desktops). During the site visit, the senior author asked for and participated in a demonstration of the VR system, copies of recent research papers and presentations, design guidelines followed in the design of the VR system, technological barriers, assessment of the state of the art of VR, and their definition of VR.

What Is Virtual Reality?

The definitions for virtual reality environments are vague and varied, making it difficult to ascertain the true meaning of the term virtual reality. Definitions range from "virtual reality is a way for humans to visualize, manipulate, and interact with computers and extremely complex data" to Wann and Mon-Williams' (1996) definition:

> a virtual environment provides the user with access to information that would not otherwise be available at that place or time, capitalizes upon natural aspects of human perception by extending visual information in three spatial dimensions, and may supplement this information with other sensory stimuli and temporal changes; which enable the user to interact with the displayed data. (p. 830)

The degree of complexity of virtual reality systems are as varied as the definitions, ranging from simplistic desktop virtual reality to immersive head mounted display with kinesthetic feedback of motion virtual reality environments. Desktop virtual reality environments use a computer monitor to display the virtual world. The user is not surrounded by the virtual environment and the experience is comparable to playing a computer-based video game. Fish tank virtual reality systems improve upon desktop displays systems with the addition of stereoscopic monitor, LCD shutter glasses, and a head tracker that introduces visual parallax effects. Many VR researchers do not consider desktop systems as virtual reality environments because the user is not immersed in the environment. "Immersive virtual reality is technology that gives the user the psychophysical experience of being surrounded by a computer generated environment" (Van Dam, Forsberg, Laidlaw, LaViola, & Simpson, 2000, p. 27). Immersive virtual reality systems submerge the user's viewpoint inside of the virtual world. This is accomplished with the use of head mounted displays or stereoscopic lenses in a CAVE. A CAVE™ is a wide-field presentation of computer-generated, multisensory information that tracks a user in real-time. In addition to the more well-known modes of virtual reality head-mounted displays and binocular omni-oriented monitor (BOOM) displays—the Electronic Visualization Laboratory at the University of Illinois at Chicago introduced a third mode in 1992; a room constructed of large screens on which the graphics are projected onto two to three walls and/or the floor. Images are projected onto all three walls. A CAVE is a multiperson, room-sized, high-resolution, 3D video and audio environment. Graphics are rear projected in stereo onto three walls and the floor, and viewed with stereo glasses. As a viewer wearing a position sensor moves within its display boundaries, the correct perspective and stereo projections of the environment are updated by a supercomputer (Silicon Graphics Power Onyx with three Infinite Reality Engines is used to create the imagery that is projected onto the walls in a room), and the images move with and surround the viewer. Hence, stereo projections create 3D images that appear to have a continuous presence both inside and outside the projection room. To the viewer with stereo glasses, the projection screens become transparent and the 3D image space appears to extend to infinity. For example, a tile pattern could be projected onto the floor and walls such that the viewer sees a continuous floor extending well outside the boundaries of the projection room. Three-dimensional objects such as tables and chairs would appear to be present both inside and outside this projection room. To the viewer, these objects are really there until they try to touch them or walk beyond the boundaries of the projection room. There are reports of viewers having forgotten to be careful when walking within these invisible boundaries and inadvertently ripping and tearing projection screens.

   This chapter only discusses the most common types of display technology CAVES.

Presence and Immersion

Important terms in VR systems/environments are *presence* and *immersion*. Although early in the history of VR these terms were a matter of controversy, the current view is that these terms refer to separate but related phenomena. Presence in the context of virtual reality refers to the user's subjective sense of "being there" (Nichols, Haldane, & Wilson, 2000; Pausch, Proffitt, & Williams, 1997; Salnas, Rassmuss-Grohn, & Sjostrom, 2000). Nichols, et al. (2000) described presence as a reflection of the user's feelings of engrossment within a VR environment. The inclusion of haptic feedback within a VR environment has been related to significantly higher sense of virtual presence (Salnas et al., 2000). There are over 100 (only a selected few studies are mentioned here to indicate the potential importance of the presence construct) studies that have examined the presence construct. They have examined ways of measuring it that vary from use of behavioral and physiological measures such as skin conductance and heart rate (Meehan, Insko, Whitton, & Brooks, 2001); what factors influence its occurrence and in fact, many VR researchers use it as a criteria to evaluate the efficacy of the VR environment (Tromp, Steed, & Wilson, 2003). Although there is not consensus on a theory of presence, Heeter (2003) and others (Shim & Kim, 2003) still contend that it is a very important construct in the design of VR systems. However, we do not know if presence has any relationship to the acquisition of knowledge or skills.

Immersion is dependent on the ability of the virtual reality environment to provide the user with a continuous stream of stimuli that promote the user's feelings of inclusion and ability to interact with the virtual reality environment in real-time (Salnas et al., 2000). Factors that can have an effect on immersion include the extent to which the virtual reality environment isolates the user from the real world and provides the user with natural and predictable modes of interaction. The user's perception of natural self-movement can be another key factor in which the illusion of immersion can be gained or lost. Participants who reported high levels of presence were less likely to recall or identify music that was played in the background during the VR environment session. Participants with higher reported levels of presence were also more likely to display a physical reaction to a startle event within the VRE. The participants' reactions to a startle event were measured by assessing their responses to a virtual startle event in which a virtual object flew toward the participants and exploded. The responses to the startle event were classified into three categories; no response, verbal response, or physically noticeable response (i.e., ducking or moving to avoid the virtual object). The distinction between "presence and immersion" is that presence refers to the viewer's subjective feeling of "being there" whereas immersion refers to the conditions that promote the subjective feeling of "being there." However, as with presence, we do not know if immersion has any relationship to the acquisition of knowledge or skills.

Simulator/Motion Sickness

A key factor in limiting the widespread use of VR technology in education and training is simulator or motion sickness. As many as 30% of the individuals exposed to VR systems have symptoms severe enough to discontinue their use (Harm, 2002). Symptoms vary in degree from a feeling of unpleasantness, disorientation, and headaches to extreme nausea. The cause of simulator sickness is not known but possible factors identified are sensory distortions such as abnormal movement of arms and heads, long delays or lags in feedback, and missing visual cues from convergence and accommodation.

A subset of VR is augmented reality (mixed reality), which merges telepresence and virtual reality to create a virtual environment. Augmented reality is defined as an advanced human–computer interface technology that attempts to blend and fuse computer-generated information with the user's sensations of the world (Barfield & Caudell, 2001). Computer-generated graphics overlap the user's viewpoint of the real world with the use of special lenses, visors, wearable computers, and so forth. Telepresence allows remote sensors on a robot or tool to be linked with the senses of a human operator, allowing the user to perform certain tasks in an environment without actually being there. Augmented reality superimposes computer-generated graphics on the world where the user is physically located. An example application is superimposing some icon that indicates the next piece of equipment that must be moved or replaced in a maintenance task.

In immersive virtual reality environments, the user is generally confined to the environment displayed on a desktop computer, HMD, or CAVE. However, the virtual world in VR may well be a representation of a real location, for example, training security agents in the layout of a convention center prior to the actual meeting. Augmented reality can provide the user with more freedom to roam around in the real world. In order to do this, the tracking system must accurately track the orientation and location of the user or else the illusion of the virtual object as a part of the real world is lost. Mobile Augmented Reality Systems (MARS) consist of a wearable computer capable of 3D graphics rendering, position and orientation trackers, a see-through head display, and a wireless network interface. Augmented reality has shown promise in military, manufacturing, education, and medical domains. However, little or no empirical data exists as the effectiveness of the use of augmented reality technologies.

HMDs and CAVEs are considered immersive VR environments, promoting the illusion of being there. Immersive virtual reality (IVR) utilizes much more of the user's peripheral vision that provides better contextual cues to the user, affording easier and faster navigation than desktop displays (Van Dam et al., 2000). Users of IVR are prone to the same mistakes in spatial visualization within an IVR as they do in the real world; users often overestimate height and width characteristics of different objects (Van Dam et al., 2000).

Brooks (1999) believed that desktop displays should not be considered as VRs because of their inability to promote immersion or block out the physical environment, or to present life-size virtual objects. Loomis and Knapp (1999) associated desktop displays with pictures, in that the user is faced with a perceptual conflict between what is actually displayed and the user's internal representations of the displayed environment. The utilization of stereoscopic techniques reduces perceptual conflicts by diminishing the user's awareness of the display surface. Given the previous comments about the limitations of desktop displays as virtual reality environments, reviews of these systems are not included in this review.

Applications of Virtual Reality

Education

Constructivist as Design in VR Systems.   Many of the VR systems that have educational goals that are described in this chapter were guided in their design by constructivist theories of learning. In constructivist theory, the learning process is viewed as one where the learner is building or constructing an internal representation of knowledge, a personal interpretation. The resultant representation is constantly open to change, its structure and the linkages forming the foundation to which knowledge structures are attached. Learning is an active process in which meaning is developed on the basis of experience. According to this theory, conceptual growth comes from the sharing of multiple perspectives and the simultaneous changing of our internal representations in response to those perspectives, as well as through cumulative experience. The design requirements for this view are that knowledge or learning must be situated in a rich context, and it must be reflective of real-world contexts for the constructive process to occur and transfer to environments beyond the education and training classroom (Duffy & Jonassen, 1992).

The Round Earth Project (Johnson et al., 1999a; Moher et al., 1999; Ohlsson, Moher, & Johnson, 2000) is an educational virtual reality system designed to teach elementary students (third graders) that the earth is round. The researchers had noted in earlier research that third graders frequently report that they believe that the earth is flat. This misconception is due, in part, to the observation that these children visually experience the world as flat. The application is a 10' cubic CAVE using a rack SGI Onyx with Infinite Reality Engines for projecting the images/graphics on the walls. The student (astronaut) wears a pair of Stereographics glasses to allow translation of the video displays to stereo imagery and a Flock of Birds tracker position sensor to track the user's head position. A wand (3D mouse) with three buttons and a joystick is used to navigate within the CAVE. An ImmersaDesk displays the CAVE user's position and orientation for a secondary user. A rack SGI Onyx using a Reality Engine 2 creates a display on a single screen. The virtual world presented to the subject is called Asteroid World and it was presented using *ImmersaDesk*. Immersadesk is a VR projection device developed at the Electronic Visualization Laboratory at the University of Illinois at Chicago. It is 6 ft by 4 ft and supports full immersive VR with stereo vision head and hand tracking and audio.

The Round Earth Project application, Asteroid World, is used to bridge a concept in one context (the asteroid) to a target context (the earth). The virtual world is a small asteroid in which the astronaut is told to search and collect fuel cells scattered upon the surface. As the astronaut explores the asteroid, the mission control student tracks an avatar representation of the astronaut walking around the asteroid and provides directions to the student. The students switch between the astronaut and the mission control scenarios after 10 min. In the astronaut condition, the students were able to see objects appear over the horizon, the curvature of the asteroid, and experience walking in one direction and eventually return to the starting point. The mission control condition afforded students the ability to see the entire asteroid at once while an avatar explored the surface (the students would often see the avatar in an upside-down or sideways position). All students in the virtual reality condition were exposed to both viewpoints.

Students were given pre and posttests, and a delayed posttest (administered 4 mo after the experiment) consisting of open-ended questions about the shape of the earth. A globe of the earth, a styrofoam model of the asteroid, and Play-Doh were also used to bridge the target learning concept. The results of the Round Earth World Project reported evidence of students learning the target concept based on improved test scores; the experimental groups score were significantly superior to the control group (non-VR treatment group). The children in the treatment group almost doubled their understanding of the shape of the earth, as measured by the knowledge test (correct answers pretest, $M = 7.3\%$; posttest, $M = 12.9\%$, and delayed, $M = 11.4\%$).

Another example of a CAVE VR system is *Correlation World*. Correlation World (Moher, Johnson, Cho, & Lin, 2000) is a room-sized CAVE VR hardware used for the virtual reality environments included a Silicon Graphics Onyx Reality Engine2, SGI workstation, VR4 head mounted display, a 3Ball, and a Polhemus magnetic tracking device. Correlation World was designed to teach children the concept of cooccurrence by using a combination of plants found in a virtual world. Students were assigned to teams, given target plants to look for, and given virtual flags to place next to the target plants when they were identified in the CAVE. After the students explored the CAVE, they were instructed to present to the class what they had learned and their conclusions.

The results of the experiment (pre and posttests) show that although students enjoyed the virtual reality experience, they did not appear to understand the purpose of the experiment. Students had problems navigating and using the CAVE.

ScienceSpace is another immersive, multisensory virtual reality environment designed to enhance the user's understanding of complex, abstract scientific concepts in three virtual worlds; Newton World, Maxwell World, and Pauling World (Dede, Saltzman, Loftin, & Ash, 1997). Newton World presents the laws of motion in the VRE; Maxwell World allows the representation and manipulation of electrostatic fields, whereas Pauling World allows users to learn about molecular structures and chemical bonding. The developers of these worlds believe that for learning to occur, there must be meaningful representations and multiple mappings of information. They achieved this by employing visual, auditory, and haptic stimuli. The hardware used for the virtual reality environments included a Silicon Graphics Onyx Reality Engine2, SGI workstation, VR4 head mounted display, a 3Ball, and a Polhemus magnetic tracking device.

Saltzman, Dede, Loftin, and Chen (1999) used ScienceSpace to study the effects of multiple frames of reference on learning within a virtual reality environment (Maxwell World). Participants (high school students) explored Maxwell World from one of three frames of reference (FOR); egocentric, exocentric, and bicentric. The egocentric condition places the participant as a test charge within a magnetic field. The exocentric frame of reference allows exploration of the magnetic field from the outside. The bicentric condition allows participants to switch perspectives between the egocentric and the exocentric while exploring the virtual electric fields. Participants studied the distribution of forces and the motion of test charges in electric fields within the virtual reality environment. A paper and pencil based mastery test was administered to the participants to measure their ability to describe phenomena and explain why the phenomena occur. The results of the study show that participants in the bicentric condition performed significantly better on the mastery test for force than the other groups; egocentric ($M = .639$); exocentric ($M = .636$); and bicentric ($M = .733$).

The ability to switch between the egocentric and exocentric frames of reference allowed the participants to acquire both global (exocentric) and local (egocentric) information pertaining to the electric fields. The provision of the egocentric viewpoint encouraged participants to adopt that viewpoint while solving the mastery test questions. Participants' responses to a simulator sickness questionnaire suggest that more simulator sickness symptoms were associated with lower levels of mastery whereas higher levels of spatial ability were associated with lower levels of simulator sickness symptoms.

Virtual reality environments do essentially provide users with a better understanding of abstract concepts by creating abstract metaphors and they allow users to manipulate and scale virtual objects to create a better understanding of the target concept. Virtual reality environments afford students the ability to visit and interact with locations that distance, time, or safety would prevent. Jackson and Fagan (2000) tested this notion using Global Change World. Global Change World is an immersive virtual reality system that teaches students the effects of global warming within a virtual environment. Global Change World is an HMD-based virtual learning environment running on networked Hewlett-Packard 9000 computers using DVISE VR software. The head mounted displays are fitted with microphones and speakers to allow users to communicate while immersed within the Global Change World. The addition of microphones and speakers within the HMDs allowed the experimenters to provide scaffolding for the participants while they were immersed in the Global Change World.

Participants were randomly assigned to one of three conditions. The first condition had participants enter the Global Change World alone and perform the required tasks. The second condition allowed one pair of participants to perform the tasks collaboratively within Global Change World. For the third condition, participants were paired with an experimenter who acted as an expert advisor, answering any questions and directly assisting the participants. A 24-question posttest was administered after the GCW session to measure the student's content knowledge of global warming. There were no significant differences in test scores among the three groups. Furthermore, all groups required a great deal of scaffolding in order to navigate and to accomplish the goals within the environment. In this section we review several VR systems whose research goals were to foster the learning of knowledge and skills in school age children. The results of experiments designed to demonstrate their effectiveness was mixed (i.e., only two of the four studies showed significant differences between the experimental and control conditions). In this regard, Roussos, Johnson, Moher, Leigh, Vasilakis, and Barnes (1999) stated that "there is a strong need for demonstrable added value to learning associated with the use of VR technologies" (p. 261). Without clear-cut evidence that virtual reality brings any "added value," there does not seem much point in investing lots of money to replace conventional teaching methods. In summary, virtual reality provides a potential avenue for transporting users to environments that they normally would not be able to visit and the experimenter can control what information and how much of it will be presented, offering even-handed interventions to channel specific learning goals. However, there is limited evidence in K–12 environments as to its effectiveness.

Training Applications of VR

A virtual reality environment has the potential to enhance training. For example, virtual reality has the potential ability to improve the methods of interaction and visualization in assembly applications. Manipulating an object in a 3D environment (virtual reality) can be more intuitive than dealing with schematic drawings. The goal of virtual reality applications in assembly is the reduction of design time and increase time needed to market a product. Participants (engineering students) were assigned to one of 4 water pump assembly training conditions. Group 1 used 2-D engineering drawings, group 2 used a desktop VR system with a monitor and a 2-D mouse, group 3 used a desktop VR system with stereoscopic glasses and a 2-D mouse, and group 4 used an immersive VR system with an HMD and a 3-D mouse. Participants trained in one of the four conditions and then completed five trials of a timed assembly of the actual water pump.

The results of the experiment show that the assembly times for the participants using the 2-D drawings were significantly slower than participants in the VR conditions. A significant difference in assembly time was not found between the different VR applications, although users of the IVR reported that the manipulation of a 3-D object in 3-D space was very intuitive. Participants also reported problems with the VR system due to slow system control and lack of haptic feedback (participants often overshot a virtual). Boud, Baber, and Steiner (2000), concluded that VR has the potential to train assembly operators. VR allows a user to train and practice a task before the real component has been developed. Designers can watch the assembly of a virtual product and identify potential problems in the assembly process, allowing modifications to be made before the product is created. Boud et al. (2000) described the technological shortcomings of VR as a trade-off between model complexity and the computational ability of the VR system. For assembly applications, VR systems must be properly calibrated, must afford real-time collision detection algorithms, and must provide the user with haptic feedback, all of which represent difficulties for VR to handle.

Jordan, Gallagher, McGuigan, McGlade, and McClure (2000) studied the effects of the Minimally Invasive Surgery Trainer Virtual Reality (MIST VR) on psychomotor skill acquisition. Novice laparoscopic surgeons must learn to compensate for the fulcrum effect where the patient's tissue acts as a fulcrum for the surgical equipment. MIST VR trains the surgeon by providing laparoscopic instruments for the manipulation of shapes displayed on a monitor. MIST VR provides trainees with a rating of their manual dexterity, how their training is progressing, objective scores based on performance and errors, and how they match up with their peers. MIST VR also fosters the development of psychomotor skills that are crucial to successful laparoscopic procedures. The application runs on a Pentium PC linked to a jig with two laparoscopic instruments attached to position-sensing gimbals. Real-time video of virtual objects and instruments is displayed on a 17-inch monitor. The users can grasp the virtual shapes with the instruments and practice the psychomotor skills required to successfully perform a laparoscopic procedure.

Participants completed a laparoscopic cutting task and were then randomly assigned to one of three training conditions; MIST VR, laparoscopic cutting task with normal laparoscopic image conditions, or laporoscopic cutting task with randomly alternating image conditions (normal laparoscopic imaging or y-axis inverted imaging). The laparoscopic cutting task uses laparoscopic instruments inserted into a box trainer. The individual watches a monitor that displays the instruments and a piece of paper with a series of black lines 1 cm apart. The trainee attempts to make as many incisions between the lines as possible within a 2-min time period. For each condition, trainees completed six training trials and then performed the laparoscopic cutting task.

Jordan et al. (2000) found that participants in the MIST VR condition made significantly more correct incisions during the cutting task. Participants in the randomly alternating condition made significantly more correct incisions than the normal laporoscopic condition. The results of this study indicate that virtual reality trainers provide a novel approach to surgical training that is superior to traditional methods that lack meaningful feedback.

Stone (2000) described a virtual reality training device developed for the Royal Air Force for the maintenance of Tornado jets. The Royal Air Force was in need of a VR-based aircraft maintenance trainer due to a dwindling number of available equipment weapons platforms. The original training system included a 13-week course that only allowed two students to use a Tornado rig at one time. The training system did not include defensive avionics and required a 3-week downtime to reset the trainer, all at a cost of $14 million. The VR-based system reduced the overall course to 9 weeks and allowed eight or more students to work at the same time. All avionics are included in the program and the system does not require any downtime, with a cost of approximately $1.5 million. Trainees also reported and displayed enhanced procedural knowledge and spatial awareness near the

midpoint of the course, assessed by comparing trainees' diagnosis and repair times in the original training system to the MUSE Virtual Presence
Training System.

The Simulator Training Research Advanced Testbed for Aviation located at Fort Rucker, Alabama (STRATA) was the system used in a series of
experiments. The apparatus is an AH-64A Apache helicopter cockpit with
an HMD in the aft cockpit and a rear projection display in the forward cockpit. For this experiment, the STRATA was not used as a helicopter simulator, but as a "virtual flying carpet." In the flying carpet mode, trainees can
traverse the simulated terrain of Hanchey Army Heliport, as if they were flying on a flying carpet. The environment created for the simulation was a virtual representation of Hanchey Army Heliport (HAH) at Fort Rucker,
Alabama. Trainees were aviators from Fort Rucker who had never visited
HAH, and were randomly assigned to one of three conditions. Condition 1
used a high resolution HMD with a wide field of view (representation of the
highly immersive VRE). Condition 2 used the same HMD with a narrow
field of view. The third condition (low immersion/low resolution display)
used the rear-projection wide screen display. Participants were administered a pretest of their knowledge of HAH, allowed to fly around the virtual
HAH, and then given a posttest of their knowledge acquisition of HAH.

The results of the experiment showed that the virtual exploration of
HAH had a significant effect on imparting spatial awareness to the participants (pretest and posttest scores). Participants in the study were able to
complete the navigation posttest with a mean error rate less than one wrong
turn per participant. The hypothesis that the high resolution, high-im-
mersive VR condition would improve knowledge acquisition was not supported by the results. The result suggests that spatial knowledge acquisition
may not rely on high-resolution, high-fidelity VRs.

Virtual Reality Methodology

The analysis of a VR system requires attention toward the application environment, how information will be presented and processed, and the design
of the human–computer interface (Kalawsky, 1999) and the specific instructional strategy being used. VRUSE was developed to provide a diagnostic
tool for usability evaluations of VRs. The aim was to collect user feedback
concerning interaction with the environment, provide feedback based on
usability feedback, and indicate where problems exist within the VR.
VRUSE is a 10-part questionnaire that measures the functionality, ease of
use, flexibility, system output, consistency, fidelity, sense of immersion, and
overall system usability of a virtual environment. VRUSE has been successfully used to identify problems with the VR that can be used to fine tune in-

terface designs. Unfortunately, no data has been generated regarding the tool's reliability or validity.

From an ergonomics perspective, HMDs need much improvement in the quality of visual displays, the reduction of system latencies, and the improvement in comfort for the user (Wilson, 1999). The design of a VR should focus on the capabilities of the user (perceptual, motor, etc.) and reduce the amount of time needed for a user to learn to use the system (Wann & Mon-Williams, 1996). VR developers must assess what tasks will be completed in the VRE and who will be using the VR. The complexity of a VR should never exceed the requirements needed to complete a task (Wilson, 1997). VREs are not constrained by the physical laws of the real world so the developers must not assume that a user will naturally perceive proper interaction and navigation within the VR (Wann & Mon-Williams, 1996). The VR should support motion parallax and provide the user with binocular vision, creating the illusion of depth within the environment. Visual perception within a VR should strive to mimic visual processes within the real world so that skills required in the context of the VR will transfer to the real world with little difficulty (Loomis et al., 1999).

VRs need to provide cues to the user that aid in orientation and navigation within the virtual world. An aid to navigation and orientation in a VR may be to include a walk-through that takes the user through the virtual environment, provides instructions on how to interact and navigate in the VR, and gives an overview of the tasks and goals to be accomplished within the VR (Sutcliffe & Kaur, 2000). Proprioceptive cues should be included to enhance the user's ability to orient and navigate within the VR (Klatsky, Loomis, Beall, Chance, & Golledge, 1998). Chance, Gaunet, Beall, and Loomis (1998) advised that if tasks require spatial orientation, real rotations and translations of movement should be afforded by allowing the user to actually walk around the VR. For movement to discontinuous places within a VR, Ruddle, Howes, Payne, and Jones (2000) suggested the use of hyperlinks that allow the user to jump from one location to another, thus reducing navigation times.

Haptic feedback (force feedback) plays an important role in the quality of interaction between a user and a virtual environment. Salnas, et al. (2000) studied the effects of haptic feedback on task performance time, immersion, social presence, and perceived task proficiency. Participants were randomly assigned to two groups (haptic feedback vs. no haptic feedback) and asked to arrange blocks in certain patterns in a virtual space while working with a virtual partner. The PHANToM was used as the manipulation device for both groups but only one group experienced the haptic feedback. Participants in the haptic feedback condition showed significantly faster task completion times (25 min vs. 35 min) and reported a higher sense of virtual presence and social presence within the VR. The haptic feedback group also rated their perceived task proficiency as higher than the no haptic feedback group. Physically touching a virtual object improves the user's experience within the VR (Hoffman, 1998). The ability to feel the environment and the interface allows the user to manipulate and interact with the environment in a more efficient manner. Other devices that support haptic feedback include instrumental objects (tactile augmentation), gloves, speakers, and vests equipped with subwoofers.

Avatar development is another important factor in the development of VRs. An avatar is a representation of another interactant in the virtual world that can be another user or a computer-based model. For social interaction to occur within a VR, the computer must create intelligent interactants that represent other users or models (Loomis et al., 1999). A major difficulty is supplying avatars with a proper range of expressive behavior. Avatars need to possess complex methods of expressiveness to foster the illusion of intelligent beings within the VR (Riva, 1999). Olveres, Billinghurst, Savage, and Holden (1998) developed an intelligent avatar representation that can infer emotions from text input using natural language parsers. The avatar can provide the appropriate facial expression and speak with the emotional intonation based on the text input. As computers display more humanlike traits, users may be more willing to treat the computer or avatar more like a human. However, very little data exists to support the effectiveness of Avatars (see Clark, Bewley, & O'Neil, chap. 8).

VR has been shown to be a potentially useful tool in multiple domains but more research must be carried out to address usability issues. Understanding of what is meant by usability in VRs is relatively poor, and there is little agreement on which attributes among the many variables of the VR interface are important to learning. Research must also be carried out on the types of training or educational domains in which VR can be applied. Researchers must focus on theory driving VR research instead of allowing the technology be the deciding factor for the type of research that is carried out.

Research Issues in VR Environments

So far, we have described a sample of the state-of the-art of virtual environments for education. We found a small number of research articles in our literature review concerned with examining the impact of VR on learning. Perhaps this is reflective of the current level of the maturity of this technology as an education and training media. By and large, the VR laboratories we visited voiced concerns with the engineering issues of VR and HCI design rather than with exploring the impact of VR on learning. This led us to the conclusion that a number of issues need to be addressed before learning studies can be seriously pursued. These research issues are described in this section. A key issue that several researchers mentioned (Loomis et al., 1999) is that visual distance perception in VR environments should mimic that of the real world as closely as possible so that skills acquired in an VR environments will transfer to the real task. VR environments should be designed to support head motion parallax and binocular vision so that the VR environment has depth perception (Wann & Mon-Williams, 1996). Stereoscopic techniques should be used in VR environments to greatly reduce the awareness of the display surface, reducing perceptual conflicts (Loomis et al., 1999).

With regard to usability issues Wilson (1997) suggested that ergonomics of VR should focus on the design of the head mounted displays to make them more comfortable for the user, that optic displays be improved, that latency effects be studies, and that interface control and feedback be developed. The design of VR environments must center on the perceptual-motor capabilities of the users. Improvements need to be made in navigation, orientation, depth cues, and visual fidelity. Transfer of training studies need to be conducted to determine the value of VR to Web-based learning application or any other training application (see Witmer et al., 2002). Studies need to be conducted that measure human performance in VR environments. However, what are the appropriate metrics to be used in assessing human performance in simulation and VR environments? The American National Standards Institute (ANSI) 1993 guide to human performance lists several issues that underlie the measurements of human performance in the context of scientific research, test, and evaluation. Although these issues are applicable to human performance assessment in general, they are of particular importance to the assessment of human performance in simulation and VR environments. These issues are:

- Lack of a general theory to guide performance measurement.
- The inverse control between operational control and realism.
- The multiple dimensions of behavior.
- The ambiguous relationship between objective and subjective data.
- Difficulty of measuring cognitive tasks (e.g., how do we assess deep understanding or knowledge of a device model).
- Lack of objective performance criteria for most tasks.
- Difficulty of generalizing results to the real world.

The critical issue for VR environments is assessing the extent of transfer and generalization of skills and knowledge acquired in the VR environment to the real world (Lampton, Bliss, & Morris, 2002) What is a reasonable transfer task? VR environments are ideal for addressing these critical issues due to the capability of VE to potentially replicate with precision real-world situations and environments. VR environments are subject to systematic experimental manipulation of variables hypothesized to influence learning. Not only is performance measurement important in demonstrating the training effectiveness of a specific VR environment (see O'Neil et al., 2000), it is critical to identifying which features or components facilitate acquisition of new skills and knowledge. Objective performance measurement is important to provide accurate, reliable, and meaningful feedback and knowledge of results to individual users.

Lastly, research needs to be performed on individual differences, and whether one's ability to visualize facilitates or hinders learning in VR environments.

Technological Issues of VR

Many of the technological shortcomings of VR are a product of the computational ability of the system and the complexity of the models produced by the system (Boud et al., 2000). According to Riva (1999), there needs to be a shift of focus from image quality to the freedom of movement that the VR affords the user. Improvements need to be made in HMD development, navigation, orientation, haptics, visual depth, and visual cues (Wilson, 1999). Users of VRs often experience magical appearance syndrome in which the user becomes disoriented and loses the ability to navigate when immersed into the VR (Robertson, Czerwinski, & Dantzich, 1997). VR development needs to be based on perceptual psychology research on visualization, improve graphical rendering performance, and improve interaction within the VR by providing system flexibility (Van Dam et al., 2000). HMDs are often cumbersome and visual displays are often low resolution that inhibits natural interaction within the VRE. Many VREs have limited tracking capabilities due to sensitivities to magnetic interference. Auditory cues and haptic feedback can be very expensive and difficult to provide to the user and may even result in simulator sickness due to multisensory inputs (Dede et al., 1997). With respect to the use of VR as a media for Web-based learning given limited band width, response speeds, security issues, and the lack of tools for building VR applications over the net, virtual environment are not a viable option as a media for education or training at this point.

Simulator sickness is a by-product of the technical limitations of VREs. Incongruencies between motion signals transmitted by the eyes, the vestibular system, and proprioceptors or optical distortions in the display medium often result in simulator sickness (Draper, Viire, Furness, & Gawron, 2001). Improvements in high-fidelity visual representation may also increase the sense of movement within a VRE, contributing to the symptomology of simulator sickness (Hill & Howarth, 2000). Draper, et al. (2001) suggested that avoiding visual deviations in displays, improving the accuracy of optic flow rates in HMDs, and limiting first time exposure to

VRs to 10 minutes will help to reduce simulator sickness. Allowing the user to physically walk around the environment will reduce symptoms as long as the visual cues match vestibular cues. Hill and Howarth (2000) suggested habituation as a means to lessen the effects of simulator sickness.

Instructional Strategies in VR design

The effectiveness of the VR technology in facilitating learning in educational and training applications is mixed. Only a few empirical studies have been performed to date in education (Bowman, Hodges, Allison, & Wineman, 1999; Johnson, Moher, Ohlsson, & Leigh, 2001; Osberg et al., 1997; Saltzman & Saltzman, 1999) have provided initial evidence of the learning gains using VR-based environments with students ranging from second grade through high school. The evidence for training effectiveness is somewhat better. Of the educational studies that measured the impact of VR on learning the focus has been on a limited range of instructional strategies from the use of a constructivist approach (e.g., Jackson & Fagan, 2000) to the design of instruction to frames of references (Saltzman et al., 1999). Two of these research studies are discussed in the following sections to provide examples of the type of research that has been performed thus far. The Round Earth World Project (Johnson et al., 2001) is one of the representatives of this research where they used a variety of VR-based learning strategies to teach mental models of science concepts to elementary school-age children. A specific learning strategy used in their research was guided by the "cross domain transfer hypothesis" or theory. The cross domain transfer theory suggests that acquired central ideas (i.e., the belief that the world is flat) are not transformed but replaced by ideas from other contexts, domains, or situations. In the Round Earth World experiments, the experimenters attempted to bring about a conceptual change in the way that their subjects perceived the shape of the earth, that the earth is round not flat. According to this theory, subjects did not have any prior knowledge about the shape of the virtual asteroid but they did about the shape of the earth. So the subjects' experiences with the virtual world of the Round Earth World caused them to replace their idea of the earth as flat to that of the earth is round. Although, the experimenters found evidence for conceptual change in these school-age children, their experimental design did not allow them to assign whether it was the virtual environment or the instructional strategy that was responsible for the conceptual change in their subjects (Johnson et al., 2001). This shortcoming can also be made of the research on frames of references (Saltzman et al., 1999) where they found that the bicentric group was superior in learning to groups that only provided the egocentric or exocentric frame of reference. However, they failed to find differential effects of FORs on learning different types of information. For example, it was hypothesized that exocentric FOR would teach global aspects and egocentric FOR would teach more local aspects of force and motion. The rationale for this prediction was not offered for these predictions nor for why these FOR did not achieve the predicted outcome. What is needed is more methodologically rigorous research to determine what variables account for facilitating learning in VR environments. The relationship of cognitive and instructional design theories to VR design are not as direct as one would expect. We would like to see in the future VR designers pull from basic principles in cognition, as well as from basic principles of instructional design. For example, Czerwinski and Larson (2002) discuss how Fitts and Posner's law (1967) and Hick's law (1952) and preattentive processing (Triesman, 1985) have been used to guide the development of the human computer interface of Web sites. Likewise, research on virtual environments for teaching and learning should involve the use of cognitive principles not only in the design of the human computer interaction and software but in the instructional content as well. Perhaps the most interesting aspect of the application of well-understood instructional strategies and variables to be investigated is how these strategies/variables interact in a dynamic three dimensional environment. For example, the use of (the when and how) auditory and visual cues, the use of various forms of visualization to represent information (see O'Neil et al., 2000), the use of scaffolding (prompts, hints), the use of spatial location of visual cues, the impact of individual differences (e.g., spatial ability and gender) on the ability to acquired skills and knowledge, and the types of direct practice and feedback can interact in entirely different fashions in a VR environment.

REFERENCES

Barfield, W., & Caudell, T. (2001). (Eds.). *Fundamentals of wearable computers and augmented reality*. Mahwah, NJ: Lawrence Erlbaum Associates.

Bliss, J. P., Tidwell, P. D., & Guest, M. A. (1997). The effectiveness of virtual reality for administering spatial navigation training to fire fighters. *Presence, 6*(1), 73–86.

Boud, A. C., Baber, C., & Steiner, S. J. (2000). Virtual reality: A tool for assembly? *Presence, 9*, 486–496.

Bowman, D. Hodges, L., Allison, D., & Wineman, J. (1999). The educational value of information-rich virtual environment. *Presence, 8*, 317–331.

Brooks, F. P., Jr. (1999, November/December). What's real about virtual reality? *IEEE, 19*, 16–27.

Burpee, J. S. (1981). Proceedings of the third inter-service/industry training equipment conference, Vol. II. *American Defense Preparedness Association, 2*, 36–42.

Chance, S. S., Gaunet, F., Beall, A. C., & Loomis, J. M. (1998). Locomotion mode affects the updating of objects encountered during travel: The contribution of vestibular and proprioceptive inputs to path integration. *Presence, 7*, 168–178.

Clark, R. E. (1983). Reconsidering research on learning from media. *Review of Educational Research, 53*, 445–459.

Clark, R. E. (2001). New directions and evaluating distance learning technologies. In R. E. Clark (Ed.), *Learning rom media: Arguments, analysis, and evidence*. Greenwich, CT: Information Age Publishers.

Czerwinski, M. P., & Larson, K. (2002). Cognition and the web: Moving from theory to web design. In J. Ratner (Ed.), *Human factors and Web development* (pp. 147–165). Mahwah, NJ: Lawrence Erlbaum Associates.

Dede, C., Saltzman, M., Loftin, R. B., & Ash, K. (1997). Using virtual reality technology to convey abstract scientific concepts. In M. J. Jacobson & R. B. Kozma (Eds.), *Learning the sciences of the 21st century: Research, design, and implementing advanced technology learning environments* (pp. 8–120). Mahwah, NJ: Lawrence Erlbaum Associates.

Draper, M. H., Viire, E. S., Furness, T. A., & Gawron, V. J. (2001). Effects of image scale and system time delay on simulator sickness within head-coupled virtual environments. *Human Factors, 43*, 129–146.

Duffy, T. M., & Jonassen, D. H. (1992). Constructivism: New implications for instructional technology. In T. M. Duffy & D. H. Jonassen (Eds.), *Constructivism and the technology of instruction a conversation* (pp. 1–17). Hillsdale, NJ: Lawrence Erlbaum Associates.

Fitts, P. M., & Posner, M. I. (1967). *Human performance: Basic concepts in Psychology Series*. Belmont, CA: Brooks/Cole.

Fletcher, J. D. (2003). Implications of advance distributed learning for education (Urban diversity series). ERIC clearing house on Urban Education. New York: Columbia University Teachers College.

Forsberg, A. (2000, November/December). Artery. *IEEE*, 35–36.

Garris, R., Ahlers, R., & Driskell, R. (2001). Games, motivation, and learning: A research and practice model. (manuscript in preparation.)

Harm, D. L. (2002). Motion sickness neurophysiology, physiological correlates and treatment. In K. M. Stanney (Ed.), *Handbook of virtual environments: Design, implementation, and applications* (pp. 637–662). Mahwah, NJ: Lawrence Erlbaum Associates.

Heeter, C. (2003). Reflections on real presence by a virtual person. *Presence, 12*(4), 333–345.

Hick, W. E. (1952). On the rate of gain of information. *Quarterly Journal of Experimental Psychology, 4*, 11–26.

Hill, K. J., & Howarth, P. A. (2000). Habituation to the side effects of immersion in a virtual environment. *Displays, 21*, 25–30.

Hoffman, H. G. (1998). Virtual reality: A new tool for interdisciplinary psychology research. *CyberPsychology & behaviour: The impact of the internet, multimedia and virtual reality on behavior and society, 1*, 195–200.

Höllerer, T., Feiner, S., Hallaway, D., Bell, B., Lanzagorta, M., Brown, D., et al. (2001). User interface management techniques for collaborative mobile augmented reality. *Computers & Graphics, 25*, 799–810.

Jackson, R. L., & Fagan, E. (2000). Collaboration and learning within immersive virtual reality. *ACM, 1*(4), 83–92.

Johnson, A., Moher, T., Ohlsson, S., & Gillingham, M. (1999a, March). The round earth project: Deep learning in a collaborative virtual world. *Proceedings IEEE Virtual Reality '99.* (pp. 112–129).

Johnson, A., Moher, T., Ohlsson, S., & Gillingham, M. (1999b, November/December). The Round Earth Project-collaborative VR for conceptual learning. *IEEE*, 60–69.

Johnson, A., Moher, T., Ohlsson, S., & Leigh, J. (2001, March). Exploring multiple representations in elementary school science education. *Proceedings of IEEE Virtual Reality*, (pp. 89–96).

Johnson, D. M., & Stewart, J. E., II. (1999). Use of virtual environments for the acquisition of spatial knowledge: Comparison among different visual displays. *Military Psychology, 11*, 129–148.

Jonassen, D., & Tennyson, R. D. (1997). *Handbook of research on educational communications and technology.* Washington, DC: Association for Educational Communications and Technology.

Jones, E. R., & Hennessy, R. T. (Eds.). (1985). *Human factors aspects of simulation.* Washington, DC: National Academy Press.

Jones, E. R., Hennessy, R. T., & Deutsch, S. (Eds.). (1985). *Human factors aspects of simulations: Work group on simulation.* National research council. Washington, DC: National Academy Press.

Jordan, J., Gallagher, A. G., McGuigan, J., McGlade, K., & McClure, N. (2000). A comparison between randomly alternating imaging, normal laparoscopic imaging, and virtual reality training in laparoscopic psychomotor skill acquisition. *The American Journal of Surgery, 180*, 208–211.

Kalawsky, R. S. (1999). VRUSE-a computerized diagnostic tool: For usability evaluation of virtual/synthetic environment systems. *Applied Ergonomics, 30*, 11–25.

Klatsky, R. L., Loomis, J. M., Beall, A. C., Chance, S. S., & Golledge, R. G. T. (1998). Spatial updating of self-position and orientation during real, imagined, and virtual locomotion. *Psychological Science, 9*, 293–298.

Lampton, D. R., Bliss, J. P., & Morris, C. S. (2002). Human performance measurement in virtual environments. In K. Stanney (Ed.), *Handbook of virtual environments: Design, implementation and applications* (pp. 701–720). Mahwah, NJ: Lawrence Erlbaum Associates.

Loomis, J. M., Blascovich, J. J., & Beall, A. C. (1999). Immersive virtual environments technology as a basic research tool in psychology. *Behavior Research Methods, Instruments, & Computers, 4*, 557–564.

Loomis, J. M., & Knapp, J. M. (1999). Visual perception of egocentric distance in real and virtual environments. In L. J. Hettinger & M. W. Haas (Eds.), *Virtual and adaptive environments* (pp. 143–164). Mahwah, NJ: Lawrence Erlbaum Associates.

Malone, T. W., & Lepper, M. F. (1987). Making learning fun: A taxonomy of intrinsic motivation for learning. In R. E. Snows & M. J. Farr (Eds.), *Aptitude, learning, and instruction* (pp. 233–253). Hillsdale, NJ: Lawrence Erlbaum Associates.

Meehan, C., Insko, B., Whitton, M. C., & Brooks, F. P. (2001). Physiological measures of presence in stressful virtual environments. *ACM transactions on Graphics, 21*(3), 645–653.

Moher, T., Johnson, A., Cho, Y., & Lin, Y. (2000). Observation-based inquiry in a virtual ambient environment. In B. Fishman & S. O'Connor-Divelbiss (Eds.), *International conference of the learning sciences* (pp. 238–245). Mahwah, NJ: Lawrence Erlbaum Associates.

Moher, T., Johnson, A., Ohlsson, S., & Gillingham, M. (1999, May). Bridging strategies for vr-based learning. *CHI '99* (pp. 536–544), Pittsburgh, PA: ACM.

Molineros, J., & Sharma, R. (2001). Real-time tracking of multiple objects using fiducials for augmented reality. *Real-Time Imaging, 7*, 495–506.

Munro, A. (2003). Simulation and online learning: Does it make sense? Can it be done? Presentation at the Online Learning Conference, Los Angeles, CA.

Nichols, S., Haldane, C., & Wilson, J. (2000). Measurement of presence and its consequences in virtual environments. *International Journal of Human-Computer Studies, 52*, 471–491.

Ohlsson, S., Moher, T. G., & Johnson, A. (2000, August). Deep learning in virtual reality: How to teach children that the Earth is round. *Proceedings of the 22 annual meeting of the Cognitive Science Society*, Philadelphia, PA.

Olveres, J., Billinghurst, M., Savage, J., & Holden, A. (1998, October). Intelligent, expressive avatars. In *Proceedings of the First Workshop on Embodied Conversational Characters (WECC'98)*. Lake Tahoe, CA.

O'Neil, H. F., Mayer, R. E., Herl, H., Thurman, R., & Olin, K. (2000). Instructional strategies for virtual aviation training environments. In H. F. O'Neil & D. H. Andrews (Eds.), Aircraft training: Methods, technologies, and assessment (pp. 105–130). Mahwah, NJ: Lawrence Erlbaum Associates.

Osberg, K., Winn, W., Rose, H., Hollander, A., Hoffman, H. & Char, P. (1997, May). The effect of having grade seven students construct virtual environments on their comprehension of science. *AERA Annual Meeting*, Chicago, IL.

Pausch, R., Proffitt, D., & Williams, G. (1997). Quantifying immersion in virtual reality. *SIGGRAPH'97, ACM*, 112–242.

Ramish, R., & Andrews, D. H. (1999). Distributed mission training: Teams, virtual reality and real-time networking. *Communications of the ACM, 42*, 65–67.

Ricci, K., Salas, E., & Cannon-Bowers, J. A. (1996). Do computer based games facilitate knowledge acquisition and retention? *Military Psychology, 8*(4), 295–307.

Riva, G. (1999). From technology to communication: Psycho-social issues in developing virtual environments. *Journal of Visual Languages and Computing, 10*, 87–97.

Robertson, G., Czerwinski, M., & Dantzich, M. (1997). Immersion in desktop virtual reality. *ACM, 40*, 11–19.

Roussos, M., Johnson, A., Moher, T., Leigh, J., Vasilakis, C., & Barnes, C. (1999). Learning and building together in an immersive virtual world. *Presence, 8*, 247–263.

Ruddle, R. A., Howes, A., Payne, S. J., & Jones, D. M. (2000). The effects of hyperlinks on navigation in virtual environments. *International Journal of Human-Computer Studies, 53*, 551–581.

Salnas, E., Rassmus-Grohn, K., & Sjostrom, C. (2000). Supporting presence in collaborative environments by haptic force feedback. *ACM Transactions on Computer-Human Interaction, 7*, 461–476.

Saltzman, M., Dede, C., Loftin, R. B., & Chen, J. (1999). A model for understanding how virtual reality aids complex conceptual learning. *Presence, 8*, 292–316.

Shim, W., & Kim, G. J. (2003). Designing for presence and performance: The case of the virtual fish tank. *Presence, 12*(4), 387–410.

Spalter, A. M. (2000, December). Color museum. *IEEE 30*.

Stone, R. (2000). Virtual reality in perspective. Retrieved June 6, 2003, from www.vrweb.com/docs/vr/vr.html.

Stone, R. (2001). Virtual reality for interactive training: an industrial practitioner's viewpoint. *International Journal of Human-Computer Studies, 55*, 699–771.

Sutcliffe, A. G., & Kaur, K. (2000). Evaluating the usability of virtual reality user interfaces. *Behaviour & Information Technology, 19*, 415–426.

Tennyson, R. D., & Breuer, K. (2002). Linking learning theory to instructional design. *Educational Technology, 42*(3), 51–55.

Thurman, R. A., & Russo, T. (2000). Using virtual reality for training. In H. F. O'Neil & D. H. Andrews (Eds.), Aircrew training: Methods, technologies, and assessments (pp. 85–109). Mahwah, NJ: Lawrence Erlbaum Associates.

Triesman, A. (1985). Preattentive processing in vision. *Computer Vision, Graphics, and Image Processing, 31*, 156–177.

Triesman, A. (1985). Preattentive processing in vision: Computer vision, Graphics, and Image Processing, 31, 156–177. Reprinted in Z. Pylyshyn (Ed.), Computational processes in human vision: An interdisciplinary perspective (pp. 341–369). Norwood, NJ: Ablex.

Tromp, J. G., Steed, A., & Wilson, J. R. (2003). Systematic usability evaluation and design issues for collaborative virtual environments. *Presence, 12*(3), 241–267.

Van Dam, A., Forsberg, A. S., Laidlaw, D. H., La Viola, J. J., & Simpson, R. M. (2000). Immersive VR for scientific visualization: A progress report. *IEEE Computer Graphics and Application, 20*, 26–52.

Waller, D., Hunt, E., & Knapp, D. (1998). The transfer of spatial knowledge in virtual environment training. *Presence, 7*(4), 129–143.

Wann, J., & Mon-Williams, M. (1996). What does virtual reality need?: Human Factors issues in the design of three dimensional computer environments. *International Journal of Human-Computer Studies, 44*, 829–847.

Wilson, J. (1997). Virtual environments and ergonomics: Needs and opportunities. *Ergonomics, 40*, 1057–1077.

Wilson, J. R. (1999). Virtual environments applications and applied ergonomics. *Applied Ergonomics, 30*, 3–9.

Wilson, P. N., Foreman, N., & Tlauka, M. (1997). Transfer of spatial information from virtual to a real environment. *Human Factors, 39*, 526–531.

Witmer, B. G., Bailey, J. H., & Knerr, B. W. (1995). Training dismounted soldiers in virtual environments: Route learning and transfer (Tech. Rep. No. 1022). Alexandria, VA: US Army Research Institute for the Behavioral and Social Sciences.

Witmer, B. G., Sadowski, W. J., & Finkelstein, N. M. (2002). VE-Based training strategies for acquiring survey knowledge. *Presence: Teleoperators and virtual environments, 11*(1), 1–18.

Chapter 8

Heuristics for Selecting Distance or Classroom Settings for Courses

Richard E. Clark
University of Southern California

William L. Bewley
CRESST/UCLA

Harold F. O'Neil
University of Southern California

When new courses are developed, a decision must be made about the "delivery media and setting" for student access to the instruction. In the past, a huge variety of instructional settings and media have been used to deliver courses including (most commonly) classrooms and teachers and (most recently) multimedia transmitted via the Web and/or recorded on CD or DVD. The purpose of this chapter is to describe a relatively simple procedure for making a cost-beneficial decision between the classroom and a distance delivery platform for any one course of instruction.

MEDIA SELECTION RESEARCH

A recent, comprehensive review by Sugrue and Clark (2000) of approximately 45 media selection schemes published over a period of 30 years concluded that most "gave an illusion of rationality and scientific precision to what were, at best, decisions driven by practical and economic considerations, and at worst, by invalid assumptions about learning, learners and the effects of media on them" (p. 208).

There are no published studies of the way that instructional designers or curriculum managers actually select media for courses but informal talks with media producers suggest that existing selection models are seldom used in practice. For example, nearly all of the published models give designers the excellent advice to delay media selection until the end of the instructional design process but before instructional materials are developed. In this way, media can be selected that will adequately carry the necessary instructional design without excessive cost. Yet, the opinion of many curriculum experts and experienced designers is that media are chosen far ahead of the design process either because the organization is focused on a specific medium or because administrators want to appear to be using the latest technology. This seemingly irrational behavior fits the evolving model of automated decision making proposed by Ellen Langer (1994) and reinforced in recent reviews by Daniel Wegner (2002). Langer suggested that rational, deliberate, conscious decision making (in any domain) may most often be a myth and argued that

> the processes that are most generally understood as leading to decisions, such as integrating and weighing information in a cost-benefit analysis, most often are post-decision phenomena, if they occur at all .... Cognitive commitments are frozen on rigidly held beliefs .... Once a cognitive commitment is reached, choice follows mechanically, without calculation. (p. 34)

Media Impact on Learning and Motivation

Sugrue and Clark (2000) concluded that existing evidence suggests that media are not expected to contribute any unique influence on learning and motivation based on reviews of media comparison studies by Clark (1983, 1994, 2001) and others (Morrison, 2001; Russell, 1999). Another way to view this conclusion is that any learning goal that can be achieved in one medium, for example in the classroom, can also be achieved at the same level in another medium or mix of media, for example in computer-based instruction or interactive televised settings. Even Kozma (1994), who is widely regarded as a critic of this point of view, acknowledged that "no significant difference" is the best view of all past comparisons of different media to teach similar learning tasks and learners. Similarly, Salomon (1984) has made a compelling case that media do not uniquely motivate learning. He presented evidence that the same media can have very different motivational qualities depending on the beliefs and expectations of learners and vice versa.

The most comprehensive and current meta-analyses of the media comparison studies to be conducted were undertaken by Bernard, et al. (2004).

In an analysis of hundreds of studies, they found no learning differences between the two media delivery platforms that were attributable to medium or instructional context. Bernard, et al. did report some very strong motivational results in their studies that indicated a dislike of asynchronous distance education by the subjects in the experiments they reviewed. Yet, this finding seems to be due not to the media employed but to the delayed feedback conditions and students' general dislike of asynchronous distance courses. Thus, the most reasonable conclusion from many studies seems to be that the media or mix of media selected for instruction cannot influence learning and/or motivation, because neither outcome seems to be influenced by the medium of instruction. So what impact does media have on the instructional process?

Access and Efficiency Benefits

Most reviewers agreed with Cobb (1997) and Clark (1983, 2001) that media may have a significant impact on student access to instruction, and the cost (Levin, 1983) and efficiency of their learning (Cobb, 1997). Presumably, distance education is a potential solution to instructional access problems when students are widely distributed geographically and when travel is either more expensive or less convenient than "distance" access via the Internet or television transmission. In addition, when large numbers of students must be served, there may be a considerable economy of scale in serving them at a distance. Both access and scale are economic issues that can and should be addressed in an a priori, cost/benefit analysis (e.g., Levin, 1983; Levin & McEwan, 2001).

A Cognitive Approach to Media Selection

Sugrue and Clark (2000) suggested a "cognitive approach [that] (a) conceives of training as a collection of [instructional] methods that support specific cognitive processes essential to learning and transfer, and (b) treats media as collections of attributes that facilitate the delivery of those methods" (p. 208). Their view of the instructional impact of media and methods is summarized in Fig. 8.1.

They recommended an analysis of the instructional methods that are required to learn in any course and then an analysis of the variety of media that will effectively and efficiently present necessary methods. Thus, they confirmed previous views by authors of the few systematic media selection schemes that media should not be chosen until a complete blueprint or instructional design for a course has been developed. Only at this point can course developers know what instructional methods are needed to teach the instructional content in a course.

	Access	Cost (Development and Delivery)	Efficiency (Time to Learn)	Learning and Motivation
Media	X	X	X	
Methods			X	X

FIG. 8.1.   Outcomes of instruction influenced by media and instructional methods.[1]

THREE INSTRUCTIONAL METHODS THAT OFTEN LIMIT INSTRUCTIONAL MEDIA SELECTION

The research evidence is that there are no learning or motivation differences when the same course is presented by live instructors teaching students in classrooms or when a variety of electronic media are utilized. Yet some instructional methods cannot be presented in all media. Designers are advised to follow the suggestions made by Sugrue and Clark (2000) and ask first what instructional methods are required to achieve course learning goals, and then ask what media are available that will present those methods at the least expensive cost? In our clinical attempts to examine this issue, we have often found that three of the most common instructional methods can only be presented via a limited number of media. Those three methods are; 1) the sensory modes required for learning concepts, processes, and procedures; 2) conditional knowledge requirements for the use of learned information; and 3) the need for synchronous feedback when complex knowledge is being learned.

Sensory Mode Requirements

Sometimes, adequate learning requires that a person be able to not only see and/or hear something, but perhaps also to smell, taste, or recognize the texture of an object or event. If sensory-based information is absolutely required to learn, it must be presented. Because most electronic media now

[1]From "Media Selection for Training," by B. M. Sugrue and R. E. Clark, 2000, *Training and Retraining: A Handbook for Business, Industry, Government, and the Military*, p. 211.

only provide visual and aural sensory information, those parts of an instructional presentation that require smelling, tasting, or touching something may have to be conducted "in person." The first author of this chapter once helped to design a specialized lesson for pastry chefs and so smell, taste, and texture were all critical to learning many of the key concepts. This fact does not imply that an entire course where one lesson may require familiarity with a smell, taste, or texture has to be entirely taught "in person"—but certainly the lesson or part of a lesson would have to be live and perhaps "classroom based."

Conditional Knowledge Requirements

Instruction not only teaches people what to do but also when and where to do it. The "when and where" information is often called "conditional knowledge" (for example, Taylor & Dionne, 2000). Another way to think about conditional knowledge is that it describes the "if" condition in "If ... Then" sequences. Some conditions that must be present before procedures are implemented or before a certain process can be said to be underway can be very complex. For example, conditional knowledge might require that we simulate a poorly lighted street at night, an electrical fire, an urban riot, or an angry confrontation between bullies and a victim. The issue that designers must consider is what media will adequately depict the key elements of the conditions that must be present for students to use the new knowledge they are learning.

Synchronous Feedback Requirements

When instruction attempts to teach complex knowledge, very detailed observation of student practice accompanied by corrective feedback must be provided to support learning. Complex knowledge is defined as requiring the integration and coordinated performance of task-specific constituent skills rather than merely recalling definitions and other conceptual knowledge about concepts, processes, and principles. In addition, complex knowledge requires what van Merrienboer (1997) called "part-task and whole-task practice." Most instructional design models emphasize instruction in relatively simple learning tasks and assume that a large, complex set of interrelated tasks are achievable as "the sum of the parts"—by sequencing a string of practice exercises focused on simplified, component task procedures until a complex task is captured and mastered. There is overwhelming evidence that this does not work (see van Merrienboer, Clark, & de Crook, 2002, for an in-depth discussion of these issues). Thus, when complex practice exercises must be undertaken, a live "expert coach" must often be available to observe each student's practice and to give supportive and corrective feedback. The media selected to support complex practice exercises therefore has to support synchronous (real time) observation of practice and both verbal (voice) and visual (demonstration by the coach) feedback to each learner. This requirement can severely limit the range of media available to deliver instruction.

A "JOB AID" FOR SELECTING DISTANCE AND CLASSROOM PLATFORMS FOR INSTRUCTION

The final part of this chapter presents a very specific, proceduralized "job aid" for deciding between classroom and distance media for instruction (see Table 8.1). In addition to analyzing the three instructional methods that often require "live" instruction, the job aid (Rosett & Gautier-Downes, 1991) described an approach to assessing the cost and benefit ratio of various options based on work by Levin (1983) and Levin & McEwan (2001).

Instruction

A Decision Procedure for Selecting Cost-Beneficial Delivery Platforms for Distance or Classroom Training.   The goal is to make a cost-beneficial selection of either classroom or distance learning delivery platforms for effective training and education.

The prerequisites include access to required learning objectives, location and number of learners, cost of delivering instruction on all platforms being considered, information about practice and feedback requirements, and sensory mode information necessary to achieve all course objectives.

Backup Information for Training Delivery Platform Selection Procedure. There are four steps in the selection procedure.

-   *Step 1.* Review the learning objectives for the course and determine whether all delivery platforms being considered can adequately simulate all of the necessary *"conditional knowledge"*—defined as *knowing when and why to select and use specific procedures, concepts, processes and principles.* Conditions are often expressed as the "If" statement in "If (this is the condition) then (do this procedure)." Conditions can be events (such as formal orders, the end of some process that signals the beginning of another, the presence of a fault in equipment or a system) and/or reasons (for example, "this fault needs to be repaired in order for this system to work more efficiently"). All conditions that lead to the implementation of knowledge and skills gained in training must be able to be simulated during instruction so that the learner will be able to recognize the conditions on the job. Some conditions are difficult but not impossible to simulate in distance education or in classrooms that are not "on or near the job site."

• *Step 2.* Determine whether the learning objectives and instructional methods required for your course specify the observation of learner practice that must be conducted by a live expert who gives immediate (or synchronous) corrective feedback about practice performance in real time. The alternative to synchronous feedback is asynchronous feedback meaning "delayed" for hours or days. Synchronous practice and feedback is most often required when highly complex knowledge is being learned. An example of complex knowledge can be found when

TABLE 8.1

Training Delivery Platform Selection Procedure

Steps	Decisions and actions (see below for explanations of concepts marked with *)
1	Can both a distance and a classroom platform simulate all of the necessary conditions* in the job setting where the learner will apply their skills and knowledge? If yes, go to Step 2. If the answer is no for any platform, select the platform that will provide the necessary conditions.
2	Can both platforms provide the required immediate (synchronous*) and delayed (asynchronous*) information and corrective feedback* needed to achieve learning objectives? If yes, go to Step 3. If the answer is no for any platform, select the platform that will provide the necessary feedback.
3	Can both platforms provide the necessary sensory mode information* (visual, aural, kinesthetic, olfactory, tactile) required to achieve all learning objectives? If the answer is no for any platform, select the platform that will provide the necessary sensory mode information.
4	If both distance and classroom platforms have survived as viable options, subject both to cost-per-student* (Steps 4A and 4B) and (if desired) value-enhanced-cost* (Step 4C) analysis:
4.A.	Derive the cost of each platform by listing and summing the costs* associated with a specific course. Derive two sums, one for distance delivery and one for classroom.
4.B	Divide the projected cost of each platform by the number of learners to be trained to determine the cost-per-student* of each platform. Either select the platform with the lowest cost per student (or go on to Step 4C).
4.C	To determine the value-enhanced-cost* for classroom or distance platforms, survey command staff and other key stakeholders to determine their preference or value for each platform. Subtract the percent of average value assigned to the preferred platform by stakeholders from the cost-per-student of that platform to derive a value-enhanced-cost.

students learn a number of different troubleshooting procedures that must often be combined in novel ways to debug problems in a set of interconnected, complex systems such as the avionics for a complex aircraft. What defines complex knowledge is that it is clearly more than the sum of its parts because it also includes the capability to coordinate and integrate those parts. In general, if it is possible to automate (with technology) the real-time (synchronous) observation of practice and corrective feedback to learners during practice in the distant alternative, and if live experts are available for classroom settings, you can select either option.

• *Step 3.* Review your objectives and ask, "Is it possible to provide all of the necessary sensory information required to learn and perform the main objectives in this course in both the classroom and distance learning options?" For example, if learning that will transfer to adequate on-the-job performance requires that during training, a learner recognize a specific set of sounds (e.g., of a broken mechanism), smells (e.g., of burning insulation), the surface texture (e.g., of a fabric or a biological or geological sample), the taste (e.g., of a well-prepared cake) or the sight (e.g., of a rapid real-time event slowed to 10% of its speed), you must ask whether the distance and classroom platforms can provide the required sensory information.

• *Step 4. Cost-per-student* is the value of all resources invested in the development and delivery of distance and classroom versions of a course divided by the number of students who must complete the course. Cost includes development, production, and transmission expenses for media and TDY or PCS travel expenses for classroom options. Divide the cost of each platform by the number of students who must be trained in the foreseeable future. For example, a course whose platform costs $850,000 and will be delivered to 15,000 trainees has a cost-per-student of $56.67.

Value-enhanced-cost is defined as the percent of value (relative strength of the preferences) stakeholders place on their preferred delivery platform above the value they place on their less preferred option multiplied by the cost-per-student. Value-enhanced-cost analysis is useful whenever developers work with a variety of stakeholders and/or managers who are concerned about whether training technology platforms are trendy or conform to public expectations. Some people believe that live trainers are essential and others emphasize the public relations value of using trendy new technology. This analysis permits you to weight the final decision about delivery platforms by assessing the strength of stakeholder values toward each of the alternative platforms being considered. This way, the final decision is influenced by a combination of instructional method, cost/benefit ratios, and stakeholder values. For example, if stakeholders prefer the distance option 23% more than the classroom option, and the cost of the distance option is $56.67 per student, the value-enhanced-cost would be $56.67 – (.23 × $56.67) or $56.67 – 13.03 = $43.64. Platform value is derived by first identifying the stakeholders (stakeholders are the individuals and teams who have an immediate responsibility for, or interest in, the success of the students who are trained). Develop a brief questionnaire made up of one or more items where you ask for agreement or disagreement on a seven-point scale from the lowest rank of 1 (*worst option*) to 7 (*best option*). Sum all responses from stakeholders and derive a mean rating for each delivery option. Divide the highest mean into the lowest mean to determine the percent difference and use that percent to derive a value-enhanced-cost estimate.

ACKNOWLEDGMENTS

The work reported herein was supported, in part, under Office of Naval Research Award Number #N00014-02-1-0179, as administered by the Office of Naval Research. The findings and opinions expressed in this report do not reflect the positions or policies of the Office of Naval Research.

REFERENCES

Bernard, R. M, Abrami, P., Lou, L., Borokhovski, E., Wade, A., Wozney, L., et al. (2004). How does distance education compare to classroom instruction? A meta-analysis of the empirical literature. *Review of Educational Research, 74*(3), 379–439.

Clark, R. E. (1983). Reconsidering research on learning from media. *Review of Educational Research, 53*, 445–459.

Clark, R. E. (1994). Media will never influence learning. *Educational Technology Research and Development, 42*(2), 21–29.

Clark, R. E. (2001). New directions: Evaluating distance-learning technologies. In R. E. Clark (Ed.), *Learning from media: Arguments, analysis and evidence* (pp. 299–318). Greenwich, CT: Information Age Publishers.

Cobb, T. (1997). Cognitive efficiency: Toward a revised theory of media. *Educational Technology Research and Development, 45*(4), 21–35.

Kozma, R. B. (1994). Will media influence learning? Reframing the debate. *Review of Educational Research, 61*, 179–211.

Langer, E. (1994). The illusion of calculated decisions. In R. C. Schank & E. Langer (Eds.), *Beliefs, reasoning, and decision making: Psycho-logic in honor of Bob Abelson* (pp. 33–53). Hillsdale, NJ: Lawrence Erlbaum Associates.

Levin, H. M. (1983). *Cost-effectiveness: A primer.* Beverly Hills, CA: Sage.

Levin, H. M., & McEwan, P. J. (2001). *Cost-effectiveness analysis: Methods and applications* (2nd ed.). Thousand Oaks, CA: Sage.

Morrison, G. (2001). The equivalent evaluation of instructional media. In R. E. Clark (Ed.), *Learning from media: Arguments, analysis and evidence* (pp. 319–327). Greenwich, CT: Information Age Publishers.

Rosett, A., & Gautier-Downes, J. (1991). *A handbook of job aids*. San Francisco, CA: Jossey-Bass/Pfeiffer.

Russell, T. L. (1999). *The "no significant difference" phenomenon: A comparative research annotated bibliography on technology for distance education*. Raleigh, NC: North Carolina State University Office of Instructional Telecommunications.

Salomon, G. (1984). Television is easy and print is "tough": The differential investment of mental effort in learning as a function of perceptions and attributions. *Journal of Educational Psychology, 76*(4), 647–658.

Sugrue, B. M., & Clark, R. E. (2000). Media selection for training. In S. Tobias & J. D. Fletcher (Eds.), *Training and retraining: A handbook for business, industry, government and the military* (pp. 208–234). New York: Macmillan Reference.

Taylor, K. L., & Dionne, J-P. (2000). Accessing problem-solving strategy knowledge: The complementary use of concurrent verbal protocols and retrospective debriefing. *Journal of Educational Psychology, 92*(3), 413–425.

van Merrienboer, J. J. G. (1997). *Training complex cognitive skills: A four-component instructional design model for technical training*. Englewood Cliffs, NJ: Educational Technology Publications.

van Merrienboer, J. J. G., Clark, R. E., & de Crook, M. B. M. (2002). Blueprints for complex learning: The 4C/ID model. *Educational Technology Research and Development, 50*(2), 39–64.

Wegner, D. (2002). *The illusion of conscious will*. Cambridge, MA: MIT Press.

Chapter 9

Putting the "Advanced"
into Advanced Distributed Learning

Susan F. Chipman
U.S. Office of Naval Research[1]

It appears that the advent of Web-based learning is resulting in a great leap forward for computer-based instruction. For the first time, truly large numbers of people are experiencing computer-based instruction. Ironically, however, the same event has brought a step backward in the quality of computer-based instruction. It has been an obstacle to the implementation of the most advanced forms of computer-based instruction, just as they became mature enough for practical use.

Computer-based instruction as envisioned in the first version of the SCORM[2] standard (discussed elsewhere in this volume), amounted to noth-

---

[1]The Office of Naval Research (ONR) is the U.S. Navy's primary research funding agency. It supports Navy-relevant research ranging from basic research that is usually performed by university recipients of research grants to more applied research that is usually performed by Navy laboratories or industrial contractors. Research related to training, especially training technology, has been supported by ONR since it was founded in 1946. Dr. Susan Chipman is a program officer who manages basic research in cognitive science as well as more applied projects in advanced training technology and serves as the primary point of contact for training-related research. The opinions expressed in this chapter are the personal professional opinions of Dr. Susan Chipman and do not necessarily represent the official policy or positions of the Office of Naval Research.

[2]Advanced Distributed Learning (ADL) is an initiative of the U.S. Office of the Secretary of Defense, a collaborative effort among government, industry, and academia to establish a new distributed learning environment that permits the interoperability of learning tools and course content on a global scale. Implementing ADL requires specifications and standards that

ing more than a sequence of PowerPoint slides with some quiz questions added. Only the most recent version of the standard (SCORM Version 1.2) allows for branching of the instruction provided in response to student performance. Yet, this type of individualization of instruction was one of the earliest goals for computer-based instruction, as it was initially developed in the late 1950s and early 1960s. For this to be an "advance" in the SCORM standard circa 2004, rather than a taken-for-granted feature in the initial development of a standard, is a sad occurrence. Similarly, in their rush to implement Web-based capability, the major vendors of authoring tools for CBT (computer-based training) simplified their offerings, eliminating much of the flexibility and capability that they had had. The authors using these tools have little choice but to produce what has long been scorned as "page-turning CBT." Books still have much to recommend them, as contrasted to computers. Their resolution is higher, making reading them easier and faster than reading text on a screen (Gould, Alfaro, Barnes, & Finn, 1987). As a consequence, students do not tolerate large amounts of text on a screen. Course content may be inadvertently simplified and compressed in response to this constraint. Books are still more portable and convenient to use than computers, as well as less expensive. So, there is not much reason to involve a computer in mere page-turning activity.

Although the Web has advantages as an efficient medium for rapid and inexpensive distribution of instructional materials, given an existing installed base of computers serving the intended audience, it has increasingly brought security problems and concerns along with it. This, too, has meant barriers to the implementation of sophisticated forms of computer-based instruction. Security concerns have led military training policymakers, and undoubtedly others in the private sector, to ban downloading of executable programs as part of instruction. But locally executable programs may be necessary to provide interactive simulations for students and trainees to work with. They may be necessary to implement the Bayesian inference networks that estimate the current state of a student's knowledge in sophisticated artificially intelligent tutoring systems. If bandwidth were not a problem, as many claimed it would not be at the advent of the Web-based learning movement, perhaps these limitations would not exist. However, bandwidth has been a problem until the present day, and it has effectively prevented the implementation of sophisticated instructional approaches in the Web environment. In the Navy environment, at least some of those responsible for the development of future training will say that bandwidth will continue to be a problem because

[2](continued)   are known as SCORM (Sharable Content Object Reference Model). As of this writing, SCORM documents were available for download from this site: http://www.adlnet.org The SCORM Best Practices Guide for Content Developers was available from this site: http://www.lsal.cmu.edu/lsal/expertise/projects/developersguide/

other material—tactical data—will always have much higher priority for the bandwidth that is available.

Despite the declining cost of computing power, in these military and business environments, individual workstations may be devolving back toward the status of dumb terminals, as we knew them in the mainframe computing era, primarily because of these security worries. It is already the case that users of the Navy-Marine Corps Intranet (NMCI) are not permitted to install software on their own machines. Soon their machines may not even have the cd or dvd readers that would permit use of instructional software distributed in cd or dvd form, reducing the installed base of computers usable for sophisticated instructional software distributed on those media. For the individual user, the need to involve other people and obtain official approvals before initiating use of instructional software raises a significant barrier that may well turn out to prevent instructional involvement from ever occurring. We may be about to take another step backward for the environment of computer-based instruction.

Other large-scale environmental obstacles associated with Web-based instruction also impede the implementation of sophisticated instructional technology. As mentioned earlier, vendors of authoring tools tended to actually simplify their authoring tools in response to the advent of Web-based learning. The change to Web-based delivery absorbed their capital investment and sapped any interest in developing improved capabilities. As a specific example, the Navy announced a so-called dual use funding opportunity that would have subsidized a commercial authoring tool company in implementing some of the authoring capabilities emerging from DoD R&D investments, such as those pioneered by the Behavioral Technology Laboratories of USC for maintenance training applications (Munro et al., 1997). Unfortunately, the announcement of this opportunity more or less coincided with the advent of Web-based learning. The authoring tool companies were putting all of their investment into conversion to the Web environment, but this opportunity required that the companies match government investment in developing new capabilities. The result was that only one bid was received and that the capabilities promised were very limited in comparison to what had been hoped for. Nevertheless an award was made. Unfortunately, in the end the company went very strongly for Web-based instruction, changed its name and its "business model," greatly simplified or handicapped its authoring tool products as compared to what they had been, and delivered very little in return for a fairly substantial government investment.

We can hope that the advent of the Web has brought only an hiatus, a temporary slowing of the advance in sophistication of computer-based instruction. The remainder of this chapter discusses what we could be doing in distributed learning if it became truly advanced, if we were to implement the best of what we can do today.

THE FRONTIERS OF COMPUTER-BASED INSTRUCTION

Artificially Intelligent Tutoring Systems

The capability to provide individualized instruction to meet the unique needs of individual students was a major promise of computer-based instruction from its outset. Early projects supported by ONR focused on the goal of individualized instruction, including mastery testing, branching instruction based on testing outcomes, and selective remedial instruction.[3] This emphasis on individualization later evolved into the effort to build artificially intelligent tutoring systems that might emulate the outstanding effectiveness of individual human tutoring (Bloom, 1984). The first ONR contract in the area of artificially intelligent tutoring was awarded in 1969 to the late Jaime Carbonell of Bolt, Beranek, and Newman, Inc. At that time, a $2M computer was required to do the research. Beginning with Carbonell's SCHOLAR program (1970) that attempted a natural language dialog approach to teaching geography, several significant projects were carried out at BBN. Collins and Stevens' (1982) WHY system extended SCHOLAR to teaching about weather, and Burton and Brown developed SOPHIE (Brown, Burton, & de Kleer, 1982) to tutor the troubleshooting of faults in electronic circuits. Brown and Burton (1978) also built the famous BUGGY program that diagnosed "bugs" or faulty procedures in children's doing of subtraction problems, pioneering the important diagnostic element of intelligent tutoring. The systems of that era did not make it into practical use. It was in the 1980s that intelligent tutoring became an important emphasis of research with substantial dedicated funding. The cost of the necessary computing power had become more reasonable ($20,000–$60,000), if still beyond what either military training organizations or civilian schools could support. Under the Defense University Research Instrumentation Program, ONR provided many members of the university research community with AI workstations to be used in intelligent tutoring research.

By the time the special funding emphasis on artificially intelligent tutoring concluded, one could fairly say that the American, and international, research community basically knew how to build highly effective tutoring systems. Among the papers and books summarizing the accomplishments of this era are Anderson, Boyle, and Reiser (1985), Clancey (1986), Lesgold, Chipman, Brown, and Soloway (1990), and Wenger (1987). There were also two notable projects demonstrating that the technology could apply to

---

[3]This and following historical statements are based on a review of old annual project books for the ONR programs, and other such resources, that was done in preparation for the following invited address: Military Special Interest Group, American Educational Research Association: *DOD Contributions to Education and Training Technology*, Atlanta, April, 1993. No written version of this address exists.

practical military maintenance training problems. One of these was the Navy's Intelligent Maintenance Training System (IMTS) (Towne, 1987) that also led to research on authoring tools to build similar systems at lower costs. The other was the Air Force's SHERLOCK (Gott, 1989), a tutor for troubleshooting of an avionics test station, which involved one of the best evaluations of the effectiveness of intelligent tutoring that has yet been done (Lesgold & Nahemow, 2001). Gott and her associates devised a good approach for measuring troubleshooting performance with simulated problems and found that about 25 hours of SHERLOCK training was equivalent to 4 years of on-the-job learning opportunities. Unfortunately no more conventional training approach was available for comparison. In addition, ONR funded a demonstration application to troubleshooting ship steam power plants (Vasandani, 1991). The National Science Foundation also began to support applications of artificially intelligent tutoring to education, mainly supporting researchers whose earlier work had been supported by ONR or other DoD agencies (such as those described in Koedinger, Anderson, Hadley, & Mark, 1995, and Schofield, 1995).

State of the art artificially intelligent tutoring systems are typically built around a highly detailed cognitive model of the knowledge and skill being taught (Anderson, 1993). Some approach, typically Bayesian inference networks today (Conati, Gertner, & VanLehn, 2002), is taken to estimate the student's mastery or lack of mastery of all the elements in the cognitive model of knowledge and skill from the evidence provided by the student's details of performance in problem solving or explanation. This is a computationally intensive function. It provides a very refined assessment function without overt "testing" or quizzes, providing the information needed to select the appropriate next instructional experience for the individual student. Tutors of academic subjects, such as high school mathematics (Koedinger et al., 1995) or college physics (Albacete & VanLehn, 2000; Shelby et al., 2001) and thermodynamics (Forbus et al., 1999), have now made it into practical use, but they are not delivering instruction over the Web. Computing the model of the student's knowledge over the Web with sufficient speed to support a timely response to the student is somewhat problematic; it would be preferable to do those computations locally on the student's machine, which is how they are being done now. In addition, these academic tutors currently focus on problem solving practice, assuming a context in which classroom teachers provide the basic conceptual instruction. These tutors would need to be supplemented with more conventional CBT that substitutes for that classroom instruction. These tutors have been shown to be highly effective in improving student learning (Anderson, Conrad, & Corbett, 1989; Corbett, 2001; Koedinger, Anderson, Hadley, & Mark, 1997); there is no fundamental reason why distance learning systems should not provide this type of sophisticated tutorial instruction.

Interactive Simulations with Intelligent Coaches

For many important military training applications, the capability to practice skills using an interactive simulation of equipment and/or the physics of the natural world is very important. Examples include flying, "ship-driving," fighting fires aboard ships, various types of tactical actions, and troubleshooting complex electronic equipment or ship steam plants. Demonstrations of systems of all of these types have been built in PC environments, and some of these systems have made it into practical use (McCarthy et al, 1994). However, they are not being run over the Web. Again, such programs are very large and computationally intensive if one wants the simulation to respond realistically to trainee actions in real time. Note that a *simulation* that responds to a trainee action is very different from, and more demanding than, a mere *animation*, however impressive and realistic the latter may look. Today, a typical PC is likely to be able to support the computational needs of such a system, so it becomes feasible for "distributed learning." If Advanced Distributed Learning[4] were truly advanced, we would see such simulation systems implemented, along with the modeling of trainee skill and adaptive selection of instructional experiences described earlier.

Intelligent coaching of dynamic skills does involve some new challenges that have not yet been fully researched. Although McCarthy of Sonalysts, one of the small businesses now producing artificially intelligent training systems, reports (personal communication) building several successful examples of systems with on-going coaching, there are as yet no design principles established by research. How does one coach or tutor in these situations without disrupting the performance? That issue is being addressed by some current research projects. John Anderson of Carnegie-Mellon University is working with a one-person simulation of AEGIS anti-air warfare (Sohn, Douglass, Chen, & Anderson, 2000), and Stephanie Doane of Mississippi State University is working on turning her successful cognitive model of instrument flying (Doane & Sohn, 2000) into a tutoring system. This tutor involves tracking of eye movements, which are also modeled by the cognitive model and used to assess trainee learning. Obviously the timing of instructional responses becomes much more critical in this type of application, a problematic aspect if one's computing is being done remotely.

---

[4]Advanced Distributed Learning (ADL) is an initiative of the U.S. Office of the Secretary of Defense, a collaborative effort among government, industry, and academia to establish a new distributed learning environment that permits the interoperability of learning tools and course content on a global scale.

The simpler approach of doing after-action review of trainee performance in a simulated dynamic system has already been implemented in Wilkins' tutor of shipboard damage control management, DC-TRAIN (Bulitko & Wilkins, 1999; Sniezek, Wilkins, & Wadlington, 2002). Recent research by Sandra Katz (Katz, 2003; Katz, Allbritton, & Connelly, 2003) of the University of Pittsburgh also suggests that after-action review (reflection) may have its place in tutoring academic skills. Coaching during problem solving, whether or not it is fast-paced and dynamic, helps the student or trainee to get through the problem successfully, but after-action review is the place for deeper explanations, generalization to promote transfer of training, and the abstraction of principles.

Virtual Reality

Advanced forms of training technology can provide stimulation to the human perceptual system that approximates experience in real environments, virtual reality. Perhaps the best example of this is an old one: The full scale flight simulator with its powerful computer driven projectors and dedicated building. Indeed one of the earliest drivers for the development of what is now called virtual reality may have been the Navy's interest in providing flight simulators aboard aircraft carriers. The rapid advance of computer technology, accompanied by drastic reductions in the cost of computing power, is making PC-based visual simulation feasible. A great deal of effort has gone into developing displays for head mounted displays (very small high resolution displays that can be mounted in goggles or helmets close to the eye) that will eliminate the need for projectors. Two such Navy applications are already in practical use, the Conning Officer's Virtual Environment (COVE; Roberts, 2001[5]), used to teach "ship driving," and a similar trainer, VE-SUB (Virtual Environment-Submarine; Hays & Vincenzi, 2000), used to train the skill of bringing submarines into harbor. A number of similar virtual reality vehicle trainers for the Marines and Special Operations forces are now under development.

As both displays and the supporting graphics computation make their way into the commercial market, resulting in much lower prices and wide distribution, driven by the market appeal of computer games, it will become feasible to think about the application of virtual reality in Web-based distance learning. This is especially true because the highest fidelity of simulation is not always necessary for effective training (AGARD, 1980). A great deal of research on flight simulation demonstrated this point, although the

---

[5]The version of COVE that was actually implemented in the field does not have an artificially intelligent coach like the one described in this chapter.

message does not seem to have been well accepted by the aviation community. Anecdotal evidence, however, recently prevailed. A young pilot trainee in the Navy, who was determined to succeed, did a great deal of work on his own with the Microsoft Flight Simulator. He then did extremely well in flight training. As a result, the Navy implemented a trainer with the Microsoft Flight Simulator, augmented with some special airplane-like controls, and this is now an FAA certified flight simulator. So, one could say the era of flight and other similar simulators that could be implemented in distance learning is already upon us. The computational and bandwidth requirements of virtual reality will pose substantial technical and organizational challenges for distance learning.

Simulators, per se, are not really trainers, although many people assume that they are. In the past, the instructional side of simulators has often been neglected, perhaps because the technical accomplishment of building the simulator seemed so impressive. Too often, the "instructional features" of a simulator have consisted of a capability to program scenarios that is very difficult to use. It is not uncommon to find very expensive simulators that no one knows how to program, after several turnovers of instructor personnel. Scenarios tend to be built in a somewhat haphazard way, striving for subjectively judged realism. This task is often left to instructors, rather than being the subject of a professional curriculum design effort. But the scenarios presented to the trainee need to be seen as carefully designed problems, meeting defined curricular objectives. Artificially intelligent coaching, delicately timed to minimize the disruption of trainee performance, should be integrated with the simulator, along with a capability for reflective after-action review. That is, we should be looking forward to the day when virtual reality simulation will be integrated with artificially intelligent tutoring. Both the design of distance learning systems and the setting of standards need to provide for these capabilities, rather than effectively prohibiting them.

True Natural Language Interaction Capability: Tutorial Dialog

Current state-of-the-art tutoring systems are very clever at avoiding the need to do true natural language interaction. It is a salient difference between them and human tutors. Therefore, it seems a promising path for closing the effectiveness gap[6] that still separates human and artificially intelligent tutor-

---

[6]The effectiveness of human tutoring is generally estimated as a 2 SD improvement in achievement as compared to standard classroom instruction (Bloom, 1984); however, it is likely that truly expert human tutors may be even more effective than that. Bloom's results applied to "good" tutors; inexpert or peer tutors are less effective (Cohen, Kulik, & Kulik, 1984), yielding an average effect size of only .4 SD. Generally, the claims for the most successful of present artificially intelligent tutoring systems are about a 1 SD improvement in effectiveness (Corbett, 2001), although the total amount of relevant evidence is small.

ing. For a little more than a decade, one of the priorities of the ONR basic research program in cognitive science has focused on understanding student inputs and generating appropriate explanations or other language to present to the student. Although some other agencies have supported work on artificial dialog systems, the focus on the special characteristics of tutorial dialog has been unique to ONR. Because program funds have been very limited, neither speech recognition nor speech generation has been included in the program. We have relied on other agencies and sources of research support, notably DARPA, to advance those technologies. When this program direction began, a Naval Studies Board convened in 1988 under the auspices of the National Research Council advised that this proposed new research direction was too difficult to attempt. Nevertheless, and despite very limited financial resources, much has been accomplished.

Investments began with detailed studies of the linguistic behavior of human tutors (Fox, 1993; Graesser, Person, & Magliano, 1995). Next, two computational linguists who also studied human tutorial language but then also attempted to emulate it in computational systems became the key figures in the tutorial dialog program. They were Martha Evens at the Illinois Institute of Technology and Johanna Moore, who was initially at the University of Pittsburgh but moved to the University of Edinburgh. The most notable accomplishment is that Martha Evens of the Illinois Institute of Technology has produced what I believe to be the first example of a tutor with true natural language interaction capability that reached a level of quality good enough to be used with real students, in this case medical students, who were not being paid to be subjects (Cho, Michael, Rovick, & Evens, 2000). These results were reported immediately after the ITS 2000 conference's keynote speaker predicted that such accomplishments were still 10 years in the future. The CIRCSIM-Tutor (Michael, Rovick, Zhou, Glass, & Evens, 2003) is now implemented as a regular feature of the curriculum at Rush Medical School in Chicago and work continues on improved versions of the system. The subject matter of this tutor is cardiac physiology. CIRCSIM was a preexisting simple simulation of the circulatory system that presents medical students with problems to exercise their knowledge of cardiac physiology that has been acquired from lectures and textbooks. For example, students are asked to specify what happens in response to a hemorrhage of 2 pints of blood. Michael and Rovick, medical school professors of cardiac physiology, had years of experience tutoring medical students as they attempt to deal with these problems. CIRCSIM-Tutor attempts to emulate their tutoring behavior. It would probably be quite feasible to implement this tutor as distance learning over the Internet. The tutor communicates in written language, does not use elaborate graphics or demanding simulations, and runs well on portable PCs.

Evens and her associates, as well as Johanna Moore, who is now at Edinburgh, have produced many interesting results about the details of the instructional strategies and linguistic forms that human tutors use (e.g., Core, Moore, & Zinn, 2003; Hume, Michael, Rovick, & Evens, 1996; Moore, Lemaire, & Rosenblum 1995). Evens' project produced a very large number of publications (listed in Evens, 2000), but most of them are in rather obscure conference proceedings. A large number of graduate students (24) also did their dissertation work under this project. Evens and her medical colleagues Michael and Rovick are now writing a book to be published by Lawrence Erlbaum Associates that sums up the lessons learned in this research effort. Although the subject matter domain of the tutor is cardiac physiology, many of the lessons learned about tutoring language and strategies, however, are quite general and already proving very influential. For example, in contrast to the haphazard sequence of hints in many computer-based training systems, even intelligent tutors, Michael and Rovick were found to have sophisticated hinting strategies, such as the "directed line of reasoning" (Hume et al., 1996), a sequence of hints that pushes the student along a desired line of reasoning. This project benefited greatly from having expert tutors who were both a subject of study and collaborators in the research.

Moore started her research by studying human tutoring within the context provided by the SHERLOCK (Gott, 1989) troubleshooting tutor. A human tutor was substituted—without face-to-face communication or speech—for the automated feedback provided by SHERLOCK. Striking differences were found (Moore et al., 1995). The human tutor referred back to earlier parts of the tutoring encounter, such as similar errors, nearly every time it was possible to do so. The relative importance of information in the feedback messages was indicated linguistically by the human tutor but not in SHERLOCK feedback. Although the early results indicated that very complex memory for and control of the tutorial dialog would be required to truly emulate what the human tutor did, aspects of Moore's early results nevertheless were used to improve the quality of feedback to trainees in the final delivered version of SHERLOCK, SHERLOCK II (Katz et al., 1998).

The primary focus of Moore's work is now on developing a clean modularized architecture for tutorial dialog, in which different types of required knowledge are cleanly separated (Zinn, Moore, & Core, 2002a, 2002b, 2003). Modular software design makes it much easier to work on improving inherently different aspects of the total system; in particular, it will make it much easier to apply what is learned about the general structure of tutorial interaction to new subject matter. Several younger researchers are now becoming independent contributors to this field, notably Barbara Di Eugenio of the University of Illinois, Chicago (Di Eugenio, 2001) and Carolyn Rose, who both worked with Moore in Pittsburgh.

For a 5-year period (2001–2005), the ONR program has been augmented by two large grants with funding from the Office of the Secretary of Defense under the Multi-Disciplinary Research Initiative (MURI) program. One of these projects, directed by Prof. Stanley Peters, a computational linguist at Stanford University, is using an intelligent tutor of shipboard damage control as a demonstration platform for natural language tutoring (Clark et al., in press; Fry, Ginzton, Peters, Clark, & Pon-Barry, 2001; Pon-Barry, Clark, Schultz, Bratt, & Peters, 2004; Schultz, Bratt, Clark, Peters, Pon-Barry, & Treeratpituk, 2003). Martha Evens is a consultant to this project, and it otherwise builds strongly on what has been learned about tutorial dialog in the past research projects. (The damage control tutor, DC-TRAIN, is itself a more applied demonstration project by David Wilkins of the University of Illinois; Bulitko & Wilkins, 1999) Peters has integrated speech recognition technology that was supported in the past by DARPA and Festival text-to-speech technology (Black & Taylor, 1997) from the University of Edinburgh with his own natural language technology. DC-TRAIN provides the natural language system with information about what the student did, what errors were made, and what should have been done. The natural language system then provides an after-action review in the form of an interactive dialog with the trainee. A domain-specific voice was built in Festival by recording quite a number of sentences in the domain: The resulting quality of the speech is so good that only a few small glitches caused by the fact that one word ("do") that was not recorded in a sentence final position reveal that it is indeed computer generated speech. It is a conspicuous improvement over the prior generic computer voice. Recent research by Atkinson (Hosie, Atkinson, & Merrill, 2004) strongly suggests that voice quality is important to instructional effectiveness, as does some earlier research (Mayer, Sobko, & Mautone, 2003). Peters' system also demonstrates new capabilities in responding to student initiatives such as the desire not to discuss a particular issue at a particular time in the after action review: The automated tutor is capable of adapting its plans to accommodate the trainee's request.

The second Tutorial Dialog MURI, Why2000, tutors qualitative reasoning about physics problems and is a collaboration between Kurt VanLehn at the University of Pittsburgh and Art Graesser at the University of Memphis (Graesser, VanLehn, Rose, Jordan, & Harter, 2001). A number of researchers who worked with Johanna Moore when she was at Pittsburgh are working on this project, as has at least one of Evens' former students. It is exploring combinations of symbolic language processing approaches with more statistical semantic approaches using Latent Semantic Analysis (Landauer, Foltz, & Laham, 1998). It also relates to considerable prior work on physics learning that ONR has supported at the University of Pittsburgh and VanLehn's physics tutor for use at the Naval Academy, described later. At times, the Why2000 tutor has been up on the Internet, in order to collect data. It communicates in written language. Thus, distance learning using natural language tutoring is feasible.

In summary, if distance learning were to be truly "advanced" in the next few years, it would not only do intelligent tutoring, but would also have the capability to do that tutoring with true natural language, perhaps including speech recognition and speech generation capability. Many computers already have the necessary microphones built in; virtually all have speakers.

OVER THE HORIZON

Eyetracking

At the present time, tracking the learner's visual attention remains primarily a research method rather than part of a routine training technology, although eyetracking has been used in flight simulators to provide high detail in the region where the trainee is actually looking, but not elsewhere, reducing computational requirements. In its research use, eyetracking has proved quite revealing. Sandra Marshall (personal communications) found that learners of a tactical decision-making task often did not read all of the task instructions—some individuals systematically skipped what was at the top of the page/screen. Similarly, John Anderson's research group has found that many of their carefully crafted explanations and hints to students in their artificially intelligent tutors are going unread (Gluck, 1999). They have also found that much of the learning in a simulated air traffic control task of sorts was perceptual learning—learning where and where not to look on the display (Lee & Anderson, 2000). There are important military tasks in which learning where and when to look is central to what one wants to train, so that knowing where the trainee is actually looking becomes very valuable information for training. Those who are responsible for training helicopter pilots in the Navy have believed that they are training "eye scan patterns" for checking flight instruments. There is actual military doctrine about what the scan pattern is supposed to be. A project that was intended to provide instructors with information about trainees' scan patterns revealed that expert pilots are more variable in the scanning they do than the doctrine would suggest. The eyes are picking up information in the service of the cognition that is controlling flying actions. Stephanie Doane was able to model eye fixations in simulated instrument flight as part of a more inclusive model of instrument flying (Doane & Sohn, 2000). Currently she is attempting to build an artificially intelligent tutor for instrument flying that uses eye-tracking information as part of the processes of modeling the trainee's state of mastery of that skill. Somewhat similarly, in training something like the tactical decision-making task involved in antiair warfare aboard ships equipped with the sophisticated AEGIS radar system, it is important to know whether failures to investigate a threatening track on the radar screen are due to failures to look or to failures of judgment. The Advanced Embedded Training project (Zachary, Cannon-Bowers, Burns, Bilazarian, & Krecker, 1998; Zachary et al., 1998), which demonstrated artificially intelligent tutoring—especially performance assessment—for the AEGIS antiair warfare team, incorporated eye-tracking on an experimental basis for that purpose. Although the technology involved in tracking eye fixations is still rather tricky for practical implementation in most training systems, we know enough to suggest that it has high promise for the future.

Cameras focused on the user are already incorporated in many computer systems and have become quite cheap. With appropriate research and software development, it is likely that eye fixation information could be derived from such images (Wang & Sung, 2002). People are very good at determining where others' eyes are fixated (Cline, 1967; Gibson & Pick, 1963; Martin & Jones, 1982; Ricciardelli, Baylis, & Driver, 2000); some of us are convinced that even cats and dogs can do it (Brauer, Call, & Tomasello, 2004; Emery, 2000). If we can solve this problem artificially, an entire new range of capabilities become possible for distance learning.

Gestures

Tutorial interaction involves gestures as well as speech, and the ONR program investigating tutorial dialog has included a small amount of investigation of the instructional use of gestures. Herbert Clark and his students are collaborators in Peters' MURI project, investigating human use of gestures and exploring ways of accomplishing the same communicative functions on computer screens. They have found that gestures are very delicately timed in coordination with the speech they accompany (Clark, 2003; Clark & Krych, 2004). Beth Littleton (Littleton, Schunn, & Kirschenbaum, 2002) of Aptima Corporation did some particularly interesting work investigating how instructors and other submariners use gestures while talking about the submarine approach officer's task, which involves very complex spatial reasoning about the localization of another submarine. The use of gestures to express uncertainty was an interesting aspect of the project findings. Quek of Wright State University (McNeill et al., 2002) has been supported by NSF in studies of tutorial gestures. Atkinson, Graesser, and others have done investigations of instructional avatars, such as those provided by Microsoft agent software; sometimes it seems to be helpful if, for example, Petey the Parrot points appropriately in conjunction with verbal instruction (Hosie, Atkinson, & Merrill, 2004), although avatars can also be distracting. Currently, Ken Forbus of Northwestern University is engaged in a DARPA-funded project in which military decision makers can draw military plans in a natural way and have the computer interpret them. This capability is being much better received by military users than previous approaches for entering such information into computers.

We do not yet have much formal knowledge about the effective use of gestures in instructional communication; it is likely that gestures have some instructional value (Goldin-Meadow, Kim, & Singer, 1999), especially when the subject matter has spatial aspects. We all gesture, but we have little conscious awareness of what we are doing. This is an area in which it will be possible for computer-based instruction to advance considerably. We already know enough to say that we want to ensure that the design of distance learning systems and standards allows for the future development of improved gestural communication in both directions.

Interpreting and Responding to Student Emotion

Having access to images of the student, and to student speech, opens up the possibility of adding an entire new dimension to computer-based instruction. Human instructors, human tutors, typically detect, respond to, adapt to what they perceive about the emotional state of the student. Effective management of the emotional state of the student is an important part of effective tutoring. Currently even artificially intelligent tutoring systems are not doing this at all. Of course, the few tutors that process student or trainee language can detect curse words or other verbal expressions of affect. (The Advanced Embedded Training project also involved speech recognition in order to determine whether trainees were asking for and providing the right information at the right time. The vocabulary developed for its speech recognition function included many curse words, not surprisingly.) One can begin to think about using that information. The interpretation of facial expressions, however, remains very difficult territory, although it is the subject of considerable research in artificial intelligence (Lissetti & Schiano, 2000; Pantic & Rothkrantz, 2000). Perhaps training applications will require some special attention to "cognitive emotions" that are not usually mentioned among the usual set of emotions that researchers are seeking to recognize. What about the bewildered look students so often have? What about the expressions indicative of cognitive effort being expended? It seems to me that recognizing these expressions is something that we are likely to be able to succeed in doing, within a relatively small number of years. Just as tutorial dialog differs from dialog in general, and required special research attention, instructionally relevant emotional expressions may require some special research attention.

Of course, emotions are also expressed in speech, to the extent that research on video teleconferencing (Olson, 1995; Whittaker, 2003) has generally found it difficult to demonstrate that the ability to see the other person contributes anything beyond what can already be accomplished with conventional telephone speech. Although people generally have highly developed skill in interpreting this information, it is another area in which conscious access to the basis of these perceptions is lacking, as is formal knowledge about and artificial emulation of the skill. (Diane Litman of the University of Pittsburgh and Lynette Hirshberg of Columbia University have just received NSF funding to pursue the monitoring of student state in tutorial spoken dialog.) Correspondingly, artificially synthesized speech, even at its best, is also lacking in this information. This entire area presents a major opportunity for advance in computer-based instruction, distributed or not.

CONCLUDING REMARKS

Let us hope that distributed learning will catch up with what we can already do with truly advanced computer-based training technology today, that the technical and organizational barriers currently limiting its quality will be overcome. There is some danger of stagnation in a technology that does not even match the best of what could be done in the 1960s, stagnation lasting long enough to endanger continued progress in the areas outlined earlier, or even to result in our losing the know-how to do what the community knows how to do today. That knowledge is embodied in a relatively small number of people, and if they do not get the opportunity to apply what they know and train others to do it, that knowledge could be lost. Let us hope that the future does hold truly *advanced* distributed learning. In this chapter, I have tried to show what it could be like.

REFERENCES

AGARD (Advisory Group for Aerospace Research and Development). (1980). *Fidelity of simulation for pilot training* (Tech. Rep. AGARD-AR-159). Neuilly-sur-Seine, France: Advisory Group for Aerospace Research and Development. (DTIC No. ADA 096825)

Albacete, P. L., & VanLehn, K. (2000). Evaluation of the effectiveness of a cognitive tutor for fundamental physics concepts. In L. R. Gleitman & A. K. Joshi (Eds.), *Proceedings of the Twenty-Second Annual Conference of the Cognitive Science Society* (pp. 25–30). Mahwah, NJ: Lawrence Erlbaum Associates.

Anderson, J. R. (1993). *Rules of the mind.* Hillsdale NJ: Lawrence Erlbaum Associates.

Anderson, J. R., Boyle, D. F., & Reiser, B. J. (1985). Intelligent tutoring systems. *Science, 288,* 456–462.

Anderson, J. R., Conrad, F. G., & Corbett, A. T. (1989). Skill acquisition and the LISP Tutor. *Cognitive Science, 13,* 467–505.

Black, A., & Taylor, P. (1997). Festival Speech synthesis system: System documentation (1.1.1) University of Edinburgh, Human Communication Research Centre (Tech. Rep. HCRC/TR-83). Retrieved from, http://www.cstr.ed.ac.uk/projects/festival/papers.html

Bloom, B. S. (1984). The 2 sigma problem: The search for methods of group instruction as effective as one-to-one tutoring. *Educational Researcher, 13*, 4–16.

Brown, J. S., & Burton, R. R. (1978). Diagnostic models for procedural bugs in basic mathematical skills. *Cognitive Science, 2*, 155–192.

Brown, J. S., Burton, R. R., & de Kleer, J. (1982). Pedagogical, natural language, and knowledge engineering techniques in SOPHIE I, II, and III. In D. H. Sleeman & J. S. Brown (Eds.), *Intelligent tutoring systems* (pp. 227–282). London: Academic Press.

Bulitko, V. V., & Wilkins, D. C., (1999, July). Automated instructor assistant for ship damage control. *Proceedings of the Eleventh Conference on Innovative Applications of Artificial Intelligence* (pp. 778–785). Orlando, FL.

Brauer, J., Call, J., & Tomasello, M. (2004). Visual perspective taking in dogs (Canis familiaris) in the presence of barriers. *Applied Animal Behaviour Science, 88*, 299–317.

Carbonell, J. (1970). AI in CAI: An artificial intelligence approach to computer-aided instruction. *IEEE Transactions on Man-Machine Systems, 11*, 190–202.

Chi, M. T. H., Bassok, M., Lewis, M. W., Reimann, P., & Glaser, R. (1989). Self-explanations: How students study and use examples in learning to solve problems. *Cognitive Science, 15*, 145–182.

Cho, B. I., Michael, J., Rovick, A., & Evens, M. W. (2000, June). An analysis of multiple tutoring protocols. *Proceedings of the Fifth International Conference on Intelligent Tutoring Systems: ITS 2000* (pp. 212–221). London, UK: Springer Verlag.

Clancey, W. J. (1986). From GUIDON to NEOMYCIN and HERACLES in twenty short lessons: ONR final report 1979–1985. *AI Magazine, 7*(8), 40–187.

Clark, B., Lemon, O., Gruenstein, A., Bratt, E. O., Fry, J., Peters, S., et al. (in press). A general purpose architecture for intelligent tutoring systems. In N. L. Bernsen, L. Dybkjaer, & J. van Kuppevelt (Eds.), *Natural, intelligent and effective interaction in multimodal dialogue systems*. Dordrecht, Netherlands: Kluwer.

Clark, H. H. (2003). Pointing and placing. In S. Kita (Ed.), *Pointing: Where language, culture, and cognition meet* (pp. 243–268). Hillsdale, NJ: Lawrence Erlbaum Associates.

Clark, H. H., & Krych, M. A. (2004). Speaking while monitoring addressees for understanding. *Journal of Memory and Language, 50*, 62–81.

Cline, M. G. (1967). Perception of where a person is looking. *American Journal of Psychology, 80*, 41–48.

Cohen, P. A., Kulik, J. A., & Kulik, C. C. (1984). Educational outcomes of tutoring: A meta-analysis of findings. *American Educational Research Journal, 19*, 237–248.

Collins, A., & Stevens, A. L. (1982). Goals and strategies of inquiry teachers. In R. Glaser (Ed.), *Advances in instructional psychology*, (Vol. 2, pp. 65–119). Hillsdale, NJ: Lawrence Erlbaum Associates.

Conati, C., Gertner, A., & VanLehn, K. (2002). Using Bayesian networks to manage uncertainty in student modeling. *User Modeling and User-Adapted Interaction, 12*, 371–417.

Corbett, A. T. (2001, July). Cognitive computer tutors: Solving the two-sigma problem. *Proceedings of the Eighth International Conference on User Modeling* (pp. 137–147). Sonthofen, Germany. London, UK: Springer Verlag.

Core, M. G., Moore, J. D., & Zinn, C. (2003). The role of initiative in tutorial dialogue. *Eleventh Conference of the European Chapter of the Association for Computational Linguistics* (EACL), Budapest, Hungary.

Di Eugenio, B. (2001). Natural-language processing for computer-supported instruction. *ACM Intelligence, 12*, 22–33.

Doane, S. M., & Sohn, Y. W. (2000). ADAPT: A predictive cognitive model of user visual attention and action planning. *User Modeling and User Adapted Interaction, 10,* 1–45.

Emery, N. J. (2000). The eyes have it: The neuroethology, function, and evolution of social gaze. *Neuroscience and Biobehavioral Reviews, 24,* 581–604.

Evens, M. W. (2000). *Language understanding and generation in complex tutorial dialogues* (Final report on grant N00014-94-1-0338). Chicago: Computer Science Department, Illinois Institute of Technology. (DTIC No. ADA384733)

Forbus, K. D., Whalley, P. B., Everett, J. O., Ureel, L., Brokowski, M., Baher, J., & Kuehne, S. E. (1999). CyclePad: An articulate virtual laboratory for engineering thermodynamics. *Artificial Intelligence, 114,* 297–347.

Fox, B. A. (1993). *The human tutorial dialogue project: Issues in the design of instructional systems.* Hillsdale, NJ: Lawrence Erlbaum Associates.

Fry, J., Ginzton, M., Peters, S., Clark, B., & Pon-Barry, H. (2001, September). Automated tutoring dialogues for training in shipboard damage control. *Proceedings of the Second ACL SIGdial Workshop on Discourse and Dialogue* (pp. 68–71). Aalborg, Denmark.

Gibson, J. J., & Pick, A. D. (1963). Perception of another person's looking behavior. *American Journal of Psychology, 76,* 386–394.

Gluck, K. A. (1999). *Eye movements and algebra tutoring.* Unpublished doctoral dissertation, Carnegie-Mellon University.

Goldin-Meadow, S., Kim, S., & Singer, M. (1999). What the teacher's hands tell the student's mind about math. *Journal of Educational Psychology, 91,* 720–730.

Gott, S. P. (1989). Apprenticeship instruction for real-world tasks: The coordination of procedures, mental models, and strategies. In E. Z. Rothkopf (Ed.), *Review of research in education, Vol. 15* (pp. 97–160). Washington, DC: American Educational Research Association.

Gould, J. D., Alfaro, L., Barnes, V., & Finn, R. (1987). Reading is slower from CRT displays than from paper: Attempts to isolate a single-variable explanation. *Human Factors, 29,* 269–299.

Graesser, A. C., Person, N. K., & Magliano, J. P. (1995). Collaborative dialogue patterns in naturalistic one-to-one tutoring. *Applied Cognitive Psychology, 9,* 495–522.

Graesser, A. C., VanLehn, K., Rose, C., Jordan, P., & Harter, D. (2001). Intelligent tutoring systems with conversational dialogue. *AI Magazine, 22*(4), 39–51.

Hays, R. T., & Vincenzi, D. A. (2000). Fleet assessments of a virtual reality training system. *Military Psychology, 12*(3), 161–186.

Hosie, T., Atkinson, R. K., & Merrill, M. M. (2004). *Measurement and evaluation of animated pedagogical agents and their use in training* (Final Rep. on Grant N00014-02-1-0120; DTIC No: ADA420184).

Hume, G., Michael, J., Rovick, A., & Evens, M. (1996). Hinting as a tactic in one-on-one tutoring. *The Journal of the Learning Sciences, 5*(1), 23–47.

Katz, S. (2003, July). Distributed tutorial strategies. *Proceedings of the 25th Annual Meeting of the Cognitive Science Society.* Boston, MA.

Katz, S., Allbritton, D., & Connelly, J. (2003). Going beyond the problem given: How human tutors use post-solution discussions to support transfer. *International Journal of Artificial Intelligence and Education, 13,* 79–116.

Katz, S., Lesgold, A., Hughes, E., Peters, D., Eggan, G., Gordin, M., et al. (1998). Sherlock II: An intelligent tutoring system built upon the LRDC Tutor Framework. In C. P. Bloom & R. B. Loftin (Eds.), *Facilitating the development and use of interactive learning environments* (pp. 227–258). Hillsdale, NJ: Lawrence Erlbaum Associates.

Koedinger, K. R., Anderson, J. R., Hadley, W. H., & Mark, M. (1995, August). Intelligent tutoring goes to school in the big city. In J. Greer (Ed.), *Artificial Intelligence in Education* (Proceedings of AI-ED 95, pp. 421–428). Washington, DC. Norfolk, VA: Association of Computers in Education.

Koedinger, K. R., Anderson, J. R., Hadley, W. H., & Mark, M. (1997). Intelligent tutoring goes to school in the big city. *International Journal of Artificial Intelligence in Education, 8*, 30–43.

Landauer, T. K., Foltz, P. W., & Laham, D. (1998). An introduction to latent semantic analysis. *Discourse Processes, 25*, 259–284.

Lee, F. J., & Anderson, J. R. (2000). Modeling eye-movements in a dynamic task. *Proceedings of the Third International Conference on cognitive modeling* (pp. 194–201). Veenendaal, The Netherlands: Universal Press.

Lesgold, A., Chipman, S., Brown, J. S., & Soloway, E. (1990). Intelligent training systems. *Annual Review of Computer Science, 4*, 383–394.

Lesgold, A., & Nahemow, M. (2001). Tools to assist learning by doing: Achieving and assisting efficient technology for learning. In S. M. Carver & D. Klahr (Eds.), *Cognition and Instruction: Twenty-five years of progress* (pp. 307–346). Mahwah, NJ: Lawrence Erlbaum Associates.

Lisetti, C. L., & Schiano, D. J. (2000). Automatic facial expression interpretation: Where human–computer interaction, artificial intelligence, and cognitive science intersect. *Pragmatics & Cognition, 8*, 185–235.

Littleton, E., Schunn, C., & Kirschenbaum, S. (2002). *Modeling distant psychological space in complex problem-solving* (Final Tech. Rep. for Office of Naval Research contract No. N00014-00-C-0340, DTIC No. ADA#: TBD).

Marshall, S. (personal communications) Confirmed by email of Feb 18, 2004.

Martin, W. W., & Jones, R. F. (1982). The accuracy of eye-gaze judgment—a signal detection approach. *British Journal of Social Psychology, 21*, 293–299.

Mayer, R. E., Sobko, K., & Mautone, P. D. (2003). Social cues in multimedia learning: Role of speaker's voice. *Journal of Educational Psychology, 95*, 419–425.

McCarthy, J. E., Pacheco, S., Banta, H. G., Wayne, J. L., & Coleman, D. S. (1994, November). The radar system controller intelligent training aid. *Proceedings of the 16th Interservice/Industry Training, Simulation and Education Conference* (Section 5, paper 2). Orlando, FL.

McNeill, D., Quek, F., McCullough, K.-E., Duncan, S., Furuyama, N., Bryll, R., et al. (2002). Dynamic imagery in speech and gesture. In B. Granstrom, D. House, & I. Karlsson (Eds.), *Multimodality in language and speech systems* (pp. 27–44). Dordrecht, Netherlands: Kluwer.

Michael, J. A., Rovick, A. A., Zhou, Y., Glass, M. S., & Evens, M. W. (2003). Learning from a computer tutor with natural language capabilities. *Interactive Learning Environments, 11*, 233–262.

Moore, J. D., Lemaire, B., & Rosenblum, J. A. (1995). Discourse generation for instructional applications: Identifying and exploiting relevant prior explanations. *Journal of the Learning Sciences, 5*, 49–94.

Munro, A., Johnson, M. C., Pizzini, Q. A., Surmon, D. S., Towne, D. M., & Wogulis, J. L. (1997). Authoring Simulation-Centered Tutors with RIDES. *International Journal of Artificial Intelligence in Education, 8*, 284–316.

Olson, J. S. (1995, April). *Groupwork and groupware: How the process and product of real-time group work changes with shared workspaces and long-distance connectivity.* Colloquium presentation in the NCARAI Seminar Series, Naval Research Laboratory, Washington, DC.

Pantic, M., & Rothkrantz, L. J. M. (2000). Automatic analysis of facial expressions: The state of the art. *IEEE Transactions on pattern analysis and machine intelligence, 22*, 1422–1445.

Pon-Barry, H., Clark, B., Schultz, K., Bratt, E. O., & Peters, S. (2004). Advantages of spoken language interaction in dialogue-based intelligent tutoring systems. In J. C. Lester, R. M. Vicari, & F. Paraguaçu (Eds.), *Intelligent tutoring systems: Proceedings of ITS 2004, 7th International Conference on Intelligent Tutoring Systems* (pp. 390–400). Berlin: Springer Verlag.

Ricciardelli, P., Baylis, G., & Driver, J. (2000). The positive and negative of human expertise in gaze perception. *Cognition, 77*, B1–B14.

Roberts, B. (2001, November). COVE—A shiphandling trainer with an attitude. *Proceedings of the 22nd Interservice/Industry Training, Simulation and Education Conference*, Orlando, FL.

Schofield, J. W. (1995). *Computers and classroom culture.* Cambridge, England: Cambridge University Press.

Schultz, K., Bratt, E. O., Clark, B., Peters, S., Pon-Barry, H., & Treeratpituk, P. (2003). A scalable, reusable spoken conversational tutor: SCoT. *Proceedings of the AIED 2003 Workshop on Tutorial Dialogue Systems: With a View Towards the Classroom* (pp. 367–377). Retrieved from http://www-cslp.stanford.edu/semlab-hold/muri/

Shelby, R. N., Schulze, K. G., Treacy, D. J., Wintersgill, M. C., & VanLehn, K. (2001, July). *The Andes intelligent tutor: An evaluation.* Paper presented at the Physics Education Research Conference, Rochester, NY.

Sohn, M-H., Douglass, S. A., Chen, M-C., & Anderson, J. R. (2000, July). Eye-movements during unit-task execution in a complex problem-solving situation. *Proceedings of the 44th Annual Meeting of the Human Factors and Ergonomics Society* (pp. 378–381). San Diego, CA.

Sniezek, J. A., Wilkins, D. C., & Wadlington, P. (2002). Training for crisis decision making: Psychological issues and computer-based solutions. *Journal of Management Information Science, 18*(4), 147–168.

Towne, D. M. (1987). The generalized maintenance trainer: Evolution and revolution. In W. B. Rouse (Ed.), *Advances in man-machine systems research* (Vol. 3, pp. 1–63). Greenwich, CN: JAI Press.

Vasandani, V. (1991). Intelligent tutoring for diagnostic problem solving in complex dynamic systems. TR CHMSR-91-4. Atlanta, Georgia: Georgia Institute of Technology, School of Industrial and Systems Engineering, Center for Human-Machine Systems Research. *Dissertation Abstracts International, 52*, 12B, 6593.

Wang, J. G., & Sung, E. (2002). Study on eye gaze estimation. *IEEE Transactions on Systems, Man, and Cybernetics, Part B—Cybernetics, 32*, 332–350.

Wenger, E. (1987). *Artificial intelligence and tutoring systems: Computational and cognitive approaches to the communication of knowledge.* Los Altos, CA: Morgan Kaufman.

Whittaker, S. (2003). Things to talk about when talking about things. *Human-Computer Interaction, 18*, 149–170.

Zachary, W., Cannon-Bowers, J., Burns, J., Bilazarian, P., & Krecker, D. (1998). An advanced embedded training system (AETS) for tactical team training. In B. P. Goettl, H. M. Halff, C. L. Redfield, & V. J. Shute (Eds.), *Intelligent tutoring systems: Proceedings of the 4th International Conference, ITS '98* (pp. 544–553). Berlin: Springer Verlag.

Zachary, W., Ryder, J., Hicinbothom, J., Santarelli, T., Scolaro, J., Szczepkowski, M., & Cannon-Bowers, J. (1998). Simulating behavior of tactical operators and teams using COGNET/GINA. *Proceedings of the 7th Symposium on computer-generated forces and behavioral representation* (pp. 365–376). Orlando, FL: Institute for Simulation and Training.

Zinn, C., Moore, J. D., & Core, M. G. (2002a, June). A 3-tier planning architecture for managing tutorial dialogue. *Intelligent Tutoring Systems, 6th. Intl. Conference, ITS 2002* (pp. 574–584). Berlin: Springer Verlag.

Zinn, C., Moore, J. D., & Core, M. G. (2002b). A 3-tier planning architecture for managing tutorial dialogue, system demonstration. *Proceedings of the sixth workshop on the semantics and pragmatics of dialogue* (EDILOG 2002; p. 200). Edinburgh, England.

Zinn, C., Moore, J. D., & Core, M. G. (2003). Multimodal intelligent information presentation for tutoring systems. In O. Stock & M. Zancanaro (Eds.), *Intelligent information presentation* (pp. 227–253). Dordrecht, Netherlands: Kluwer Academic Publishers.

Chapter 10

Beyond Content and Design: Employment Processes as the Missing Link in Web-based Distance Learning Success

Wayne Zachary
Christopher McCollum
Jennifer McNamara
James Stokes
CHI Systems, Inc.

Elizabeth Blickensderfer
Embry-Riddle Aeronautical University

Janet Schofield
University of Pittsburgh

Web-based technology has become increasingly widespread in the workplace over the last decade. Driving this rapid introduction are expectations of *universal availability* (i.e., potential to provide anytime, anywhere access to people, services, and information), and potential for *cost-savings*. Web-based distance learning is a case in point, where workplace applications have been motivated both by the hope for reduced training costs and by the promise of flexible, just-in-time training. This is particularly true in the U.S. military, one of the largest workforces in the world. The U.S. Department of Defense has embarked on ambitious and broad-reaching revisions to its traditionally classroom-based training processes, seeking instead to bring the training to the trainee by moving the major portion of training to the Web and other forms of computer-based distance learning (CDL). A potential Achilles' heel for such large-scale transformations is a tacit assumption underlying the expectations of universal availability and cost savings: That those in the workplace (in the training case, the learners and the organizations in which they work) are able to successfully use the application to achieve their work (i.e., training) goals, a process we call *employment* of the technology. When the technology cannot be successfully employed, the expected benefits are reduced or even eliminated, resulting in an essentially wasted investment.

It is thus surprising that while issues of Web-based CDL design, technological implementation and delivery have been widely studied both theoretically (e.g., Keegan, 1993; Lea & Nicoll, 2002) and empirically (e.g., Steeples & Jones, 2002), there is remarkably little research into employment issues in the workplace, such as how, or even whether, individuals and organizations are able to make CDL technology work for them. There is even less information available on what employability of Web-based CDL entails, or that offers guidance on how the process of CDL employment should be understood and even engineered across the development life cycle.

The lack of insight into CDL employment issues is worrisome. Virtually every past technological and pedagogical advance in education has been accompanied by predictions of "revolutions" in the way that education, training, and ultimately learning, occur (Cuban, 1986, 2001). But virtually all of these advances have encountered practical problems, mostly unexpected, in their employment. As employment challenges overburden and sometimes overwhelm end-users, organizations often abandon the new approach and return to familiar instructional tools and strategies (Rosenberg, 2001). Thus, it may be that without successful employment (and methods to ensure or at least encourage it), the entire investment in a CDL course or curriculum would effectively be lost.

This chapter addresses these issues with findings from a 3-year study of CDL-employment in the U.S. Navy and Marine Corps, undertaken with the overall goal of developing practical advice and procedures to support effective employment of their new CDL training systems. The first section of the chapter provides two examples that illustrate what can go wrong when employment issues are not handled effectively. The section that follows summarizes the larger study from which the examples are taken, and outlines the concepts and issues that are central to employment analysis. The remainder of the chapter discusses the implications of the study's findings for both creators and end-users of CDL. This section includes a description of the employment guidelines and other support tools that are being developed to facilitate more effective use of these new training systems.

CASE EXAMPLES

Before discussing the overall study and its conclusions, it is useful to present some examples of employment, and consider what a CDL course or curriculum that is successfully employed (or not) looks like. The following cases were all studied by the project team; each is briefly described in terms of the focus of the CDL course or curriculum, why it was developed, and what happened when users tried to employ it. In each case, there were unexpected and to some degree negative results, and the final part of each description takes advantage of the luxury of hindsight to suggest some reasons why problems arose that impeded effective CDL use. The subsequent sections also refer back to these cases.

Case 1: Physical Skill Refresher Training

The CDL and Motivation

Virtually all military personnel receive training (in most cases, both initial and regular refresher training) in marksmanship, which is both a highly cognitive and motor skill (see Bewley et al., 2003). A CDL course was created for the cognitive portions of the marksmanship refresher training course. These cognitive portions are supposed to precede the physical skill testing and (re-)qualification process on a shooting range. The course was intended to augment or replace traditional classroom training, allowing on-demand learning as trainees' schedules permitted, and enabling more individualized instruction and remediation than might be possible in large classroom settings (McCollum, 2003). The CDL course was of a high quality from both the instructional design and the multimedia implementation perspectives.

What Happened

The course was receiving little or no use months after its distribution.

Why it Happened That Way (The 20/20 Hindsight)

The course developers focused heavily, if not exclusively, on the instructional and technical content of the course, and did not provide the marksmanship training organizations with either an explicit model of how the course was intended to be used in the refresher training process or a model of how the transition from current training to CDL-based training should unfold. The developers preferred, instead, to allow those in charge of the training to be free to use it as they best saw fit. However, the large number of students receiving the refresher training (hundreds at a time) and the high throughput that the training process had to maintain left the training supervisors with little time to develop an employment plan and/or to experiment with different strategies. Moreover, previous unfavorable encounters with hardware simulator technology had left them with a reluctance to rely too heavily on the new (CDL) technology, given their need to maintain the throughput of trainees. Finally, there was a severe mismatch of trainees to equipment at the refresher training site (with only 20 computers v. several hundred trainees). As a result, the CDL course was never put into use.

Case 2: Blended Learning While Deployed

The CDL and Motivation

Junior Naval officers complete a broad initial training curriculum before reporting to their first ship assignment, but the classroom-based delivery of the curriculum had grown to well over a year, delaying officers' arrival for duty at sea. A blended curriculum, involving CDL and supported by on-the-job-training (OJT) and mentoring, was developed to allow some cohorts of junior officers to report directly to their ships and receive initial training there. The CDL courses within the curriculum were of very high quality from both the instructional design and the multimedia implementation perspectives.

What Happened

Months after the deadline for having an entire training cohort progressing through the course, administrators were having difficulty confirming that even a single trainee had begun working on the curriculum.

Why it Happened That Way (The 20/20 Hindsight)

The mobile nature of ships made delivery and installation of the CDL portions of the curriculum difficult, and made custom installations by the developers themselves impractical. The CDL was therefore designed to self-install and execute on the official "lowest common denominator" system—technology that all ships were presumed to have. The reality, however, was that many ships had evolved away from (or never gotten to) this lowest common denominator for various reasons; that the technological environments aboard ships were far more technically inconsistent (with each other as well as with written standards) than had been anticipated; and that training uses were constrained in ways that varied from ship to ship. In addition, the installation packages were received by information technology specialists without any direct integration of the training supervisors on board ship, who were responsible for implementing the new blended curriculum.

Underlying Commonalities

Tolstoy mused that "All happy families resemble one another, each unhappy family is unhappy in its own way." (Tolstoy, 1875–1877/1992, p. 1), and from even the two simple cases previously described, it might be tempting to conclude that the same principle applies to CDL. There are, however, clear commonalities across these and the other cases studied. These examples demonstrate how successful employment of Web-based and other forms of distance-learning technology depends not only on the technology itself but also on the individuals and organizations that must make it work. They also show how development of potentially useful learning technology, by itself, does not guarantee that the product will ever be used effectively. For CDL to satisfy training goals, the creators and end-users of the technology must take into account the employment factors that, if left unaddressed, can impede or even derail a new training system.

STUDY GOALS AND METHOD

The case summaries given earlier were developed as part of a multiyear study of the individual and organizational effects of Web-based (and other forms of) distance learning in the military. The two main goals of the research were:

1. to collect data on what happened when different CDL courses or curricula were employed to provide training in the military work setting, and
2. to create guidance on how organizational processes need to adapt to effectively employ CDL tools and methods.

The data collected to meet the first goal were obtained through multiple interrelated field studies. To choose candidate sites for the study, researchers used an approach to selecting cases that sought to capture and describe the central themes or factors that cut across a great deal of variation in CDL-training sites. Specifically, researchers targeted cases for in-depth study that maximized variation along two primary dimensions:

1. *the setting in which training occurred*—of particular interest was whether the setting was *deployed* (e.g., aboard a ship that was at sea or unit away from home base) or *nondeployed* (e.g., a ship at home port or a unit at its home base).

2. *the level of instructional and/or organizational support provided for train-ees*—this dimension involved the degree to which the CDL incorpo-rated the presence of such support features as access to human in-structors, mentors or other learners, technical (troubleshooting) support, and so forth.

Each dimension was scaled in a binary manner (deployed v. nondeployed for the first dimension, and high support available v. little/no support avail-able on the second) to create a matrix with four cells. An informal census was done of CDL courses/curricula fielded in military units. From this census, individual cases were selected for detailed field study, based on the pres-ence of three criteria:

1. *logistical availability*—the ability of the research team to gain access to and study users of the CDL course/curriculum;
2. *dimensional categorization*—its categorization according to the two di-mensions previously described; the cases studied had to be balanced across the four cells created by these two dimensions; and
3. *available classroom comparisons*—the availability for comparative study of a traditional (e.g., classroom-based) setting in which the same con-tent had recently been or was currently being taught, so that any ef-fects of content could be understood and controlled for in the analysis.

Ultimately, eight CDL cases (ranging from stand-alone CDL courses to in-tegrated CDL-based curricula) were selected and studied, two in each cell of the matrix. (Human subject protection protocols of the research prohibit disclosure of any information about the specific organizations, units, or in-dividuals who acted as subjects of the research.)

Qualitative methods were used in the field studies of these eight cases. Where possible, the qualitative methods were combined with surveys in or-der to enhance the representativeness of the data. Researchers used the qualitative techniques of comparison and triangulation to analyze data (e.g., field notes, interviews, surveys) and produced narrative accounts of the situations under investigation (see Strauss & Corbin, 1998 for discus-sion of qualitative analysis). In addition, the surveys were analyzed using statistical techniques. These analytic processes revealed the complex em-ployment factors at work at each site and suggested explanations for these local dynamics. These techniques were also used to identify patterns in the data that cut across different employment sites, and to develop the guide-lines that are discussed later.

The study found moderate to severe employment problems in three of the eight cases studied, along the lines of those illustrated by the case examples in the preceding section. According to the standards used, "moderate" meant significant impairment in the use of technology (e.g., increased training time and/or costs, significant delays in distributing technology to end-users and/or implementing technology after receiving it); and "severe" meant the technology was not used in a systematic or effective way at all. The frequency of employment problems confirmed the importance of identifying and resolving employment issues before they undermine the success of a new training system. (Indeed, a surprising observation, which is discussed further in the conclusions, is how detrimental a single oversight in employment planning could be to an otherwise well-designed and well-implemented instructional system.)

Additional details of the individual cases, the data collected for each case, and the data analysis process are not included here due to space limitations. Rather, the focus for the remainder of the chapter is on the results that were obtained from the analysis of the field site data. For more information on the sites and data analysis, the reader is referred to McCollum, Zachary, McNamara, Stokes, and Schofield (2004), McNamara et al. (2004), McNamara and McCollum (2004), and McCollum (2003).

COMMON BARRIERS AND ENABLERS FOR CDL EMPLOYMENT

The analysis of the data from the field studies revealed a variety of common themes in both successful and problematic employment of CDL. Employment problems were associated with one or more instances of four general problems:

1. *Developers not fully understanding the end-user training environment*—this included situations as diverse as failing to understand the local history at the end-user site (as in Case 1), or not knowing how computing resources or time allocations were managed in the end-user organization (as in both Cases 1 and 2); or making tacit or explicit assumptions about the end-user environment that were not based on current data and that led to mismatches between the CDL and its use environment (e.g., Case 2).

2. *Organizations not recognizing secondary requirements created by CDL*—in virtually all cases, the organization at which the CDL was used found that the employment of the CDL gave rise to other varying needs. Important among these were secondary training needs, such as the need for end-user organizations to acquire more or different equipment; or to change their training processes (e.g., Case 1).

3. *Lack of planning for transition from traditional training*—the change from existing classroom-based processes to CDL-based training seldom

occurs instantaneously. Typically, the process involves a period in which the CDL is phased in, or in which some other partial transition precedes the full CDL use. When the need for this process was unrecognized, or when no plan for it was provided to the end-user organization, employment problems often ensued (e.g., Cases 1 and 2).

4. *Unrecognized evolutions of end-user organizations during CDL design/development*—CDL courses typically are developed in a relatively short time (e.g., taking months, rather than the years that high-fidelity simulation-based trainers can involve). Nonetheless, substantial technological and/or organizational changes could and did occur at end-user sites after the initial understanding of the end-user training process and organization was developed. One subtle but important type of change that almost always occurs in military training is the rotation of personnel. This repeatedly disrupts the channels of communication between the CDL design/development team and the end-user organization, making it easier to miss key changes that are occurring in the end-user organization while development is underway.

When a CDL curriculum or course was employed successfully, most of the following enabling conditions or processes were typically involved:

1. *Effective front-end employability analysis*—the developers gathered data on the setting in which the CDL would be used, identifying potential problems and pitfalls, as well as requirements for a CDL product that would be employable in the end-user setting and included these alongside the instructional requirements as inputs to the design/development process.

2. *Active consideration of employment issues and needs as part of CDL design and development*—throughout the development and transition process, the teams involved in creating and fielding the CDL thought about and planned around who was going to use the CDL, how it would be used, and how that would affect the learner and the learner's organization. During the design/development process, employment, as well as instructional issues, were routinely considered at each decision point.

3. *Clear, structured, and actively used lines of communication between developers and CDL end-user organizations regarding employment*—rather than relying on communications during only one part of the process (typically the front-end analysis) or on communications based only on personal relationships (e.g., the design team subject matter expert has a former colleague in the target organization), successful processes were more often systematic about maintaining multiple lines of communication and about managing those lines of communication over time.

SYNTHESIS: IMPLICATIONS FOR PRACTICE

The main concern of this research was enabling practitioners to achieve better employment outcomes in the future. This section of the paper provides a data synthesis answering three key questions: (1) Who are the stakeholders that need to be involved in ensuring successful CDL employment? (2) What processes need to occur for a CDL course/curriculum to have the best chance of being successfully employed? (3) What specific guidance and supporting information can be provided to stakeholders to help them carry out these processes?

Stakeholders in CDL Employment

The barriers and enabling factors described earlier help identify the broad range of stakeholders involved in CDL employment. CDL stakeholders are clustered into four broad groups, which include both roles involved in CDL creation and roles involved in end-use of CDL.

The managers and administrators of CDL development include individuals who provide funds for the development or acquisition of a CDL course or curriculum, and who manage the CDL development team, either through a direct line or contract management relationship. These stakeholders define the scope of the development team's activities and allocate resources (particularly funding) to those activities. If activities for planning and facilitating employment (as discussed in the next section) are not included in the work breakdown, schedule, funding and management oversight provided to the development team and end-users, then it will be more difficult and sometimes impossible for them to identify and address employment concerns. Further, manager/administrator stakeholders are ultimately held accountable for the success or failure of the CDL product making it in their interest to ensure that employability is part of their purview.

The extended CDL development team includes roles involved in instructional systems creation—instructional designers, subject-matter experts, content developers, and CDL software designers, developers, maintainers, and user-support specialists. People in these roles need to understand the end-use environment and the way the CDL will be integrated into that environment as context for design and development. Ignoring this context greatly reduces the likelihood that the CDL product will be effectively employed.

The learner/trainee and his/her management or command structure includes the individual in the trainee role, as well as his/her coworkers, and management chain including immediate supervisors through the overall executive (e.g., site manager, ship commander, etc.). The learner/trainee is perhaps the most obvious CDL stakeholder because he or she requires the training. In the workplace, CDL must coexist and be compatible with the business of the organization. Coworkers are stakeholders because the involvement of the trainee in CDL activities can burden coworkers by reducing the trainee's availability overall and at key times. The management line in the workplace has a strong stake in the trainee to achieving his or her training goals. At the same time, this same line management has an interest in keeping CDL from interfering with the organization's business processes, or requiring changes in business processes to accommodate CDL introduction. Thus, management cannot be passive in employment, but needs to develop a mutual understanding with CDL creators of the constraints, needs, and opportunities of the workplace environment.

The learners' training and technology support structure includes roles in the end-user organization that support the trainee's learning, such as training manager, instructor or mentor, or that support the trainee's work processes, such as the local information technology support person, team, or help desk. The roles of training support stakeholders need to be clearly defined with respect to each CDL program and then accommodated in employment. The work process support roles can be greatly affected by introduction of CDL and the way it is employed, as shown by two case examples. Personnel in these roles can acquire responsibilities for installing, fixing, maintaining connectivity to, and/or updating the CDL software, as well as find themselves having to provide advice and user support to trainees trying to use the CDL. All of these kinds of involvement can and do affect the workload and work situation of work-support personnel, giving them a strong stake in the way the CDL is employed.

Factoring Employment Thinking into the CDL Development Process

Our theme, which should be emerging at this point, is that successful employment of CDL does not "just happen." Rather, it is the product of a larger process involving all of the previously mentioned stakeholders. Later, we suggest a method for incorporating employment issues and concerns into the CDL development process. This method is built on existing instructional systems development approaches, but is also based on the empirical data and the lessons learned from the field studies and their comparative analysis. Our employment method assumes that the CDL course or curriculum is being created through a structured approach such as the widely used Instructional Systems Development/Systems Approach to Training and Education or ISD/SAT method (Department of Defense, 2001). To incorporate employment concerns in existing methods, three general extensions are required.

First, explicit communication channels and relationships between the extended development team stakeholders and the end-user environment stakeholders must be established and maintained during the CDL development and fielding. These are used to identify issues, opportunities, and potential barriers to employment that may be present initially or that may arise during the CDL design/development. Second, traditional front-end analysis must be extended to include a separate employability analysis that identifies issues in the end-use environment(s) that may affect the CDL's employment. Third, the remaining design, development, implementation, and evaluation steps must be augmented to explicitly address the case-specific employment issues identified from the employability analysis. Each extension is discussed in more detail.

Managing Communication Between CDL Creators and CDL User Stakeholders

Successful CDL employment is unlikely without explicit and on-going communication between the development team and the end-user organization stakeholders (both the trainee management/command structure and the training/technology support structure). It is important that the relationship not be dependent on specific individuals or their relationships, but rather be made more explicit and formal. Systems engineering methods (see International Council of Systems Engineering, 2004) suggest a way of accomplishing this. Modern system engineering processes are organized by functional stages of the life cycle, with integration across the functional teams/roles maintained by crosscutting Integrated Product/Process Teams (IPTs). IPTs focus on specific aspects of the whole product or process being engineered, and their membership explicitly includes a range of stakeholders. Although individual members of the IPT come and go, the IPT persists through time. Creating and maintaining an employment IPT (or equivalent) is a valuable and visible means for keeping an on-going flow of information between and among the stakeholders. This IPT serves different functions in different life cycle stages—such as facilitating the flow of information from the end-user environment to the development team during the front-end analysis, and later from the development team to the end-user environment as design features and employment concepts emerge. The employment IPT can also be a focal structure throughout the life cycle for obtaining commitment for the CDL's introduction and success management from the end-user organization and its leader.

The physical skills refresher training example illustrated what can go wrong when this communication fails to occur. Involving end-users from the training site in the CDL design and development process would have alerted CDL creators to the access issues while there was still time to modify the training delivery method to circumvent the problem. Better communication between creators and end-users also would have alerted CDL creators to the low level of organizational support for new training technology at the site. Creators of the technology could have then countered or ameliorated this negative sentiment through a marketing/publication effort, before the technology was delivered to the site.

Analyzing the Training Environment for Employability

Traditional instructional systems design methods incorporate various forms of front-end analysis to gather information needed to define the instructional content and model. A separate and explicit employability analysis must be undertaken as part of the end-analysis process to identify and address specific employment barriers, issues, and opportunities in the end-use environment. At a minimum, the employability analysis should include the following items.

First, the existing training processes and training needs in the end-user's work environment must be documented, along with the constraints under which the existing training processes must operate; such as time available for training, size of the time units allocated to training, how training activities are incorporated into the overall work schedule. The analysis should also identify how the training support personnel function (e.g., Are they full time or supporting training as a collateral duty? Are they skilled in training and instruction methods, or just in subject matter and content?) and how the trainee will expect to interact with these personnel.

Next, the existing business rules and work processes that govern the (work) activity where the trainees will be using the CDL must be identified. From these, the analysis identifies opportunities for the CDL to fit into the work processes and flow. Transition from traditional classroom-based training (especially where trainees travel from their work setting to a schoolhouse) to forms of workplace-based CDL introduces a potential conflict with primary work activities. When this occurs, it is usually the CDL that suffers, so it is incumbent on the employability analysis to anticipate any such conflicts. This part of the analysis should include not just the trainee's perspective but the view of the trainee's management/command structure, and even the vision of the leader on the organization's mission and how training process and content supports that mission. These latter items can be key to obtaining management/command support for the employment process.

The front-end analysis should also document the history, both good and bad, of training changes in that workplace, and any prevalent attitudes, either positive or negative, that may linger in individuals or in the oral history of the workplace. These can affect how training innovations such as CDL will be perceived within the organization. The analysis should also document the role of technical and work support personnel and functions, such as information technology department, help desk, and so forth, in the work environment. These people may affect, in a secondary but nonetheless significant way, the introduction of a new workplace-situated CDL curriculum. The analysis needs to uncover how the trainees might interact with these personnel in the context of the new CDL, and the constraints this may place on their time and responsibilities.

This analysis process is not just a "front-end" process; it should not end when the instructional design begins. Instead, it should assume a background role, and with revised goals, throughout the remainder of the development process. Later-stage analysis functions include determining if CDL is an appropriate medium to suit the training need, identifying changes in the end-user environment that occur while instructional systems development is proceeding, identifying design/development team assumptions about the end-user environment or employment process and testing them, and validating possible employment models or strategies.

Because CDL technology is not tied to any specific classroom or training environment, a given CDL course/curriculum may be intended for use in many different workplaces. This can pose a challenge for the employability analysis. In general, the employability analysis can be adapted to consider employment in multiple settings by directly analyzing only a sample of the environments in detail. Survey methods can then be used to validate or generalize the analysis findings with the remaining work environments (or broader sample of them). In these cases, the employability analysis must identify the set of "least common denominator" constraints that the CDL design must meet in order to be employable in the desired range of work environments.

Meeting Case-Specific Employment Issues

Front-end analysis is traditionally followed by interrelated steps of systems design, development, implementation, and testing. As the examples showed, the successful completion of these steps does not guarantee that the resulting CDL will be successfully employed and used. We suggest that employment be explicitly addressed in these core steps of CDL creation by creating and evolving an employment model—a representation of how the CDL being created is expected to be introduced and used by trainees in their workplace. The employment model identifies how the training process is intended to unfold in terms of when, where, how, and in what manner trainees are expected to be able to train and integrate training with other responsibilities. It also identifies how training support personnel are expected to support the learning process of CDL users; for example, by installing the CDL, by making the existing computing environment compatible with the CDL, by troubleshooting problems that might develop, by guiding or helping trainees having learning or user-interface difficulties, or by interacting with the CDL software maintainers. This latter part of the employment model helps identify secondary training needed by training or support personnel to make the employment model work.

The employment model provides a reference point for making or evaluating various design and implementation decisions during the on-going CDL development. It is analogous to the "use model" in the human–computer interface literature (Flach & Dominguez, 1995; Rubenstein & Hersh, 1984) or the "concept of operation" in the system engineering literature (Institute of Electrical and Electronic Engineers, Inc., 1998). It facilitates communication between the extended development team and the end-user organization stakeholders. The employment model gives the end-user organization stakeholders a clear statement of what the CDL product will be and how they are expected to employ it. This, in turn, gives them a concrete basis for identifying problems and suggesting corrections. It is important, however, that the employment model be continuously converged with evolutions in the workplace(s) in which the CDL will be used, as they are uncovered through the on-going employability analysis. Established communication channels such as the employment IPT provide a forum to frequently review the employment model in light of changing processes and structures in the workplace, and adapt it as necessary.

Guidelines to Support Application of the Enhanced Development Process

Although the extended development process described earlier provides a general approach for including employment planning as part of CDL development, it suffers from a problem common to design methods in that it lacks specific guidance to complement its comprehensive but abstract structure. To that end, we developed a set of CDL employment guidelines. The guideline structure is similar to the structure used in the "What works in distance learning" guidelines discussed elsewhere in this volume (O'Neil, 2003). Each guideline has a guideline summary that provides a simple imperative statement of the guideline followed by the guideline detail, which provides a broader statement of the guideline detailing its purpose, use, and insight into the data on which it rests. A set of application strategies is included to provide the practitioner with some actionable advice on how to apply the guideline in real-world settings. A unique feature in the CDL employment guidelines is mapping from each guideline to two or more synoptic real-world examples. Not unlike the case examples given earlier, the examples show what could happen when the guidelines are applied or ignored. Although the CDL employment guidelines are not based on literature, citations to theoretical, experimental, and literature review publications that provide support for, or additional insight into, the guidelines are included in a literature support section. Finally, key terms are provided for each guideline to allow indexing, search, and retrieval of appropriate guidelines. There are 27 CDL employment guidelines, and they are organized into broad categories of analyzing the training environment for CDL employability, managing the CDL creator–CDL user relationship, and recognizing and meeting organizational needs resulting from CDL employment. Space precludes an exhaustive listing and discussion of the guidelines. However, one guideline example is presented and discussed later to give a flavor of the content and level of detail of the full set. The full guideline set is available in McCollum et al. (2005).

Guideline Example

Table 10.1 presents an example guideline related to CDL technology resources. In its summary form, it recommends environmental analysis to ensure resource accessibility. At first glance this may seem an obvious concern, but the possible complexity in this area is often overlooked, resulting in rather simple assessments of the relationship between number-of-computers and number-of-trainees. As noted in the guideline detail, a wide range of issues may need to be addressed, from network bandwidth to computer-use priorities. The guideline's real-world examples (omitted here for space reasons) discuss accessibility problems and solutions observed in the course of the field research on which the guideline is based. The first real-world example referenced is drawn from data on the physical skill refresher training example. The example points out how a learning center with 20 or so computers was to provide CDL access for several hundred trainees. Although trainees' access to the technology could conceivably be staggered during the week-long time frame of the training, the example goes on to point out that the course was intended to be completed before the hands-on training. Because the hands-on phase accounts for the majority of the time spent in the course, it was thus predictably impossible for all trainees to access the CDL with so few computers.

The second real-world example was drawn from the data on the CDL curriculum to train naval officers on ship, summarized in the blended learning while deployed example. Unlike the preceding real-world example, trainees in this setting were not involved in full-time training, but rather had to interweave training with primary work duties. The example points out how trainee's experiences with CDL varied with the way in which computer resources were provided (e.g., always available, sometimes available, shared first-come/first-served for general usage). The competition

TABLE 10.1

Example Guideline

Guideline summary: Analyze training environment to ensure that CDL resources are sufficiently accessible to all learners.

Guideline detail: Quantity and kind of technological resources needed (e.g., numbers of computers, bandwidth, etc.) and their actual availability to learners (e.g., priority of uses, hours of operation/availability, etc.) must be evaluated to determine if all learners will have sufficient access to training/educational materials.

Strategies: Employment strategy for a CDL course/curriculum should provide precise requirements for the technology's general accessibility, as well as analysis/projections of the technology's availability at times when training is likely to occur. The analysis should include identifying the number of computers and network bandwidth available in the training environment; determining the time required to complete the course work—total course and individual session modules; defining the number of learners expected to share the computer resources; mapping out learners' schedules—to determine when each learner is available for training and the likely number of users at any given time; and estimating existing technology reliability—to determine the proportion of technology likely to be inoperable at any given time.

Real-world examples:

1. Too few technological resources preclude CDL course from meeting training need

2. Limited technological accessibility impedes employment process for CDL

3. Access to CDL is impeded by technological constraints in training environments

Literature support:

Muilenburg, L. Y., & Berge, Z. L. (2001). Barriers to distance education: A factor-analytic study. *The American Journal of Distance Education, 15*(2): 7–22.

Bates, A. W. (2000). *Managing technological change*. San Francisco: Jossey-Bass.

Key terms: Educational environment, Educational technology, Access to computers.

with other uses/users combined with the need to give primacy to work duties severely undermined the training experience; CDL usage was limited (and hence poor employment resulted) if computing resources were not available, on a guaranteed basis, when trainees had training time available.

Strategies for implementation of this accessibility-analysis guideline are directed, in particular, to CDL developers and operational personnel involved in the development process (perhaps via the employment IPT). In order to evaluate constraints in the environment, accessibility requirements of the CDL's instructional approach must be known. For example, what are the requirements for uninterrupted CDL use: Can the training be performed in 10-min chunks or is an uninterrupted session of several hours required? In light of this information, potential mismatches between computer availability and trainee work schedule must be assessed. As indicated in the strategies, this assessment must go well beyond a simple count of computers and trainees—one computer for five trainees may work out if trainee availability can be effectively staggered, whereas five computers for one trainee may fail if higher priority activities occupy these machines whenever the trainee is available to train.

CONCLUSIONS

Our research has several broad implications for Web-based distance learning and other forms of computer-based distance learning. The first is that employment is what the chapter title suggests—the (heretofore missing) link between (good) CDL development and (successful) training results. Simply put, if no one uses the system (for whatever the reason), there are no training benefits. The case examples described at the beginning of the chapter exemplify how the potential benefits of good instructional design can be undermined or completely lost by a poor employment process. The converse is, interestingly, not entirely true. Although the best employment process may not be able to "save" a poorly designed CDL course, the field studies clearly showed that a CDL course with only average or even below-average instructional design can be productively used, if its employment strategy was well conceived and well executed.

A consistent finding from the field studies is that even a single significant oversight or incorrect assumption in the employment process or planning can result in an unsuccessful employment outcome. This leads to the second implication, which is that employment strategy and planning must be an explicit and integrated part of the CDL analysis, design, development, implementation, and evaluation process. Successful employment outcomes do not simply happen, but rather are the result of a deliberate process. The research has developed a model employment process with supporting guidelines and examples. Although these materials are complementary to the existing large body of research and methods on CDL instructional design (see O'Neil, 2003 for review of the literature), the employment process should not be viewed as an independent, parallel process to instructional systems design. The model and guidelines have been framed as an augmented design or development method, in which employment thinking is interwoven through the entire life cycle. The pervasiveness of employment awareness is crucial (even though the amount of actual time or effort explicitly devoted to employment may remain comparatively small), because of the point noted—the need to avoid that single problem that could undermine the entire investment in the system design.

The third implication of the research is to underscore the importance of lines of communication to a successful employment outcome. Both the field study data and the resulting model point out how multiple groups of stakeholders must interact and cooperate to identify and resolve employment problems and issues. It should be noted, though, that the typical social organization of the development process can work against the formation and use of the needed communication channels. The vendor organizations to which the extended development team belongs usually do not have ready access to the end-user organizations for employment planning and preparation purposes. At the same time, the stakeholders in the end-user organizations typically have neither time, nor authority, nor a suitable reward structure for interacting with the CDL developers in the employment planning process. Ad hoc organizations such as the employment IPTs may help lower the organizational barriers to communication, but the structural forces that separate the two types of stakeholders are deep and strong, and reassert themselves if the focus on maintaining effective communication falters.

A final implication concerns the relationship between complexity and employability. The field study data showed that a sizeable number (five of the eight) of courses/curricula studied did have a successful employment, but also that these successful courses were (generally) the least complex (in content, instructional design, and technology) of those studied. All but one of them involved self-directed instructional models devoid of instructor or colearner interactions, relied on simple didactic presentation, and organized learning into small units that could be completed in limited time segments. They were not blended with mentoring, on-the-job training, exploratory learning, or other more complex models. The resulting CDL products were simple in structure and had a minimum numbers of points of articulation with the end-user organization or work environment. Put another way, they had fewer opportunities for things to go wrong, for that "single problem in employment" to arise. The more complex courses and curricula had more complicated interactions with the end-use environment and work processes and, predictably, generated more employment problems. Thus, the final implication of this research is that careful attention to employment processes is particularly important for the "high end" of the CDL complexity curve, if such richer yet more complex courses are to achieve widespread use and success in the workplace. If not, the implication is that workplace CDL be left to the least common denominator of simple low-end CDL instructional models.

ACKNOWLEDGMENTS

This research was supported by the Office of Naval Research as part of the Capable Manpower Program/Future Naval Capabilities Program. The authors gratefully acknowledge the contributions and suggestions of Susan Chipman, Ray Perez, and Jan Dickieson of the Office of Naval Research; Sandra Hughes and Joan Johnston of the Naval Air System Command, Training Systems Division; Judy Wyne of the Naval Education and Training Command, and all of the many individuals who took the time to talk with us about distance learning employment and who allowed us to observe and participate in their learning and instructional development processes. Thanks also go to Chris Volk for her work on manuscript preparation. All opinions expressed here are those of the authors and not the U.S. Navy, and any errors or omissions remaining are the sole responsibility of the authors.

REFERENCES

Bates, A. (2000). *Managing technological change*. San Francisco: Jossey-Bass.

Bewley, W., Chung, G., Delacruz, G., Munro, A., Walker, J., Zachary, W., & McCollum, C. (2003). *Research on USMC Marksmanship training assessment tools, instructional simulations, and qualitative field-based research*. Interim report. Los Angeles, CA: Graduate School of Education & Information Studies, UCLA.

Cuban, L. (1986). *Teachers and machines: The classroom use of technology since 1920*. New York: Teachers College Press.

Cuban, L. (2001). Why are most teachers infrequent and restrained users of computers in their classrooms? In J. Woodward & L. Cuban (Eds.), *Technology, curriculum and professional development* (pp. 121–137). Thousand Oaks, CA: Corwin Press.

Department of Defense. (2001). *Handbook instructional systems development/systems approach to training and education* (Part 2). Retrieved August 31, 2005 from http://www.dtswg.org/Tutorials/Tutorial4/-2%20hdbk.pdf

Flach, J., & Dominguez, C. (1995). Use-centered design. *Ergonomics in Design*, July, 19–24

Institute of Electrical and Electronic Engineers, Inc. (1998). *IEEE Guide for information technology-systems definition-concept of operations (ConOps) document*. New York: Author.

International Council of Systems Engineering (INCOSE), (2004). *Systems engineering handbook*. Seattle, WA: Author.

Keegan, D. (1993). *Theoretical principles of distance education*. London: Routledge.

Lea, M. R., & Nicoll, K. (2002). *Distributed learning: Social and Cultural approaches to practice*. New York: Routledge/Falmer.

McCollum, C. (2003, December). Importance of employment strategy to ADL success: A case study. *Proceedings of the 25th Interservice/Industry Training, Systems & Education Conference (I/ITSEC)*. Orlando, FL.

McCollum, C., McNamara, J., Stokes, J., Zachary, W., Blickensderfer, B., Schofield, J., & Hughes, S. (2005). *Advanced distance learning assessment tools: Guidelines*. (Tech. Rep. No. 050131.00001-019). Ft. Washington, PA, CHI Systems, Inc.

McCollum, C., Zachary, W., McNamara, J., Stokes, J., & Schofield, J. (2004). Individual and organizational factors that affect successful employment of CDL courses and curricula. *Proceedings of the Human Factors and Ergonomics Society (HFES) 48th Annual Meeting* [CDROM]. Santa Monica, CA.

McNamara, J., & McCollum, C. (2004, August). Putting computer-based distance learning to work. *Proceedings of the Washington Interactive Technologies Conference 2004.* [CDROM] Warrenton, VA: Society for Applied learning Technology (SALT).

McNamara, J., Szczepkowski, M., McCollum, C., Stokes, J., & Zachary, W. (2004, December). Beyond content and design: Employment of computer-based distance learning. *Proceedings of the 26th Interservice/Industry Training, Systems & Education Conference* (I/ITSEC). [CDROM]. Arlington, VA: National Training Systems Association.

Muilenburg, L. & Berge, Z. (2001). Barriers to distance education: A factor-analytic study. *The American Journal of Distance Education, 15*(2), 7–22.

O'Neil, H. (2003). *What works in distance learning.* Retrieved February 9, 2004, from http://www.adlnet.org/index.cfm?fuseaction=DLGuid

Rosenberg, M. (2001). *E-learning: Strategies for delivering knowledge in the digital age.* New York: McGraw-Hill.

Rubenstein, R., & Hersh, H. (1984). *The human factor: Designing computer systems for people.* NY: Digital Press.

Steeples, C., & Jones, C. (2002). *Networked learning: Perspectives and issues.* New York: Springer.

Strauss, A., & Corbin, J. (1998). *Basics of qualitative research: Techniques and procedures for developing grounded theory* (2nd ed.), Thousand Oaks, CA: Sage.

Tolstoy, L. (1992). *Anna Karenina* (L. Maude et al., Trans.). New York: Knopf. (Original work published 1875–1877)

Part II

THEORY AND RESEARCH ISSUES

Chapter 11

Becoming a Self-Regulated Learner: Implications for Web-Based Education

Myron H. Dembo
Linda Gubler Junge
University of Southern California

Richard Lynch
Woosong University, South Korea

Web-based learning or training is a contemporary form of distance learning or training that is providing new opportunities for educational institutions and their students as well as for public and private organizations and their employees. Distance learning may be defined as learning that occurs in a different place than teaching, utilizing special aspects of course design, instructional methods, and delivery modalities (Moore & Kearsley, 1996). Kjeldsen, Krogsdal, and Gomme (2003) characterized Web-based learning (WBL) as any learning that uses Web-based content or communication via the Internet focusing on flexibility and the demands of individual learners.

A U.S. Department of Education report indicated that during the 2000–2001 academic year, 56% (2,320) of all 2-year and 4-year Title IV-eligible, degree-granting institutions offered distance learning courses employing diverse delivery modalities for various audiences. Asynchronous Internet courses were offered at 90% of those institutions, with 43% offering synchronous Internet instruction (Waits & Lewis, 2003).

Distance learning has traditionally faced higher student dropout rates (between 10%–50%) than classroom-based courses (Phipps & Merisotis,

1999). The situation is similar with Web-based distance learning, with non-completions in some online corporate university courses as high as 70%–80% (Martinez, 2003).

Interventions are clearly needed to reduce dropouts and incompletes in distance learning. Gibson (1998) identified three categories of factors that predict dropout in distance learning; student factors (e.g., educational preparation, motivational and persistence attributes), situational factors (e.g., family support and changes in life circumstances), and educational system factors (e.g., quality and difficulty level of instructional materials, quality and availability of instructional feedback). This discussion focuses on student factors, which have implications for dealing with situational and educational system factors as well.

Frustration is a common problem for asynchronous Web-based learners who are left to their own devices when trying to use new technologies (Hara & Kling, 2002; O'Regan, 2003). The responsibilities required in Web-based learning often exacerbate problems with time management (Loomis, 2000), procrastination (Lavoie & Pychyl, 2001), motivation (Hofmann, 2003); and anxiety (Kazmer & Haythornthwaite, 2001).

If Web-based learners take responsibility for their own learning through acquiring important motivation and learning strategies, they will acquire the skills to deal with a broad range of issues and problems in distance learning. Initiative and self-discipline are two important learner characteristics that are needed for success in distance learning. These characteristics are often identified by proponents of self-directed learning who focus on learner autonomy, or on the freedom of the learner to control his or her goals and activities in the learning process. Garrison's (2003) review of the research into self-directed learning in asynchronous online learning indicated, however, that this construct offers little assistance in improving learning. Garrison discussed the limitations of autonomy and control to fully understand learner behavior, and pointed out that the psychological or cognitive aspects of the learning process have been generally ignored in the conceptualization and adoption of self-directed learning in distance education. The terms self-directed learning and self-regulated learning are not synonymous. The former refers to the initial motivations prompting learners to begin learning on their own, whereas the latter refers to the cognitive, metacognitive, and affective strategies self-regulated learners employ while learning and that describe the learning process (Kerlins, 1992). It is necessary, therefore, to move beyond the generally accepted notion that successful Web-based learning entails a high level of learner autonomy, or self-direction, and to investigate precisely what processes the concept of autonomy involves.

One problem in the issue of learner autonomy is the assumption by some educators that mere exposure to motivation and learning strategies is sufficient for their independent use by learners. A second issue is that learners should come to Web-based courses with autonomous behavior. The first point of view is represented by Mehrotra, Hollister, and McGahey (2001), who recommend the importance of discussing effective learning strategies in the course syllabus or study guide:

> Including such a discussion in the beginning motivates students to do well in the course, reminds them of effective study skills, and helps them remain focused on the task at hand .... In addition students should be reminded that beyond reading about how to study, they need to learn the study skills by putting them into practice. (pp. 44, 47)

This statement illustrates the assumption that if learners are simply exposed to learning strategies or reminded about how to learn effectively, they should be able to apply the strategies. Unfortunately, there is no evidence that such exposure improves students' learning strategies in either the traditional classroom or in Web-based contexts. Learners need to be taught directly how to use the strategies and then monitored while practicing them. In addition, there is no evidence that brief exposure to learning strategies will motivate students to complete courses.

Major and Levenburg (1999) took a stronger position by stating:

> It is the learner's responsibility to be an active learner .... They must have the self-discipline and time-management skills to "keep up" with the expected learning schedule and pace. Learners must accept the importance of this demand, or opt out of the distance education environment. (p. 5)

This point of view also was heard when more diverse students were entering higher education in the 1960s. The argument went something like: "If they can't hack it, they shouldn't be in college!" It did little to improve access or success in higher education and it will not do much to improve learning and retention in Web-based learning.

There is, however, a useful area of research that can offer assistance to educators. Self-regulation theory has been applied to diverse areas of human functioning, including classroom-based learning (Bandura, 1997; Boekaerts, Pintrich, & Zeidner, 2000). There is a need to apply it to Web-based learning by identifying the self-regulatory psychological processes and related learning strategies that can enable successful Web-based learning to occur. This perspective is particularly important given the potential of asynchronous Web-based learning to provide a learning environment conducive to higher order learning, reflection, and collaboration through the development and support of reflective, self-regulatory skills (Garrison, 2002). Identification of specific processes and strategies will assist those responsible for Web-based instruction to design and conduct courses which learners are more likely to successfully complete.

SELF-REGULATION

Self-regulation may be defined as the ability of learners to control the factors or conditions affecting their learning. Research indicates that learners' self-regulatory beliefs and processes are highly correlated with academic achievement (Zimmerman & Martinez-Pons, 1990; Zimmerman & Risemberg, 1997). Zimmerman and Kitsantas (1997) pointed out that in self-regulated learning, the student must incorporate a combination of cognitive, metacognitive, motivational, and behavioral processes to attain the highest possible level of academic achievement. Cognitively, they use effective learning strategies to comprehend and retain information. Metacognitively, they plan, set goals, and monitor and evaluate their performance. Motivationally, they learn how to self-motivate and take responsibility for their own successes and failures. They develop a high level of self-efficacy that leads to greater effort and persistence on tasks. Behaviorally, they seek help when needed and create optimal learning environments for studying. Throughout the entire process of self-regulation, they constantly monitor their progress, reflect, react, and adapt to feedback. Researchers have demonstrated that it is possible to teach self-regulatory behaviors that increase learners' achievement and enhance their sense of efficacy (Tuckman, 2001; Zimmerman, Bonner, & Kovich, 1996).

Although self-regulated learning has only been recently mentioned in the distance learning literature, it can provide a useful framework for understanding and dealing with many of the learning problems currently identified in the field. A Web-based learner's ability to self-regulate his or her own behavior clearly fits into Gibson's (1998) first (i.e., student factors) and second (i.e., situational factors) categories related to student retention identified earlier. However, a highly self-regulated learner will also be better equipped to deal effectively with negative educational system factors as well because of the ability to make adaptive learning adjustments.

Components of Self-regulation

The usefulness of self-regulation to improve Web-based distance learning is based on the fact that researchers have identified specific components that need to be addressed. Zimmerman (1994, 1998) presented a conceptual framework of self-regulation that consists of six underlying psychological dimensions that learners can self-regulate by employing specific processes. The psychological dimensions of self-regulation in Zimmerman's model and related research questions include motive (Why?), method (How?), time (When?), behavior (What?), physical environment (Where?), and social environment (With Whom?). Table 11.1 identifies these dimensions and provides examples of motivation and

TABLE 11.1

Self-Regulatory Dimensions and Related Motivation and Learning Strategies

Self-Regulatory Dimensions	Motivation and Learning Strategies
Motives (Why?)	Setting proximal, challenging but achievable goals, self-talk, and behavioral and cognitive intervention strategies dealing with emotions
Methods of learning (How?)	Elaboration and organizational learning strategies: Summarization, annotation, outline-formatted notes, higher level questions, elaborative interrogation, elaborative rehearsal, visual representation
Use of time (When?)	Dealing with procrastination and time management: Prioritizing tasks, planning and scheduling time, setting specific tasks for each study period, starting longer tasks early, focusing on more difficult tasks before easier tasks
Physical environment (Where?)	Environmental selection and restructuring: Ensuring the study environment is conducive to learning and restructuring or changing it as necessary
Social environment (With Whom?)	Help seeking: Knowing when help is needed, identifying potential sources of help, knowing how to obtain help (through which medium), knowing how to frame help request, and evaluate the help received
Performance (What?)	Observing, reflecting upon, judging, and reacting to present performance compared to short-term and long-term goals, making adjustments as necessary on the basis of self-assessment of learning

Note. From *Self-Regulation of Learning and Performance* (p. 8), by D. H. Schunk & B. J. Zimmerman (Eds.), 1994, Hillsdale, NJ. Copyright 1994. Adapted with permission.

learning strategies that can be taught to learners to develop their self-regulatory skills. Each component is identified and related to the distance learning literature. Some key self-regulatory skills that can be taught to learners either before they take a distance course or by embedding the skills within the course itself are suggested. Detailed information for how to teach these skills can be found in Dembo (2004).

Motive.   Motive addresses the question of why learners choose to learn, that is, their motivation for learning. Problems in motivation are the most frequently mentioned student characteristic influencing success in distance learning (Hofmann, 2003; Qureshi, Morton, & Antosz, 2002).

Pintrich and Schunk (2002) have identified three observable behaviors that can be used as indicators of motivation—active choice (i.e., what tasks learners decide to engage in), persistence (i.e., the willingness of learners to maintain behavior when tasks are difficult, challenging, or boring), and effort (i.e., how hard learners work on a task). Clark (2003) pointed out that each of these indices may play an important role in, or relate differently to, learning processes. For example, it is possible that active choice (e.g., enrollment) may be facilitated by optimistic expectations about scheduling and completing Web-based courses. However, this aspect of motivation deals with access, not learning. Delays in finishing Web-based courses and high dropout rates indicate the need for more research on persistence and effort in distance learning.

Salomon's (1984) research is important to consider in this regard. He found that learners who express a preference for instruction using media tend to expect that it will be a less demanding way to learn. This expectation results in lower investment of effort and lower achievement levels compared to instructional conditions that are perceived as more demanding (e.g., traditional instruction).

A major difference between successful and less successful individuals in any field or specialization is that successful individuals know how to motivate themselves even when they do not feel like performing a task, whereas less successful individuals have difficulty controlling their motivation. Therefore, less successful individuals are less likely to complete a task, more likely to quit, or complete a task at a lower level of proficiency. Although successful learners may not feel like completing required tasks, they learn how to motivate themselves to completion in order to maintain progress toward achieving their goals.

Several self-regulatory strategies can be used to develop and maintain these important motivational beliefs and behaviors. The first is goal setting. Research indicates that high achievers report using goal setting more frequently and more consistently than do low achievers (Zimmerman & Martinez-Pons, 1986). When individuals establish and attempt to attain personal goals, they are more attentive to instruction, expend greater effort, and increase their sense of efficacy when they see themselves making progress. It is difficult to be motivated to achieve without having specific achievement goals (Gollwitzer, Fujita, & Oettingen, 2004).

Goals direct attention, mobilize effort, increase persistence, and motivate strategy development. As students select and pursue goals, they are able to progress personally, gain feedback, and self-monitor their progress.

They become more self-motivated. Students with specific, challenging goals outperform those with general, easy, or no goals. Effective goals are short term (current) and ask learners to accomplish specific tasks today or, at the most, this week (longer term goals do not necessarily help performance). It is important that students have the ability to attain or at least approach the specific, challenging goal; it must not be out of reach and unrealistic for academic benefits to accrue (Locke & Latham, 2002).

Learning goals increase learning if learners believe that (a) the goals are possible to achieve with the time and resources available; (b) they have, or will acquire, the knowledge to achieve the goal; and (c) the goals are specific, explicit, and difficult. In addition, the more the skills and knowledge that students are learning are directly relevant to goal achievement, the more students will be motivated to invest maximum effort and to use effective learning strategies. This rule does not apply to highly novel learning tasks where "do your best" goals tend to be best for learning.

There is some evidence (Kanfer, Ackerman, Murta, Dugdale, & Nelson, 1994) that when learners face extraordinarily challenging tasks with a minimum of training and a great deal of motivation, "three C" goals (Concrete, Current and Challenging) may interfere with their learning. Except for highly novel and complex tasks, however, three C goals seem to help both learning and motivation. On the motivation side, Locke and Latham (2002) suggested that specific three C goals facilitate active choice by encouraging "relevant" activities for goal achievement; they encourage appropriate mental effort because adults need to adjust their effort to the level of the goal and people tend to persist in the face of distractions until they attain their goals.

Independent goal setting is an important element of Web-based learner autonomy. Curry et al. (1999), in a study of online learners, pointed out that in hypertext learning environments, specific proximal learning goals, whether set by the instructor or, preferably, by the students themselves, contributed significantly to efficient and effective learner navigation of the course content. Whipp and Chiarelli (2001) studied online learners in a teacher education course and found that, among other attributes, the ability to set specific learning goals and to devise and execute specific strategies to attain those goals, were important elements of student success.

In Web-based learning, self-selected goals can give the student a sense of control, as well as structure. There is generally minimal interaction with an instructor, and the pace at which material is covered will depend almost entirely on the individual learner. In order to set and maintain an appropriate pace, goal setting and self-monitoring must occur. The material to be covered must be broken down into monthly and weekly goals. Daily tasks and schedules need to be set up, adhered to, evaluated, reevaluated, and adjusted as necessary. These processes can be taught to learners and, through practice and reflection, acquired as elements of life-long learning skills.

A second self-regulatory strategy for motivation is self-verbalization or self-talk. Some of our speech motivates us to try new tasks and to persist in difficult situations; other self-talk is unproductive and inhibits our motivation to succeed. One of the most common forms of self-talk is verbal reinforcement or praise following desired behavior. Learners can be taught responses like: "Great! I did it!" or "I'm doing a great job concentrating on my readings!" Students who control their motivation by giving themselves rewards and punishments outperform students who do not use this control technique (Zimmerman & Martinez-Pons, 1986).

For learners prone to learning and test anxiety, there are elaborate cognitive-behavioral training programs available to help them control anxiety, mood, and other emotional responses (Clark, 2002). One such program, rational emotive therapy, attempts to teach individuals to recognize and change their irrational belief system (Ellis, 1998).

In summary, to control motivation, learners need to set goals, develop positive beliefs about their ability to perform academic tasks (self-efficacy), and maintain these beliefs while faced with the many disturbances, distractions, occasional failure experiences, and periodic interpersonal conflicts in their lives. This is especially critical for Web-based learners who lack the extrinsic support structures available to classroom-based learners. When learners realize they are responsible for their own motivation, they may be more willing to initiate strategies to control it.

Method.   Method addresses questions relating to *how* learners self-regulate learning. The key underlying process regulating method is the use of learning strategies. Learning strategies are the methods students use to acquire information. Research indicates that higher achieving students use more learning strategies than do lower achieving students (Zimmerman & Martinez-Pons, 1988). Learning strategies are significant factors for success in distance learning (Bonk & Dennen, 1999; Harris, 2003; Saba, 2004).

Weinstein and Mayer (1986) identified three different categories of learning strategies that learners must acquire. The first type, rehearsal strategies, can be effective for learning factual material. Copying, taking verbatim notes, reciting words or definitions are all examples of rehearsal strategies. Their limitation, however, is that they make few connections between new information and the knowledge that is already in long-term memory.

The second type, elaboration strategies, helps retention by linking new information with knowledge already in long-term memory. These strategies are useful for improving the recall of names, categories, sequences, or groups of items. Students in asynchronous Web-based learning work independently, without the direct assistance of peers and/or instructors. Therefore, it is important that they be able to monitor their own learning, to elaborate on it, and to organize it in order to recall it later and improve comprehension. There are several elaboration strategies that have proven effective for the integration and retention of new knowledge; summarization, annotation, outline-formatted notes, higher level questions, elaborative interrogation, and elaborative rehearsal (see Simpson & Nist, 2000, for a discussion of these comprehension strategies). All of these strategies are especially effective when learning from written text, the primary form of information transmission on the Internet, although they may also be employed with Web-delivered video and graphics.

The third category of learning strategies is organizational strategies (Weinstein & Mayer, 1986). These strategies help learners remember information by allowing them to structure academic content. Students can learn to structure content through visual representations like diagrams, matrices, sequences, and hierarchies (Dembo, 2004).

Visual representation of text material is helpful in improving comprehension of complex material. If synthesizing and elaborating information contained in complex expository texts is required, then visual representations can be used to increase comprehension of the material. Reading involves two processes; comprehension and retention. Just because reading material is comprehended does not mean that it will be retained. Additional steps such as visual representations improve comprehension of detailed material, and also improve retention and performance. When students are left primarily to themselves to read, comprehend, and retain material, as is the case in asynchronous Web-based learning, visual representations are especially helpful.

In summary, many learners who have difficulty in Web-based instruction may attribute their problem to a lack of ability when it actually may be that they have never been properly taught how to learn. Some students use one or two major learning strategies for all tasks in all courses. These students often do not have the necessary tools to learn the complex material they encounter in the courses they are required to take. It is imperative that Web-based learners be taught not only course content, but also how to most efficiently acquire that content.

Time.   The time dimension addresses questions relating to when and for how long to study. An essential element of distance learner success is the ability to effectively manage learning time (Loomis, 2000; Parker, 2003; Wang, Kanfer, & Hinn, 2001). This management is particularly important in asynchronous Web-based learning where learners must decide when to access the learning materials and how long to spend working with them.

In considering the causes of online learner dropouts, Cookson (2000) noted the inability to manage learning time as a primary factor. Gibson

(1998), in reviewing distance learner persistence studies, pointed out that a key construct relating to learners' persistence was their self-efficacy for learning at a distance, which was related to learners' perceptions of their ability to manage time effectively.

Tuckman (2002) studied procrastination in a Web-based course with many performance deadlines. He found that more serious procrastinators were more likely to utilize rationalizations, less likely to self-regulate, and earned lower grades. Marron (2000) reported that in a poll taken by a career Web site, greater than 90% of the 1,244 employees sampled surfed the Internet for information irrelevant to their jobs at work. Lavoie and Pychyl (2001) found that over half of their 208 subjects reported frequent Internet procrastination, which was positively correlated with trait procrastination and negative emotions. Their investigation was based on Postman's (1992) notion of technological bias, the misconception that the use of technology intrinsically allows for greater human efficiency. Postman argued that procrastination using the Internet may be easily justifiable to the user because the procrastination activity involves exposure to information. Procrastinators may believe that they are obtaining some value from their online activities even while procrastinating because of the incorrect belief that work was being accomplished.

Students who use their time efficiently are more likely to learn and/or perform better than students who do not have good time management skills. Self-regulated learners know how to manage their time because they are aware of deadlines, how long it will take to complete each assignment, and their own learning processes. They prioritize learning tasks, evaluating the more difficult from easier tasks in terms of the time required to complete them. They are aware of the need to evaluate how their study time is spent and to reprioritize as necessary. The greater such awareness is, the better time management skills will be, meaning that more material will be read, reviewed, and elaborated on (Zimmerman, Greenberg, & Weinstein, 1994; Zimmerman & Martinez-Pons, 1986). In this way, time management improves achievement.

Time management skills can be learned, and subsequent efforts by students to manage their study time does make a difference academically. As time management skills are refined, more time is spent on task, procrastination decreases, tasks are completed on time, and chances of academic achievement and success improve. Additionally, as use of time improves, individuals show increased intrinsic interest and enhanced personal perceptions of satisfaction with the specific task and with their performance overall (Kelly, 2002).

Learners need to acquire time management skills in order to manage interactions associated with the course (e.g., by setting aside time each day to check the course bulletin board and/or course e-mail). Because many

Web-based courses generate a large number of e-mails, learners need to set priorities in reading course related messages, that is, knowing when to skim for content as opposed to reading for detail, while respecting the individual (peer learner or instructor) who shared the information (Hill, 2001).

In asynchronous Web-based learning, goal setting, planning, and time management are often the sole responsibility of the student, who may have little interaction with either other students or the instructor. In order to successfully complete all assignments, acquire the necessary information, and attain their self-set learning goals, students in such settings need to be able to pace themselves, using time management skills to distribute learning and complete assigned work over time.

Physical Environment.   Physical environment concerns where learners learn and which instructional supports they employ. Zimmerman and Martinez-Pons (1986) found that high achievers reported greater use of environmental restructuring than did low-achieving students. Self-regulated learners are proactive in choosing where they will study and take appropriate steps to ensure that they have regulatory control over their learning environment. They are sensitive to their environment and resourceful in altering it as necessary.

In terms of physical space, Web-based learners generally have the option of accessing their courses via computers at home or elsewhere (e.g., library or computer lab). If they are working at home, they have the option of which room the computer is situated in—a quiet place such as a den or bedroom, or a louder more distracting environment, such as a living room or kitchen. If learners are unable to restructure their learning environment at home, they can access their course from a university or library computer. Learners must also ensure that they have access to and are proficient at using the equipment they require in order to study effectively, such as a computer of sufficient RAM and with the necessary software to access course materials, whether they be text, video, and/or graphic. Mastery of these elements contributes to the learner's control over the virtual space within which Web-based learning occurs.

As Web-based learners, through direct instruction and monitored practice, acquire the metacognitive skills of setting learning goals, monitoring learning progress, and evaluating learning goal attainment, they develop the ability to determine whether both their physical and virtual learning spaces are supportive of their learning or whether one and/or the other environments requires adjustment in order to facilitate more efficient goal attainment (Wang et al., 2001).

Social Environment.   Social environment refers to with whom the learner studies (Zimmerman, 1998). Active learners who are motivated to achieve tend to seek help when it is needed. Web-based learners must be able to determine where and how to seek help, and make decisions concerning the most appropriate sources for such help. When collaboration with other online learners or the instructor is required, learners need to know or to learn how to most efficiently interact in a Web-based environment.

Self-regulated learners are aware of the important role other people can play in their learning. If students are mastery oriented, goal directed, and have positive perceptions of their ability to achieve, then they are likely to seek help from social (i.e., instructors or classmates) or nonsocial sources (i.e., written sources or Web-based help functions) when faced with complex or difficult tasks. One of their distinguishing characteristics is their ability to seek academic assistance in an adaptive manner to optimize learning.

There are a number of motivational factors that could limit adaptive help-seeking behavior. The factors that appear to be most relevant for Web-based learning are the students' goal orientation, self-perceptions of ability, and desiring and valuing challenge and mastery of material rather than simply getting a good grade (Aleven, Stahl, Schworm, Fischer, & Wallace, 2003). Research suggests that the students who need help the most are generally the least likely to ask for it (Newman, 1994).

Because an element of asynchronous Web-based learning is social isolation, learners need to be proactive in employing the technology, through e-mail, chat rooms, bulletin boards, and any embedded help functions to lessen the social distance involved in their learning situation. Effective use of instructional technology systems requires that the learner be sufficiently motivated and self-regulated to effectively and efficiently utilize the features of the technology. In Web-based learning, this means that learners either have or mindfully develop their skills in using the specific elements of the technology that permit interaction with other learners and with instructors. In terms of help seeking, Newman (1994) noted that it is a key way that self-regulated learners exercise control over the learning process in order to achieve their learning goals. Self-regulated learners take action to focus and target their help-seeking requests in order to overcome any frustrations they encounter in meeting their objectives when it is needed or when faced with complex or difficult tasks. They know when help is needed, make the decision to seek help, identify sources of help, use appropriate strategies to obtain the help, and finally, they evaluate the help received (Aleven et al., 2003).

Hill (2001) presented several strategies and techniques that instructors and course designers can employ to develop a sense of community in Web-based learning environments. Such a sense of community assists Web-based instructors and learners build a learning environment that mitigates the social isolation of distance study and fosters shared learning activities, including mutual helping behaviors (Rovai, 2002). An emotionally "safe," comfortable online environment enables learners to communicate openly without fear of negative criticism. It is also important to provide as part of course structure both the means and the encouragement for learners to maintain regular contact with one another and with the instructor throughout the course. A well-organized, easily navigated, course structure and interface is also vital in facilitating and encouraging efficient interaction among course learners. Learners should also be provided with multiple means of accessing and sharing information. Given the relative novelty of Web-based learning, creation of a sense of adventure, a "we are all in this together," attitude among learners will encourage a sense of community (Hill, 2001). All of these strategies can foster an atmosphere where learners will be enabled to efficiently seek help from instructors and peers.

Performance.   Performance addresses questions relating specifically to overt behavior, or what learners do in pursuit of their learning goals. Self-regulated learners are aware of the learning outcomes they expect (have set for themselves), are sensitive to not having achieved those outcomes (if such is the case), and are able to adjust their behavior accordingly in order to make up for any behavioral deficiency in attaining their learning goals (Zimmerman, 1998). Successful distance learners largely choose their own learning goals and self-monitor and self-evaluate their learning performance, being able to effectively adjust their behavior based on feedback. The fact that successful students tend to be aware of how well they have done on a test, even before getting it back from an instructor, indicates the importance of monitoring performance (Zimmerman & Martinez-Pons, 1988). In most classrooms, the teacher assumes responsibility for monitoring students' performance. The task is determining how to shift from a teacher-directed to a learner-managed and controlled learning environment. Learning autonomy occurs when students learn how to regulate their own behaviors so they can control their performance outcomes.

Assisting learners to develop self-assessment strategies is one way to help them acquire this skill. Learners can be taught to regulate their learning performance through setting learning goals, monitoring learning progress, and evaluating learning. Initially, self-assessment checklists keyed to specific learning task goals can be given to learners to complete. As the course progresses, learners can be taught to develop their own daily progress logs and self-assessment checklists keyed to their learning goals and to employ them regularly during the monitoring and evaluation phases of their learning. Acquisition of these metacognitive strategies enhances development of learner autonomy and life-long learning skills (Clark & Shatkin, 2003; Kassop, 2003).

SUMMARY

Although an increasing number of students are enrolling in Web-based courses, dropout rates remain problematic. Many authors have identified the importance of autonomy, initiative, and self-discipline in Web-based learning and have identified learner characteristics that lead to failure or low achievement. Unfortunately, there are few models to guide educators in identifying learner problems and in providing successful remediation to overcome potential obstacles in successful completion of Web-based learning classes.

While there is a wealth of literature investigating the role of self-regulation in classroom-based learning, there is to date little literature concerning self-regulation in Web-based learning. However, the key learning processes involved in both types of learning are essentially the same regardless of how the learning content is delivered, face-to-face or at a distance via communications technologies.

Six important components of self-regulatory behavior and related motivation and learning strategies derived from classroom-based research have been identified and applied to Web-based learning. This model can be used both for identifying possible Web-based learner characteristics that can limit successful learning (i.e., prevention) and as a guide to developing intervention strategies to deal with learning problems. It is important that educators realize that low achieving students may lack important self-regulatory skills that must be taught either before enrolling in a Web-based course or while taking courses. The key point is that these skills can and must be directly taught to learners and acquired by them through guided practice.

REFERENCES

Aleven, V., Stahl, E., Schworm, S., Fischer, F., & Wallace, R. (2003). Help seeking and help design in interactive learning environments. *Review of Educational Research, 73*(3), 277–320.

Bandura, A. (1997). *Self-efficacy: The exercise of control*. New York: W. H. Freeman.

Boekaerts, M., Pintrich, P. R., & Zeidner, M. (Eds.). (2000). *Handbook of self-regulation*. San Diego: Academic Press.

Bonk, C. J., & Dennen, V. (1999). Learner issues with WWW-based systems. *International Journal of Educational Telecommunications, 5*, 410–411.

Clark, L. (2002). *SOS help for emotions: Managing anxiety, anger and depression*. Bowling Green, KY: SOS Programs & Parents Press.

Clark, P. G., & Shatkin, L. (2003, March/April). A new challenge for education: Addressing the needs of lifelong learners. *The Technology Source*. Retrieved August 30, 2004, from http://ts.mivu.org/

Clark, R. E. (2003). Research on web-based learning: A half-full glass. In R. Brunning, C. Horn, & L. M. Pytlikzillig, (Eds.), *Web-based learning: What do we know? Where do we go?* (pp. 1–22). Greenwich, CT: Information Age Publishers.

Cookson, P. (1990). *Persistence in distance education.* Retrieved August 30, 2004, from www-wbweb4.worldbank.org/disted/Teaching/Design/kn-01.html

Curry, J., Haderlie, S., Ku, T., Lawless, K., Lemon, M., & Wood, R. (1999). Specified learning goals and their effect on learners' representations of a hypertext reading environment. *International Journal of Instructional Media, 26*(1), 43–51.

Dembo, M. (2004). *Motivation and learning strategies for college success* (2nd ed.). Mahwah, NJ: Lawrence Erlbaum Associates.

Ellis, A. (1998). *How to control your anxiety before it controls you.* New York: Kensington.

Garrison, D. R. (2002, September). Cognitive presence for effective online learning. *The role of reflective inquiry, self-directed learning and metacognition.* Paper presented to the Sloan Asynronous Learning Network Invitational Workshop, Lake George, NY.

Garrison, D. R. (2003). Self-directed learning and distance education. In M. G. Moore & W. G. Anderson (Eds.), *Handbook of distance education* (pp.161–168). Mahwah, NJ: Lawrence Erlbaum Associates.

Gibson, C. C. (1998).The distance learner in context. In C. C. Gibson (Ed.), *Distance learners in higher education: Institutional responses for quality outcomes* (pp. 113–126). Madison, WI: Atwood.

Gollwitzer, P. M., Fujita, K., & Oettingen, G. (2004). Planning and the implementation of goals. In R. F. Baumeister & K. D. Vohs (Eds.), *Handbook of self-regulation: Research, theory and applications* (pp. 211–228). New York: Guilford.

Hara, N., & Kling, R. (2002). Students' distress with a web-based distance education course: An ethnographic study of participants' experiences. *Information, Communication & Society, 3*(4), 557–579.

Harris, V. (2003). Adapting classroom-based strategy instruction to a distance learning context. *TESL-EJ, 7*(2). Retrieved August 27, 2004, from http://www-writing.berkeley.edu/TESL-EJ/ej26/toc.html

Hill, J. R. (2001, April). *Building community in Web-based learning environments: Strategies and Techniques.* Paper presented at the Southern Cross University AUSWEB annual conference. Coffs Harbour, Australia.

Hofmann, J. (2003). Motivating online learners. *Learning Circuits.* Retrieved August 30, 2004, from www.learningcircuits.org/2003/aug2003/hofmann.htm

Kanfer, R., Ackerman, P. L., Murta, P. C., Dugdale, P., & Nelson, L. (1994). Goal setting, conditions of practice and task performance: A resource allocation perspective. *Journal of Applied Psychology, 79,* 826–835.

Kassop, M. (2003, May/June). Ten ways online education matches, or surpasses, face-to-face learning. *The Technology Source.* Retrieved August 30, 2004, from http://ts.mivu.org/

Kazmer, M., & Haythornthwaite, C. (2001). Juggling multiple social worlds: Distance students online and offline. *American Behavioral Scientist, 45,* 510.

Kelly, W. E. (2002). Harnessing the river of time: A theoretical framework for time use Efficiency with suggestions for counselors. *Journal of Employment Counseling, 39*(1), 12–21.

Kerlins, B. (1992). *Cognitive engagement style, self-regulated learning and cooperative learning.* Retrieved August 27, 2004, from http://kerlins.net/bobbi/research/myresearch/srl.html

Kjeldsen, T., Krogsdal, M. B., & Gomme, J. (2003). *Towards an operational definition of WBL*. Retrieved August 27, 2004, from www.ku.dk/wbl/om_WBL/WBL_definition_rev_25AUG03.pdf

Lavoie, J., & Pychyl, T. (2001). Cyberslacking and the procrastination superhighway: A web-based survey of online procrastination, attitude, and emotion. *Social Science Computer Review, 19*, 431–444.

Locke, E. A., & Latham, G. P. (2002). Building a practically useful theory of goal setting and task motivation. *American Psychologist, 57*, 705–717.

Loomis, K. D. (2000). Learning styles and asynchronous learning: Comparing the LASSI model to class performance. *Journal of Asynchronous Learning Networks, 4*(1). Retrieved August 30, 2004, from http://www.aln.org/publications/jaln/v4n1/index.asp

Major, H., & Levenberg, N. (1999). Learner success in distance education environments: A shared responsibility. *Commentary*. Retrieved August 30, 2004, from http://ts.mivu.org/default.asp?show=article&id=71

Marron, K. (2000, January 20). Attack of the cyberslackers. *The Globe and Mail*, p. T5.

Martinez, M. (2003). High attrition rates in e-learning: Challenges, predictors, and solutions. *The E-Learning Developers' Journal*. Retrieved August 30, 2004, from www.elearningguild.com

Mehrotra, C., Hollister, C. D., & McGahey, L. (2001). *Distance learning: Principles for effective design, delivery, and evaluation*. Thousand Oaks, CA: Sage.

Moore, M. G., & Kearsley, G. (1996). *Distance education: A systems view*. Belmont, CA: Wadsworth.

Newman, R. S. (1994). Adaptive help seeking: A strategy of self-regulated learning. In D. Schunk & B. Zimmerman (Eds.), *Self-regulation of learning and performance: Issues and educational applications* (pp. 283–301). Hillsdale, NJ: Lawrence Erlbaum Associates.

O'Regan, K. (2003). Emotion and e-learning. *Journal of Asynchronous Learning Networks, 7*(3). Retrieved August 30, 2004, from www.aln.org/publications/jaln/v7n3/pdf/v7n3_oregan.pdf

Parker, A. (2003). Identifying predictors of academic persistence in distance education. *USDLA Journal, 17*(1). Retrieved August 27, 2004, from www.usdla.org/html/journal/JAN03_Issue/article06.html

Phipps, R., & Merisotis, J. (1999). *What's the difference?: A review of contemporary research on the effectiveness of distance learning in higher education*. Washington, DC: The Institute for Higher Education Policy.

Pintrich, P. R., & Schunk, D. (2002). *Motivation in education: Theory, research, and applications* (2nd ed.). Upper Saddle River, NJ: Pearson.

Postman, N. (1992). *Technopoly: The surrender of culture to technology*. New York: Knopf.

Qureshi, E., Morton, L. L., & Antosz, E. (2002). An interesting profile—University students who take distance education courses show weaker motivation than on-campus students. *Online Journal of Distance Learning Administration, 5*(6). Retrieved August 30, 2004, from www.westga.edu/~distance/ojdla/winter54/Qureshi54.htm

Rovai, A. P. (2002). Building a sense of community at a distance. *International Review of Research in Open and Distance Learning*. Retrieved August 27, 2004, from www.irrodl.org/content/v3.1/rovai.html

Saba, F. (2004). Strategies to succeed in distance learning. *Distance-Educator.com*. Retrieved August 27, 2004, from www.westga.edu/~distance/ojdla/winter54/Qureshi54.htm

Salomon, G. (1984). Television is "easy" and print is "tough": The differential investment of mental effort in learning as a function of perceptions and attributions. *Journal of Educational Psychology, 76,* 647–658.

Simpson, M., & Nist, S. (2000). An update on strategic learning: It's more than textbook reading strategies. *Journal of Adolescent & Adult Literacy, 43,* 528–542.

Tuckman, B. W. (2001, April). *The effect of learning and motivation strategies training on college students' achievement.* Paper presented at the National Meeting of the American Educational Research Association, Seattle, WA.

Tuckman, B. W. (2002, April). *Academic procrastinators: Their rationalizations and web-course performance.* Paper presented at the Annual Meeting of the American Psychological Association, Chicago, IL.

Waits, T., & Lewis, L. (2003). *Distance education at degree-granting postsecondary Institutions: 2000–2001* (NCES 2003017). Washington, DC: National Center for Education Statistics.

Wang, C. X., Kanfer, A. & Hinn, D. M. (2001). Stretching the boundaries: Using ALN to reach off-campus students during an off-campus summer session. *Journal of Asynchronous Learning Networks, 5*(1). Retrieved August 30, 2004, from www.aln.org./publications/jaln/v5n1_arvan.asp

Weinstein, C. E., & Mayer, R. E. (1986). The teaching of learning strategies. In M. C. Wittrock (Ed.), *Handbook of research on teaching* (3rd ed.; pp. 315–327). New York: Macmillan.

Whipp, J. L., & Chiarelli, S. (2001). *Self-regulation in web-based courses for teachers.* Retrieved August 30, 2004, from http://edtech.connect.msu.edu/Searchaera2002/viewproposaltext.asp?propID=1696

Zimmerman, B. J. (1994). Dimensions of academic self-regulation: A conceptual framework for education. In D. H. Schunk & B. J. Zimmerman (Eds.), *Self-regulation of learning and performance* (pp. 3–21). Hillsdale, NJ: Lawrence Erlbaum Associates.

Zimmerman, B. J. (1998). Academic studying and the development of personal skill: A self-regulatory perspective. *Educational Psychologist, 33,* 73–86.

Zimmerman, B. J., Bonner, S., & Kovich, R. (1996). *Developing self-regulated learners: Beyond achievement to self-efficacy.* Washington, DC: American Psychological Association.

Zimmerman, B. J., Greenberg, D., & Weinstein, C. E. (1994). Self-regulating academic study time: A strategy approach. In D. H. Schunk & B. J. Zimmerman (Eds.), *Self-regulation of learning and performance* (pp. 181–199). Hillsdale, NJ: Lawrence Erlbaum Associates.

Zimmerman, B. J., & Kitsantas, A. (1997). Developmental phases in self-regulation: Shifting from process to outcome goals. *Journal of Educational Psychology, 89,* 29–36.

Zimmerman, B. J., & Martinez-Pons, M. (1986). Development of a structured interview for assessing student use of self-regulated learning strategies. *American Educational Research Journal, 23*(4), 614–628.

Zimmerman, B. J., & Martinez-Pons, M. (1988). Construct validation of a strategy model of student self-regulation. *Journal of Educational Psychology, 80,* 284–290.

Zimmerman, B. J., & Martinez-Pons. (1990). Student differences in self-regulated learning: Relating grade, sex, and giftedness to self-efficacy and strategy use. *Journal of Educational Psychology, 82,* 51–59.

Zimmerman, B. J., & Risemberg, R. (1997). Self-regulatory dimensions of academic learning and motivation. In G. D. Phye (Ed.), *Handbook of academic learning: Construction of knowledge* (pp. 105–125). San Diego, CA: Academic Press.

Chapter 12

The Importance of Motivation, Metacognition, and Help Seeking in Web-Based Learning

Sigmund Tobias
Teachers College, Columbia University

This chapter examines whether such student characteristics as motivation and interest, metacognition, and readiness to use help, such as auxiliary instructional resources, are differentially beneficial for student success in Web-based learning (WBL). Furthermore, the importance of studying the relationships among these variables in understanding individuals' learning in general, and especially their effects on outcomes in WBL is discussed.

Duffy and Kirkley (2004a, p. 3) described the rate of WBL development as "explosive" echoing the findings of others (NCES, 2003; Shea, Fredericksen, Pickett, & Pelz, 2004). In addition, the government, the military, and agencies in the health and professional sectors, among others, are also increasingly delivering WBL courses. WBL enables students in urban or rural environments who cannot travel to a campus for instruction to receive it. Such convenience is important to caregivers, students, and trainees, as well as to anyone working in unsatisfying positions who needs instruction but is unable to leave home to receive it. From the institution's perspective, WBL is cost effective because it does not require campus resources or human instructors, nor do organizations have to defray travel costs of sending employees to remote sites for training (Duffy & Kirkley,

2004b). These factors suggest that WBL development in both the public and private sector is likely to continue and perhaps increase for the future.

Despite its popularity, relatively little is known empirically about WBL, especially its effectiveness for students with different characteristics. The high student drop out rate from WBL (Bernard, Lou, & Abrami, 2003) suggests that learning from the Web is not ideal for all types of students. Phipps and Merisotis (1999) estimated attrition from WBL to be 32%, compared to only 4% in face-to-face settings. These attrition rates may be underestimates because drop out data are rarely available from commercial software vendors who portray their products in the most favorable terms.

High attrition from WBL also raises questions about the "typical" finding (Phipps & Merisotis, 1999; Lockee, Burton, & Cross, 1999; Russell, 1999) of no difference, or trivial differences (Bernard et al., 2003) between WBL and face-to-face instruction. Of course, such findings do not demonstrate the equivalence of the two because the null hypothesis cannot be proved. It should be noted that WBL achievement data might be inflated because students who drop out probably have more difficulties with their courses than those who persist. The attrition and achievement results indicate that WBL is not equally effective for all students and contribute to the widespread agreement among researchers (Bernard et al., 2003; Dillon & Gabbard, 1998; Hartley & Benddixen, 2001; Wisher& Champagne, 2000) that there is an urgent need to study the effectiveness of WBL for different types of students.

OVERVIEW

The effects of motivation on learning have been studied intensively in educational and training contexts, but much less frequently in WBL even though suggestive evidence indicates that motivation may be even more important in Internet settings. Sankaran and Bui (2001) found that motivation was the most important student characteristic related to achievement in WBL courses. Similar findings were reported by Oxford, Park-Oh, Ito, and Sumrall (1993). Another study (Shih & Gamon, 2001) found that motivation was the only characteristic significantly related to WBL achievement.

Motivation, like all affective characteristics, can affect learning only indirectly by engaging the cognitive and metacognitive processes controlling learning (Tobias, Galvin, & Michna, 2002). Clarifying the effects of cognitive variables on learning provides an understanding of how learning occurs; it is equally important to know why students choose and pursue different learning goals, that is, to understand people's motivation, as well as to study the relationships between cognitive and affective variables. Surprisingly the motivation–cognition or metacognition relationship has received little attention in WBL.

Metacognition is perhaps the most thoroughly investigated construct in contemporary instructional psychology. However, there has been little study of the effects of metacognition on WBL and the few existing studies (Hannafin & Hill, 1997; Land & Greene, 2000) are based on a handful of participants. The scarcity of such research is surprising especially because metacognition was demonstrated (Hill & Hannafin, 1997, p. 38) to be "fundamental to successful learning" in environments such as WBL where students work largely by themselves, often with requirements that may seem ambiguous and are not readily clarified, and where learners can easily lose their bearings (Beasley & Waugh, 1995) and become disoriented (Beasley, 1994; Hill, Hannafin, & Land, 1997) by the flood of information confronting them.

Suggestive findings indicate that students with "undirected" learning strategies, (Sankaran & Bui, 2001) learn poorly from WBL. Undirected was defined as students having problems processing and coping with large amounts of material and discriminating between important and unimportant content. Those results suggest that such students have ineffective metacognitive processes such as monitoring of learning, evaluating it, and selecting appropriate learning strategies. Clearly such metacognitive processes may be critical for success in WBL.

There has also been little study of the effect of WBL students' access to supplementary instructional resources, such as extra help, hints, examples, or "hot" buttons providing links to supplementary instructional resources. This chapter examines this issue and relates it to existing research on help seeking.

REVIEW OF THEORETICAL AND EMPIRICAL ISSUES

Research on motivational goal orientation and interest is reviewed, followed by studies of metacognition and metacognitive monitoring, and by a review of problems with students' self-reports of these processes. Finally, the importance of studying the interactions among these variables and their relationships with prior knowledge is discussed.

Motivation

It is generally agreed that motivation initiates, directs, and maintains the activities controlling learning. However, motivation must engage the cognitive and metacognitive processes controlling learning in order to affect it. Prior research, largely in classrooms, has studied motivation's effect on metacognition with self-reports usually defining both the independent and dependent variables. The limitations of such research are discussed later.

Many of the phenomena reviewed here have also been examined from the perspective of self-regulated learning (Boekaerts, Pintrich, & Zeidner, 2000; Hong, O'Neil, & Feldon, in press; O'Neil & Abedi 1996; Zimmermann, 2004), which may be seen as a combination of metacognitive and motivational processes (Winne & Perry, 2000). Typically that research also relies on self-report questionnaires or structured interviews. "Unpacking" these variables and examining the metacognitive and motivational components separately may lead to greater clarity in understanding their effects on learning.

Motivational Goal Orientation.   Motivational goal orientation has been at the center of motivational research for the last two decades. Motives are seen as stable dispositions to achieve or avoid specific outcomes, desires, or wishes that give rise to the adoption of various goals (Pintrich & Maehr, 2001); once the goals are accounted for, motivation has no residual effects (Elliot & Church, 1997). Motives may "arouse or activate certain types of goals, but the goals then serve to guide and direct behavior and achievement" (Pintrich & Maehr, 2001, p.16). In the most recent research on goal orientation, two types of goals, mastery and performance, have been identified and each has both approach and avoidance valences (Barron, Finney, Davis, & Owens, 2003; Elliot & McGregor 2001; Pintrich & Maehr, 2001; Zuscho & Pintrich, 2000).

Mastery approach goals describe students' desires to learn and understand, whereas the avoidance element portrays their hope to evade misunderstanding or completing a task incorrectly. Performance approach goals describe the desire to outdo others, whereas the avoidance valence focuses on evading the appearance of being less able than peers. It has been shown (Barron et al., 2003; Meece, Blumenfeld, & Hoyle, 1988; Pintrich, 2000) that more than one goal may be pursued simultaneously. Space constraints make a complete summary of this voluminous research impossible. Therefore, a recent project is described in detail followed by summaries of the results of similar studies.

Pintrich and Maehr (2001) reported two studies; the first conducted in actual college chemistry classrooms and the second involved college psychology students performing a mathematics task. Both studies used self-report measures to assess motivational goal orientation, cognitive and metacognitive strategies, and related variables. Performance approach goals had few negative and many positive outcomes, whereas performance avoidance goals were related to poor consequences in both studies. Interest was positively related to mastery approach goals in both studies and negatively related to mastery avoidance goals; performance approach goals had a positive impact on achievement whereas that of avoidance goals was negative. Despite some inconsistencies in the findings for the two performance approach goals, both types of avoidance goals reported use of surface strategies such as rehearsal. In contrast, and with some exceptions, students with high approach tendencies (mastery and performance) used deeper elaboration and organizational strategies than those high on avoidance. Mastery approach goals were positively related to self-reported metacognition; similarly, and surprisingly, so were all avoidance goals. The results for mastery avoidance goals were somewhat mixed, although both studies found that they led to more cognitive engagement and greater use of cognitive and metacognitive strategies than did performance goals. There were no interactions among goals.

Pintrich and Maehr's (2001) research paradigm and findings are typical of a great deal of goal orientation research. For example, mastery goals have been associated with self-reported intrinsic behavior (Elliot & Harackiewicz, 1996) and greater use of both cognitive and metacognitive strategies (Archer 1994; Ford, Smith, Weissbein, Gully, & Salas, 1998; Pintrich, 2000; Pintrich & Maehr, 2001; Schraw, Potenza, & Nebelsick-Gullet, 1993). On the other hand, performance goals typically led to negative attributions, use of superficial strategies, and failure avoidance behavior. Other researchers (Ablard & Lipschultz, 1998; Ames, 1992; Somuncuoglu & Yildirim, 1999) had similar findings. In a dissertation study (Stavrianopoulos, 2005), goal orientations were induced by instructions and assessed by questionnaire (Elliot & Church, 1997). The results indicated that neither instructions nor questionnaire responses affected students' metacognitive monitoring, raising questions about the effectiveness of varying goal orientation experimentally.

There is ample support for the impact of motivation generally, and the mastery orientation specifically on self-reported use of metacognitive processes in classroom learning contexts, although not in WBL. Mastery oriented students, compared to those with performance orientations, typically also use more cognitive strategies, have greater engagement in and enjoyment of learning activities, use deeper learning processes, and seek more challenging tasks than those with performance orientations. Performance approach goals have a positive impact on learning. On the other hand, performance avoidance goals lead to evading activities that could make students appear to be incapable, to seeking easy problems, and to using surface rather than deep processing strategies.

In summary, the results suggest that WBL may be differentially effective for students with mastery orientations, who tend to work on content until it is comprehended, and use "deeper" cognitive, metacognitive and organizational strategies. Performance avoidance oriented students tend to use shallower strategies, they compare themselves to their peers, and tend to learn more in classroom contexts where exceeding peers is more salient.

Interest

The impact of interest, or individuals' preferences for various activities, on learning, retention, and cognitive processing is important because results (Elliott & Church, 1997; Elliot & McGregor, 2001; Harackiewicz, Barron, & Elliot, 1998; Pintrich & Maehr, 2001) have shown a link between interest and mastery orientations. Because interest improves both learning and recall, and induces deeper processing (Boekaerts & Boscolo, 2002) adapting instruction to students' interests can improve learning. Results suggest (Tobias, 1994a) that about 20% of the variance in interest is attributable to prior knowledge indicating that prior knowledge should be assessed in interest research so that its unique contribution may be estimated. There are at least two types of interest (Renninger, Hidi, & Krapp, 1992). Situational interest is elicited by the novelty or intensity of situations, and the presence of different human interest factors contributing to the attractiveness of content. Topic interest refers to relatively enduring preferences for topics, tasks, or contexts.

There is very little research relating interest to metacognition. Tobias (1994b) found that including students' names in math problems, a procedure that had previously been found to enhance interest, also increased metacognitive accuracy. In a second study (Tobias, 1995), students for whom a text passage was expected to be more interesting made more accurate metacognitive assessments of their vocabulary knowledge than did others. McWhaw and Abrami (2001) found that students with high topic interest selected more main ideas and reported using more metacognitive strategies than did less interested students. Clearly, further research is needed that assesses both students' interests and prior knowledge and then examines their relationships to goal orientation, metacognition, and help seeking.

Metacognition

Metacognition may be defined as the ability to monitor, evaluate, and plan one's learning (Brown, 1980; Flavell, 1979). Metacognitive processes may be divided (Pintrich, Woters, & Baxter, 2000) into three components; knowledge about metacognition, monitoring of learning processes, and control of those processes, that is, self-regulation. Metacognition may be a hierarchical process in which monitoring of prior learning is a prerequisite for more complex metacognitive control processes (Tobias & Everson, 2000a, 2000b). If students cannot differentiate between what they know or do not know, they can hardly engage in more complex metacognitive activities that control learning directly.

Metacognitive control processes may be especially important in WBL because evaluating progress, selecting learning strategies, and planning may be more important than in classroom instruction where instructors and peers assist students with these activities. Findings (Tobias & Everson 2000a, 2002) indicate that metacognitive monitoring of prior knowledge is a crucial component for learning; that may be especially true in WBL where a great deal of new material must be acquired with relatively little external support. There, students who differentiate accurately between the known and unknown have an advantage because they can omit or skim the familiar and concentrate on the unknown. Less accurate students spend valuable, usually limited time on the familiar at the expense of the unknown and fall behind more accurate peers.

Metacognition is usually assessed by inferences from observations of performance, by interviews, or by self-report inventories (Schraw & Impara, 2000). Assessments based on observation are labor intensive (Royer, Cisero, & Carlo, 1993) because they require recording students' work, rating it for metacognitive processes, and obtaining and analyzing "think aloud" protocols. Self-report scales of metacognition (Everson, Hartman, Tobias, & Gourgey, 1991; Hong et al., in press; Jacobs & Paris, 1987; O'Neil & Abedi 1996; Pintrich, Smith, Garcia, & McKeachie, 1991; Schraw & Dennison, 1994) are less labor intensive but are subject to the problems discussed later.

Concerns Regarding Self-Reports of Motivation and Metacognition.
Self-report scales are easily administered and scored. Unfortunately, their use in assessing motivation or metacognition raises serious questions such as the following. Are students aware of the motivational or metacognitive processes used during learning? Because metacognition involves monitoring, evaluating, and coordinating cognitive processes, do students know, and can they recall, describe, and report these processes? Finally, do students report candidly on them?

In a series of studies using ethnographic interviewing coupled with grounded theory procedures, Pressley, Van Etten, Yokoi, Freebern, and Van Meter (1998) found that achieving good grades was an overarching goal of students rather than mastery of the material. "Students made it quite clear that all other goals were secondary" (p. 353). Students may check off mastery responses to questionnaires in research settings, and with the large number of participants often used in such studies, significant results may be obtained. However, that does not necessarily mean that mastery motivation is of major importance in their school work (Pressley et al., 1998).

Finally, data also raise questions about self-reports of metacognition. Tobias and Everson (1998) found low, nonsignificant relationships between

students' grade point average (GPA) and all scales of the Motivated Strategies Learning Questionnaire (MSLQ; Pintrich et al., 1991). In that study,
the Learning and Study Skills Inventory (LASSI; Weinstein, Palmer, &
Schulte, 1987) was also given and factor analyzed. None of the resulting factors correlated significantly with GPA. In contrast, the correlation between
grades and the metacognitive knowledge monitoring assessment (KMA), a
partially performance-based metacognitive task that is described further,
was significant. Furthermore, relationships between the KMA and the
self-report questionnaires were not significant, indicating that somewhat
different characteristics were being measured by the two assessment approaches. In another study (Tobias, Everson, & Laitusis, 1999) the KMA
had higher relationships with SAT scores than did either the LASSI or a
metacognitive self-report scale (Schraw & Dennison, 1994). In a review of
existing measures of metacognition, Pintrich et al. (2000), reported that the
KMA had higher relationships with external criteria than did any of the
other metacognitive assessments.

These findings suggest that results from self-reports of motivational goal
orientation or metacognition should be viewed with caution. These concerns stimulated the development of a procedure expected to be less subject to the problems of the other metacognitive assessments.

Assessing Metacognitive Knowledge Monitoring.   The KMA may be administered to groups, via computers, or over the Internet, and is objectively
scored. On the KMA students estimate their declarative or procedural
knowledge and are then tested on the same content. For example, participants check whether they know or do not know any of the words on a vocabulary list, or on a set of mathematical problems, and are then tested on the
same items. The hamann coefficient (Romesburg, 1984; Schraw, 1995) is
then computed to determine the accuracy of the estimates compared to
demonstrated knowledge on the test.

Research findings of some 25 studies to date (Tobias & Everson, 2000b,
2002; Tobias et al., 2002) have confirmed that the more accurate students'
knowledge estimates are, compared to test performance, the better their
metacognition. Among elementary school students the KMA was highly related to reading ability and learning of mathematics (Tobias & Everson,
2000b, 2002). Moderate relationships were found between the KMA and
both prior and future college grades, and with grades for vocational high
school students (Everson & Tobias, 2001). Learning disabled students or
those with attention deficit disorders were less accurate knowledge monitors than are regular students (Tobias & Everson, 2000b), and high school
dropouts were less accurate than continuing students (Gerrity & Tobias,
1996). Interest was found to (Tobias, 1994a, 1995) enhance monitoring accuracy, whereas test or mathematics anxiety (Everson, Smodlaka, & Tobias,

1994; Nathan & Tobias, 2000) lowered it. Accurate monitors required less external feedback (Seignon & Tobias, 1996) for the correctness of answers to a cloze task than less accurate peers, presumably because of their internal confirmation of answer correctness.

In summary, research in classrooms demonstrated considerable generality for the KMA over a variety of populations including elementary, junior, vocational, and regular high school, and college students. Also, similar results were obtained using KMAs in various domains including vocabulary, verbal analogies, mathematical calculation and word problems, and scientific terms associated with oceanography. The KMA's construct validity was supported by consistent and significant positive relationships with reading comprehension, mathematics achievement, learning, scholastic aptitude, and GPAs (concurrently and predictively). There have been no prior KMA studies of WBL.

The KMA paradigm is similar to methods used in research on metamemory (Koriat, 1993; Nelson & Nahrens, 1990), and reading comprehension (Glenberg, Sanocki, Epstein, & Morris, 1987). Because the KMA does not require self-reports of cognitive processes, it is less likely to be affected by the difficulties of other metacognitive appraisals, probably contributing to the reported (Pintrich et al., 2000) superiority of the KMA compared to other metacognitive assessments.

Help Seeking Research

"Those who sought help were denigrated as dependent, and the act of relying on others was considered the antithesis of what it means to strive for excellence .... That view has changed dramatically, however, with the recognition of help seeking's strategic value in the learning process" (Karabenick, 1998, p. 1). Nelson Le Gall's research (1981) was important in changing those views. She found that seeking help was an important skill and differentiated between two types of assistance. Instrumental help is the assistance (e.g., prompts, hints) necessary to complete tasks independently and has long-term strategic value by increasing future competence and independence. In contrast, executive help assists students in solving immediate problems but does not decrease their future dependence. Most help seeking research was conducted in classrooms although Aleven, Stahl, Schworm, Fischer, and Wallace (2003) reviewed a number of such studies in interactive learning environments, including WBL. Their review suggests that "an increasing number of studies provide evidence that learners often do not use help functions very effectively or even ignore them totally" (p. 278).

In classrooms, help seeking research has been conducted largely with self-report scales. Some studies (e.g., Butler, 1998) used both self-reports and observations; others were based largely on observation—although these usually occurred in elementary schools (e.g., Nelson-Le Gall & Jones, 1990). Results indicate (Karabenick, 1998) that mastery students seek more needed assistance whereas students with performance avoidance orientations often do not seek help fearing that it makes them seem incompetent. Paradoxically, those needing help most are least likely to seek it (Aleven et al., 2003; Karabenick & Knapp, 1988; Newman & Goldin, 1990). Students often avoid seeking help because of perceived threats to self-esteem and fears of embarrassment (Karabenick & Knapp, 1991; Newman, 1990; Newman & Schwager, 1993).

Arbreton's study (1998) is similar to much help seeking research. She administered a scale assessing executive and instrumental help seeking, help avoidance, and students' goal orientations. Multiple regression analysis found that the orientations had significant impact on self-reports of seeking help. The highest significant relationships were between learning focus (similar to mastery) and instrumental help seeking whereas ability focus (similar to performance) had low correlations with executive help seeking.

Help seeking research results indicate, with some exceptions, that performance avoidance students feel that seeking assistance reflects negatively on them, whereas mastery oriented students are less prone to report such threats. Thus, it is not surprising that mastery oriented students seek more help, especially instrumental assistance, than their performance oriented peers who, when they do seek it, are more likely to look for executive help. Aleven et al. (2003) indicated that students who sought help in WBL tended to be more successful than those who did not.

Seeking assistance is composed of two hierarchical components. First, students must recognize making a mistake, having a misconception, or hitting a learning impasse. Second, they must try to overcome the problem with help. Virtually all help seeking research has investigated only the motivational component; awareness of error has received little explicit study. Most of the KMA help seeking studies, reviewed later, also did not specifically investigate students' metacognitive awareness of a learning problem. The failure to study students' metacognitive realization of a learning impasse is important because assistance may be sought for social reasons, out of idle curiosity, or to escape from the task at hand, rather than to clarify misconceptions. Clearly, students' recognition of an impasse should be addressed explicitly in future research.

KMA and Help Seeking. Five studies related metacognitive knowledge monitoring to help seeking by letting students obtain assistance after completing a multiple choice test. A correct definition and use of the word in a sentence provided help in two vocabulary based studies. In three mathematics studies, help provided the correct answer and the steps needed to derive it.

Romero and Tobias (1996) found that accurate monitors sought more needed help, that is, on words estimated to be unknown. Less accurate students asked for more help when it was not needed, that is, on items estimated as known. In a succeeding study using math problems (Tobias & Everson, 1998) accurate knowledge monitors sought more help than others on two types of items where it seemed to be needed; those originally estimated as soluble and failed on the test; here, help probably assisted students to find the reasons for wrong estimates; and those estimated to be insoluble and failed on the test. Another study (Nathan & Tobias, 2000) also used mathematical problems and found that math anxiety correlated negatively with monitoring accuracy. Anxious students sought more unnecessary help, that is, on items passed on test. Monitoring accuracy and necessary review correlated positively in a control group not subjected to stress instructions, although that result failed to reach significance because of the few cases in that group. A negative relationship between help and monitoring accuracy for those getting stress instructions before a math test suggested that accurate knowledge monitors were least strategic in their help seeking.

In general, the KMA help seeking studies found that accurate monitors tended to seek more necessary help. There were some inconsistent results attributable to some differences among the studies. Help appeared on the same page as the test in four studies and was obscured by yellow tabs, a potentially troublesome procedure because students could "cheat" by peeking under the tabs covering the assistance. Stavrianopoulos (2005) gave the KMA by computer, making "cheating" impossible, and found that accurate students recognized significantly more nonwords and sought help more strategically than others. Specifically, more assistance was sought on words estimated as unknown and failed on test, and fractionally more help on items estimated as known and failed on test, presumably to correct misconceptions.

Most of the KMA help seeking studies ignored the motivational component, whereas help seeking research in classrooms has ignored the metacognitive component. Clearly both variables should be studied in order to have an accurate picture of students' help seeking.

SUGGESTIONS FOR FURTHER RESEARCH

The findings document the importance of metacognitive and motivational variables for learning generally and for WBL specifically, although very few studies examined both variables simultaneously other than by self-report scales. Studying cognitive or metacognitive variables in the absence of motivation is analogous to clarifying different machine components without studying the energy sources that make it work. Examination of the joint effects of both variables is especially important in WBL where knowing why individuals chose to receive instruction over the Internet, and understanding the variables leading to success are equally important. Investigating both motivational and metacognitive variables in studies of seeking help is especially important because the metacognitive recognition of a learning impasse, not generally investigated, must precede the desire to overcome the problem.

There are few studies of metacognition or motivation in WBL, and they often use questionnaires developed for that investigation that have unknown construct validity, and often unknown reliability as well. Motivational research in WBL would profit from studies employing the motivational goal orientation perspective, especially because the scales to assess it are widely used and their construct validity and reliability are well known (Barron et al., 2003; Pastor, Barron, Miller, & Davis, 2004). Motivational orientation seems especially important in students' learning from the Internet because they often work in isolation without the social support of instructors or fellow students. In WBL, students may feel more anonymity than they do in classes, hence performance oriented students should feel that seeking assistance poses little threat to their self-esteem, a finding reported by Schofield (1995) in computer-based learning environments.

Metacognition has been investigated even less frequently in WBL than motivation. That scarcity is also surprising because students' ability to organize and evaluate what they have learned, and their selection of effective strategies are likely to be more important in WBL than during face-to-face instruction where students can turn to both instructors and to peers for help.

Understanding learning, especially in WBL, probably also requires consideration of the effects of students' prior knowledge (Shapiro, 2004), in addition to motivation and metacognition. Furthermore, clarification of students' help seeking during instruction, and the types of help sought are probably also affected by their prior knowledge. Aleven, et al. (2003) concluded that students "with low prior knowledge—those who need help the most—are least likely to use help appropriately when help is under student control" (p. 298). It has been suggested (Tobias, 1989a) that such students need instructional support most in order to succeed, but Aleven, et al's. review suggests that they are least likely to seek it voluntarily. In a computer assisted instructional context, it was found (Tobias, 1989b) that students with comprehension problems and limited prior knowledge performed optimally when they were required to review their reading. Perhaps studies varying optional and mandated help for students with different levels of prior domain knowledge may also be helpful in WBL. Fletcher and Tobias (in press) also document the importance of prior knowledge in multimedia learning environments.

Findings that students with limited prior knowledge seek help less often than others seem similar to the results relating goal orientation to help seeking. Because mastery oriented students typically learn more than their performance oriented peers, they are more likely to have high prior knowledge and seek more help. An intriguing finding reported by Dochy, Segers, and Buehl (1999) is that high interest can compensate for low prior knowledge, perhaps because highly interested students may work harder than those with lower interest, a finding that should also be investigated in WBL contexts.

The results point to the importance of examining interest, metacognition, goal orientation, and prior knowledge simultaneously in studies dealing with student characteristics and WBL. Such research may clarify both the variables accounting for success in WBL and make it possible to identify the types of students who may profit maximally from Internet-based instruction. Furthermore, research combining these variables is equally scarce in studies of instruction generally and, therefore, will also clarify the effects of the interaction of these variables on the outcomes of learning in varying contexts.

REFERENCES

Ablard, K., & Lipschultz, R. E. (1998). Self–regulated learning in high-achieving students: Relations to advanced reasoning, achievement goals, and gender. *Journal of Educational Psychology, 90*, 94–101.

Aleven, V., Stahl, E., Schworm, S., Fischer, F., & Wallace, R. (2003). Help seeking and help design in interactive learning environments. *Review of Educational Research, 73*, 277–320.

Ames, C. (1992). Classroom: Goals, structures, and student motivation. *Journal of Educational Psychology, 84*, 261–271.

Arbreton, A. (1998). Student goal orientation and help-seeking strategy use. In S. A. Karabenick (Ed.), *Strategic help seeking: Implications for learning and teaching* (pp. 95–116). Mahwah, NJ: Lawrence Erlbaum Associates.

Archer, J. (1994). Achievement goals as a measure of motivation in university students. *Contemporary Educational Psychology, 19*, 430–446.

Barron, K. E., Finney, S. J., Davis, S. L., & Owens, K. M. (2003) *Achievement goal pursuit: Are different goals activated and more beneficial in different types of academic situations?* Paper presented at the annual convention of the American Educational Research Association, Chicago, IL.

Beasley, R. E. (1994). *The effects of three browsing devices on learner structural knowledge, achievement, and perceived disorientation in a hierarchically organized hypermedia environment.* Unpublished doctoral dissertation, University of Illinois, Urbana-Champaign.

Beasley, R. E., & Waugh, M. L. (1995). Cognitive mapping architectures and hypermedia disorientation: An empirical study. *Journal of Educational Multimedia and Hypermedia, 4*, 239–255.

Bernard, R. M., Lou, Y., & Abrami, P. C. (2003, April). *Is distance education equivalent to classroom instruction? A meta-analysis of the empirical literature*. Paper presented at the annual convention of the American Educational Research Association, Chicago IL.

Boekaerts, M., Pintrich, P. R., & Zeidner, M. (Eds.). (2000). *Handbook of self-regulation*. San Diego: Academic Press.

Boekaerts, M., & Boscolo, P. (2002). Interest in learning, learning to be interested. *Learning and Instruction, 12*, 375–382.

Brown, A. L. (1980). Metacognitive development and reading. In R. J. Spiro, B. B. Bruce, & W. F. Brewer (Eds.), *Theoretical issues in reading comprehension* (pp. 453–481). Hillsdale, NJ: Lawrence Erlbaum Associates.

Butler, R. (1998). Determinants of help seeking: Relations between perceived reasons for classroom help-avoidance and help-seeking behaviors in an experimental context. *Journal of Educational Psychology, 90*, 630–643.

Dillon, A., & Gabbard, R. (1998). Hypermedia as an educational technology: A review of the quantitative research literature on learner comprehension, control, and style. *Review of Educational Research, 68*, 322–349.

Dochy, F. J. R. C., & Seeger, S. M. S. R. (1997). *The effects of prior knowledge and its assessment on learning in classroom practice*. Keynote address presented at the Deustche Gesellschaft fuer Psychologie Conference, Frankfurt, Germany.

Dochy, F., Segers, M., & Buehl, M. (1999). The relation between assessment practices and outcomes of studies: The case of research on prior knowledge. *Review of Educational Research, 69*, 145–186.

Duffy, T. M., & Kirkley, J. R. (2004a). Introduction: Theory and practice in distance education. In T. M. Duffy & J. R. Kirkley (Eds.), *Learner centered theory and practice in distance education: Cases from higher education* (pp. 3–13). Mahwah, NJ: Lawrence Erlbaum Associates.

Duffy, T. M., & Kirkley, J. R. (2004b). Learning theory and pedagogy applied in distanced learning: The case of Cardean University. In T. M. Duffy & J. R. Kirkley (Eds.), *Learner centered theory and practice in distance education: Cases from higher education* (pp. 107–141). Mahwah NJ: Lawrence Erlbaum Associates

Elliot, A. J., & Church, M. (1997). A hierarchical model of approach and avoidance achievement motivation. *Journal of Personality and Social Psychology, 72*, 218–232.

Elliot, A. J., & Harackiewicz, J. M. (1996). Approach and avoidance achievement goals and intrinsic motivation: A mediational analysis. *Journal of Personality and Social Psychology, 70*, 461–475.

Elliot, A. J., & McGregor, H. A. (2001). A 2 × 2 achievement goal framework. *Journal of Personality and Social Psychology, 3*, 501–519.

Everson, H. T., Hartman, H., Tobias, S., & Gourgey, A. (1991, June). *A metacognitive reading strategies scale: Preliminary validation evidence*. Paper presented at the annual convention of the American Psychological Society, Washington, DC.

Everson, H. T., Smodlaka, I., & Tobias, S. (1994). Exploring the relationship of test anxiety and metacognition on reading test performance: A cognitive analysis. *Anxiety, Stress, and Coping, 7*, 85–96.

Everson, H. T., & Tobias, S. (2001). The ability to estimate knowledge and performance in college: A metacognitive analysis. In H. J. Hartman (Ed.), *Metacognition in learning and instruction: Theory, research and practice* (pp. 69–83). Amsterdam: Kluwer.

Flavell, J. (1979). Metacognition and cognitive monitoring: A new area of cognitive developmental inquiry. *American Psychologist, 34*, 906–911.

Fletcher, J. D., & Tobias, S. (in press). The multimedia principle. In R. Mayer (Ed.), *Cambridge handbook of multimedia learning*. New York: Cambridge University Press.

Ford, J. K., Smith, E. M., Weissbein, D. A., Gully, S. M., & Salas, E. (1998). Relationship of goal orientation, metacognitive activity, and practice strategies with learning outcomes and transfer. *Journal of Applied Psychology, 83*, 218–233.

Gerrity, H., & Tobias, S. (1996, October). *Test anxiety and metacognitive knowledge monitoring among high school dropouts*. Paper presented at the annual convention of the Northeastern Educational Research Association, Ellenville, NY.

Glenberg, A. M., Sanocki, T., Epstein, W., & Morris, C. (1987). Enhancing calibration of comprehension. *Journal of Experimental Psychology: General, 166*, 119–136.

Hannafin, M. J., Hill, J. R., & Land, S. (1997). Student centered learning and interactive multimedia: Status, issues, and implications. *Contemporary Education, 68*, 94–99.

Harackiewicz, J. M., Barron, K. E., & Elliot, A. J. (1998). Rethinking achievement goals: When are they adaptive for college students and why? *Educational Psychologist, 33*, 1–21.

Hartley, K., & Bendixen, L. D. (2001). Educational research in Internet age: Examining the role of individual characteristics. *Educational Researcher, 30*(9), 22–26.

Hill, J. R., & Hannafin, M. J. (1997). Cognitive strategies and learning from the World Wide Web. *Educational Technology, Research and Development, 45*, 37–64.

Hong, E., O'Neil, H. F., Jr., & Feldon, D. (in press). Gender effects on mathematics achievement: Mediating role of state and trait self-regulation. In A. M. Gallagher & J. C. Kaufman (Eds.), *Mind the gap: Gender differences in mathematics*. Cambridge: Cambridge University Press.

Jacobs, J. F., & Paris, S. G. (1987). Children's metacognition about reading: Issues in definition, measurement, and instruction. *Educational Psychologist, 22*, 255–278.

Karabenick, S. A. (1998). Help seeking as a strategic resource. In S. Karabenick (Ed.), *Strategic help seeking: Implications for learning and teaching* (pp. 1–12). Mahwah, NJ: Lawrence Erlbaum Associates.

Karabenick, S. A., & Knapp, S. R. (1988). Help seeking and the need for academic assistance. *Journal of Educational Psychology, 83*, 221–230.

Koriat, A. (1993). How do we know that we know? The accessibility model of the feeling of knowing. *Psychological Review, 100*, 609–639.

Land, S. M., & Greene, B. A. (2000). Project-based learning with the World Wide Web: A qualitative study of resource integration. *Educational Technology, Research and Development, 48*, 45–67.

Lockee, B. B., Burton, J. K., & Cross, L. H. (1999). No Comparison: Distance education finds a new use for "No Significant Difference." *Educational Technology Research and Development, 47*, 33–42.

McWhaw, K., & Abrami, P. C. (2001). Student goal orientation and interest: Effects on students' self-regulated learning strategies. *Contemporary Educational Psychology, 26*, 311–329.

Meece, J. L., Blumenfeld, P. C., & Hoyle, R. H. (1988). Students goal orientations and cognitive engagement in classroom activities. *Journal of Educational Psychology, 80*, 514–523.

Nathan, J., & Tobias, S. (2000, August). *Metacognitive knowledge monitoring: Impact of anxiety*. Paper presented at the annual meeting of the American Psychological Association, Washington, DC.

National Center for Educational Statistics. (2003). *Distance education at degree-granting post-secondary educational institutions: 2000–2001*. Retrieved August 31, 2004, from http://nces.ed.gov/pubsearch/pubsinfol.asp?pubid=2000013

Nelson-Le Gall, S. (1981). Help-seeking: An understudied problem-solving skill in children. *Developmental Review, 1*, 224–246.

Nelson-Le Gall, S., & Jones, E. (1990). Cognitive-motivational influences on children's help-seeking. *Child Development, 61*, 581–589.

Nelson, T. O., & Nahrens, L. (1990). Metamemory: A theoretical framework and new findings. In G. H. Bower (Ed.), *The psychology of learning and motivation* (pp. 125–173). New York: Academic Press.

Newman, R. S. (1990). Children's help seeking in the classroom: The role of motivational factors and attitudes. *Journal of Educational Psychology, 82*, 71–80.

Newman, R. S., & Schwager, M. T. (1993). Student's perceptions of the teacher and classmates in relation to reported help seeking in math class. *Elementary School Journal, 94*, 3–17.

O'Neil, H. F., Jr. (1991, August). *Metacognition: Teaching and measurement.* Paper delivered at the annual convention of the American Psychological Association, San Francisco, CA.

O'Neil, H. F., Jr., & Abedi, J. (1996). Reliability and validity of a state metacognitive inventory: Potential for alternative assessment. *Journal of Educational Research, 89*, 234–245.

Oxford, R., Park-Oh, Y., Ito, S., & Sumrall, M. (1993). Factors affecting achievement in a satellite-delivered Japanese language program. *The American Journal of Distance Education, 7*, 11–25.

Pastor, D. R., Barron, K. E., Miller, B. J., & Davis, S. L. (2004, April). *College students' achievement goal profiles.* Paper presented at the annual convention of the American Educational Research Association, San Diego, CA.

Phipps, R. A., & Merisotis, J. O. (1999). *What's the difference? A review of contemporary research on the effectiveness of distance learning in higher education.* Washington, DC: The Institute of Higher Education Policy.

Pintrich, P. R. (2000). Multiple goals, multiple pathways: The role of orientation in learning and achievement. *Journal of Educational Psychology, 92*, 544–555.

Pintrich, P. R., & Maehr, M. L. (2001, April). *Motives, goals, and context: Sources for motivation, self-regulation, and achievement.* Paper presented at the convention of the American Educational Research Association, Seattle, WA.

Pintrich, P. R., Smith, D. A., Garcia, T., & McKeachie, W. J. (1991). *A Manual for the Use of the Motivated Strategies for Learning Questionnaire (MSLQ).* Ann Arbor, MI: National Center for Research to Improve Postsecondary Teaching and Learning.

Pintrich, P. R., Woters, C. A., & Baxter, G. P. (2000). Assessing metacognition and self regulated learning. In G. Schraw & J. C. Impara (Eds.), *Issues in the measurement of metacognition* (pp. 43–98). Lincoln, NE: Buros.

Pressley, M., Van Etten, S., Yokoi, L., Freebern, G., & Van Meter, P. (1998). The metacognition of college studentship: A grounded theory approach. In D. Hacker, J. Dunlosky, & A. G. Grasses (Eds.), *Metacognition in educational theory and practice* (pp. 347–366). Mahwah, NJ: Lawrence Erlbaum Associates.

Renninger, K. A., Hidi, S., & Krapp, A. (1992). *The role of interest in learning and development.* Hillsdale, NJ: Lawrence Erlbaum Associates.

Romesburg, H. C. (1984). *Cluster analysis for researchers.* London: Wadsworth, Inc.

Romero, R., & Tobias, S. (1996, October). *Knowledge monitoring and strategic study.* Paper presented at annual convention of the Northeastern Educational Research Association, Ellenville, NY.

Royer, J. M., & Cisero, C. A., & Carlo, M. (1993). Techniques and procedures for assessing cognitive skills. *Review of Educational Research, 63*, 201–243.

Russell, T. L. (1999). *The no significant differences phenomenon.* Chapel Hill, NC: North Carolina State University.

Sankaran, S. R., & Bui, T. (2001). Impact of learning strategies and motivation on performance: A study in Web-based instruction. *Journal of Instructional Psychology, 28,* 191–201.

Schofield, J. W. (1995). *Computers and classroom culture.* New York: Cambridge University Press.

Schraw, G. (1995). Measures of feeling of knowing accuracy: A new look at an old problem. *Applied Cognitive Psychology, 9,* 329–332.

Schraw, G., & Dennison, R. S. (1994). Assessing metacognitive awareness. *Contemporary Educational Psychology, 19,* 460–475.

Schraw, G., & Impara, J. C. (2000). *Issues in the measurement of metacognition.* Lincoln, NE: Buros.

Schraw, G., Potenza, M., & Nebelsick-Gullet, L. (1993). Constraints on the calibration of performance. *Contemporary Educational Psychology, 18,* 455–463.

Seignon, N., & Tobias, S. (1996, April). *Metacognitive knowledge monitoring and need for feedback.* Paper presented at the annual meeting of the American Educational Research Association, New York, NY.

Shapiro, A. S. (2004). How including prior knowledge as a subject variable may change outcomes of learning research. *American Educational Research Journal, 41,* 159–189.

Shea, P. J., Fredericksen, E. E., Pickett, A. M., & Pelz, W. E. (2004). Faculty development, student satisfaction, and reported learning in the SUNY learning network. In T. M. Duffy & J. R. Kirkley (Eds.), *Learner centered theory and practice in distance education: Cases from higher education* (pp. 343–377). Mahwah, NJ: Lawrence Erlbaum Associates.

Shih, C. C., & Gamon, J. (2001). Web-based learning: Relationships among student motivation, attitude, learning styles, and achievement. *Journal of Agricultural Education, 42,* 12–20.

Somuncuoglu, Y., & Yildirim, A. (1999). Relationship between achievement goal orientations and use of learning strategies. *Journal of Educational Research, 92,* 267–277.

Stavrianopoulos, K. (2005). *Relationship between achievement goal orientations, knowledge monitoring and academic help seeking.* Unpublished doctoral dissertation, Fordham University, New York.

Tobias, S. (1989a). Another look at research on the adaptation of instruction to student characteristics. *Educational Psychologist, 24,* 213–227.

Tobias, S. (1989b). Using computers to study consistency of cognitive processing of instruction. *Computers in Human Behavior, 5,* 107–118.

Tobias, S. (1994a). Interest, prior knowledge, and learning. *Review of Educational Research, 64,* 37–54.

Tobias, S. (1994b, April). *Interest and metacognition in word knowledge and mathematics.* Paper presented at the annual convention of the American Educational Research Association, New Orleans, LA.

Tobias, S. (1995). Interest and metacognitive word knowledge. *Journal of Educational Psychology, 87,* 399–405.

Tobias, S., & Everson, H. T. (1998, April). *Research on the assessment of metacognitive knowledge monitoring.* Paper presented at the annual convention of the American Educational Research Association, San Diego, CA.

Tobias, S., & Everson, H. T. (2000a). Cognition and metacognition. *Educational Issues, 6,* 167–173.

Tobias, S., & Everson, H. T. (2000b). Assessing metacognitive knowledge monitoring. In G. Schraw & J. C. Impara (Eds.), *Issues in the measurement of metacognition* (pp. 147–222). Lincoln, NE: Buros.

Tobias, S., & Everson, H. T. (2002). *Knowing what you know and what you don't: Further research on metacognitive knowledge monitoring.* (College Board Research Report No. 2002-3). Retrieved from http://iume.tc.columbia.edu/downloads/tobias/CBR2001-3.pdf

Tobias, S., Everson, H. T., & Laitusis, V. (1999, March). *Towards a performance based measure of metacognitive knowledge monitoring: Relationships with self-reports and behavior ratings.* Paper presented at the annual meeting of the American Educational Research Association, Montreal, Canada.

Tobias, S., Galvin, K., & Michna, G. (2002, April). *Metacognition, motivation, and help seeking.* Paper presented at the annual meeting of the American Educational Research Association, New Orleans, LA.

Weinstein, C. E., Palmer, D. R., & Schulte, A. C. (1987). *LASSI: Learning and study strategies inventory.* Clearwater, FL: H & H Publishing.

Winne, P. H., & Perry, N. E. (2000). Measuring self-regulated learning. In M. Boekaerts, P. H. Pintrich, & M. Zeidner (Eds.), *Handbook of self-regulation* (pp. 531–566). San Diego, CA: Academic Press.

Wisher, R., & Champagne, A. (2000). Distance learning training systems. In S. Tobias & J. D. Fletcher (Eds.), *Training and retraining: A handbook for business, industry, government, and the military* (pp. 385–409). New York: Macmillan.

Zimmerman, B. J. (2004). Sociocultural influences and students' development of academic self-regulation: A social-cognitive perspective. In D. M. McInerney & S. Van Etten (Eds.), *Big theories revisited* (pp. 139–164). Greenwich, CT: Information Age.

Zuscho, A., & Pintrich, P. R. (2000, April). *Fear of not learning? The role of mastery avoidance goals in Asian American and European American college students.* Paper presented at the annual meeting of the American Educational Research Association, New Orleans, LA.

Chapter 13

Learning and Transfer in Two
Web-Based and Distance Applications

Adrienne Lee
New Mexico State University

In recent years, the advancement of technology has resulted in the need for people to acquire highly complex skills in order to use and maintain that technology (Barry & Runyan, 1995; Greenspan, 2001). Consequently, the demand for ongoing innovations including Web-based and distance training has increased. Although Web-based training can be in a classroom (i.e., students in a computer lab all using Web-based training software together) or at a distance (i.e., students at their homes using Web-based software with no interaction), distance training can be Web-based or it can take many other forms (such as correspondence or video courses). Although sending personnel to training sites can be costly, recent surveys have found that considerable cost savings with comparable training outcomes can be acquired through the use of distance learning (Russell, 1999/2001). For example, the Asynchronous Computer Conferencing used by the Army resulted in comparable performance between resident and Asynchronous Computer Conferencing students but cost less (Hahn, 1990). However, even though distance learning in some form has been available for many years (e.g., correspondence courses), studies focusing on the Internet/Web-based training have only recently been performed and relatively few have examined the effectiveness of the technology for knowledge acquisition (Boling & Robinson, 1999;

Kerka, 1996).[1] With increasing use of these technologies, research focused on the factors that improve learning from this type of training would be beneficial.

In order to study Web-based distance learning, two main research projects were conducted in our lab to examine individual and team learning. In the first project, the research was based on the idea that individuals could use Web-based tutors to supplement learning outside of classroom instruction. To assess whether learning occurred, students were asked to write answers to essay questions, and issues of type of question, use of tutoring system, and material complexity could be addressed. In the second project, we focused on learning and transfer (a measure of learning) in face-to-face and distance training situations. Because interest in group learning has increased recently and because group or team learning is considered to be different from individual learning, focusing on group or team learning may produce results that differ from individual learning. These projects are discussed in the next sections.

STUDYING LEARNING THROUGH WRITING USING WEB-BASED TUTORS

Instructors are always looking for ways to increase student learning and computer-based instruction can be one way to provide additional training outside of the classroom. With improvements in technology and the Internet, students can now use Web-based tutors on their own time and from any location (as opposed to one organized lab session at the university or one central university's computer lab room). However, in spite of increasing use of computer technology, evaluation of both the technology and student's learning from those new technologies has not kept pace. Most studies focus on satisfaction or just report on how the technology was used, not how well students learned compared to more traditional training approaches. One exception has been the work of John Anderson and colleagues where tutoring systems have been used both to evaluate Anderson's learning theory and to improve student learning both at the university and in local Pittsburgh schools (Anderson, Corbett, Koedinger, & Pelletier, 1995; Anderson & Gluck, 2001; Baker, Corbett, & Koedinger, 2001; see also Parr, 2000 and Emurian & Durham, 2002). The success of these tutors

---

[1]This article is making a distinction between general computer-based instruction, for which empirical studies of effectiveness beyond satisfaction can be found and the recent Web-based technology. Interest in evaluating Web-based systems does exist (Chang, 1999) but even in a recent database search, very few citations of studies that empirically evaluate what was learned (as opposed to student satisfaction) could be found (two exceptions include Chang, 2001; Psaromiligkos & Retalis, 2003). Assessing what is learned is far more difficult than assessing satisfaction or self-reported learning.

suggests that Web-based tutors used with classes should also result in better learning.

Evaluating Student Learning Using Tutoring Systems

The primary way to assess whether learning has occurred is to ask students questions (Graesser, 1985; Lauer, Peacock, & Graesser, 1992). When students answer questions, they reveal not only the knowledge that they have acquired, but also what their overall knowledge representation contains and how new knowledge has been integrated into their previous knowledge structure (Foltz & Lee, in press). However, many previous computer-based training systems have been limited to using multiple choice questions, entering numbers, or entering words from a limited vocabulary for assessing students' knowledge representations (Foltz & Lee, 2005; see also Edelson, 1996; Graesser, 1985; Polson & Richardson, 1988; Sleeman & Brown, 1982; Wenger, 1987).

Current advances in technology (particularly in computational linguistics) have allowed for assessing student's knowledge based on analyzing essay answers to open-ended questions (e.g., Foltz, Gilliam, & Kendall, 2000; Landauer, Laham, & Foltz, 2000; see also Foltz, 1996; Landauer, Foltz, & Laham, 1998). Latent semantic analysis (LSA) is a computational technique that can provide measures of the quality of a student's knowledge representation based on analyses of a corpus of textual information on a domain and a student's essay. LSA is both a computational model of knowledge representations and a method for determining the semantic similarity between pieces of textual information. LSA generates a high dimensional semantic representation of a body of knowledge based on a statistical analysis of textual information of that domain. The assumption is that there is some underlying or latent structure in the pattern of word usage across texts. Based on an analysis of the occurrences of words in contexts, a representation can be formed in which words that are used in similar contexts will be more semantically related. To perform the analysis, a corpus of text is first represented as a matrix in which the columns stand for passages (usually paragraphs or sentences), and rows stand for unique word types found in the text. The cell entries represent the frequency with which a given word appears in a given context, transformed to provide a measure of the information value of that word. A singular value decomposition (SVD), which is a variant of factor analysis, is performed on this matrix. (For a review of singular value decomposition, see Golub & van Loan, 1996.)

This approach permits assessment to be done based entirely on essays. Essays can more accurately capture a student's current knowledge representation because they require the creation of the answer by the student rather than just a choice of answers provided by an instructor. As a student's knowledge representation changes, so too should their essay responses change, including more knowledge and improvement in quality. Providing accurate information about the state of a student's changing knowledge representation can be used to provide individualized instruction (scaffolding) and specific feedback. Because writing requires more recall and organization of information than other means of question answering (such as multiple choice or fill in the blank questions with limited vocabulary choices), it also can induce a richer knowledge representation in a student and can improve writing abilities (Lee & Hutchison, 1998). Thus, one goal of this project was to demonstrate that writing answers to essay questions could be used for assessing learning and that the evaluation of these written responses could be performed automatically using LSA. We wished to demonstrate that the tutors could be effective classroom tools and that basic factors in what affects whether learning occurs through writing could be examined concurrently.

Cognitive Tutors.   A series of Web-based tutors were developed based on basic concepts in cognitive psychology: Sperling effect, serial position, priming, perceptual processes, and judgment and decision making. The tutors consisted of pages that integrated text, visuals, and animated sample experiments. To support the basic cognitive principles discussed, students could run themselves in these sample experiments that allowed them to get a feeling for the actual experiments performed. A sample screen is shown in Fig. 13.1. Reflection questions were embedded throughout the text. The question appeared on the right side of the screen and students could reference the text on the left side.

Evaluating the Web-Based Tutors.   The advantage of Web-based tutors is that students can access the tutors at any time and from any location where a computer and bandwidth are available. Instructors can assign the tutors as lab assignments with deadlines or merely as supplements. The cognitive tutors described have been used in several classes over the last 3 years. Students take from 45 minutes to 2 hours on some of these tutors. They report finding these tutors as very useful and as good learning experiences. Even though they were not designed for test review, many students report using them for this purpose. Some of the problems include slow connections or lost connections (due to storms or other reasons) and the length of the tutoring sessions.

In order to evaluate the effectiveness of the tutors, a series of studies varying the type and quantity of both the questions and feedback were performed (Lee, Biron, & Foltz, 2003). These experiments have identified critical factors to learning: (a) What type of question is presented (multiple choice or essay); (b) individual differences in initial knowledge; (c) com-

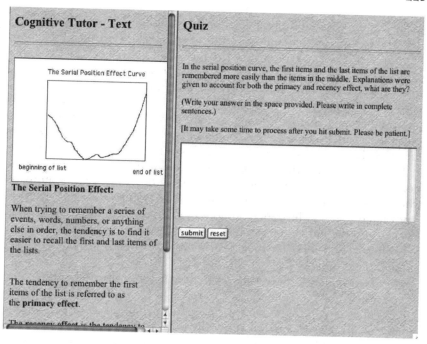

FIG. 13.1. Example interface from cognitive Web-based tutor on the serial position topic. A correct answer will describe both the primacy and recency effect. An example response might be, "The serial position effect is being better able to learn and recall the first and last numbers in a long list better than those in the middle. The primacy effect can be explained by the first few items suffering no interference by later learning, thus making them easier to store in long term memory. The higher recall of the last few items can be explained by the fact that they were just heard/read and are still being held in one's short term memory."

plexity of material; and (d) type of response an individual makes (oral versus written).

Three of the experiments are summarized here. In a first experiment, writing answers to reflection questions produced increased learning as compared to answering multiple choice questions or not answering any questions at all. No significant differences were found regarding the number of reflection questions, but differences were found regarding initial knowledge. Experiment 2 extended the results by comparing groups who merely read reflection questions with those who answered questions, and the effects of feedback. Results indicate that overt responses are better than covert responses and that feedback also increases the amount of learning; however, although these results were found for low initial knowledge participants, no significant differences among conditions was found for high initial knowledge participants. Overall, writing does seem to facilitate learning, and feedback appears to provide an additional benefit. In a third experiment, the complexity of the material was varied (simple vs. complex) with writing versus no writing and high and low knowledge students. High knowledge students performed well despite the complexity of the material; on the other hand, low knowledge students performed well only on the simple material and writing helped these low knowledge students on complex material. This study is currently being replicated to verify the results.

In summary, the results of the studies indicate that multiple choice questions are not as effective as essay questions and writing quality improves when students are asked to write answers to essay questions. However, the type of question may be dependent on the complexity of the material to be learned and the individual's initial knowledge, as well as on other individual difference factors. Further, the inclusion of feedback increases the amount of learning.

We also evaluated the tutors through classroom use. All students received instruction on the material covered in the cognitive tutor and then a specific question on their exam was used for evaluation. Four classes were compared; the classes were all upper division cognitive psychology classes, with a mean size of 23 students. In three classes, taught by the same instructor, students did not use the Web-based tutors but received a test question based on those tutors on one of their exams. (These three classes served as the control groups.) Students in these classes received an in-class exercise on the topic and discussion on the exercise. For the fourth class, students were required to use the tutor as part of a lab exercise. Students wrote answers to embedded essay questions and half of the time, the students received automated feedback using LSA-based essay scoring. The other half of the students received general feedback on their answer. Feedback to both conditions was provided after the student hit the submit button. Class 4 students received the same test question on one of their exams as the control classes. (Data from students who did not take the exam were not included in the analyses. Twenty four students were included in this analysis; half in the LSA condition and half in the general feedback condition.)

The question responses were scored by two independent graders (not the instructor for these classes) and graders were blind to condition and purpose of the experiment. Post hoc analyses (Fisher's PLSD) for class showed that Class 4's performance on the exam was better than Class 2 and 3 (mean difference class 2; $M = 2.83$, $p < .01$; mean difference class 3; $M = 1.46$, $p < .02$) and marginally better than Class 1 (mean difference; $M = 1.18$, $p = .05$). Post hoc analyses (Fisher's PLSD) for type of test question showed that the curve question was answered correctly more often than either the primacy or recency question (mean difference primacy; $M = 1.79$,

$p < .01$; mean difference recency; $M = 1.23$, $p < .01$). Results indicate that using a Web-based tutor to supplement classroom activities results in increased learning for students, with the LSA tutor outperforming the regular tutor (Fig. 13.2). Thus, the distance Web-based tutor was quite effective in helping students learn the material needed for the exam.

Summary of Individual Learning Using Web-Based Tutors.
In summary, this project focused on the development of Web-based tutors, incorporating essay writing and automatic grading. Initial findings indicate that learning is increased when students use these Web-based tutors to supplement classroom instruction. In addition, students not only used these tutors for their assigned labs but also used them to review for exams and appreciated the asynchronous nature of the Web-based tutors.

The results of these studies are quite promising. They indicate that efforts by instructors to supplement student learning can be eased through the use of Web-based tutors, which can provide both additional instruction and practice problems to students. Because feedback on student responses is so important, these studies also indicate that automatic essay grading (LSA) incorporated into these tutors can produce good results with minimal instructor effort (at least for the grading).

As promising as these results are, learning rarely occurs in isolation, and more instructors are incorporating some type of group learning into their

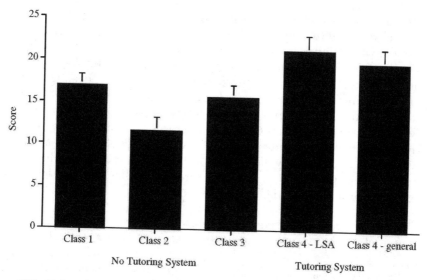

FIG. 13.2. Results of classroom study showing better performance by classes using tutors.

courses. Therefore, studying how Web-based training could occur for groups or teams seems to be necessarily in order to present a complete picture as to how Web-based distance learning occurs generally. In particular, focusing on team learning and transfer can help us to gain a greater understanding as to what aspects of learning theories developed based on the individual apply to groups or teams.

Team Learning and Transfer Through Distance Training

As Internet and communication technology has improved and Web-based training has increased, a parallel development has occurred in the area of team training and cognition (Salas & Fiore, 2004; see Smith-Jentsch, Campbell, Milanovich, & Reynolds, 2001). Teams play an increasingly large role in many aspects of military work. In particular, the growing complexity of tasks frequently surpasses the cognitive capabilities of individuals and thus, necessitates a team approach (Cooke, Salas, Cannon-Bowers, & Stout, 2000; Salas, Cannon-Bowers, Church-Payne, & Smith-Jentsch, 1998). However, most individuals have little formal training in how to work within a group, much less on how to learn within one. Moreover, the move toward distributed mission training[2] for many military training programs creates new challenges for collaborative learning by teams. Trainers are faced with the problem of training both the skills directly needed for the job and the interpersonal skills needed for successful team performance. In addition, trainers and trainees must adapt to distributed training programs.

At the heart of both individual and team training, however, is the ability to accurately and reliably assess learning and measure the knowledge that results from training. Although progress has been made on knowledge measurement at the individual level, the measurement of team knowledge, and team cognition in general, is still in its infancy (Cooke et al., 2000). In addition, extensive research has been performed on individual's cognitive skill acquisition; however, team learning and computer supported cooperative learning have only recently become the focus of attention, especially for groups larger than two individuals (Salas & Fiore, 2004). A greater understanding of what an individual learns within collaborative learning situations and, as opposed to or in conjunction with, what the team learns is needed in order to provide information for trainers.

Issues for Teams Learning at a Distance. Under ideal training situations, multiple individuals can be trained together to form effective teams.

---

[2]Distributed mission training is defined as training that uses simulations and provides individual and aggregate training at single or multiple places. Individuals can train individually, they can train with a team, or they can train within a full theater of battle. (For further information, please see Fawcett, 2004.)

However, the constraints of distance and time often play a role in limiting team training. Furthermore, limitations in available personnel and the need to spread these personnel over wide geographic areas also impede the ability to train effective teams. One solution to these problems is distance learning.

Studies performed in military settings have tended to show no difference in achievement between distance learners and resident learners (Russell, 1999/2001). Distance training is cost-effective because individuals do not need to travel to training sites with the associated costs of that travel and it can be efficient because many students at different locations can learn asynchronously (i.e., training can occur at the convenience of the individual rather than at a specifically scheduled time and place). There were three studies that compared distance and resident learners, as reported in Barry and Runyan (1995) using Army participants: (a) Hahn (1990) used asynchronous computer conferencing and found no differences between distance and resident trainees; (b) Phelps, Wells, Ashworth, and Hahn (1991) used a computer-mediated communication system and also found no differences; and (c) Keene and Cary (1992) showed a benefit for distance learners over resident learners in using interactive video teleconferencing training. A fourth study by Bramble and Martin (1995) found that community colleges could provide adequate training for the military when using the U.S. Army's two-way audio/video teletraining network. Thus, distance learning can be both a cost effective and an efficient way to provide training.

On the other hand, distance learning may have a different meaning in the context of group (collaborative) or team training. Few studies have examined collaborative (group) distance learning and even fewer studies have examined team distance training (Frost & Fukami, 1997; Kerka, 1996). Computer Internet/Web environments have tended to be built for the individual (Calvani, Sorzio, & Varisco, 1997); however, groupware and computer-mediated communication has allowed for the possibility of the delivery of team distance learning. Results from studies comparing computer-mediated communication to face-to-face have found mixed results. For example, studies have suggested that computer-mediated communication can reduce social norms (Sproull & Kiesler, 1986), can be a hindrance to the creation of meaning (Mantovani, 1996) and can lead to lengthy decision making (Hedlund, Ilgen, & Hollenbeck, 1998) in comparison to face-to-face communication. These studies are limited because they tended to focus on organizational and social factors rather than on team process, cognition, and performance. Also, military teams tend to be populated by hierarchical teams of individuals each with his or her own role, as opposed to homogeneous groups of individuals making the same judgments or decisions. Therefore, in order to study team distance learning, new techniques may need to be developed.

In educational settings, students tend to know each other before being placed into groups. However, in the new distance education paradigm, it is likely that students at different campuses could be paired together. In this case, the students may not know each other before being placed into a group and must get to know each other over the period of the course. In the military, a similar situation can arise, where ad hoc teams are quickly formed from workforces who do not know each other. Also, in distributed mission environments, team members are less likely to be familiar with one another, must often communicate in ways other than face-to-face communication, and due to a lack of copresence, may not easily share displays or information conveyed through gestures. These factors should affect team cognition (i.e., team decision making, team situation models, and team knowledge) for both education within and outside of the military. Distributed mission training (DMT) is a shared training environment in which multiple individuals (teams) can engage in training at multiple sites with realistic training scenarios (battles, all levels). As with collaborative distance learning, few studies have been performed to examine the effectiveness of DMTs.

One benefit of distance instruction is that the individuals can learn at their own pace, in their own time (on-demand, real-time training). However, if the members of the team train without any knowledge of the other individuals or of the individuals' part in the total task, then how can they develop team knowledge and teamwork skills? We would predict that distance team training should be worse than face-to-face (colocated) team training. However, recent technology such as the development of chat rooms and shared virtual spaces may provide one solution, but the effectiveness of those technologies for complex tasks is not well understood (Barab, Kling, & Gray, in press; Schlager, Fusco, Koch, Crawford, & Phillips, 2003; Sen & Al-Hawamdeh, 2001).[3] Therefore, the summarized experiments examined both the effects of distance learning on teams and how to improve this type of training.

Empirical Study Examining Distance Learning for Teams.   In order to study distance learning, teams were trained either together (colocated)

---

[3]The references provided in the text are studies and discussions about virtual chat rooms and virtual spaces for education. Chat rooms on the Web are defined as spaces where people can go to interact with others. This can take the form of text messaging or an actual cartoon character interaction. Many sites define and discuss chat rooms; interested readers could go to the American Library Association site (http://www.ala.org/rusa/mars/glossary.html) or the Information Security and Crime Prevention site (http://www.infosec.gov.hk/engtext/general/glossary.htm). Virtual spaces are known by many names including virtual learning spaces, virtual environments, virtual educational environment, or multiuser domain. Although some of the Web sites come and go, the interested reader could visit Dr. Schlager's site at http://ti2.sri.com/tappedin/.

or apart (distance); however, after training, teams were transferred to either a different context than training (colocated to distance or distance to colocated) or they stayed in the same context (Fig. 13.3 illustrates the design.) Teams were asked to learn how to fly an unmanned air vehicle (UAV) to various sites and take pictures of those sites. An unmanned air vehicle is a small airborne vehicle that is not operated by a flight crew (and is not a model aircraft). These aircraft can be operated at a distance and can provide reconnaissance and surveillance in places in complex environments where it may be difficult for individuals to travel.

In the missions flying these simulated aircraft, each team member had a different role but these roles interacted with each other. For example, one person flew the plane but had to interact with the person who navigated and with the person who took the pictures. The three roles are the air vehicle operator (AVO), the payload operator (PLO), and the DEMPC (data exploitation, mission planning and communication operator). The AVO controls

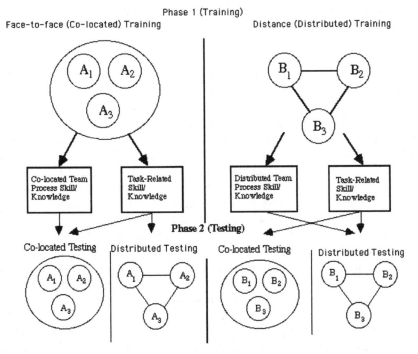

FIG. 13.3. Design of face-to-face versus distance training of teams. (The letters, A and B, have subscripts to represent different teams. The individual circles around these letters represent these individual teams. The larger circle surrounding three smaller circles represents the idea that 3 teams are working together in the same room or are colocated.)

airspeed, heading, and altitude, and monitors UAV systems. The PLO adjusts camera settings, takes photos, and monitors the camera equipment. The DEMPC oversees the mission and determines flight paths under various constraints. To complete the mission, the team members need to share information with one another and work in a coordinated fashion. Each person was trained individually on the basics of the UAV system and was required to reach criteria on the questions that appeared after training before being given hands-on training on his or her role.

Training was separated into sections: The individual reading portion that provided basic information took about 45 min and included answering questions provided by the computer training. Then participants experienced 30 min of hands-on training on the equipment.

Only after each individual had learned his or her role in the hands-on training did the team perform its first mission. Each mission consisted of flying the UAV to various sites and taking pictures. For training, teams flew the same task for five missions and then for testing/transfer, the teams switched to another task for three more missions. (Missions were limited to 30 min, regardless of completion.) The two tasks were counterbalanced for training and transfer across teams. A performance score was provided at the end of each mission by the software (i.e., a formula that takes into account number of targets, amount of time, fuel used, etc.).

Each team consisted of three participants who were assigned different roles. Twenty eight teams were run. Individuals did not know each other before being placed in a team. Colocated teams trained and performed missions in the same physical location whereas distributed teams (individuals who trained and performed in separate locations at a distance) did not physically see each other during either experiment day.

Figure 13.4 illustrates the mean results for each mission by each condition. (For statistical details, please see Lee & Bond, 2003). Results showed that distance teams learned more quickly (reached asymptote) than colocated teams, even though all individuals in each team received the same declarative and hands-on training before the first mission. Similar to Singley and Anderson's (1989) results for individuals, all teams suffered a decrement in performance at transfer, but distance teams recovered more quickly and performance was higher than for colocated teams on the two missions following transfer. Thus, distance can be more effective in some training situations. For transfer, change in task appeared to play a larger role than did the change in context. All teams changed to a test task but some teams changed context, distance to colocated or colocated to distance, as well. If context had played a larger role, we would have expected to see a larger reduction in performance for the change in context conditions. Thus, the results may have been because the task itself was very complex; in complex tasks, the task itself may form the context to which

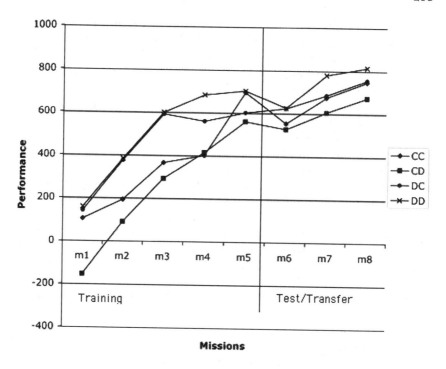

FIG. 13.4. Team training and test/transfer results. *Note.* CC stands for colocated for both training and test; CD stands for colocated training and distance test/transfer; DC stands for distance training and colocated test/transfer and DD stands for distance for both training and test.

subjects attend. Currently, we are replicating this study in a different but equally complex context to further refine these ideas.

Summary of Distance Learning for Teams. In summary, the results of this study indicate that team learning generally may be similar to individual learning. For example, the interference found for change between training and transfer tasks was similar to that obtained by Singley and Anderson (1989). These results make sense if one thinks of teams as a unit, similar to an individual, and teams that perform well together should mimic the performance of individuals who perform well. Teams that do not perform well together may cripple the overall performance and this may also result in performance that resembles poorly performing individuals. Further, a team's performance can often be predicted by one individual within the team. For example, if a team is relying on the navigator to organize the most efficient route and the navigator gives incorrect directions, then the plane could run out of fuel before the mission is complete or the plane may never reach the target. The other team members could perform their tasks well, but the one individual could handicap the others, with a resulting poor team performance score.

Although these team results are similar to previous literature on individual performance, both distance learning and context transfer findings were not consistent with previous research. In the first case, distance training appeared to be more effective than colocated training and in the second, change in context was not detrimental (as compared with those who stayed in the same context for training and test). In both cases, the role of task complexity may affect what is learned and what transfers. Therefore, theories of training and transfer may have to be extended by these results to incorporate other factors. For example, in addition to the cognitive aspects of team learning, theories need to consider individual differences, team process and behavior, and social–cultural cognition.[4]

OVERALL SUMMARY OF WEB-BASED, DISTANCE TRAINING

Web-based, distance instruction holds many benefits for instructors and students, including the ability to provide additional instruction outside of class that students can access wherever and whenever they choose. Research is just beginning to examine factors other than instructor or student satisfaction; however, studies using diverse populations, such as those described in this chapter, are still not very widespread.

The challenge for Web-based and distance education is not just in the containment of costs or the dissemination to populations that may not have access to advanced technology. Indeed, more research needs to be performed to determine what factors are involved for successful delivery of this type of instruction and training. Specifically, what characteristics of individuals, groups, and teams might affect distance learning, what characteristics of the materials of technology might affect distance learning, and what interactions will we find between these types of learners, the media, and the mode of delivery. Theoretical models of individual learning can be extended to some extent in order to help inform answers. However, more

---

[4]The idea that all of these factors play a role in learning derives from a combination of sources. The interested reader could start with Schwartz and Reisberg (1991) or Tobias and Fletcher (2000). Essentially, researchers modeling learning, found in computational modeling of human behavior (Anderson, 1993; Newell, 1990), have argued that one should consider all the factors that are involved in an aspect of human behavior. The cognitive factors include physical or developmental abilities, individual differences, and previous knowledge. Aside from cognitive factors, social factors (Hollingshead, 1998; Moreland, Argote, & Krishnan, 1996) and social–cultural factors (Nisbett & Norenzayan, 2002) could also play a role in learning as a team.

complete theoretical models of team learning as well as additional empirical testing is required.

ACKNOWLEDGMENTS

Funding for the experiments summarized in the section on individual and Web-based tutors was partially provided by the National Science Foundation and funding for the experiments described in the section on team learning was partially provided by the Army Research Institute. Additional support of this researcher has come from the Office of Naval Research, the Army Research Laboratory, and New Mexico State University. The findings and opinions expressed in this report do not reflect the positions or policies of any of the agencies listed.

I would like to thank Peter Foltz for help with all of these projects and with comments on drafts of this chapter. Also, thanks to Harry O'Neil and Ray Perez for their support and advice over the last 2 years. I would also like to thank Douglas Gillan and Nancy Cooke, as well as graduate students, Heidi Biron, Sara Gilliam, Gary Bond, and Sunny Lee, for their help on these projects, and the undergraduates who participated in the experiments and who took my cognitive class.

REFERENCES

Anderson, J. R. (1993). *Rules of the mind*. Hillsdale, NJ: Lawrence Erlbaum Associates.
Anderson, J. R., Corbett, A. T., Koedinger, K. R., & Pelletier, R. (1995). Cognitive tutors: Lessons learned. *The Journal of the Learning Sciences, 4*(2), 167–207.
Anderson, J. R., & Gluck, K. (2001). What role do cognitive architectures play in intelligent tutoring systems? In D. Klahr & S. M. Carver (Eds.), *Cognition & instruction: Twenty-five years of progress* (pp. 227–262). Mahwah, NJ: Lawrence Erlbaum Associates.
Baker, R. S., Corbett, A. T., & Koedinger, K. R. (2001). Toward a model of learning data representations. *Proceedings of the Cognitive Science Society Conference* (pp. 45–50). Mahwah, NJ: Lawrence Erlbaum Associates.
Barab, S., Kling, R., & Gray, J. (in press). *Designing virtual communities in the service of learning*. Cambridge, MA: Cambridge University Press.
Barry, M., & Runyan, G. B. (1995). A review of distance-learning studies in the U.S. Military. *The American Journal of Distance Education, 9*, 37–45.
Boling, N. C., & Robinson, D. H. (1999). Individual study, interactive multimedia, or cooperative learning: Which activity best supplements lecture-based distance learning? *Journal of Educational Psychology, 91*, 169–174.
Bramble, W., & Martin, B. (1995). The Florida Teletraining Project: Military training via two-way compressed video. *The American Journal of Distance Education, 9*, 6–26.
Calvani, A., Sorzio, P., & Varisco, B. (1997). Inter-university cooperative learning: An exploratory study. *Journal of Computer Assisted Learning, 13*, 271–280.

Chang, C.-C. (2001). A study on the evaluation and effectiveness analysis of web-based learning portfolio. *British Journal of Educational Technology, 32*, 435–458.

Chang, V. (1999). Evaluating the effectiveness of online learning using a new web based learning instrument. *Proceedings Western Australian Institute for Educational Research Forum 1999*. http://education.curtin.edu.au/waier/forums/1999/chang.html

Cooke, N. J., Salas, E., Cannon-Bowers, J. A., & Stout, R. (2000). Measuring team knowledge. *Human Factors, 42*, 151–173.

Edelson, D. C. (1996). Learning from cases and questions: The Socratic case-based teaching architecture. *The Journal of the Learning Sciences, 5*(4), 357–410.

Emurian, H. H., & Durham, A. G. (2002). Computer-based tutoring systems: A behavioral approach. In J. A. Jacko & A. Sears (Eds.), *The human-computer interaction handbook: Fundamentals, evolving technologies, and emerging applications* (pp. 677–697). Mahwah, NJ: Lawrence Erlbaum Associates.

Fawcett, J. (2004). Distributed mission operations and distributed mission training. *Military Technology, 28*, 24–30.

Foltz, P. W. (1996). Latent semantic analysis for text-based research. *Behavior Research Methods, Instruments and Computers, 28*(2), 197–202.

Foltz, P. W., Gilliam, S., & Kendall, S. (2000). Supporting content-based feedback in online writing evaluation with LSA. *Interactive Learning Environments, 8*(2), 111–129.

Foltz, P. W., & Lee, A. Y. (2005). Adaptive learning systems. In H. van Oostendorp, L. Breure, & A. Dillon (Eds.), *Creation, use and deployment of digital information* (pp. 157–175). Mahwah, NJ: Lawrence Erlbaum Associates.

Frost, P. J., & Fukami, C. V. (1997). Teaching effectiveness in the organizational sciences: Recognizing and enhancing the scholarship of teaching. *Academy of Management Journal, 40*(6), 1271–1281.

Golub, G., & van Loan, C. (1996). *Matrix computations*. 3rd Edition. London: The John Hopkins University Press.

Graesser, A. C. (1985). An introduction to the study of questioning. In A. C. Graesser & J. B. Black (Eds.), *The psychology of questions* (pp. 1–14). Hillsdale, NJ: Lawrence Erlbaum Associates.

Greenspan, A. (2001). The growing need for skills in the 21st century. Retrieved February 28, 2004, from http://www.federalreserve.gov/boarddocs/speeches/2001/20010620/default.htm

Hahn, H. (1990). Distributed training for the reserve component: Remote delivery using asynchronous computer conferencing (Report No. 2Q263743A794). Boise, ID: Army Research Institute.

Hedlund, J., Ilgen, D. R., & Hollenbeck, J. R. (1998). Decision accuracy in computer-mediated versus face-to-face decision making teams. *Organizational and Behavior and Human Decision Processes, 76*, 30–47.

Hollingshead, A. B. (1998). Distributed knowledge and transactive processes in decision-making groups. In M. A. Neale, E. A. Mannix, & D. H. Grunfeld (Eds.), *Research on Managing Groups and Teams* (Vol. 1, pp. 103–123). Greenwich, CT: JAI.

Keene, D., & Cary, J. (1992). Effectiveness of distance education approach to U.S. Army reserve component training. In M. G. Moore (Ed.), *Distance education for corporate and military training* (ACSDE Research Monograph No. 3, pp. 97–103). University Park, PA: Pennsylvania State University, American Center for the Study of Distance Education.

Kerka, S. (1996). *Distance learning, the Internet, and the World Wide Web* (ERIC Digest No. 168). Columbus, OH: ERIC Clearinghouse on Adult, Career, and Vocational

Education, Ohio State University. (ERIC Document Reproduction Service No. ED395214)

Landauer, T. K., Foltz, P. W., & Laham, D. (1998). An introduction to latent semantic analysis. *Discourse Processes, 25*(2/3), 259–284.

Landauer, T. K., Laham, D., & Foltz, P. W. (2000). The intelligent essay assessor. *IEEE Intelligent Systems, 15,* 27–31.

Lauer, T., Peacock, E., & Graesser, A. (1992). *Questions and information systems.* Hillsdale, NJ: Lawrence Erlbaum Associates.

Lee, A. Y., & Bond, G. (2003, November). *Team learning and transfer in different contexts.* Poster session presented at the annual meeting of the Psychonomics Society, Vancouver, Canada.

Lee, A. Y., Biron, C. A., & Foltz, P. W. (2003). *The effects of learning on writing.* Manuscript submitted for publication.

Lee, A. Y., & Hutchison, L. (1998). Improving learning from examples through reflection. *Journal of Experimental Psychology, 4,* 187–210.

Mantovani, G. (1996). *New communication environments from everyday to virtual.* Bristol, PA: Taylor & Francis.

Moreland, R. L., Argote, L., & Krishnan, R. (1996). Socially shared cognition at work: Transactive memory & group performance. In J. L. Nye & A. M. Brower (Eds.), *What's social about social cognition?* (pp. 57–84). Thousand Oaks, CA: Sage.

Newell, A. (1990). *Unified theories of cognition.* Cambridge, MA: Harvard University Press.

Nisbett, R. E., & Norenzayan, A. (2002). Culture and cognition. In D. Medin & H. Pashler (Eds.), *Stevens' handbook of experimental psychology: Vol. 2. Memory and cognitive processes* (3rd ed., pp. 561–597). New York: Wiley.

Parr, J. (2000). *A review of the literature on computer-assisted learning, particularly integrated learning systems, and outcomes with respect to literacy and numeracy.* Wellington, New Zealand: Ministry of Education.

Phelps, R., Wells, R., Ashworth, R., & Hahn, H. (1991). Effectiveness and costs of distance education using computer-mediated communication. *The American Journal of Distance Education, 5*(3), 7–19.

Polson, M. C., & Richardson, J. J. (1988). *Foundations of intelligent tutoring systems.* Hillsdale, NJ: Lawrence Erlbaum Associates.

Psaromiligkos, Y., & Retalis, S. (2003). Re-evaluating the effectiveness of a web-based learning system: A comparative case study. *Journal of Educational Multimedia and Hypermedia, 12,* 5–20.

Russell, T. L. (1999). *No significant difference phenomenon.* Montgomery, AL: IDECC (Updated 2001). Retrieved from http://www.nosignificantdifference.org/nosignificantdifference/

Salas, E., Cannon-Bowers, J. A., Church-Payne, S., & Smith-Jentsch, K. A. (1998). Teams and teamwork in the military. In C. Cronin (Ed.), *Military psychology: An introduction* (pp. 71–87). Needham Heights, MA: Simon & Schuster.

Salas, E., & Fiore, S. M. (2004). *Team cognition: Understanding the factors that drive process and performance.* Washington, DC: American Psychological Association.

Schlager, M., Fusco, J., Koch, M., Crawford, V., & Phillips, M. (2003, July). *Designing equity and diversity into online strategies to support new teachers.* Presented at National Educational Computing Conference 2003, Seattle, WA.

Schwartz, B., & Reisberg, D. (1991). *Learning and memory.* New York: W. W. Norton & Company, Inc.

Sen, L. C., & Al-Hawamdeh, S. (2001). New mode of course delivery for virtual classrooms. *Aslib Proceedings: New information perspectives, 53,* 238–242.

Singley, M. K., & Anderson, J. R. (1989). *The transfer of cognitive skill*. Cambridge, MA: Harvard University Press.

Sleeman, D., & Brown, J. S. (1982). *Intelligent tutoring systems*. New York: Academic Press.

Smith-Jentsch, K. A., Campbell, G. E., Milanovich, D. M., & Reynolds, A. M. (2001). Measuring teamwork mental models to support training needs assessment, development, and evaluation: Two empirical studies. *Journal of Organizational Behavior, 22*, 179–194.

Sproull, L., & Kiesler, S. (1986). Reducing social context cues: Electronic mail in organizational communication. *Management Science, 32*, 1492–1512.

Tobias, S., & Fletcher, J. D. (2000). Training and retraining: A handbook for business, industry, government, and the military. New York: Macmillan Library Reference.

Wenger, E. (1987). *Artificial intelligence and tutoring systems*. Los Altos, CA: Morgan Kauffman.

Chapter 14

Role of Task-Specific Adapted Feedback on a Computer-Based Collaborative Problem-Solving Task

San-hui (Sabrina) Chuang
University of Southern California/CRESST

Harold F. O'Neil
University of Southern California/CRESST

Many research studies on collaborative problem solving have shown a positive effect on students' cognitive improvement (e.g., Arts, Gijselaers, & Segers, 2002). Recently, computer networks and simulations have been used and proven effective as an assessment tool to measure collaboration skills and problem-solving skills (e.g., Hsieh & O'Neil, 2002). Another influence brought about by advances in computer technology is the new emphasis on the skills needed for electronic information seeking and processing (Covington, 1998). However, many students and teachers alike still lack basic information technology knowledge and skills (Smith & Broom, 2003). Current curriculum, instruction, and assessment do not adequately make use of the capabilities of today's networked information systems. Research has shown that expert searchers locate information faster and use more search logic, such as Boolean operators, in their queries than do novice searchers (Lazonder, 2000). Thus, research has pointed to a need for training on Boolean search strategies, and a few studies have also demonstrated its effectiveness. However, in Hsieh and O'Neil's 2002 study, searching was unexpectedly negatively related to performance on a team knowledge mapping task.

By combining Hsieh and O'Neil's (2002) methodological approach with instruction in search strategies, this study investigated student collaborative problem-solving processes and teamwork processes on a computer-based knowledge mapping team task with special attention to the effectiveness of feedback. In Hsieh and O'Neil's study, two levels of feedback, adapted feedback and knowledge of response feedback, were compared. Knowledge of response feedback is feedback that informs the learner whether the answer is correct. Adapted feedback was designed in computer-based instruction with attention to customizing feedback for the user's needs rather than providing just one fixed form of feedback. Hsieh and O'Neil demonstrated that adapted feedback teams outperformed knowledge of response feedback teams. Continuing in the same fashion, the current study compared two levels of adapted feedback—adapted feedback and task-specific adapted feedback.

The measurement of teamwork processes and problem-solving processes in this study was based on the model developed by the National Center for Research on Evaluation, Standards, and Student Testing (CRESST). The teamwork model consists of six teamwork skills; "(a) adaptability, (b) coordination, (c) decision making, (d) interpersonal, (e) leadership, and (f) communication" (O'Neil, Chung, & Brown, 1997, p. 413). The problem-solving model consists of three subelements; (a) content understanding; (b) problem-solving strategies; and (c) self-regulation.

In the current study, content understanding was measured by a knowledge map created with and recorded by computer software. A knowledge map is a graphical representation consisting of nodes and links. Nodes represent terms (standing for a concept) in the domain of knowledge. Links represent the relationships between nodes. A proposition is the combination of two nodes joined by a link.

Hsieh and O'Neil (2002) used a simulated Internet Web to evaluate student collaborative problem-solving strategies and outcomes in a computer-based knowledge mapping environment. They successfully showed that adapted feedback was more effective in improving students' performance than knowledge of response feedback. The current study used the same simulated Internet Web space, in which students searched to find information to improve their knowledge maps, and the same simulation also provided students with feedback on their maps.

In the literature, feedback is regarded as an important resource to assist the learning process. Hsieh and O'Neil (2002) demonstrated that feedback access was positively related to outcome performance. However, even though their feedback provided participants with a direction as to "what" area to improve on their knowledge map, it did not provide practical tips on "how" to improve the map. The present study argued that if search tips were provided in the feedback, students would become more effective and efficient in locating pertinent information and in turn, improve the overall result of their map. Therefore, we modified Hsieh and O'Neil's (2002) original task by providing examples of how to use Boolean operators in addition to information on the area(s) into which participants should put more effort.

Because feedback with search tips was provided, participants in the current study were expected to perform better than Hsieh and O'Neil's (2002) participants in general. In addition, increased use of Boolean operators when doing the simulated Web search was expected.

There were four hypotheses in this study:

Hypothesis 1:   Students will perform better on the environmental science knowledge mapping task if they receive task-specific adapted feedback than if they receive adapted feedback.

Hypothesis 2:   Students who receive task-specific adapted feedback will be more likely to use decision-making and leadership team processes than students who receive adapted feedback.

Hypothesis 3:   Information seeking will have positive effects on team outcome in environmental science knowledge mapping.

3.1   Browsing and searching will be positively related to team outcome.

3.2   The number of requests for feedback will be positively related to team outcome.

Hypothesis 4:   Searching using Boolean operators will have positive effects on students' problem-solving strategies and team outcome on the knowledge mapping task.

4.1   The more frequently Boolean operators are used, the higher the map score on the knowledge map.

4.2   The task-specific adapted feedback team will use Boolean operators more frequently in their searching than the adapted feedback team.

METHOD

Participants

Participates were 120 college students (60 dyads), 18 years of age or older.

Networked Knowledge Mapping System

The mapping system was based on the networked knowledge mapping system developed by Schacter, Herl, Chung, Dennis, and O'Neil (1999) and furthered modified by Hsieh and O'Neil (2002). Using this system, teams of two participants (dyads) created a knowledge map on environmental science by exchanging messages in a collaborative environment and by searching for relevant information in a simulated World Wide Web environment. The participants in a dyad were randomly assigned to the role of leader or searcher. The leader was solely responsible for creating the knowledge map, and the searcher was solely responsible for accessing the simulated World Wide Web to find information and to request feedback.

The knowledge map concepts were 18 important predefined concepts identified by content experts; atmosphere, bacteria, carbon dioxide, climate, consumer, decomposition, evaporation, food chain, greenhouse gases, nutrients, oceans, oxygen, photosynthesis, producer, respiration, sunlight, waste, and water cycle. The links for the knowledge map were also predefined by content experts; CAUSES, INFLUENCES, PART OF, PRODUCES, REQUIRES, USED FOR, and USES. There were altogether 37 predefined messages with 37 corresponding buttons. When a participant clicked on a button, the corresponding message was sent instantly to both team members' computers. The simulated World Wide Web environment contained more than 200 Web pages with approximately 500 images and diagrams about environmental science.

Feedback

The searcher was allowed to access feedback to find out how well his or her team was performing. Feedback was provided in one of two categories; adapted feedback and task-specific adapted feedback; both were based on comparing students' knowledge map performance to experts'. Adapted feedback in the present study was identical with Hsieh and O'Neil's (2002) feedback condition. It pointed out concepts that needed improvement. For example, as can be seen in Fig. 14.1, "atmosphere" needed a lot of improvement according to the feedback.

Task-specific adapted feedback, used in the current study, included the information contained in adapted feedback and Boolean search strategy tips. Figure 14.2 shows an example of task-specific adapted feedback provided in the present study. Search tips were adapted from the Firstsearch help guide at http://newfirstsearch.oclc.org/

As seen in Fig. 14.2, the feedback provided participants a direction as to what area to improve for search and task performance, and also how to improve the performance. It should be noted that the search tips were task-specific adaptive knowledge of results response feedback to help teams to improve their searches.

Your map has been scored against an expert's map in environmental science. The feedback tells you:

- How much you need to improve each concept in your map (i.e., A lot, Some, A little)

Use this feedback to help you search to improve your map.

A Lot	Some	A Little
atmosphere,	food chain,	photosynthesis,
carbon dioxide,	decomposition,	oxygen,
respiration,	consumer,	waste,
evaporation,	producer	climate
sunlight,		
water cycle,		
oceans,		
bacteria		
greenhouse		
gases		

Improvement: You have improved the "food chain" from needing "A lot of improvement" to "Some improvement" category.

Strategy: It is most useful to investigate information for the "A lot" and "Some" categories rather than the "A little" category. For example, improving "atmosphere" or "climate" first rather than "evaporation."

FIG. 14.1.   Example of adapted feedback in Hsieh and O'Neil's (2002) study.

MEASURES

Team Outcome Measure

Team outcome measures were computed by comparing the semantic content score of a team's knowledge map to that of a set of four experts' maps (Schacter et al., 1999). The following description shows how these outcomes were scored. First, the semantic score was based on the semantic propositions in experts' knowledge maps and was calculated by categorized map scoring (Herl, O'Neil, Chung, & Schacter, 1999). Using this method, all seven links were categorized into four classifications. CAUSES and INFLUENCES were classified as the "casual" category and marked as string 1. REQUIRES, USED FOR, and USES were classified as the "conditional" category and marked as string 2. PART OF and PRODUCES, the remaining two links, were classified individually and marked as strings 3 and 4 respectively. Every proposition in a student map was compared against each proposition in the four experts' maps using strings 1–4. One match was scored as one point. The average score across all four experts was the semantic score of the map. For example, if a student team made a proposition such as "Oceans PART OF Water cycle," this proposition would be first categorized into "Oceans 3 Water cycle" and then compared with the four experts' propositions. A score of 1 meant this proposition was the same as a

Your map has been scored against an expert's map in environmental science. The feedback tells you:

How much you need to improve each concept in your map (i.e., A lot, Some, A little).

Use this feedback to help you search to improve your map

A Lot	Some	A Little
atmosphere,	food chain,	photosynthesis,
carbon dioxide,	decomposition,	oxygen,
respiration,	consumer,	waste,
evaporation,	producer	climate
sunlight,		
water cycle,		
oceans,		
bacteria		
greenhouse		
gases		

Improvement: You have improved the "food chain" from needing "A lot of improvement" to "Some improvement" category.

General Strategy: It is most useful to investigate information for the "A lot" and "Some" categories rather than the "A little" category. For example, improving "atmosphere" or "climate" first rather than "evaporation."

Search strategy 1: Use the Boolean operators AND to combine search terms when you need to expand or narrow a search. AND retrieves only records that contain all search terms. Use this operator to narrow or limit a search.

oxygen AND atmosphere

If you type: oxygen AND atmosphere
   It searches for: Only records containing both oxygen and atmosphere

If you type: oxygen AND atmosphere AND carbon dioxide
   It searches for: Only records containing all three search terms—oxygen, and atmosphere, and carbon dioxide

Search strategy 2: If using the Boolean operator AND ends up with no relevant pages found. Use the Boolean operator OR to retrieve all records that contain one or both of the search terms. Use this operator to expand a search.

oxygen OR atmosphere

If you type: Oxygen OR atmosphere
It searches for: Records containing oxygen, records containing atmosphere, and records containing both

FIG. 14.2.   Example of task-specific adapted feedback in the present study.

proposition in the map of an expert. A score of zero meant this proposition was not the same as any of the experts' propositions.

Teamwork Process Measures

Teamwork process scores were calculated by adding the number of messages both members in a team sent from each teamwork process category. That is, if a team leader sent seven messages from the adaptability category, then that person's individual-level adaptability score was 7. If both the leader and the searcher in a team each sent seven messages from the adaptability category, the team-level adaptability score was 14.

Information Seeking and Feedback Behavior Measures

Information seeking and feedback behavior were measured by three activities; browsing, searching, and requesting feedback. Browsing was measured by how many times a searcher selected Web pages or clicked on any hypertext within the Web pages. Each time a searcher selected a page or clicked on any hypertext, a point was added. For searching, one point was awarded for simple searches. For example, when a searcher typed "oxygen" as the search string, one point was awarded. An additional point was awarded if the search used Boolean search strategies. For example, "oxygen AND sunlight" would be counted as 2 points; one for a simple search and one for using the Boolean operator AND. The score for feedback request was calculated as the number of times the team requested feedback.

RESULTS

Teamwork Process Measure

Table 14.1 presents teamwork process measure frequency counts for all six teamwork processes. In general, the reliability of the teamwork process measure was unacceptably low. Alpha reliability ranged from –.03 (leadership) to .48 (interpersonal). Examination of the "alpha if item deleted" data indicated that deletion of some messages would improve the reliability. After deleting items, the final alpha reliability for these processes ranged from .29 for decision making to .65 for coordination. Alpha reliability for the other subscales was .37 for adaptability, .56 for interpersonal, .46 for leadership and .48 for communication.

The frequency counts were calculated by adding the number of usage for the individual messages in each teamwork process, after item deletion, and then dividing by the number of teams. In addition, because some team processes had more messages than others, a new metric was created by using a mean. The means in Table 14.1 were calculated by taking the mean of the frequency count for a category and dividing it by the number of messages left in that category after item deletion. Using adaptability as an example, the mean of 4.80 was divided by 3, the number of messages left after item deletion; therefore, the final mean was calculated to be 1.60.

Table 14.2 shows the intercorrelations for the teamwork process variables and the two feedback condition teams. For the adapted feedback team, six significant correlations were found. First, decision making was significantly correlated with adaptability ($r = .39, p < .05$). In addition, a significant correlation was found between communication and leadership

TABLE 14.1

Frequency Count of Teamwork Processes: Team Level ($N = 60$)

Teamwork Process	No. of Messages	M	SD	Min.	Max.
Adaptability	3	1.60	3.26	.00	18.00
Coordination	2	.50	1.71	.00	8.00
Decision making	4	2.01	7.98	.00	39.00
Interpersonal	5	1.39	5.32	.00	23.00
Leadership	2	.73	1.78	.00	7.00
Communication	2	.79	2.22	.00	10.00

TABLE 14.2

Intercorrelations for Team-Level Teamwork Process Measures
and Team Outcome for the Adapted Feedback Team ($n = 30$)
and for the Task-Specific Adapted Feedback Team ($n = 30$)

	1	2	3	4	5	6	7	8
1. Adaptability	− .31	−.24	.16	.37*	.52**	.43*	.16	
2. Coordination	.10	−	−.34	.60**	−.18	−.15	.22	.21
3. Decision making	.39*	.14	−	−.18	−.11	.00	.59**	.12
4. Interpersonal	.17	.32	.34	−	−.16	−.04	.47**	.49**
5. Leadership	−.19	.03	−.04	.02	−	.43*	.13	.18
6. Communication	−.09	−.12	−.01	−.02	.76**	−	.39*	.15
7. All messages sent	.47**	.35*	.80**	.71**	.27	.27	−	.48**
8. Outcome performance	.27	.08	−.05	.33	−.39*	−.31	.06	−

Note. Intercorrelations for the adapted feedback team are shown below the diagonal.
*$p < .05$, two-tailed. **$p < .01$, two-tailed.

($r = .76$, $p < .01$). Moreover, "all messages sent" significantly correlated with adaptability ($r = .47$, $p < .01$), decision making ($r = .80$, $p < .01$), and interpersonal ($r = .71$, $p < .01$). Because "all messages sent" was calculated as the sum of all messages in the six individual categories, these results were expected. Last, team outcome was negatively correlated with leadership ($r = −.39$, $p < .05$). This correlation indicates that the greater the number of leadership messages sent, the worse the team outcome was. This result was unexpected.

For the task-specific adapted feedback team, 10 significant correlations were found. First, adaptability was significantly correlated with leadership ($r = .37, p < .05$) and communication ($r = .52, p < .01$). Second, coordination was significantly correlated with interpersonal ($r = .60, p < .01$). Leadership, in addition to being significantly correlated with adaptability, as mentioned earlier, was also significantly correlated with communication ($r = .43, p < .05$). These significant relationships indicate that an increase in the number of leadership messages sent resulted in an increase in the number of adaptability messages and communication messages sent, or vice versa, by the task-specific adapted feedback team.

In addition, "all messages sent" was significantly correlated with adaptability ($r = .43, p < .05$), decision making ($r = .59, p < .01$), and interpersonal ($r = .47, p < .01$) processes. Communication ($r = .39, p < .05$) was significantly correlated with "all messages sent." Last, team outcome was significantly correlated with interpersonal messages sent and with "all messages sent." This set of correlations indicates that the greater the number of interpersonal messages sent, the better the team outcome.

Team Outcome Measure

The mean team outcome for the adapted feedback team was 10.96, and for the task-specific adapted feedback team it was 12.96. The mean difference for team outcome for the two feedback treatment teams was statistically significant ($t(29) = 2.09, p = .046$).

The maximum possible team outcome score was 23.31. This score was calculated as the average of the four expert map scores. Thus, the students in this study demonstrated 51% of the experts' knowledge, whereas the students in Hsieh and O'Neil's (2002) study demonstrated 42% of the experts' knowledge. The mean difference for team outcome in this study and Hsieh and O'Neil's study was statistically significant ($t(59) = 3.75, p < .01$). In Hsieh and O'Neil's study, the participants were high school students, whereas in this study, the participants were college students.

Problem-Solving Process Measures

Table 14.3 presents descriptive statistics for problem-solving variables in this study. As can be seen in Table 14.3, for the total team ($N = 60$), the mean score for content understanding (knowledge map score) was 11.97. For problem-solving strategies for the total team, the mean for "browsing" was 113.31, the mean for "searching" was 17.15, the mean for "Boolean operators used" was 5.62, and the mean for feedback was 20.01. A two-tailed t test showed a significant difference between treatment and control teams for browsing ($t(29) = 2.52, p = .02$), and number of Boolean operators used

TABLE 14.3

Descriptive Statistics for Problem-Solving Variables

Information seeking and feedback behavior	Total (N = 60)		Adapted Feedback Team (n = 30)		Task-Specific Adapted Feedback Team (n = 30)	
	M	SD	M	SD	M	SD
Content understanding						
Knowledge map score	11.97	3.67	10.96	3.26	12.96	3.84
Problem-solving strategies						
Browsing	113.31	73.79	88.47	54.53	138.17	82.62
Searching	17.15	12.84	16.17	12.61	18.13	13.21
Boolean operators used	5.62	5.06	4.00	3.90	7.23	5.62
Feedback	20.01	15.07	19.53	15.38	20.50	15.01
Self-regulation						
Planning (8 items)	3.14	.44	3.19	.45	3.08	.42
Self-checking (8 items)	3.03	.50	3.11	.52	2.93	.46
Effort (8 items)	3.09	.47	3.17	.49	3.01	.45
Self-efficacy (8 items)	2.93	.60	3.04	.61	2.80	.58

($t(29) = 2.52, p = .02$), both for the task-specific adapted feedback team. No significant difference was found for searching ($t(29) = .57, p = .58$), or for feedback accessing ($t(29) = .24, p = .82$).

There were many significant correlations found among the problem-solving process measures. As may be seen in Table 14.4, for the total team ($N = 60$), knowledge map score (content understanding) was significantly related to browsing ($r = .40, p < .01$), searching ($r = .43, p < .01$), Boolean operators used ($r = .42, p < .01$), and feedback accessing ($r = .38, p < .01$). Furthermore, the four problem-solving strategies (browsing, searching, Boolean operators used, and feedback accessing) were correlated to one another significantly. Not shown in Table 14.4, browsing was significantly related to searching ($r = .72, p < .01$), Boolean operators used ($r = .75, p < .01$), and feedback accessing ($r = .74, p < .01$). Searching was significantly related to Boolean operators used ($r = .92, p < .01$) and feedback accessing ($r = .84, p < .01$). Boolean operators used was significantly related to feedback accessing ($r = .79, p < .01$). As for the four self-regulation measures (planning, self-checking, effort, and self-efficacy), they were all significantly related to one another. However, no significant correlation was found among the four self-regulation measures (Hong, O'Neil, & Feldon, in press; O'Neil & Herl, 1998) and the three problem-solving strategies. In addition, there was no significant correlation found among the four self-regulation measures and the team outcome.

As is shown in Table 14.4, for the adapted feedback team, knowledge map score (content understanding) was significantly related to browsing ($r = .36, p < .01$), searching ($r = .44, p < .01$), Boolean operators used ($r = .41, p < .01$), and feedback accessing ($r = .35, p < .01$). There was no significant relationship found between knowledge map score and self-regulation measures (planning, self-checking, effort, and self-efficacy). However, each of the four self-regulation measures was significantly correlated with the other three, and each of the four problem-solving strategies (browsing, searching, Boolean operators used, and feedback accessing) was significantly correlated with the other three. Nevertheless, none of the

TABLE 14.4

Correlations of Team Outcome and Problem-Solving Variables

		Team Outcome—Knowledge Map Score	
Problem-Solving Variables	Total (N = 60)	Adapted Knowledge of Response Feedback Team (n = 30)	Task-Specific Adapted Knowledge of Response Feedback Team (n = 30)
Problem-solving strategies			
Browsing	.40**	.36**	.36**
Searching	.43**	.44**	.40**
Boolean operators used	.42**	.41**	.37**
Feedback	.38**	.35**	.42**
Self-regulation			
Planning	û.11	−.08	−.07
Self-checking	.05	.04	.18
Effort	−.06	−.04	.00
Self-efficacy	−.12	−.08	−.07

$*p < .05$, two-tailed. $**p < .01$, two-tailed.

self-regulation measures was correlated significantly with any of the prob-
lem- solving strategies (browsing, searching, Boolean operators used, and
feedback accessing).

The significant correlations found for the task-specific adapted feedback
team were similar to those found for the adapted feedback team. For the
task-specific adapted feedback team, knowledge map score (content understanding) was also significantly related to browsing ($r = .36, p < .01$),
searching ($r = .40, p < .01$), Boolean operators used ($r = .37, p < .01$), and
feedback accessing ($r = .42, p < .01$). No significant relationship was found
between knowledge map score and self-regulation measures (planning,
self-checking, effort, and self-efficacy). Each of the four self-regulation
measures significantly correlated with the other three, and each of the four
problem-solving strategies significantly correlated with the other three.
Nevertheless, none of the self-regulation measures was correlated significantly with any of the problem-solving strategies (browsing, searching,
Boolean operators used, and feedback accessing).

In Hsieh and O'Neil's (2002) study, for the adapted feedback team,
searching was unexpectedly negatively related to team outcome ($r = -.40$,
$p < .05$). This was not the case in the current study. All four problem-solving strategies were significantly positively related to team outcome
(knowledge map score) in both feedback conditions. One difference between the two studies is that searching was explicitly taught in the current
study but was not taught in the Hsieh and O'Neil study.

TESTS OF HYPOTHESES

For Hypothesis 1, the results indicate that the task-specific adapted feedback team performed significantly better on the knowledge map than did
the adapted feedback team. A t test (two-tailed) on team outcome between
the adapted feedback team and the task-specific adapted feedback team
showed a significant difference between the means, $t(29) = 2.09, p = .046$.
As expected, students who received task-specific adapted feedback ($M =
12.96$) performed better than those who received adapted feedback only
($M = 10.96$). Thus, Hypothesis 1 was supported.

For Hypothesis 2, the results indicate that students receiving task-specific adapted feedback used approximately the same number of decision-making and leadership messages in their communications as students
receiving adapted feedback. The difference between the two teams was not
significant for the decision-making team process, $t(29) = .31, p = .76$, or for
the leadership team process, $t(29) = -1.51, p = .14$. Thus, Hypothesis 2 was
not supported.

For Hypothesis 3, Table 14.4 shows the correlations between informa-
tion-seeking variables and team outcome. As expected, browsing was signifi-

cantly related to team outcome (knowledge map score). In addition, feedback accessing was positively related to team outcome. In other words, the more browsing students did, the higher their team outcome (map score). Furthermore, the more feedback students requested, the better their team outcome (map score). Thus, Hypotheses 3.1 and 3.2 were supported.

For Hypothesis 4, as may be seen in Table 14.4, significant positive correlations were found for the total team ($N = 60$; $r = .42$, $p < .01$), the adapted feedback team ($r = .41$, $p < .01$), and the task-specific adapted feedback team ($r = .37$, $p < .01$). Thus, Hypothesis 4.1 was supported.

Also, as shown in Table 14.3, students in the task-specific adapted feedback team used more Boolean operators than did students in the adapted feedback team. A t test (two-tailed) showed the mean difference in number of Boolean operators used between the two feedback teams to be significant, $t(29) = 2.52$, $p = .02$. Thus Hypothesis 4.2 was supported.

DISCUSSION

First, results from the study provide evidence indicating that students who received task-specific adapted feedback performed significantly better than did students who received adapted feedback. This finding was consistent with several themes in the feedback literature. For example, adapted feedback was suggested by Sales (1993) to customize along one or more dimensions to compensate for the weakness of generic feedback that lacks capacity to communicate with learners. Hsieh and O'Neil's (2002) study showed that such adapted feedback was better in assisting students in knowledge map construction than in knowledge of response feedback. Moreover, Ross and Morrison (1993) defined task-specific feedback as elaboration feedback that concentrates on the current test item. They found task-specific feedback was better than general feedback in assisting learning. Other than Ross and Morrison's study and the current study, there has been no research that has investigated task-specific adapted feedback. Our results support the efficacy of such task-specific adapted feedback.

In addition, in regard to feedback presentation style, Kalyuga, Chandler, and Sweller (2000) found that low-knowledge learners or inexperienced learners benefited most from feedback combining diagrams with additional text-based information. Foster and Macan (2002) showed that providing information about a process or strategy could optimize learning during practice. In their study, participants who received this type of feedback (called attentional advice) had significantly higher achievement than those receiving no advice at all.

Finally, the results are consistent with a theoretical framework of dynamic testing. According to Grigorenko and Sternberg (1998), "Dynamic testing is a collection of testing designed to quantify not only the products or even the processes of learning but also the potential to learn" (p. 75). In other words, dynamic testing not only provides students with accuracy reports on how they are doing on a test but also provides them with information on how to improve the quality of their work on the test during the time of the testing. Dynamic testing can do so because it assigns a different role to feedback than the one assigned in traditional, static testing. In traditional static testing, feedback about performance is usually not given during the test. In dynamic testing, feedback is given during the test to help assess learning. In this study, the students were considered to be low prior knowledge students in environmental sciences. Combining the research findings on feedback and dynamic testing, two types of feedback were created. Adapted feedback was presented in a graphical format with extra text based on general task improvement strategies. Task-specific adapted feedback was presented in a graphical format with extra text based on general task improvement strategies and task-specific strategies. In this study, the feedback was given not after the test but during the test to help students learn. As predicted, the task-specific adapted feedback team performed significantly better than the adapted feedback team. Students who received feedback with task-specific information constructed better knowledge maps than students with no task-specific information. The claim made by dynamic testing about the role of feedback as a learning strategy to assist students' performance during the task was shown to be feasible and successful. Students with task-specific information showed a higher use of the Boolean search strategy than did students without that information.

The finding that information searching and use of Boolean search operators was beneficial for team outcome was in line with the search literature. Baker and O'Neil (2003) included use of search engines as one of the requirements of technological fluency. In addition, they listed use of Boolean operators as an example of a cognitive strategy for use in a problem-solving search task. In an observational study of novice users searching information on the World Wide Web, Lazonder (2000) suggested instructing students in search logic such as use of Boolean operators to improve the quality of their searching. The results from the current study support the literature on searching with Boolean operators and training in their use.

Our study has confirmed that computer-based performance assessment in collaborative problem solving is effective. In this study, both collaboration between team members and problem-solving processes were effectively measured, administered, scored, and reported by computer. However, the results from this study should not be generalized to other types of teams due to the fact that a dyad is different from other types of teams and team size is an important variable in the teamwork literature.

ACKNOWLEDGMENTS

The work reported herein was funded in part under the Educational Research and Development Centers Program, PR/Award Number R305B960002, as administered by the Institute of Education Sciences, U.S. Department of Education. The findings and opinions expressed in this report do not reflect the positions or policies of the National Center for Education Research, the Institute of Education Sciences, or the U.S. Department of Education.

REFERENCES

Arts, J. A. R., Gijselaers, W. H., & Segers, M. S. R. (2002). Cognitive effects of an authentic computer-supported, problem-based learning environment. *Instructional Science, 30*, 465–495.

Baker, E. L., & O'Neil, H. F., Jr. (2003). Technological fluency: Needed skills for the future. In H. F. O'Neil, Jr. & R. Perez (Eds.), *Technology applications in education: A learning view* (pp. 245–265). Mahwah, NJ: Lawrence Erlbaum Associates.

Covington, M. V. (1998). *The will to learn: A guide for motivating young people.* Cambridge, England: Cambridge University Press.

Foster, J., & Macan, T. H. (2002). Attentional advice: Effects on immediate, delayed, and transfer task performance. *Human Performance, 15*, 367–380.

Grigorenko, E. L., & Sternberg, R. J. (1998). Dynamic testing. *Psychological Bulletin, 124*, 75–111.

Herl, H. E., O'Neil, H. F., Jr., Chung, G. K. W. K., & Schacter, J. (1999). Reliability and validity of a computer-based knowledge mapping system to measure content understanding. *Computers in Human Behavior, 15*, 315–333.

Hong, E., O'Neil, H. F., Jr., & Feldon, D. (in press). Gender effects on mathematics achievement: Mediating role of state and trait self-regulation. In A. M. Gallagher & J. C. Kaufman (Eds.), *Mind the gap: Gender differences in mathematics.* Cambridge, England: Cambridge University Press.

Hsieh, I. G., & O'Neil, H. F. (2002). Types of feedback in a computer-based collaborative problem-solving task. *Computers in Human Behavior, 18*, 699–715.

Kalyuga, S., Chandler, P., & Sweller, J. (2000). Incorporating learner experience into the design of multimedia instruction. *Journal of Educational Psychology, 92*, 126–136.

Lazonder, A. W. (2000). Exploring novice users' training needs in searching information on the WWW. *Journal of Computer Assisted Learning, 16*, 326–335.

O'Neil, H. F., Jr., Chung, G. K. W. K., & Brown, R. S. (1997). Use of networked simulations as a context to measure team competencies. In H. F. O'Neil, Jr. (Ed.), *Workforce readiness: Competencies and assessment* (pp. 411–452). Mahwah, NJ: Lawrence Erlbaum Associates.

O'Neil, H. F., Jr., & Herl, H. E. (1998, April). *Reliability and validity of a trait measure of self-regulation.* Presented at the annual meeting of the American Educational Research Association, San Diego, CA.

Ross, S. M., & Morrison, G. R. (1993). Using feedback to adapt instruction for individuals. In J. V. Dempsey & G. C. Sales (Eds.), *Interactive instruction and feedback* (pp. 177–195). Englewood Cliffs, NJ: Educational Technology Publications.

Sales, G. C. (1993). Adapted and adaptive feedback in technology-based instruction. In J. V. Dempsey & G. C. Sales (Eds.), *Interactive instruction and feedback* (pp. 159–176). Englewood Cliffs, NJ: Educational Technology Publications.

Schacter, J., Herl, H. E., Chung, G. K. W. K., Dennis, R. A., & O'Neil, H. F., Jr. (1999). Computer-based performance assessments: A solution to the narrow measurement and reporting of problem-solving. *Computers in Human Behavior, 15*, 403–418.

Smith, M. S., & Broom, M. (2003). The landscape and future of the use of technology in K–12 education. In H. F. O'Neil, Jr. & R. S. Perez (Eds.), *Technology applications in education: A learning view* (pp. 3–30). Mahwah, NJ: Lawrence Erlbaum Associates.

Chapter 15

Teaching Procedural Knowledge in Distance Learning Environments

Allen Munro
David Surmon
Quentin Pizzini
University of Southern California

Adult learning is often motivated by the need to learn how to perform complex tasks are important to carrying out one's job. In some cases, the procedures that must be learned to perform these tasks can be defined as a specific sequence of actions. In other cases, a procedure can be thought of instead as a network of conditional branchings that associate sets of actions that can be performed to accomplish the task goal in a variety of contexts. And in some cases, tasks are so complex that they cannot be taught in terms of predefined observations and actions, but must instead be represented as a set of strategies, tactics, and heuristics that are sufficiently abstract that they can be applied to new circumstances that cannot be anticipated by the developers of training materials.

Whatever the complexity of the procedural or applied problem solving subject matter, practice at the task under a variety of conditions will improve the chances that the learner will apply what has been learned to actual tasks. Certain types of procedural skills cannot be taught economically using distance learning technology at this time. In particular, where specialized motor skills must be learned (applying a precise twisting force during an assembly process, for example), distance learning cannot address the entire learning requirement. Cognitive components of procedural knowledge can be taught with distance learning, however. In fact, both what Fitts and Posner (1967) termed *first stage* or *cognitive* learning and *second stage* or *associative* learning occur during practice carrying out procedures. First, students learn in the context of interactive demonstrations and explanations; they are engaged in cognitive learning. As they begin to practice more rapid procedure execution, they experience associative learning.

Most procedures require learning about sequences of actions, learning about the conditions under which actions could be taken, or learning how to address complex problems in the context of a task environment. These cognitive components of procedural learning can be taught in a practice environment that provides an opportunity for interactive practice in the context of a functionally realistic task environment, such as a graphical simulation. Such an environment must provide realistic interactive behavior, but typically does not need to be photo-realistic. When a computer delivers the training, it is possible for it to tirelessly observe and offer pedagogically relevant responses to the actions that students take in that practice environment. Task practice can be interactively assessed in real time, rather than being postponed for "after-action reviews," as is common in simulation-based training in the U.S. military forces.

A special type of procedural learning is *troubleshooting training*. The U.S. armed forces research community has devoted considerable resources to the study of effective approaches to teaching maintenance technicians how to engage in effective troubleshooting of complex systems. Troubleshooting is a cognitive task that has as its goal the identification of probable causes of faults in a potentially huge problem space of possible causes. One dimension that can be used to compare research products (such as experimental tutors) for troubleshooting training is the *specificity* dimension. Must effective training deal with the particulars of systems that will be the context for troubleshooting tasks, or can troubleshooting be taught as a generic skill? One of the differences between expert and non-expert troubleshooters in real world contexts is that the experts have much more familiarity with and knowledge of the systems that they are troubleshooting. Hunt and Rouse (1981) proposed that context-free diagnostic skills could be developed that could productively transfer to specific troubleshooting contexts, and Rouse's (1979) FAULT system provided a training environment for context-free troubleshooting training. Swezey, Perez, and Allen (1988) showed that students receiving a procedurally oriented, step-by-step training regime performed more accurate troubleshooting and carried out more correct tests. On the other hand, students given conceptually oriented training, with information about system structure, exhibited better transfer of training to related tasks. Morris and Rouse (1985) also showed that:

- Instruction in theoretical principles does not produce good trouble-shooters.
- Proceduralizing troubleshooting can ensure that particular strategies are used.
- Explicit guidance in applying system knowledge or troubleshooting strategies improves performance.
- Task related knowledge is more important than aptitude.

In practice, of course, task performance does not depend on only one layer of analysis or on skills at only one level of abstraction. That is, learning about a procedure will usually require learning about the structure and functions of the system in which the procedure is conducted, but it may also demand the acquisition of meta-knowledge about how to conduct certain types of procedures (such as half-splitting or expected value analysis, in the context of troubleshooting). Perez (1991) proposed a cognitive model for troubleshooting. A useful cognitive model must represent several different kinds of knowledge relevant to troubleshooting, including the structural topology of a system, the functional topology of the system, specific facts about the system (possibly based on case knowledge), knowledge about the standard procedures that are carried out in this system, knowledge about how such procedures are structured in general, and tactical and strategic knowledge relevant to these types of procedural tasks. All these types of knowledge can be taught in the context of interactive graphical simulations.

In our laboratory, a body of work on the topic of machine-based teaching and tutoring in the context of interactive simulations has produced two sets of specifications that may have wide application to the field of teaching cognitively loaded tasks using computers. One of these is a set of techniques that have been found effective for organizing and delivering automated instruction about procedures and complex tasks. The other is a set of specifications that action-centered environments, whether they be simulations or embedded training systems, can adhere to in order to support machine observation and remediation of learner actions during task practice. These specifications are introduced in this chapter. Systems built on these principles are now being applied to distance learning (Munro, 2003; Walker et al., 2004).

WHAT CHARACTERIZES PROCEDURAL INSTRUCTION?

Procedural instruction has much in common with other types of instruction, such as the need for frequent assessment and for customized pedagogy. In addition, however, procedural instruction has a number of characteristics that are not found in other types of instruction. Procedural instruction can include specialized *modes of instruction* and specialized *types of assessment*.

Procedural instruction is often carried out in a master-apprentice context. A tutor, who knows very well how the procedure should be performed and (ordinarily) why each action should be taken, works to convey that knowledge to a student or trainee. In many cases, procedural training is carried out in a work environment, which makes it possible to demonstrate actions and procedures, to point out relevant observations that should be made, and to assess student knowledge by observing the student carry out sequences of actions. As is described herein, it is also possible to develop and deliver distance-learning procedural instruction that performs the same kinds of functions.

Special Instruction Modes

Consider the following possible major modes of instruction in procedural training:

- Demonstration.
- Supervised practice.
- Monitored but unsupervised practice.

These modes are in addition to conventional instructional modes such as presenting explanations (in text, graphics, or animations) or assessing students' answers to questions.

Special Types of Assessment

A type of assessment that is found in procedure training is a *procedural performance assessment*. In a procedural performance assessment, a student is directed to carry out a procedure in one or in a variety of contexts. The student's approach to the procedure is observed and assessed. Detailed assessments can be used to guide instruction. Summative assessments can be used to determine whether a student can be credentialed as a competent performer of the targeted procedure.

A procedural tutor can carry out a set of *micro-assessments* during training. Micro-assessments are simple interaction events that can be assessed to provide estimates of knowledge about particular facts and skills that are required for competence in the procedure as a whole. Examples of micro-assessments can include:

- Observing actions (in a procedural environment; here we are discussing actions that may be part of the procedure to be learned, not actions such as answering a multiple choice question).
- Observing effects (in the procedural environment).
- Observing the attainment of states of interest in the procedural environment.

Just as a human tutor must observe actions, pose questions, explain relationships, carry out actions and sequences of actions, set up practice contexts, and pose challenges to be attained by a learner, so, too must a Web-delivered training system.

TEACHING PROCEDURAL KNOWLEDGE IN THE CONTEXT OF A SIMULATION

During the 1980s there was an enthusiasm for so-called *microworlds* as learning environments (Forbus, 1984; Hollan, Hutchins, & Weitzman, 1984; Papert, 1980). It was widely expected that providing students rule-governed interactive graphical environments would afford learners sufficient opportunity to acquire deep understandings of these rule-based systems, which they could interact with, conducting "experiments" and observing the outcomes. Microworlds in topics such as microeconomics (Shute & Glaser, 1990), gravity and Newtonian motion (Smith, 1987), and complex electronic equipment (Lesgold, Lajoie, Bunzo, & Eggan, 1992) were developed. In the long run, the microworld approach was not much applied to real-world procedural training. There appear to be two primary reasons for this. The first is that developing high-quality microworlds for learning proved to be an expensive programming problem. Each microworld was typically created from scratch in a fairly low-level development environment (typically, using a programming language). There were substantial expenses re-implementing core simulation features and student interaction interfaces anew for each such project.

The second reason for the lack of ubiquitous success with microworlds is that it turns out that not every student has the intellectual and emotional makeup that drives them to experiment boldly, relentlessly, and imaginatively in the microworld. It is probably not a coincidence that one of the few surviving centers of educational microworld research is at MIT, where there is no shortage of students who exhibit such characteristics. To expect every electronics technician to derive or intuit important electronic principles as a result of experimenting with simulated electronic environments seems naïve, at best. In fact, subsequent work has found it necessary to supply pedagogical interactions with microworld simulations (Rieber, 1992; Self, 1995).

Similarly, to expect every schoolchild to derive the basic principles of velocity and acceleration as a result of using (real or simulated) ramps and rolling balls of different masses but equal rolling resistance is simply unrealistic. After all, people had access to ramps and balls to experiment with for thousands of years before Galileo worked out the basic principles of acceleration using such an apparatus. And he did not do so in the course of a single 2-hour "discovery learning" session. Not every student is a Galileo. Most people need guidance if they are to learn about the behavior of complex systems and about how to carry out procedures in those contexts. For most students, exposure to a microworld by itself will never bring about such learning. Students need to receive instruction in the procedural context. Clark (2004) states that: "Touvinen and Sweller (1999) demonstrated that, when properly designed, worked examples are superior to discovery learning for all but the most advanced learners, and that even advanced experts get equal benefit from discovery learning and worked examples and so seem not to be harmed by examples." Van Merrienböer, Clark, and de Croock (2002) provide an illustration of such a worked example for training.

What does instruction typically consist of in an interactive procedural context? Students can be presented worked examples (demonstrations), or they can be guided through exercises, or they can be given problems to solve with varying degrees of guidance or support. Clark (2004) suggests that "how to" procedural training should include:

- Clear descriptions of actions and decisions that must be taken to achieve a goal.
- Demonstration of the procedure (a worked example).
- Concepts, processes, and principles that explain why the procedure works.
- Practice in the procedure in behaviorally realistic contexts.

There are many possible sequences of instruction, and many types of "instructional primitives" that can be used in such sequences. Some of these instructional primitives will be of types that are commonly used in non-procedural instruction. For example, a teacher (or an artificial tutor) could begin by posing a simple yes–no question, such as "Have you ever seen an electronic heart defibrillator, such as this one?" In this chapter, the topic is the types of instructional interactions that take place in procedural learning contexts, but that are not used in many other contexts, such as conventional page-based CBT/CBI/CBL.

In the following section, a set of universal primitives for teaching the cognitive elements of procedures is presented. For each primitive, brief examples from ordinary tutoring or teaching are described. For each primitive, an example from a computer-based tutor follows. Then the requirements for implementing such a capability in a computer-based system are presented.

THE ARCHITECTURE
OF PROCEDURAL LEARNING ENVIRONMENTS

Whether instruction about procedures involves a human tutor and real-world systems and devices, or an artificial tutorial component and a computer simulation, essentially the same systems architecture can be described. See Fig. 15.1, which shows two possible instructional modes in the context of a simulation. On the left, a human tutor observes the way that a student interacts with a Navy Destroyer propulsion control system and provides appropriate instructional feedback. On the right, an artificial tutor observes the student's interactions in the same system and instructs the student. In both cases, there are three major entities interacting: a student, a responsive environment (e.g., a simulation, or a real system), and a tutor, whether human or an instructional software component.

The nature of an architectural viewpoint is independent of particular implementations. For example, one distance learning implementation of the architecture of Fig. 15.1 might push a simulation program from the server to the student's computer but run a tutor component on the server itself, while another implementation might send both the artificial tutor component and the simulation component to the student's computer. The core architectural issues about how tutorial components and training simulations should interact with each other is independent of any particular implementation. (That said, the observations presented here are informed by the experience of developing and making use of a particular implementation of

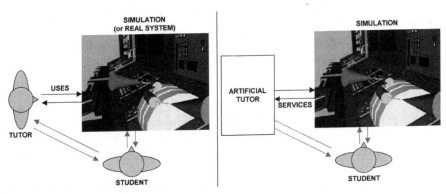

FIG. 15.1. Pedagogical services of simulations for tutors.

this architecture. This implementation, *iRides*, which was described in a preliminary form by Munro, Surmon, Johnson, Pizzini, & Walker, 1999, is briefly discussed later in this chapter.)

We can describe the uses that a human tutor makes of a simulation or a real system during procedural training as requiring certain *services* of the simulation or the real system. Simulations must provide a similar set of services to an artificial tutor, if that tutorial component is to make effective use of the simulator for training. While it may seem odd to speak of a real system providing the service of permitting that the tutor manipulate one of its controls, a systematic approach to describing the interactions between tutors and simulations (or real systems) makes it possible to identify universals of procedural instruction.

During procedural training, many types of instructional interactions take place. Some of these are not unique to procedural instruction, but can be found in many types of education and training that do not involve interactions with behaving systems (simulations or real systems). Examples of such instructional interactions include verbal explanations, questions to the student and the corresponding answers, and so on. In Fig. 15.1, these types of interactions are represented by the light gray arrows between the tutors and the students. Other instructional interactions are of types that require the presence of an interactive environment, such as a simulation. The focus of this discussion is those types of instructional interactions, the ones that make direct use of features of the behaving environment. In particular, we are interested in identifying the simplest types of instructional interactions, which we call *instructional primitives*, and especially the instructional primitives that are required for effective instruction in the context of interactive simulations. More elaborate types of frequently observed instructional interactions can be analyzed as being composed of sequences of the simpler or *primitive* types.

Conventional page-centered computer-based instruction is not concerned with these types of instructional primitives, because the environment in such systems is the *page*, not a simulated system.

THE INSTRUCTIONAL PRIMITIVES
OF PROCEDURAL LEARNING

We propose eight instructional primitives for procedural learning.

Require Indication

When a human tutor begins a session with a student, one way of pre-assessing basic knowledge is to ask the student to indicate an object, often by pointing to it. This can be done to ascertain that the student will understand technical terms that will be used, as in:

Point to the blade retract sequence valve.

or

Point to the term of the linear equation that specifies the Y-intercept of the line.

Requiring an indication can also be used to assess whether the student understands how a system works. For example:

Which button is used to turn on the defibrillator? Point to it.

When a human tutor uses this instructional primitive, it is only necessary for the tutor to watch the student in order to see which object is indicated. If the student points to the correct object, the tutor can be reasonably assured that the student knows that fact, and the session can proceed on that basis. If the student points to an incorrect object or fails to respond or admits ignorance, the instructor may decide to give the answer and to present a body of related information.

Interactions like the three preceding examples are examples of *micro-assessments*, brief interactions that are used to gauge very specific knowledge and/or skill elements during instruction. Frequent use of micro-assessments during training helps students to maintain attention, and it allows the teacher to constantly customize instruction to the needs of the students. The Require Indication instructional primitive is an essential component of many micro-assessments in procedural training.

Just as human tutors make use of micro-assessments during instruction, so can artificial tutors in a computer-based procedural learning system. For example, a tutor can check that a student understands a technical term by asking the student to point to or "touch" an object designated by that term. In Fig. 15.2, a tutor requires an indication from the student ("Click on the function plot line") that will reveal whether the student has read the immediately preceding statement (" … The blue line shown here plots this function"). In such a case, the micro-assessment tests whether the student has been paying attention and has learned the term. This is an example of Require Indication in action.

The interactive graphical environments shown in Figs. 15.2, 15.3, and 15.5 were developed using VIVIDS (Munro 2003; Munro & Pizzini, 1998) and *iRides Author* (Munro, Pizzini, & Johnson, 2004), and can be delivered for distance learning using iRides, a system implemented in Java that runs on Windows, Macintosh, and Linux, and other platforms. In iRides, there is an interactive graphical component, called the simulator, which works collaboratively with a tutorial component. Both the simulator component and

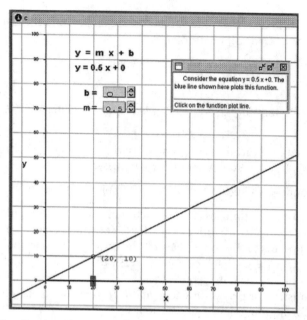

FIG. 15.2. *Require Indication* example.

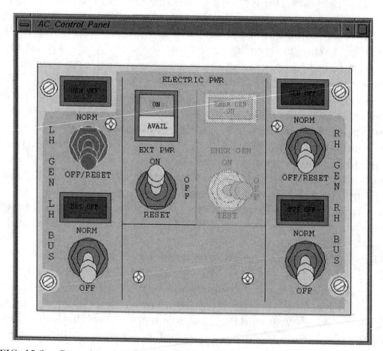

FIG. 15.3. *Draw Attention To* in VIVIDS.

the tutorial components of iRides interpret authored specifications that determine what kind of simulation and what instruction is delivered. This approach makes it possible for the core, unchanging simulator component to handle all the low-level service calls that the instructional system places on it. It is not necessary to modify the iRides delivery component in any way when presenting a completely new kind of interactive graphical environment and/or new instruction for that environment. The iRides program itself is identical for every tutorial delivered with it.

The iRides simulator must provide a number of specific services to the tutorial component in order to support *Require Indication*, including these:

- *Ignore Manipulations*—In a graphical simulation, a student ordinarily indicates an object by selecting it with a pointing device. In most desktop graphics simulations, that means clicking on the object with the mouse. But the simulation has behavior of its own. For example, clicking on the function plot line in Fig. 15.2 ordinarily activates the line, so that it can be manually dragged into a desired angle and position. This is not a desirable behavior at this point during the instruction, however. The tutorial component therefore asks the simulation component to ignore student manipulations, to the extent that the behavior rules that would ordinarily be triggered by such manipulations are not activated.
- *Report Object Selection*—The simulator must still report back to the instructional component that an object has been selected. The identity of a selected object is returned to the tutorial component, so that it can evaluate whether the target object was correctly indicated.
- *Resume Manipulations*—Once the *Require Indication* instructional interaction has ended, the simulator needs to be told that it can once again allow behaviors to follow from student actions in the interactive graphical environment.

The tutorial component itself must also have a number of low-level services that are employed to make the instructional primitive *Require Indication* work. These include catching timeouts, providing hints and answers, giving additional chances to the student, and so on. These sorts of low-level services are required for all computer-based instructional delivery systems, not just for those that interact with graphical simulations. As such, these services are not the focus of this discussion.

Draw Attention To

A kind of mirror image to the *Require Indication* instructional primitive is *Draw Attention To*. When a human tutor is teaching a procedure, he or she is likely to draw the student's attention to particular objects. For example, a tutor might say:

This handle controls the port turbine speed.

At the same time, the instructor is likely to touch or point to that control. The action of touching or pointing is an instance of the *Draw Attention To* primitive.

Of course, even a page-based CBT system is likely to make some use of attention-directing techniques. Different text characteristics, including font family, size, color, and style (bold, italic, and so on) may be used to direct a student's attention to particular words or phrases in a text. In a simulation-centered training system, what distinguishes the *Draw Attention To* primitive is that its usage is transitory, not static. In model-centered or simulation-centered instruction, text and other presentations are presented and removed while a simulation view remains open. At times, it is necessary to clarify to students exactly what is being referred to in those presentations. This is the role of an implementation of *Draw Attention To* in that instructional process.

The *Draw Attention To* primitive can be implemented in different ways. In the RIDES (Munro, 1994) and VIVIDS (Munro, 2003; Munro et al, 1998; Munro & Pizzini, 1998) simulation-centered training systems, graphical objects were highlighted by rapidly alternating the colors of the objects (from off-white to salmon to the natural colors of the object, repeatedly). In the screenshot shown in Fig. 15.2, the left-hand bus generator switch of a VIVIDS aviation control panel is being highlighted in order to draw student attention to it. (At the instant of the screenshot, that switch, at the upper left, was in the salmon-colored phase.)

In iRides, the *Draw Attention To* primitive is implemented in a different way; a flashing green oval is drawn around the object that the tutor is drawing to the attention of a student.

A simulation system that is designed to collaborate with a tutorial component must provide a variety of specific services to the tutorial component to support *Draw Attention To*, including:

- *Highlight Object*—When an instructional component asks the simulation to highlight an object, the simulator adds that object to the list of currently highlighted objects. The highlight process is responsible for rendering periodic graphical effects that are expected to draw attention to those graphics on the highlighted object list.
- *Unhighlight Object*—The simulator removes the specified object from the highlighted objects list. The object is restored to its normal appearance.
- *Cleanup Highlight List*—When a lesson is completed, any objects remaining on the highlighted objects list are removed.

Using these services, the simulation component can draw attention to objects and can stop drawing attention to them, in response to requests from a tutorial component.

Set Value/Set Values

During advanced procedural training, human instructors will set up system states or interaction contexts that they want their students to experience as part of their training. A nurse needs to be able to set up a pulse oximeter for patient use no matter what state it was previously left in. Requiring that the student perform the set-up starting from a variety of initial states provides job-relevant practice. In some cases, instructors will insert exceptional states, such as equipment malfunctions, in order to provide special practice to trainees.

This instructional primitive can be more effectively provided in simulation-based procedure training than in many real-life training contexts. For example, training for the maintainers of complex military equipment sometimes includes the insertion of malfunctions into real systems. Instructors could place a malfunctioning valve into a helicopter rotor control system used in training, for example. Where real equipment is used for training, however, policy and safety concerns often prohibit fault insertion. Some faults lead to cascading failures that can be very expensive to repair in real systems. For this reason, simulation-based training can be used to give learners the opportunity to experience working with many types of malfunctioning systems that they would not otherwise encounter during training.

The *Set Values* instructional primitive is used by the tutorial component of a simulation-based trainer to establish a simulation state for instruction or practice purposes. During a discursive presentation, *Set Values* may be repeatedly invoked to depict system states of interest, in order to illustrate the topics being discussed. Before a practice session, this primitive can be used to put a simulation in an appropriate state for the type of skill and knowledge that is about to be exercised.

The simulator in such a system must provide an underlying *Set Attribute Values* service that makes it possible for the tutorial controller to request a new state of the simulation.

Perform Manipulation

During procedural training, it is often necessary for a tutor to demonstrate how a sequence of actions is to be carried out. In many cases, the tutor does this by actually performing that set of actions. When a human tutor carries out an action, it is ordinarily obvious to a student what is being done. The tutor may provide a narrative that makes clear the reasons for the action:

I'm unlocking the ejection seat control guard, so that I can flip it out of the way, exposing the control button itself.

Now I'm flipping up the guard. If I press the ejection seat button now, explosive bolts will pop off the canopy, and a rocket engine under the seat will eject the seat, and me, out of the cockpit.

While this narrative is presented, two instances of *Perform Manipulation*—unlocking the guard and flipping it up—are carried out.

There are a few types of procedure training in which it is not naturally easy for a student to observe the tutor's *Perform Manipulations*. For example, processes such as mental multiplication involve a number of steps, but a tutor cannot illustrate them in exactly the same way that he or she would normally perform the task (silently, mentally). Instead, the tutor must do something to make the actions apparent to the student, perhaps by saying each step aloud or by writing it down as it is carried out mentally.

In the case of simulation-based training, there is an issue of how to make actions apparent to the student when the actions are performed by the artificial tutor. When the tutorial component directs that a *Perform Manipulation* take place, there are several techniques that a simulation can employ to make clear what is being done. One possibility is to employ an artificial avatar for the tutor, a moving graphical construct that can perform motions that correspond to human manipulations. See Fig. 15.4.

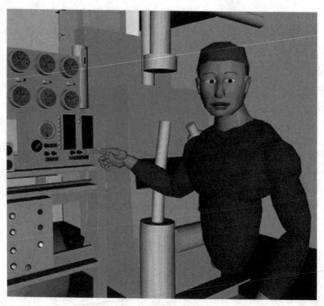

FIG. 15.4. *Perform Manipulation* in the virtual environment trainer.

Creating graphical avatars that are appropriate for a variety of graphical simulations can be a labor-intensive and expensive task. In iRides, a simpler approach has been implemented, one that has proved adequate for the *Perform Manipulation* instructional primitive in a variety of simulation contexts. In this approach, an alternative graphical "pointer," somewhat different in appearance from the usual mouse pointer, appears on the screen. This is the mouse pointer for the artificial tutor or coach. It moves to the object that must be manipulated. When the tutor "presses" the mouse button, this second "mouse pointer" becomes graphically more intense. In this way, the simulator component can provide visual feedback about the manipulation that is being demonstrated to the student. Fig. 15.5 shows a simple 2D graphics trainer for learning how to connect the components of a high tech land warfare system. At a point in training in which the procedure is demonstrated to the student, a new "mouse pointer" appears that is visually distinct from the actual mouse pointer that the student controls. This pointer moves according to specifications supplied to the simulator by the tutorial component. When the virtual mouse button is depressed, this pointer is shown with white fill, and blue edges. Here, the manipulation of dragging one end of a cable to a connector on another object is being simulated. The tutor's mouse is seen "performing the work"; note that it is visually distinct from the ordinary mouse pointer, which is under the control of the student.

Of course, it is even more important that the simulator's *Perform Manipulation* service must result in the desired simulation effects. This should be implemented in such a way that the simulator engine itself will behave no differently in response to these artificial actions than it would to actual interactions, such as mouse button actions, by a human user.

Many low-level simulation services support the *Perform Manipulation* instructional primitive in the simulation system shown in Fig. 15.5, including these:

> *Pointer Visible / Pointer Invisible*—The simulation environment must offer the service of making the pointer visible when it is needed. When it is no longer needed, it must be invisible.

> *Button Down / Button Up*—Instruction must be able to specify button actions for the virtual mouse. When these actions are taken, the simulation must respond just as it would if a human user carried out the same action using the real mouse. For example, every rule that begins with "If MouseDownIn (self)" must fire in response to pressing the virtual mouse button by the tutorial component. In this way it can be assured that the same behavior that takes place in real sessions will also occur in demonstrations. In addition, in most implementations of *Perform Manipulation*, something must be done to convey that the mouse button is now down. In

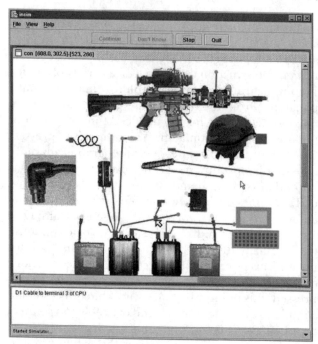

FIG. 15.5. Special "mouse pointer" for *Perform Manipulation*.

the iRides system, this is done by changing the pointer's physical appearance when it is down.

Move Pointer on Path—The simulation must be able to provide the service of moving though a set of vertexes, beginning at the first and ending at the last, within a specified time.

A simulation that offers these services can support the *Perform Manipulation* instructional primitive.

Pause/Resume Simulation

During the course of a tutorial session, it is sometimes necessary to freeze a simulation so that an instructional point can be made. For example, a simulation that replicates Galileo's experiments with gravity might be frozen to show that a light and a heavy sphere have moved the same distance down their tracked ramps at a given point in time. Ephemeral, quickly changing states of systems can be pointed out to students if the instructional system can detect the occurrence of such states and pause the simulation so as to point out the relevant transitory characteristics. Once the pedagogical point has been made, the tutorial component can tell the simulation to continue from the point at which it was paused. We call instruction that occurs because of the occurrence of a triggering state in the simulation *opportunistic* instruction.

In order to provide this service to a tutorial component, a simulation must have several features. In addition to low-level *Start* and *Stop* features, the simulator must maintain a clock that is partially independent of the computer's own real time clock. In many simulations, certain behavioral rules refer to the current time. However, if a simulation is paused, the passage of time must also be paused in the simulation. Were it otherwise, Galileo's spheres would already be at the bottom of their ramps when the simulation was unpaused. A simulation must keep track of cumulative pause time and deduct that time from the value found in the computer's system clock.

The *Pause/Resume* facility is one example of a feature that makes it possible for simulation-based tutors to provide learning experiences that are not easily achieved without simulations. In real life, a tutor cannot roll two spheres down ramps and then freeze time so that their identical positions can be discussed.

Require Manipulation

When a tutor needs to have a student indicate an object, the *Require Indication* instructional primitive is used, as described above. A simulation may disable user manipulations in order to support this primitive. At other times, a tutorial specifies that the student must carry out an action in the simulation. For example, if a tutor wants to walk a student through a procedure step-by-step, it may be useful to have the student carry out each action in turn. This type of practice can be a precursor to a less supervised form of practice that permits deviation from a fixed order of actions.

With complex systems, there is a problem with giving students the opportunity to carry out actions incorrectly. In real life, if the student presses a "Launch Missile" button when he was supposed to press a "Stand Down" button, the consequences of the error may be serious indeed. Even in a simulation, however, incorrect actions have the potential to derail step-by-step procedure training. Once the simulated missile has been launched, how can it be recalled? VIVIDS and iRides provide different solutions to this problem in their implementations of *Require Manipulation*. In VIVIDS, when the tutorial component begins a *Require Manipulation*, it asks the simulation to begin archiving all attribute value changes. If an incorrect action is taken by the student, the tutor tells the simulation to restore the initial values of all those attributes. This has the effect of backing the simulation up (including the clock value) to where it was when the action was required. At this point the tutor can give the student another chance (perhaps with a hint) or the tutor can use a *Perform Manipulation* to demonstrate what should have been done. The step-by-step instruction can then continue. In iRides, the tutor asks the simulator to stop responding to manipulations (as it does in a *Require Indication*). When the student indicates the correct object, the tutor immediately carries out the core of a *Perform Manipulation* action. To the student, it appears that an ordinary manipulation took place. If, on the other hand, the student attempts an incorrect manipulation, the tutorial can respond appropriately without having to be concerned about restoring the state of the simulation.

The ability of a simulation with pedagogical services to permit fail-safe practice creates opportunities for instruction that would not be possible using real systems, where student errors could result in a risk of injury or serious damage to expensive equipment systems.

Require State

The *Require State* instructional primitive makes it possible to offer practice that is less constrained than the step-by-step supervised practice just discussed. The tutorial component can ask the student to achieve a particular state of the simulated system. In this type of instructional interaction, a student is allowed to carry out actions without interference from the tutor. In the case of human tutoring, the tutor watches to determine whether the target state is achieved. When and if the student achieves the desired state, the tutor may confirm the student's success, or the tutor may wait for the student to claim success. (Demanding that the student make the claim helps to ensure that he or she has not simply stumbled into the target state without understanding what had to be done.) A tutor may also point out to the student what are the crucial features of the system that define the target state.

Artificial tutors need to be able to have this type of instructional interaction with students as well. In VIVIDS and iRides, a low-level service called *Register Expression* is provided to the tutorial component by the simulation. Using this call, the tutorial component passes to the simulator an expression in the native language of the simulator. When the simulator receives this service request it parses the expression, as though it were a behavior rule for an attribute. When the value of the expression changes, the tutor is informed. The value of the expression determines whether or not the desired state has been achieved. The tutor's *Require State* instructional primitive compares that value with the target value and thereby recognizes whether the state has been achieved.

The *Register Expression* service has other uses in simulation-based training, as well. It can be used to set up callbacks for other states of interest in the simulation. For example, potential safety violations can be detected based on changes in expressions that define such violations. This type of opportunistic instruction could not be authored without the Register Expression service.

All the *Require* instructional primitives must have access to an instructional timer. (Not to the simulation clock, which is frozen during periods when the simulator is paused.) This makes it possible for the artificial tutor to offer help or to provide hints or instruction if the student takes too long to respond to a requirement presented by the tutor.

Do Magic

As its frivolous name suggests, *Do Magic* provides a back door for using special features of a simulation that are intended to support instruction. It allows the tutorial component to invoke an arbitrarily named feature of the simulation.

In VIVIDS, simulation authors can create procedures written in the simulation specification language. These procedures can be, and are, used for core simulation functions, whenever authors must ensure specific orders of evaluation of behaviors or when certain event-based, rather than relational, behaviors must be specified. In addition, however, these procedures can be invoked by the tutorial component of VIVIDS, using the *Do Magic* facility.

In iRides, a more powerful facility is available. In addition to being able to invoke procedures, the instructional component can call author-defined functions that return computed values to that tutorial component. (The instructional specifications of iRides can include computable statements written in Javascript. Values returned by a *Do Magic* invocation of iRides simulation functions can be stored in Javascript variables.)

One might ask, "Why not use *Do Magic* to handle all the interactions between an instructional component and a simulation?" The major reason is that doing so would substitute crude remote procedure call functionality for all the different types of standard interactions that simulation contexts provide to tutorial components. The use of a standard vocabulary of services makes it possible to build instructional specifications that work with different types of simulation systems. All that is necessary is that the different simulation systems provide the standard services that the instructional primitives depend upon. In fact, the iRides tutorial component has already been used independently of the iRides simulation component. The XCATT Crisis Action Planning Tutor developed at the Air Force Research Laboratory makes use of the iRides tutorial component and the standard iRides instructional specification format, but the XCATT simulator is hard coded in Java, not specified using the iRides simulation specification language. Even so, instructional specifications written in the XML-compliant LML language can be delivered using the same instructional component as in iRides.

HIGHER LEVEL STANDARD STRUCTURES
FOR PROCEDURAL TRAINING

Naturally, successful tutors use higher level tactics and strategies to teach procedures. These higher level tactics, such as:

- Demonstrate procedure while explaining steps.
- Guide student to carry out procedure.
- Explain conditioned variations of the procedure (alternative forms of the procedure that are to be used in certain contexts).
- Provide practice with loose guidance.
- Provide unguided practice with remediation.
- Test procedural competence.

These tactics themselves can be expressed as instructional control structures with instances of instructional primitives (described earlier) providing the content-related interactions. For example, the second tactic listed here, "Guide student to carry out the procedure," consists primarily of a sequence of textual directives interleaved with instances of the *Require Manipulation* instructional primitive.

Still higher level structures for teaching can be composed out of instances of the tactics structures. For example, a "Train procedure to criterion" strategy could make use of all of the tactics templates listed previously. Control structures would specify that certain tactics or sequences of tactics would loop until criterion performance was achieved.

REASONS FOR SEPARATING SIMULATION BEHAVIOR
FROM PEDAGOGICAL BEHAVIOR

The separation of simulation "code" (or, in the case of iRides, executable simulation specifications) from instructional control coding or specifications has a number of advantages for controlling development costs, ensuring pedagogical quality, and supporting the maintainability of the training materials. These include the following:

- Although a simulation will be most useful if its author has some understanding of how it will be used in instruction, it is not necessary that the simulation author be an expert in pedagogy. Furthermore, all the details of the instructional uses of the simulation do not have to be specified in advance of its development.
- A simulation intended for one purpose may later be employed for a different purpose. For example, a simulation originally designed for

cockpit maintenance crews might find a new life as a cockpit familiarization trainer for pilots. To make this work, a new instructional specification that makes use of the simulation must be developed. Because the original instructional code is not embedded in the simulation code, it does not need to be removed in order to reuse the simulation for a different purpose.

- A simulation that provides a core set of well-designed services to a tutorial component is a simulation that is protected from ill-thought-out modifications by the developers of instruction. Ad hoc "meddling" by the instructional developers is not necessary in the simulation code. This helps to reduce the incidence of bugs late in the product development cycle.

There are additional reasons for having the instructional services of simulations be reusable, either by using a library of routines that provide these services or by using a simulation-specification execution shell, as iRides does. In the latter case, the shell provides universal services that know how to deliver the required functionality in the context of an iRides simulation specification. In the former case, the simulation code for the specific behaviors of a simulation must be designed in a way that provides the library routines with the requested content.

- Reused instructional services code is likely to be more thoroughly tested than special purpose code created for a novel instructional use. This means both that the code is likely to execute properly and not raise execution exceptions, and that the services will have already been found to be effective in a variety of tutorials.
- Reusable instructional services will have consistent parameter types that support references to particular content. This will encourage the development of instructional authoring systems that provide authors with a reliable toolbox of instructional prototypes that can be used to assemble particular lessons.

WHAT ABOUT THE ADL (ADVANCED DISTRIBUTED LEARNING) STANDARDS?

The ADL standards (see http://www.adlnet.org/) are primarily concerned with how learning management systems can find and utilize shareable content objects (SCOs) to meet the learning needs of students. A reference model, the Shareable Content Object Reference Model (SCORM), shows how learning management systems can interact with content units, such as Web pages. The required services of SCOs are simply (a) initializing and announcing to learning management systems that they have begun working, (b) reporting student performance, and (c) announcing when they have finished.

iRides has been designed to be able to deliver simulation-based tutoring in several different run-time environments. One of these is as a SCORM-compatible applet. All the simulation services detailed above in this chapter take place *within* an iRides SCO. Both the tutorial component and the simulation component of an iRides training object are part of that SCO. A SCORM-compliant LMS engages in simple interactions with a SCO, not the more complex tutorial interactions described in this chapter. It would be possible, however, to create an advanced LMS-like instructional controller that combined conventional learning management functionality and detailed tutorial management of simulation SCOs. Such an instructional controller would be a server-based learning management system that was also itself an interactive tutor.

CONCLUSIONS

Procedures are often learned in the context of interactive systems, whether these systems are real devices or simulations. It is possible to identify a set of instructional primitives that can be used to bring about learning in the context of such interactive systems. Eight putative universal instructional primitives for procedural training are described in this chapter. Certain of these primitives require the support of a simulation that offers specific services. Examples of such services are also presented here. The iRides simulation-centered training delivery system incorporates a reusable simulation engine that offers the required services to a tutorial component. The reusable tutor component implements the eight instructional primitives (together with other primitives that are not unique to teaching in the context of interactive systems). These instructional primitive implementations make use of the pedagogical services of the simulation delivery component. Typologies of instructional interactions and of the low-level services that must be available to support them support a systematic approach to the design of reusable, authorable training systems.

ACKNOWLEDGMENT

The research described here was supported by Office of Naval Research Grant N00014-02-0179.

REFERENCES

Clark, R. (2004). What works in distance learning: instructional strategies. In H. F. O'Neil (Ed.), *What works in distance learning: Guidelines* (pp. 25–40). Greenwich, CT: Information Age Publishing.

Fitts, P. M., & Posner, M. I. (1967). *Human performance*. Belmont, CA: Brooks/Cole.

Forbus, K. (1984). *An interactive laboratory for teaching control system concepts*. (Technical Report No. 5511). Cambridge, MA: Bolt Beranek and Newman Inc.

Hollan, J., Hutchins, E., & Weitzman, L. (1984). Steamer: An interactive inspectable simulation-based training system, *AI Magazine, 5*(2), 15–27.

Hunt, R. M., & Rouse, W. B. (1981). Problem-solving skills of maintenance trainees in diagnosing faults in simulated powerplants. *Human Factors, 23*(3), 317–328.

Lesgold, A. M., Lajoie, S. P., Bunzo, M., & Eggan, G. (1992). SHERLOCK: A coached practice environment for an electronics troubleshooting job. In J. Larkin & R. Chabay (Eds.), *Computer assisted instruction and intelligent tutoring systems: Shared issues and complementary approaches* (pp. 201–238). Hillsdale, NJ: Lawrence Erlbaum Associates.

Morris, N. M., & Rouse, W. B. (1985). The effects of type of knowledge upon human problem solving in a process control task. *IEEE Transactions on Systems, Man, and Cybernetics, 15*, 698–707.

Munro, A. (1992). Authoring interactive graphical models for instruction. In T. de Jong, D. M. Towne, & H. Spada (Eds.), *Simulation-based experiential learning* (pp. 33–45). Berlin: Springer Verlag.

Munro, A. (2003). Authoring simulation-centered learning environments with Rides and Vivids. In Murray, T., Blessing, S., & Ainsworth, S. (Eds.), *Authoring tools for advanced technology learning environments* (pp. 61–91). Dordrect, The Netherlands: Kluwer Academic Publishers.

Munro, A., Johnson, M. C., Pizzini, Q. A., Surmon, D. S., Towne, D. M., & Wogulis, J. L. (1997). Authoring Simulation-Centered Tutors with RIDES. *International Journal of Artificial Intelligence in Education, 8*, 284–316.

Munro, A., & Pizzini, Q. A. (1998). *VIVIDS Reference manual*. Los Angeles: Behavioral Technology Laboratories, University of Southern California.

Munro, A., Pizzini, Q. A., & Johnson, M. C. (2004). *The iRides simulation language: Authored simulations for distance learning*. Los Angeles: Behavioral Technology Laboratories, University of Southern California.

Munro, A., Surmon, D., Johnson, M., Pizzini, Q., & Walker, J. (1999). An open architecture for simulation-centered tutors. In S. P. Lajoie & M. Vivet (Eds.), *Artificial intelligence in education: Open learning environments: New computational technologies to support learning, exploration, and collaboration* (pp. 360–367). Amsterdam: IOS Press.

Papert, S. (1980). *Mindstorms: children computers, and powerful ideas*. New York: Basic Books.

Perez, R. S. (1991). A view from troubleshooting. In M. U. Smith (Ed.), *Toward a unified theory of problem solving* (pp. 115–153). Hillsdale, NJ: Lawrence Erlbaum Associates.

Rieber, L. P. (1992). Computer-based microworlds: A bridge between constructivism and direct instruction. *Educational Technology, Research, and Development, 40*(1), 93–106.

Rouse, W. B. (1979). Human problem solving performance in a fault diagnosis task. *IEEE Transactions on Systems, Man, and Cybernetics, 12*(5), 649–652.

Self, J. (1995). Problems with unguided learning. *Proceedings of the International Conference on Computers in Education*. ICCE'95.

Shute, V. J., & Glaser, R. (1990). A large-scale evaluation of an intelligent discovery world: Smithtown. *Interactive Learning Environments, 1*, 55–77.

Smith, R. B. (1987). *Experiences with the alternate reality kit: An example of the tension between literalism and magic*. (Proceedings CHI + GI 1987). New York: Association for Computing Machinery.

Swezey, R. W., Perez, R. S., & Allen, J. (1988). Effects of instructional delivery system and training parameter manipulations on electromechanical performance. *Human factors, 30*(6), 751–762.

Touvinen, J. E., & Sweller, J. (1999). A comparison of cognitive load associated with discovery learning and worked examples. *Journal of Educational Psychology, 91*, 334–341.

van Merrienböer, J. J. G., Clark, R. E., & de Croock, B. M. (2002). Blueprints for complex learning: The 4C/ID-model. *Educational Technology Research and Development, 50*(2), 39–64.

Walker, J., Pizzini, Q. A., Johnson, M., Darling, D., Munro, A., & Surmon, D. (2004). *Rifle marksmanship coaches toolset databook training module: Instructor guide*. Los Angeles: Behavioral Technology Laboratories, University of Southern California.

Chapter 16

Why Understanding Instructional Design Requires an Understanding of Human Cognitive Evolution

John Sweller
University of New South Wales

The information structures and processes that underlie and drive evolution by natural selection bear a striking resemblance to the structures and processes that constitute human cognitive architecture (Sweller, 2003). The manner in which humans learn, solve problems, and create all have close analogues to descriptions of biological evolution. The relevant processes may be universal with human cognitive architecture having evolved to mimic the information processes of evolution by natural selection. Thus, evolution by natural selection has the dual functions of shaping human cognitive architecture and providing a template to understand that architecture. Because the processes of evolution by natural selection are well known, any analogy between biological evolution and human cognitive architecture can serve to reveal structures and processes relevant to human cognition that otherwise would remain obscure. Human cognitive architecture, in turn, may create both restrictions and opportunities for how learners can acquire information. The manner in which learners can acquire information provides a foundation for instructional design.

This chapter both establishes the analogy between biological evolution and human cognition and provides an evolutionary explanation of some of the well-known structures of human cognitive architecture. Those informa-

279

tion structures are then used to indicate appropriate instructional design principles relevant to Web-based learning.

THE INFORMATION STRUCTURES THAT UNDERLIE BIOLOGICAL EVOLUTION AND HUMAN COGNITIVE ARCHITECTURE

Both biological processes and human cognitive activity are governed by extremely large stores of information. Although there is no consensus on a relevant metric for measuring the relative size of those aspects of species' genomes that determine individual characteristics, any plausible measure indicates massive complexity. The human genome contains about 3 billion base pairs and 30,000 genes (International Human Genome Sequencing Consortium, 2001). Whatever measure is used, a very large store of genetic information is required to govern biological activity.

Similarly, human cognitive activity requires a huge store of information held in long-term memory. For example, Simon and Gilmartin (1973) indicated that the skill of chess grand masters derived from a knowledge of 50,000–100,000 board configurations memorized from real games. The initial evidence that a large knowledge base held in long-term memory provides the basis of chess playing skill came from De Groot (1946/1965) and Chase and Simon (1973). They demonstrated that chess experts could reproduce briefly seen board configurations taken from real games but chess novices could not. The difference disappeared when using random board configurations rather than configurations taken from real games.

Whereas most humans are not chess grand masters, the knowledge base held in long-term memory required to function in most substantive areas, including areas commonly mastered, is likely to be similarly large (e.g., Egan & Schwartz, 1979; Jeffries, Turner, Polson, & Atwood, 1981; Sweller & Cooper, 1985). For example, the ability to read text fluently requires many years of practice and a large knowledge base. If any reader of the current text is briefly shown the massively complex squiggles that constitute this written sentence, he or she would be able to effortlessly reproduce those squiggles whereas a novice would fail. Of course, the central function of that knowledge base is to provide the basis of reading competence in the same way that knowledge of board configurations provides the basis of chess-playing competence.

Although the centrality of massive stores of information provides the most obvious point of analogical similarity between biological evolution and human cognitive architecture, the manner in which those stores of information are constructed, altered, and used provides further points of similarity. The details of this analogy continue to be elucidated in the remainder of this section.

Alterations to Information Stores

Environments frequently alter and a mechanism for alterations to a genome is required. Similarly, under new circumstances, human knowledge may become obsolete.

Central Executive

Biological evolution has no central executive function determining the nature of genetic changes required to permit a species to more effectively coordinate its biological activities with its environment. Indeed, if we were to postulate such a central executive, we would immediately be faced with a logical conundrum: If a central executive were available to determine the nature of genetic changes, a second executive would be required to determine the activities of the first and a third to determine the activities of the second, and so forth. This infinite regress indicates a logical flaw in the concept of a central executive determining the nature and direction of change. Information held in the genetic code does, of course, act as a central executive governing activity but this central executive does not and cannot deal with change.

While sometimes postulated, the concept of a central executive governing human learning has the same logical flaw. Although knowledge held in long-term memory can act as a central executive determining cognitive activity, nevertheless, by definition, when a change in cognitive activity (i.e., learning) is required due to changed circumstances, such knowledge held in long-term memory is no longer available. Using Web navigation as an example, new, unfamiliar sets of pages may mean a new unfamiliar route must be found for which information in long-term memory is not available. If information in long-term memory is unavailable to act as a central executive governing activity, then no viable candidate is available. Any knowledge-free central executive will require a second executive to govern the first and a third to govern the second, and so forth, as was the case for biological evolution. The concept of a central executive separate from knowledge held in long-term memory is not viable for this system.

Random Generation of Alternatives

If a central executive does not generate alterations to information stores, by what process are alterations generated? In evolution by natural selection, random mutation is central. All differences between species and all differences between individuals of a species can ultimately be sourced back to random mutation. The theory permits no other natural source for the generation of change.

Similarly, the ultimate source of novel cognitive activity is random. Novel cognitive activity occurs during problem solving. When solving a problem, all activity is generated either by previously acquired knowledge or by random factors with most, probably all problems being solved by a combination of knowledge and random factors. In other words, failing knowledge, random factors provide the only conceivable method for generating problem-solving moves. Furthermore, those random factors are the ultimate and only conceivable source of all novel cognitive activity just as random mutation is the only ultimate source of genetic variation. For the new sets of Web pages example, barring information already held in long-term memory concerning routes between pages, information on each page indicating possible routes, a set of site maps or someone else who can communicate knowledge, the initial choice of a possible route must be random (and frequently is for poorly designed sites!). If some knowledge is available from one or more of these sources, the choice can be purely cognitive without physical progress in order to see the consequences of the choice. If such knowledge is not available, the random choice must be followed physically.

Critically, it needs to be noted that the type and nature of random mutation is dependent on the initial genome that is being altered, and similarly, the type and nature of random problem-solving moves is dependent on the initial knowledge base brought to bear on the problem. Without an appropriate genome, some required alterations are improbable and without an appropriate knowledge base, some problem solutions are equally improbable. Finding a good route through a set of Web pages may be difficult without considerable knowledge of the links between them.

Testing the Effectiveness of Random Alternatives

Random mutation is only important because the consequences of mutations are tested against the environment. Successful mutations are retained in subsequent generations while unsuccessful mutations are lost. In the case of problem solving, randomly generated moves must be tested for effectiveness with ineffective moves lost and effective moves retained. A knowledge base in long-term memory is altered to the extent that effective moves become part of that knowledge base. Each alternative set of links between Web pages must be tested for effectiveness (do I reach the page I want?) either mentally or physically. Successful routes may be retained in long-term memory for future use; unsuccessful routes are unlikely to be retained.

Each Alteration to the Information Store Must be Minor

Whether a genome can survive and contribute to the next generation with a particular mutation depends in part on the extent of that mutation. A muta-

tion that substantially alters one or more critical genes is statistically unlikely to survive and reproduce. The statistical probability that a function
such as sight will evolve in one generation is effectively zero.

Learning can properly be defined as a change in long-term memory.
Nevertheless, just as changes to a genome are very slow, so are changes to
long-term memory. Learning is slow for the same reasons that genetic alterations are slow—a large random alteration to long-term memory is statistically unlikely to be adaptive.

Human cognitive architecture has a specific structural adaptation, working memory, to ensure that alterations to long-term memory are small and
cumulative. When dealing with novel information, this structure is very limited in both capacity and duration. Only a few items of novel information
can be processed simultaneously in working memory (Miller, 1956) and
those items can remain in working memory for no more than a few seconds
unless they are rehearsed (Peterson & Peterson, 1959). A limited working
memory ensures that all alterations to long-term memory are limited.
Large alterations can only occur by a slow accumulation with each step
tested for effectiveness. A really complex new set of links between Web
pages with each link determined by chance is most unlikely to be successful.
Nor can it be held in its entirety in working memory in order to be tested for
effectiveness. It can easily be held in working memory after learning has occurred but such learning is pointless until the effectiveness of what has been
learned is assured. Testing the effectiveness of small alterations to previously used information systems known to be effective provides a much
higher probability of success. A limited working memory when dealing with
new information ensures that only small alterations are considered.

These limitations of working memory only apply to new information.
Previously organized and learned information, held in long-term memory,
has no apparent limitations when transferred to working memory (Ericsson
& Kintsch, 1995). Massively complex routes between Web pages can be
brought from long-term memory and processed effortlessly in working
memory. It is only necessary for working memory to have limitations when
it is dealing with new, unstructured information that must be organized by
randomly imposing a structure and testing it for effectiveness.

INSTRUCTIONAL IMPLICATIONS
OF HUMAN COGNITIVE ARCHITECTURE

Cognitive load theory (Paas, Renkl, & Sweller, 2003, 2004; Sweller, 1999;
Sweller, van Merrienboer, & Paas, 1998) is an instructional theory based on
the information processing assumptions that underlie human cognitive architecture and discussed in the previous section. The suggestion that those
assumptions are general and also underlie evolution by natural selection

strengthens the theoretical base. The intricate relations between working and long-term memory are central to cognitive load theory. As indicated earlier, working memory is limited in capacity and duration but those limitations apply only to new material that is yet to be learned. When working memory must process new information, there is no central executive available in long-term memory to act as a guide and so relations between elements are random. It is essential that only small amounts of information be dealt with simultaneously to avoid an explosion in the number of possible random combinations. A limited working memory ensures that this condition is met. In contrast, previously learned information held in long-term memory can be processed in working memory with no discernible limitations. Experts in an area are experts precisely because knowledge held in long-term memory can act as a central executive allowing information to be processed in working memory without being affected by capacity limits. There is no requirement for capacity limits when dealing with well-learned, no longer random material because previous learning has established the appropriate relations between elements of information.

Cognitive load theory describes how instruction should be organized in order to take into account these aspects of human cognitive architecture. In general, instruction should facilitate the acquisition of knowledge held in long-term memory by reducing the heavy working memory load (or cognitive load) faced by learners dealing with novel information. One way of reducing cognitive load is to reduce or eliminate the random components that need to be dealt with by the information processing system and to replace those random components with elements whose structure is known. Using previously learned information held in long-term memory when dealing with a new task is one way of reducing random components. We know the relations between elements of previously learned information. Faced with a current problem, we will normally attempt to solve it using previous solutions to other problems, if at all possible, in order to avoid analyzing the otherwise random relations between elements. Of course, such analogous problem solutions are not always available. Interaction between humans is designed, in part, to have the function of providing previously organized information to another person who has not yet learned and organized that information. A human who has learned something of importance to other humans by the random generation and testing for effectiveness procedures discussed in the previous section can communicate what has been learned to others and so eliminate the otherwise unavoidable random components. Cognitive load can be reduced by such direct presentation of information and knowledge can be acquired at a rate that would otherwise be inconceivable.

On this analysis, information should always be presented in direct rather than indirect form. Learners should never be required to discover what can be communicated directly to them. Failing appropriate instruction, random generation and testing is unavoidable under novel conditions but is rarely likely to be an effective learning technique. Accordingly, humans will normally use the procedure as a last rather than a first resort. When faced with having to find a new route between Web pages, we will almost always attempt to obtain information from another person, either directly or via written information produced by someone else. Generate and test will only be used when no other alternative is available because it is inefficient and if the required route is complex, will impose a cognitive load that inevitably exceeds working memory capacity (Mayer, 2004).

This principle applies equally to all educational content areas but flies in the face of much educational theory of the last few decades. Beginning with discovery learning in the 1960s (Bruner, 1961) and extending to the constructivist learning techniques of the 1980s and 1990s (National Council of Teachers of Mathematics, 1989), inquiry-based instructional techniques have garnered a considerable following among educational theorists. Whereas the nomenclature has altered over the decades, the techniques are indistinguishable. In all cases, learners are required to discover information that needs to be learned rather than having the same information presented to them. There is no aspect of human cognitive architecture that suggests that inquiry-based learning should be superior to direct instructional guidance and much to suggest that it is likely to be inferior. A requirement to randomly generate problem-solving moves and then test them for effectiveness can result in virtually nothing being learned over long periods of time despite considerable cognitive effort, where cognitive effort is defined as the subjective mental effort required by students learning a task (Paas & van Merrienboer, 1993). That cognitive effort is necessary because, depending on the precise version of generate and test being used, a very heavy working memory load that interferes with learning can be imposed (Sweller, 1988).

Theoretical prognostications have little value without empirical support. If there was a large body of evidence from controlled, experimental studies demonstrating the advantages of inquiry-based learning in terms of knowledge acquired, predictions that the technique should be ineffective would be vacuous. In fact, despite inquiry-based learning having a history stretching over decades, there is no body of cumulative evidence from multiple studies demonstrating its relative effectiveness in assisting student learning compared to direct, instructional guidance. Instead, the evidence points unambiguously in the opposite direction (Moreno, 2004; Tuovinen & Sweller, 1999). Provided they are novices in the area, students given problems to solve will perform more poorly on subsequent tests of knowledge than students given the same problems presented as worked examples to study (e.g., Cooper & Sweller, 1987). This effect is called the worked example effect. With increased expertise in an area, the effect first disappears and can eventually reverse (Kalyuga, Chandler, Tuovinen, & Sweller, 2001) because knowledge held in long-term memory can act as a central executive guiding the choice of problem-solving moves. The development of a knowledge-based central executive allows elimination of random generation and testing. Problem solving with such a central executive is effective because it acts to buttress knowledge held in long-term memory. (As indicated earlier, learning is defined as a change in long-term memory.)

There are many other cognitive load effects. All were generated from the cognitive architecture described in this chapter and provide a variety of instructional designs (see Sweller, 2003). All assume the basic information processes and structures that underlie biological evolution and human cognitive architecture. They are summarized next.

The Problem Completion Effect. The worked example effect usually involves presenting each worked example followed by a very similar problem to solve. In contrast, completion problems do not require this pairing of worked examples and problems. Rather, each problem is presented in partially completed form and learners must complete the solution. The guidance provided by the partial worked example reduces problem-solving search with its random generation of moves and so reduces cognitive load whereas problem completion ensures learners are cognitively active. Evidence for the effectiveness of the completion effect comes from van Merrienboer, Schuurman, de Croock, and Paas (2002).

The Split-Attention Effect. Some worked examples are ineffective because their structure itself imposes a heavy cognitive load preventing learning. Consider a conventional geometry worked example consisting of a diagram and statements. Alone, neither the diagram nor the associated statements have any instructional value. They only take on value once they have been mentally integrated but mental integration imposes a cognitive load. That load can be avoided by physically integrating the statements within the diagram. The split-attention effect is demonstrated if a comparison of conventionally structured worked examples with physically integrated examples demonstrates an advantage for the integrated versions. Furthermore, the effect applies to any instructional material, including material in which attention must be split between temporally (e.g., Mayer & Anderson, 1992) as well as spatially noncontiguous information (e.g., Sweller, Chandler, Tierney, & Cooper, 1990).

The Modality Effect. Only the visual modality is used to demonstrate the split-attention effect. Working memory capacity may be increased if the auditory modality is used as a substitute for some of the visual materials because the auditory and visual channels are partially independent (e.g., Penney, 1989). Rather than presenting a diagram and written text under split-attention conditions, a diagram and spoken text may be used with a consequent increase in working memory capacity. If the dual mode presentation technique is superior, the instructional modality effect has been demonstrated (e.g., Brünken, Plass, & Leutner, 2004; Moreno & Mayer, 1999; Tindall-Ford, Chandler, & Sweller, 1997). For obvious reasons, dual mode presentations require modern technology to coordinate visual and auditory information.

The Redundancy Effect. The split-attention and the modality effects are only obtainable when multiple sources of information refer to each other and are unintelligible in isolation. For example, if a diagram provides all the required information with the text merely recapitulating the information, the text is redundant and neither the split-attention nor the modality effects are obtainable. The redundancy effect occurs when processing such additional information imposes a cognitive load that interferes with learning. For example, redundant text should be eliminated rather than integrated with a diagram or presented in auditory form because the diagram can be understood in isolation and processing the text increases working memory load, which interferes with learning. Examples of the redundancy effect have been provided by Chandler and Sweller (1991, 1996) and Craig, Gholson, and Driscoll (2002), among others.

The Element Interactivity Effect. The split-attention, modality, and redundancy effects only occur where the material being learned imposes an intrinsically high cognitive load because it consists of many interacting elements that must be processed simultaneously in working memory. If individual elements can be learned in isolation because they do not interact, an additional working memory load due to flawed instructional designs may be less important. Chandler and Sweller (1996) and Sweller and Chandler (1994) demonstrated that the split-attention and redundancy effects, demonstrated using high element interactivity material, disappeared using low element interactivity material. Tindall-Ford, Chandler, and Sweller (1997) found that the modality effect also disappeared using low element interactivity material. Marcus, Cooper, and Sweller (1996) and Carlson, Chandler, and Sweller, (2003) found that diagrammatic schemas facilitated understanding when compared to text using high but not low element interactivity material. Thus, whether cognitive load effects can be obtained depends on the complexity of the material being learned. Cognitive load effects are only obtainable using high element interactivity materials that impose a heavy cognitive load irrespective of instructional design flaws.

The Isolated Interacting Elements Effect.   Consider a learner faced with new material that is sufficiently high in element interactivity to substantially exceed working memory capacity. Understanding occurs when all interacting elements are simultaneously processed in working memory but cannot occur in this case because the number of interacting elements exceed working memory capacity. Once a large number of interacting elements are embedded in knowledge held in long-term memory, that knowledge can be brought into working memory and treated as a single element that will not overload working memory capacity. Under these circumstances, understanding and learning appear impossible. To be understood, high element interactivity material must have been learned (i.e., held in long-term memory) but it cannot be learned because it exceeds working memory capacity. The only possibility seems to be that initially, the elements must be learned as isolated, noninteracting elements. In this way, they can be processed in working memory. Only later might the interactions between the elements and thus understanding occur. If so, very complex information may need to be initially presented to students in isolated elements form ignoring interactions between elements. Once learned, presentation of the full information may permit understanding to occur. Presentation of the complete information during initial instruction may retard learning or understanding. Precisely this effect was obtained by Pollock, Chandler, and Sweller (2002).

The Goal-Free Effect.   This effect occurs when learners, instead of being presented goal specific problems such as "calculate the value of angle ABC" or "calculate the final velocity of the vehicle," learn less than learners presented nonspecific or goal-free problems such as "calculate the value of as many angles as you can" or "calculate the value of as many variables as you can." The goal-free effect can be readily demonstrated (e.g., Ayres, 1993; Sweller, Mawer, & Ward, 1983; Vollmeyer, Burns, & Holyoak, 1996). The effect occurs because with a normal goal, problem solvers must extract differences between the current problem state and the goal state, use knowledge or random choice to find a problem-solving operator to reduce that difference, test whether the desired effect has occurred, and then repeat these operations until a solution has been obtained. The working memory load of all of these activities can prevent learning. Using goal-free problems, randomly choosing any potential move, and determining whether it can be made is the only cognitive activity, minimizing working memory load. It should be noted that the procedure is only effective if categories of problems are used in which all moves made under goal-free conditions are useful and need to be learned. Goal-free problems should not be used on problems without this characteristic.

The Imagination Effect. Cooper, Tindall-Ford, Chandler, and Sweller (2001) and Ginns, Chandler, and Sweller (2003) found that learners asked to "imagine" a set of procedures learned more than learners given conventional "study" instructions. Imagining a set of procedures requires them to be processed in working memory and so this imagination effect is only obtainable using learners with some degree of knowledge of the materials being imagined. Complete novices are unable to process high element interactivity material in working memory and so for these learners, studying the materials is superior to imagining them giving a reverse imagination or "study" effect. The presence of the study materials can serve to reduce working memory load. Once sufficient information has been accumulated in long-term memory, that information can be imagined in working memory resulting in further learning. This reversal effect with increased expertise is general. As indicated next, cognitive load effects depend on the use of novices and first disappear and then reverse with increases in expertise.

The Expertise Reversal Effect. Other than the imagination effect, all of the previously described effects were intended to be used with novices only. Of course, learners continue to improve after initial learning. For learners other than complete novices, many of the effects described earlier, reverse. In each case, the reversal is due to the redundancy effect. There are several examples of the expertise reversal effect summarized by Kalyuga, Ayres, Chandler, and Sweller (2003). In all cases of the expertise reversal effect, information that is essential for novices becomes redundant for more expert learners. On becoming redundant, processing that information, initially essential, now imposes an extraneous cognitive load compared to not processing it.

The Guidance Fading Effect. The expertise reversal effect suggests that as expertise increases, instructional guidance should be faded out. Renkl and his associates (e.g., Renkl & Atkinson, 2003) have provided support for this hypothesis using combinations of worked examples, completion problems, and full problems. Guidance provided by worked examples was the best form of instruction for novices but as expertise increased, worked examples needed to be replaced with completion problems and at higher levels of expertise, with full problems. In effect, guidance provides a central executive for novices but with increasing expertise, that role can be taken over by knowledge held in long-term memory. In this way, random choice followed by effectiveness testing is reduced during the entire learning sequence with a consequent minimization of extraneous cognitive load.

PROBLEM SOLVING, CREATIVITY, AND INTELLIGENCE

It may be argued that problem solving and creativity, frequently seen as the apex of human intellectual activity, are downplayed in the current treatment. In fact, the analogy between human cognitive architecture and evolution by natural selection leads naturally to a universal explanation of creativity and intelligence. That explanation provides a marked departure from other explanations of human creativity and intelligence (Sweller, 2003).

Biological evolution is a spectacularly successful creative process. Its function is to create new functions and procedures that permit life to continue. The complexity of much that has been created is immense with many of the entities created by evolution by natural selection still beyond the full understanding of human beings. We are far from understanding the full functioning of the human brain, or even animal brains. Turning vegetable matter into flesh is beyond us. Doing so in a factory a few cubic millimeters in size is even further beyond us. We are not only unable to create most biological processes, we are unable to even understand them when presented with examples. We do, nevertheless, understand the mechanism—evolution by natural selection—that underlies this creativity.

If the analogy between biological evolution and human cognitive architecture is valid, we have an explanation of human creativity. Creativity occurs when successive, minor alterations to a very large knowledge base are tested for effectiveness with effective alterations added to the base and ineffective ones rejected. Most such alterations to the knowledge base result in a base that differs little from the knowledge held by other humans and is not recognized as creative. If alterations are made to a very extensive knowledge base that exceeds that of most other humans, those alterations may be labeled "creative."

It needs to be noted that if this perspective is valid, education can assist in the building of a knowledge base using the procedures discussed in the last section. It cannot be used to teach "creativity." The processes of creativity are identical between "creative" and "noncreative" individuals and consist of the random generation followed by testing for effectiveness of problem-solving moves. The differences between people occur in the knowledge base, not the processes used to generate moves. Accordingly, education can only be used to build that knowledge base using the procedures discussed in the previous section. It cannot be used to teach people how to generate good or "creative" problem-solving moves because all problem-solving moves for which knowledge is unavailable must be generated randomly. As a consequence, all attempts to directly teach "creativity" or general problem-solving skill can be expected to continue to fail.

In the same way, although evolution by natural selection may be a highly creative process, increasing its creativity makes little sense. Genetic codes may be altered just as a human knowledge base may be altered. All the intelligence of the system resides in a combination of those genetic codes and the process by which they are altered, just as all human intelligence, on the current perspective, resides in knowledge held in long-term memory and the process by which it is altered.

CONCLUSIONS

Evolution by natural selection, in conjunction with knowledge concerning genetic processes, is a detailed, highly specified, widely accepted theory. In contrast, whereas some of the structures that constitute human cognitive architecture are relatively well known, theories associated with human cognition are much less specific and much less detailed than evolution by natural selection. Accordingly, if many of the information processes that underlie biological evolution and human cognition are common, allowing an analogical comparison between them, that analogy may be used to reveal cognitive processes and general structures that otherwise would remain hidden and obscure. If the information processes humans use to learn, solve problems, and create can be found in the procedures that constitute evolution by natural selection, then we can conclude that in the science of life (that human cognition is part of), there may be a single, universal information processing system. By studying that system, light may be cast on human cognition.

There are several examples of the usefulness of the analogy. One example is provided by the suggestion that working memory has no central executive when dealing with new information. Random combinations of elements tested for effectiveness act as a substitute for a central executive. This system may be analogous to aspects of biological evolution, which has no central executive either. A central executive is not required (nor logically possible without an infinite regress) with random mutation followed by effectiveness testing acting as a substitute. As another example, the suggestion that knowledge accumulated in long-term memory provides a substitute for a general central executive when dealing with well-known information may be analogous to an evolved (or analogously, a "learned") genetic code. Genetic codes may determine biological behavior in the same way as knowledge determines psychological behaviour.

Of course, no system is perfectly analogous with any system other than itself. All useful analogies break down beyond a certain point. The issue is whether useful information may be extracted at the points where the analogy holds—the points where commonalities exist between the information processing procedures of evolution by natural selection and human cognition.

There are powerful instructional design issues that flow from the analogy. All problem solving and learning by individuals have random components unless the information is obtained from other individuals. In part, cognitive load theory may be used to determine how information can best be obtained from other individuals. Although using previously acquired knowledge, either one's own or the knowledge of someone else, eliminates random generation, that random generation may be the initial basis of all creativity, just as random mutation is the initial basis of the creativity of evolution by natural selection. If so, attempting to teach general problem-solving techniques or creativity do not constitute appropriate instructional processes. The proper function of instructional design should be to assist learners accumulate knowledge in long-term memory despite a limited working memory. Cognitive load theory was designed with that goal in mind. Web-based instruction is likely to be most effective when it is based on our knowledge of human cognitive architecture.

REFERENCES

Ayres, P. (1993). Why goal-free problems can facilitate learning. *Contemporary Educational Psychology, 18*, 376–381.

Bruner, J. (1961). The act of discovery. *Harvard Educational Review, 31*, 21–32.

Brünken, R., Plass, J., & Leutner, D. (2004). Assessment of cognitive load in multimedia learning with dual-task methodology: Auditory load and modality effects. *Instructional Science, 32*, 115–132.

Carlson, R., Chandler, P., & Sweller, J. (2003). Learning and understanding science instructional material. *Journal of Educational Psychology, 95*, 629–640.

Chandler, P., & Sweller, J. (1991). Cognitive load theory and the format of instruction. *Cognition and Instruction, 8*, 293–332.

Chandler, P., & Sweller, J. (1996). Cognitive load while learning to use a computer program. *Applied Cognitive Psychology, 10*, 151–170.

Chase, W. G., & Simon, H. A. (1973). Perception in chess. *Cognitive Psychology, 4*, 55–81.

Cooper, G., & Sweller, J. (1987). The effects of schema acquisition and rule automation on mathematical problem-solving transfer. *Journal of Educational Psychology, 79*, 347–362.

Cooper, G., Tindall-Ford, S., Chandler, P., & Sweller, J. (2001). Learning by imagining. *Journal of Experimental Psychology: Applied, 7*, 68–82.

Craig, S., Gholson, B., & Driscoll, D. (2002). Animated pedagogical agents in multimedia educational environments: Effects of agent properties, picture features, and redundancy. *Journal of Educational Psychology, 94*, 428–434.

De Groot, A. (1965). *Thought and choice in chess.* The Hague, Netherlands: Mouton. (Original work published 1946)

Egan, D. E., & Schwartz, B. J. (1979). Chunking in recall of symbolic drawings. *Memory and Cognition, 7*, 149–158.

Ericsson, K. A., & Kintsch, W. (1995). Long-term working memory. *Psychological Review, 102*, 211–245.

Ginns, P., Chandler, P., & Sweller, J. (2003). When imagining information is effective. *Contemporary Educational Psychology, 28*, 229–251.

International Human Genome Sequencing Consortium. (2001). Initial sequencing and analysis of the human genome. *Nature, 409*, 860–921.

Jeffries, R., Turner, A., Polson, P., & Atwood, M. (1981). Processes involved in designing software. In J. R. Anderson (Ed.), *Cognitive skills and their acquisition* (pp. 255–283). Hillsdale, NJ: Lawrence Erlbaum Associates.

Kalyuga, S., Ayres, P., Chandler, P., & Sweller, J. (2003). Expertise reversal effect. *Educational Psychologist, 38*, 23–33.

Kalyuga, S., Chandler, P., Tuovinen, J., & Sweller, J. (2001). When problem solving is superior to studying worked examples. *Journal of Educational Psychology, 93*, 579–588.

Marcus, N., Cooper, M., & Sweller, J. (1996). Understanding instructions. *Journal of Educational Psychology, 88*, 49–63.

Mayer, R. (2004). Should there be a three-strikes rule against pure discovery learning? The case for guided methods of instruction. *American Psychologist, 59*, 14–19.

Mayer, R., & Anderson, R. (1992). The instructive animation: Helping students build connections between words and pictures in multimedia learning. *Journal of Educational Psychology, 84*, 444–452.

Miller, G. A. (1956). The magical number seven, plus or minus two: Some limits on our capacity for processing information. *Psychological Review, 63*, 81–97.

Moreno, R. (2004). Decreasing cognitive load for novice students: Effects of explanatory versus corrective feedback in discovery-based multimedia. *Instructional Science, 32*, 99–113.

Moreno, R., & Mayer, R. (1999). Cognitive principles of multimedia learning: The role of modality and contiguity. *Journal of Educational Psychology, 91*, 358–368.

National Council of Teachers of Mathematics. (1989). *Curriculum and Evaluation Standards for School Mathematics*. Reston, VA: National Council.

Paas, F., Renkl, A., & Sweller, J. (2003). Cognitive load theory and instructional design. *Educational Psychologist, 38*, 1–4.

Paas, F., Renkl, A., & Sweller, J. (2004). Cognitive load theory: Instructional implications of the interaction between information structures and cognitive architecture. *Instructional Science, 32*, 1–8.

Paas, F., & van Merrienboer, J. (1993). The efficiency of instructional conditions: An approach to combined mental effort and performance measures. *Human Factors, 35*, 737–743.

Penney, C. (1989). Modality effects and the structure of short term verbal memory. *Memory and Cognition, 17*, 389–422.

Peterson, L., & Peterson, M. (1959). Short-term retention of individual verbal items. *Journal of Experimental Psychology, 58*, 193–198.

Pollock, E., Chandler, P., & Sweller, J. (2002). Assimilating complex information. *Learning and Instruction, 12*, 61–86.

Renkl, A., & Atkinson, R. K. (2003). Structuring the transition from example study to problem solving in cognitive skill acquisition: A cognitive load perspective. *Educational Psychologist, 38*, 15–22.

Simon, H., & Gilmartin, K. (1973). A simulation of memory for chess positions. *Cognitive Psychology, 5*, 29–46.

Sweller, J. (1988). Cognitive load during problem solving: Effects on learning. *Cognitive Science, 12*, 257–285.

Sweller, J. (1999). *Instructional design in technical areas*. Melbourne, Australia: ACER Press.

Sweller, J. (2003). Evolution of human cognitive architecture. In B. Ross (Ed.), *The psychology of learning and motivation* (Vol. 43, pp. 215–266). San Diego: Academic Press.

Sweller, J., & Chandler, P. (1994). Why some material is difficult to learn. *Cognition & Instruction, 12*, 185–233.

Sweller, J., Chandler, P., Tierney, P., & Cooper, M. (1990). Cognitive load and selective attention as factors in the structuring of technical material. *Journal of Experimental Psychology: General, 119*, 176–192.

Sweller, J., & Cooper, G. A. (1985).The use of worked examples as a substitute for problem solving in learning algebra. *Cognition and Instruction, 2*, 59–89.

Sweller, J., Mawer, R., & Ward, M. (1983). Development of expertise in mathematical problem solving. *Journal of Experimental Psychology; General, 112*, 634–656.

Sweller, J., van Merrienboer, J., & Paas, F. (1998). Cognitive architecture and instructional design. *Educational Psychology Review, 10*, 251–296.

Tindall-Ford, S., Chandler, P., & Sweller, J. (1997). When two sensory modes are better than one. *Journal of Experimental Psychology: Applied, 3*, 257–287.

Tuovinen, J., & Sweller, J. (1999). A comparison of cognitive load associated with discovery learning and worked examples. *Journal of Educational Psychology, 91*, 334–341.

Van Merrienboer, J., & Krammer, H. (1987). Instructional strategies and tactics for the design of introductory computer programming courses in high school. *Instructional Science, 16*, 251–285.

Van Merrienboer, J., Schuurman, J., de Crook, M., & Paas, F. (2002). Redirecting learners' attention during training: effect on cognitive load, transfer test performance and training efficiency. *Learning & Instruction, 12*, 11–37.

Vollmeyer, R., Burns, B., & Holyoak, K. (1996). The impact of goal specificity on strategy use and the acquisition of problem structure. *Cognitive Science, 20*, 75–100.

Chapter 17

Scalability and Sociability
in Online Learning Environments

David Wiley
Utah State University

THE PROBLEM: SOCIALITY IS BLOOMING

Instructional designers are frequently asked, "to which learning theory do you subscribe?" And like the famously unanswerable question "do you still beat your wife?" no answer to the query generally seems satisfactory. Behaviorism, cognitivism, and social constructivism (see Jonassen, 1996) present significantly differing views of the educational universe. And although persuasive arguments are made that integrity of character requires an educator to adhere permanently to one view or another, I believe an individuals' choice of a learning theoretic view of the world must always be as transient as it is pragmatic.

The Sociality Axiom

In the past few years I have come to realize that there is a reason I move fickly from one learning theory to another as my instructional design framework. My seeming inability to commit is best explained by reference to Bloom's taxonomy (Bloom & Krathwohl, 1956), recently updated by Anderson and Krathwohl (2001). The updated taxonomy includes information about both the kind of information to be learned (e.g., factual vs.

procedural knowledge) and the process by which it is learned (e.g., apply-ing vs. analyzing), as summarized in Table 17.1.

When faced with the design challenge of helping students learn material at the top left of the updated taxonomy, behavioral methods seem most appropriate. As the subject of the design challenge moves diagonally to-ward the center of the taxonomy, behavioral approaches give way to cogni-tive methods in my design inclinations. By the time the target material has reached the bottom right corner of the taxonomy, cognitive approaches have completely acquiesced to my social constructivist ideas about facilitat-ing learning.

Imagine the following two nonexamples of these connections between the elements of Bloom's taxonomy and the popular learning theories. First, imagine using a social constructivist approach to helping students learn a long list of facts. Would you personally want to learn the capitals of the 50 states through a process of discussion and negotiation in small groups of five to seven peers? Probably not; although this approach may eventually be effective, it would be neither efficient nor appealing. At the other end of the spectrum is using behavioral methods to teach students to make complex evaluative judgments. Can you imagine using only flashcard-style drill and practice methods to help students learn to evaluate the ethics of the current U.S. war in Iraq? This approach would probably completely fail to be effec-tive, efficient, or appealing.

There are many implications to draw from this linking of Bloom's taxon-omy to the historical progression in learning theory, but the implication most important to this chapter I posit as an axiom (for short, the socializa-tion axiom): The further up Bloom's taxonomy a desired learning outcome is, the more important social interaction will be in promoting student achievement of the outcome. [Importance here is judged in terms of help-ing instruction meet Reigeluth's (1999) desiderata for instructional de-signs—that they be as effective, efficient, and appealing as possible.]

TABLE 17.1

A Tabular Representation of Anderson and Krathwohl's Taxonomy

Type of Knowledge	Cognitive Process				
	Remember	Understand	Apply	Analyze	Evaluate
Create					
Factual					
Conceptual					
Procedural					

The First Corollary

Instructional designers in settings from military to higher education seek to make their educational materials scale to larger numbers of learners using automated database-driven software or intelligent tutoring systems. For example, the SCORM 2004 Overview states:

> ... as a training strategy in government, academic or industrial environments, individually tailored instruction involving one-on-one attention is often too costly and logistically challenging. Using information technology in instruction may solve this problem because its capabilities for real-time, on-demand adaptation can provide individualized instruction at affordable cost and apply consistent content that reliably leads to objectively measurable learning outcomes. (ADL, 2004, p. 19)

The removal of human-to-human interaction from automated instruction results in a problem. The degree to which instructional episodes utilize automated agents is the degree to which these episodes are restricted to effectively, efficiently, and appealingly facilitating learning at the top left of the taxonomy. In Gibbons words, one of the main problems with this instruction is that it commits a "failure to recognize that instruction is a conversation" (Gibbons, in press).

"But wait!" a contending voice clamors. "Intelligent tutoring systems can teach incredibly complex material very effectively!" Yes they can, particularly material that is meaningfully computable (mathematics, physics, chemistry, bioinformatics, music theory, etc.). But complex learning outcomes are not necessarily the same as learning outcomes at the top left of Anderson and Krathwohl's taxonomy. As we see in self-organization, extremely rich complexity can emerge from the application of a small number of very simple rules. NetLogo, a popular educational simulation environment, contains a sample model that simulates complex flocking behavior in birds. The model's online documentation explains:

> The flocks that appear in this model are not created or led in any way by special leader birds. Rather, each bird is following exactly the same set of rules, from which apparent flocks emerge. The birds follow three rules: "alignment," "separation," and "cohesion." "Alignment" means that a bird tends to turn so that it is moving in the same direction that nearby birds are moving. "Separation" means that a bird will turn to avoid another bird which gets too close. "Cohesion" means that a bird will move towards other nearby birds (unless another bird is too close). When two birds are too close, the "separation" rule overrides the other two, which are deactivated until the minimum separation is achieved. (NetLogo, 2004)

Through the simultaneous application of these three simple rules, great complexity and even seeming intelligence emerge. Computing systems are very capable of generating and interpreting this sort of complexity, and therefore they are capable of modeling, teaching, and assessing similarly complex learning outcomes. But as the NetLogo example shows, extremely rich complexity requires moving no further up the taxonomy than application. Therefore, I posit the first corollary to the socialization axiom—automated systems are only capable of effectively, efficiently, and appealingly facilitating the achievement of learning outcomes in proportion to the learning outcomes' proximity to the top left of Anderson and Krathwohl's taxonomy.

Teacher Bandwidth

For years I have described the bandwidth problem in distance education as having nothing to do with capacity as measured in bits transmitted per second. Rather than worrying about how many full-screen videos we can simultaneously stream to students' desktops, we should concern ourselves with a pedagogical aspect of the system that is far more constraining—instructional capacity as measured in students taught per instructor. I term this constraint the "teacher bandwidth problem." Preserving classroom-like teacher to student ratios in online courses prevents organizations—be they universities with extension or outreach commitments, corporations with significant training needs, or militaries with demands for high levels of readiness—from "teaching" as many students as need to learn. In order to reach all the learners necessary, many organizations have selected automating instruction and feedback as the prime candidate for solving the teacher bandwidth problem.

The automated solution that relies on artificial intelligence, learning objects, or other enabling technologies displays the strengths implied by the first corollary—to the extent that the learning outcomes to be taught by the system are classified close to the top left of Anderson and Krathwohl's taxonomy, the automated system is theoretically capable of facilitating this learning with effectiveness, efficiency, and appeal. However, to the extent that the learning outcomes to be taught by the system are classified closer to the bottom right, the automated system suffers the weaknesses described in the first corollary. The question becomes, "how can we scale educational opportunities for large numbers of learners while keeping the learning environment highly social, so as to enable the achievement of learning goals near the bottom right of Anderson and Krathwohl's taxonomy?"

SCALING SOCIALLY

The dichotomy between meaningful teacher-to-student interaction and the complete automation of teaching and feedback is false in a number of respects. Foremost among the faults of this thinking is the obvious overlooking of students as a valuable source of socialization. Whereas some might argue that interaction with peers is vastly inferior to teacher-to-student interactions in facilitating learning near the top of Bloom, research indicates otherwise. Lave and Wenger (1991) relate that in traditional apprenticeship learning situations, apprentices spend the majority of their time working with other apprentices, as opposed to the idealized one-on-one relationship between the apprentice and master. Also, in distinguishing between "authoritative discourse" and "internally persuasive discourse," Wertsch (1998) argued convincingly that students learn more effectively from peers whose statements and feedback are expected to be judged on their own merits than they do from professors who expect their statements to be blindly accepted due to their positions of power in the classroom.

Environmental Affordances and Group Size

One could easily imagine that if instruction were designed in such a manner as to utilize students as an educational resource, traditional problems with oversized classes might disappear. However, physical constraints frequently prevent teachers from taking effective advantage of the significant amount of expertise distributed throughout their classrooms. Whether a student sits in a class of 30 or a lecture hall seating 300, when the teacher asks students to take 10 min to discuss an important topic, any given student can only feasibly converse with the students in their immediate surroundings. The face-to-face environment works against individuals' attempts to work with anyone else. Gibson called the possibilities presented by the environment "affordances" (Gibson, 1979). Online settings provide instructors with a very different set of environmental affordances. In an asynchronous environment, individuals have the capacity to interact with any person in the group, opening access to the expertise of the entire collection of students as opposed to the expertise of those seated around an individual student.

Another hypothesis can be stated here: Just as there exists a class of instructional approaches that lose effectiveness as the number of students involved grows very large (think of just about any traditional teaching strategy here), there also exists a class of instructional approaches that lose effectiveness as the number of students involved grows very small. Due to the affordances of physical spaces, we have never been able to witness or study this second class of methods. However, online environments like massively multiplayer online games demonstrate that significant learning can take place in very large groups when their communication is mediated by networked, as opposed to physical, space. Wikipedia defines a massively multiplayer game as "a type of computer game that enables hundreds or thousands of players to simultaneously interact in a game world they are connected to via the Internet. Typically this kind of game is played in an online, multiplayer-only persistent world" (Various, 2004).

"But wait!" one might object. "There certainly would be access to more expertise, but there would also be hundreds of thousands of voices all sounding simultaneously. How would an individual learner cope with what would have to be a very low signal-to-noise ratio associated with such a group?" Several years ago a website called Slashdot faced that very question.

Of Slashdot and K5

Slashdot (http://slashdot.org/) is a website that carries items of interest to "geeks." The site's tagline reads, "News for Nerds. Stuff that Matters." Launched in 1997, in late 2004 Slashdot boasts over 350,000 registered users posting over 6,500 messages per day in the site's threaded discussion areas. As Slashdot grew to a very large number of users, in the fall of 1999 the signal-to-noise ratio became unacceptably low for site users and administrators. With the number of posts pouring into the site, it was impossible for the site's administrators to monitor each post.

Slashdot administrators struck upon the idea of distributing the workload for monitoring comments over the entire community. Based on five criteria defined by them, "moderators" were selected and given access to a comment rating system, by which they could reward excellent comments with points and punish ill-meaning comments by assigning negative points. In the site's FAQ the five criteria are listed as logged in user, regular slashdot readers, long-time readers, willing to serve, and positive contributors (Malda, 2003). Add to this distributed rating system a real-time filter by which users could determine the level of comments they wanted to see (e.g., only comments rated 3 or higher on a scale of 1 to 5) and the signal-to-noise problem on Slashdot largely disappeared. The secret of the solution was to turn the burden into a boon—more users posting more comments? Great, that means there are more moderators, too!

Another website called kuro5hin (http://kuro5hin.org/) or k5 has taken the distribution of work over the group one step further. In addition to enabling users to rate comments posted on the site by other users, k5 users also completely control all the content that appears on the site through a voting system. Any time new content is recommended for the site (content about which threaded discussion will shortly occur), the entire community votes on whether to accept the content or not. Votes of —1, 0, or +1 are tallied in real time and acceptance or rejection is based on the total score crossing a threshold calculated according to the total number of registered users. For example, for a given number of registered users, if a submission's total score drops below –20, it is rejected. On the other hand, if its total score surpasses +75, it is accepted.

Self-Organization

As described in the literature, self-organization sounds very similar to the manner in which these large social websites function (Maturana & Varela, 1980; Whitaker, 1995; Winograd & Flores, 1986;). Whitaker (1995) listed the facets of self-organization as self-creation, self-configuration, self-regulation, self-steering, self-production, and self-reference. Very large websites like Slashdot and k5 exhibit many of these characteristics, as do many online massively multiplayer games. These similarities led Wiley and Edwards (2002) to describe very large groups of individuals who gather in online settings to provide peer support for problem solving and other learning goals as "online self-organizing social systems" or OSOSS.

Self-organization as an explanatory framework for social phenomena is most often used in the context of social insects such as ants or bees. How is it that a hole full of ants is capable of carrying out tasks necessary to the colony's survival without direction from a central coordinating authority? Who guarantees that the jobs get done? As in Slashdot and k5, the answer is no one and everyone. The key that enables the ant collective to self-organize is the massive number of interactions that occur between individual ants. Some of these interactions are direct, others are not.

> Self-Organization in social insects often requires interactions among insects: such interactions can be direct or indirect. Direct interactions are the "obvious" interactions: antennation, trophallaxis (food or liquid exchange), mandibular contact, visual contact, chemical contact (the odor of nearby nestmates), etc. Indirect interactions are more subtle: two individuals interact indirectly when one of then modifies the environment and the other responds to the new environment at a later time. Such an interaction is an example of stigmergy. (Bonabeau, Dorigo, & Theraulaz, 1999; p. 14)

Slashdot and k5 allow for a massive number of both of these types of interactions between its users. Direct communication takes place as individuals post messages and replies to other messages. Indirect communication occurs through the rating of comments, as one user modifies a comment's score and another user responds by ignoring or reading the comment based on that modification.

The number of interactions is important as well. Just as 20 ants wandering in a 100 sq ft area may never interact with each other, the success of an OSOSS is heavily dependent on a critical mass of participants. There must be sufficient direct and indirect interaction between system users for self-organization to occur. This recalls the hypothesis posited earlier in this section—that there are strategies for working with large groups of students that were completely indiscoverable until technology mediated a minimum number of interactions among a minimum number of people. We currently understand very little about the lower bound in terms of critical mass numbers.

But why is self-organization so important? Why should it be a desideratum of large online groups? When online groups are small, they can be centrally controlled, the way a moderator or instructor directs a 25 student chat in an online course. As the group grows in size, it becomes impossible for a small number of people to focus its activities in a single direction (it also becomes prohibitively expensive, as per the teacher bandwidth discussion). For the group to remain organized, cohesive, regulated, and on a steady course, an organizing principle must obtain in the group. In other words, for learning environments to scale to numbers larger than faculty can control, and still remain necessarily social, we must rely on principles of self-organization to emerge within the group.

OPEN LEARNING SUPPORT

In partnership with MIT's OpenCourseWare project (http://ocw.mit.edu/), members of the Open Sustainable Learning Opportunity (OSLO) Group at Utah State University are now piloting social software intended to facilitate self-organization among large groups of learners. MIT OpenCourseWare is a project in which MIT is making available over the Internet the materials supporting nearly all 2,000 on-campus courses, for free. The OSLO Group's Open Learning Support (OLS, http://mit.ols.usu.edu/) system was integrated into seven MIT OpenCourseWare courses in April of 2004 and made available to the public.

Evolution

Self-organization is, of a necessity, directed by its agent participants who make individual decisions based solely on the information available to them locally. Although the characteristics of the supersystem will play a role in the direction in which an OSOSS evolves, to assume that a group can be coerced into self-organizing in a specific manner would be oxymoronic at least (and perhaps simply moronic). In designing OLS, we have taken a just-in-time approach to software design. Linus Torvalds (2001) said it best in an email to the kernel development listserv:

> And don't EVER make the mistake that you can design something better than what you get from ruthless massively parallel trial-and-error with a feedback cycle. That's giving your intelligence _much_ too much credit.

Rather than assume that we could divine "in the beginning" all the features that the community of OLS users would need, we have chosen to implement very few features. In fact, we believe we have implemented the minimum feature set necessary to facilitate the emergence of an OSOSS around a collection of reusable digital educational materials.

Forcing those who want to post to *login* creates stable identities that can accrue histories of activity, and reifies the system agents that will interact with one another. A *comment* feature allows users to post questions, answers, and other messages, enabling direct interaction between system users. Finally, the *real-time peer review* (RPR) system allows users to award points to useful messages or report messages that violate the site's Terms of Service, enabling indirect interaction between system users.

By integrating individual OLS forums with individual collections of course material from MIT OpenCourseWare, we intend to encourage discussions to focus on specific academic topics like linear algebra and applied microeconomics. However, because our primary design criterion has been to facilitate self-organization among the very large group of MIT OpenCourseWare users, there is no certain way to predict how the groups will use the OLS forums.

How OLS Evolves

During the pilot phase of OLS, the OSLO Group will carry out two distinct sets of activity. First, the research group will carry out computer-mediated discourse analyses (Herring, 2004) of conversations in the OLS system to anticipate community needs and how they can be built into the OLS software. Second, the engineering group will build additional functionality so that it can be made available at critical junctions in the groups' evolution.

Stable user identities and the OLS RPR system enable many "advanced" features that we anticipate the community eventually desiring. For example, plain keyword searching can be enhanced by ranking results according to the number of points returned comments have received. Tracking and displaying the number of points awarded to a users' messages facilitates a reputation management system (similar to Ebay's color-coded stars) by which system users can gain a positive reputation for making significant contributions to the community. Also, individual users' distribution of point awards can be mined to enable a collaborative filtering system (similar to Amazon's book recommending feature) by which a user who awarded points to 23 comments can be notified of seven additional comments she might find useful based on similarities between points she has awarded and those awarded by other OLS users.

The Future of OLS

Although OLS is currently integrated only with MIT OpenCourseWare materials, the OSLO Group is already working with other organizations to integrate OLS into their content collections. OLS is open source software. We hope that by enabling self-organization among large groups and organically growing site features as needed by the community, we are able to demonstrate successful teaching and learning interactions within a very large, academically focused, self-organized group.

CONCLUSION

The achievement of higher order learning outcomes, such as those near the bottom right of Anderson and Krathwohl's taxonomy, requires social interaction to be an integral part of the learning experience. As institutions seek to scale their educational offerings over great distances to large numbers of people, social interaction has traditionally been seen as too expensive to include. Although the automation or dehumanization of online courses does improve their scalability, it also hampers their ability to facilitate these inherently social higher order learning outcomes. Online self-organizing social systems (OSOSS) are one method of scaling educational offerings to large numbers of people while keeping the educational experience very social. OSOSS may therefore be an important key to scalable online programs that are capable of facilitating the mastery of learning outcomes across the entire range of learning outcomes.

In this chapter, I introduce open learning support or OLS, social software designed to wrap around educational materials and enable learners to support each other in their learning, and describe a pilot project in which we integrated OLS with seven collections of course material from MIT's OpenCourseWare. The pilot has been successful in terms of the number of registered users in OLS over the first 6-month period (over 900 users making over 200 comments). The integration project with MIT is therefore expanding, and will hopefully provide means of many, many more individuals receiving support and socialization as they pursue their educational interests.

In the longer run, however, it is difficult to say how one might predict the success of OLS. Envisioned as a system that would respond to user needs and demands, the only success metrics I can safely determine for it at present are use, use, and use. If the software is wrapped around several collections, with thousands of users posting thousands of messages and indicating that many of the messages are helpful, that is what I will call success.

ACKNOWLEDGMENTS

The development of this chapter was funded in part by a grant from the William and Flora Hewlett Foundation and National Science Foundation CAREER Award #0133246. Any opinions, findings, and conclusions or recommendations expressed in this material are those of the author and do not necessarily reflect the views of the William and Flora Hewlett Foundation or the National Science Foundation.

REFERENCES

ADL Technical Team (2004). *Sharable Content Object Reference Model (SCORM™) Version 2004 The SCORM Overview*. Retrieved September 13, 2005, from http://www.adlnet.org

Anderson, L. W., & Krathwohl, D. R. (Eds.). (2001). *A taxonomy for learning, teaching, and assessing: A revision of Bloom's taxonomy of educational objectives*. New York: Longman.

Bloom, B. S., & Krathwohl, D. R. (1956). Taxonomy of educational objectives: The classification of educational goals. *Handbook I: Cognitive domain*. New York: Longman.

Bonabeau, E., Dorigo, M., & Theraulaz, G. (1999). *Swarm intelligence: From natural to artificial systems*. New York: Oxford University Press.

Gibbons, A. S. (in press). *The interplay of learning objects and design architectures*. Englewood Cliffs, NJ: Educational Technology.

Gibson, J. J. (1979). *The ecological approach to visual perception*. Boston: Houghton Mifflin.

Herring, S. (2004). Computer-mediated discourse analysis: An approach to researching online communities. In S. A. Barab, R. Kling, & J. H. Gray (Eds.), *Designing for virtual communities in the service of learning* (pp. 338–376). Cambridge, MA: Cambridge University Press.

Jonassen, D. H. (Ed.). (1996). *Handbook of research on educational communications and technology*. New York: Macmillan.

Lave, J., & Wenger, E. (1991). *Situated learning: Legitimate peripheral participation*. Cambridge, England: Cambridge University Press.

Malda, R. (2003). *Frequently asked questions—comments and moderation*. Retrieved November 23, 2004 from http://slashdot.org/faq/com-mod.shtml#cm520

Maturana, H., & Varela, F. (1980). *Autopoiesis and cognition: The realization of the living*. Dordrecht, Holland: Reidel.

NetLogo. (2004). *Flocking model in the Models Library* (v2.0.0). Retrieved April 8, 2004 from http://ccl.northwestern.edu/netlogo/

Reigeluth, C. M. (1999). What is instructional design theory and how is it changing? In C. M. Reigeluth (Ed.), *Instructional design theories and models: A new paradigm of instructional theory* (pp. 5–29). Hillsdale, NJ: Lawrence Erlbaum Associates.

Torvalds, L. (2001, November 30). Coding style—a non-issue. Retrieved April 28, 1997 from http://www.uwsg.indiana.edu/hypermail/linux/kernal/0111.3/1957.html

Various. (Ed.). (2004). *Wikipedia*. Retrieved November 23, 2004 from http://en.wikipedia.org/wiki/Massively_multiplayer_online_game

Wertsch, J. (1998). *Mind as action*. New York: Oxford University Press.

Whitaker, R. (1995). *Self-Organization, autopoiesis, and enterprises*. Retrieved April 8, 2004 from http://www.acm.org/sigois/auto/Main.html

Wiley, D. A., & Edwards, E. K. (2002). Online self-organizing social systems: The decentralized future of online learning. *Quarterly Review of Distance Education, 3*(1), 33–46.

Winograd, T., & Flores F. (1986). *Understanding computers and cognition*. Norwood, NJ: Ablex.

Chapter 18

Role of Simulation in Web-Based Learning

Klaus Breuer
René Molkenthin
Johannes Gutenberg-Universität Mainz

Robert D. Tennyson
University of Minnesota

Simulations have been an area of interest and development since the early days of computer-based instruction and learning (1960s). Biological, physical, economic, and social phenomena have been depicted within simulation models that are executable on a computer. Such phenomena can be derived from a real, a theoretical, or a fictitious context. Regardless of context, a more or less sophisticated interaction component enables learners to access the model, to change parameters, to modify routines, or even to modify the structure; and, to receive feedback on the status of the model reflecting the various types of interventions (Lierman, 1993). The interaction between the learner and the model occurs in a sequence over time. From interactions over time, the learner acquires knowledge, skills, or strategies about the content depicted and its dynamics.

From those early simulations, there has been a continuous stream of developments enhancing and creating new design approaches (de Jong 1991; Edwards, 1995; Kass, Burke, & Fitzgerald, 1996; van der Boom, Paas, van Morriënboer, & van Gog, 2004). Outcomes of these efforts over the past decades are readily seen in the application of simulations in technical skills education and training. For example, railroad engineers are trained to run today's high-speed trains via simulators. Mechanics are certified for the utilization of CNC (Computer Numerically Controlled) technologies based on exercises with simulators. Business executives improve their decision making in complex, dynamic markets based on business market simulators. Students acquire knowledge and skills in subject matter domains based on (simulated) microworlds. There is application variance with respect to levels of fidelity between simulations. The successful integration of analogue media into the digital format is an example of contemporary differences. The level of fidelity presented within simulations has been extended to the full multimedia repertoire.

In addition, improved learning based on simulations is shown by the growing use of simulations as research and development tools. An example from research is given in the studies on complex problem solving abilities performed in educational psychology (Tennyson & Breuer, 2002). Experimental subjects are requested to cope with complex, dynamic environments represented by means of microworlds. The research end is not findings in instructional design but the study of human problem-solving abilities. This includes the study of learning activities within problem-solving activities, but not primarily from an educational perspective.

Given the above background and the growing technological milieu, there is no surprise about the extension of simulation-based instructional approaches into Web-based formats. The formats allow the dissemination of simulations throughout the Internet to users at any workstation within the Web environment. The lower level application formats provide for downloading of simulation programs. This makes use of the Internet as a distribution platform. More enhanced approaches target the interactive use of a simulation via the Internet. The technical solution has been achieved since the development of the World Wide Web in the early 1990s.

LEARNING/INSTRUCTIONAL THEORY FOUNDATIONS

At its core, the interactive solution comprises three basic elements: A simulation model is run as a resident on a central server. A data exchange process is established via the Internet or an intranet providing the necessary interaction between the user and the model. The network connection makes use of a standard browser providing a graphical user interface (GUI). The GUI represents the status of the model and the variables on which the participant can make her or his decisions. The three elements, a model on a server, a network connection, and a GUI within a browser, establish the necessary technical basis for using simulations at any workstation on the Web or on any notebook in a wireless LAN. The realization of such a set-up is not a trivial task but from the authors' perspective, it does not provide an educational asset in itself. The technical platform is a necessary prerequisite; any educational approach is dependant from its functionality. Meaningful instructional and learning activities however need more than a technical platform. They require a foundation in learning–teaching theory (Tennyson, 2002). Web-based simulations need design approaches making use of both simulation tools and learning foundations to achieve significant objectives of learning. This orientation defines the perspective of this chapter.

The proposed approach looks first at the framework of objectives for using simulations in educational environments. It addresses basic types of simulations in accordance with such objectives. It reflects on the approach to use simulations as a tool for problem-based learning activities. It refers to the notion of adaptivity for customized interaction processes. Such interaction may be established by using real-time, intelligent 4th generation instructional design evaluation (Tennyson & Foshay, 1998). This demand feeds back into requirements for the architecture of Web-based simulations. A basic assumption of our thesis is that the Web-based approach to simulations can bring a major technical advantage. The use of a central server can make available processing speed and processing capacity with almost no limits for Web-based simulations.

The background of our thesis is derived from three disciplines. First, there is a root in educational psychology. Second, there is a link to educational technology. And, third, there is a tie to vocational education and training (VET). The latter may result in specific arguments and examples that differ from general education. We trust that the reader has a chance for drawing generalizations and for transfer into other educational domains.

OBJECTIVES FOR INSTRUCTIONAL-LEARNING PROCESSES BASED ON WEB-SIMULATIONS

The spectrum of potential learning activities is extensive. Among these activities there are the acquisition and recall of knowledge, the automation of motor as well as of cognitive skills, the construction of problem-solving strategies, the elaboration of methods for learning or metacognition, the development of transfer strategies, the shaping of attitudes, the enhancement of motivation and interest, the creation of mental models, and the modification of behavior. From an instructional design perspective (Merrill, 1997), this variety of learning activities should be analyzed to identify distinct classes of outcomes and then to define specific instructional methods and strategies that will effectively result in the desired outcome of learning.

Our perspective on the use of Web-based simulations is that in general, they do not focus on narrow, specific results of learning. Rather, they open up a spectrum of potential objectives, which can be targets of learning. The set-up of Web-based simulation approaches needs a major investment in educational design and development as well as in information technology. The latter will provide its best return when instructional approaches are open and when they allow options for the setup of learning environments. The options can stress different objectives. An example may be given by the time a simulation is used in a learning activity. That is, a Web-based simulation can be offered at the beginning of a learning activity as a source of motivation for follow-up study efforts on the subject matter. Within that approach, a Web-based simulation may also function as an advance organizer for follow-up learning.

A Web-based simulation may be used for studying the model that it is based on. This way, a core objective can be the development of an appropriate mental model, which allows perceiving the variables involved, their interrelations, and the corresponding dynamics. The mental model may become the basis for decision-making processes within the simulated as well as in the real, depicted environment.

A simulation may also be used at the end of a learning activity for assessing the level of performance achieved by a student. This can be done, for example, by exposing participants to a scenario at a specific level of difficulty. The three approaches (advance organizer, mental model, and assessment) may make use of the same simulation environment. The decision for using a specific approach is up to the user given that the simulation environment allows such an open approach.

The use of Web-based simulation environments can target different objectives. Without the attempt at being a comprehensive list, such objectives may include:

- Acquisition of structural knowledge
- Development of domain-specific problem-solving competencies
- Elaboration of holistic views toward complex phenomena (systems thinking)
- Fostering of subject-matter interest and/or metacognitive competencies (self-regulation, self-monitoring)
- Support for the ability of role-taking
- Build-up of the ability for coping with dynamics

The acquisition of structural knowledge points to the need of making knowledge and skills applicable in a flexible way. Concepts, which become merely memorized, can hardly be used in the process of explaining a certain situation. Likewise, skills that become acquired as a mechanical, not situated, procedure can hardly be used for performing within a specific context (Renkl, Gruber, Mandl, & Hinkhofer, 1994). Such components of knowledge have to be linked within semantic networks. They have to be contextualized. In addition to the conceptual and the procedural facets of knowledge, learning needs the contextual or conditional component (Tennyson, in press). Knowledge becomes applicable in a flexible mode when it is used in varying situations. When students can apply concepts and procedures within different situations and can elaborate on the usefulness and appropriateness of such experiences, they can construct a flexible, structured knowledge base. One efficient way of providing respective contexts can be through the use of simulations in learning environments.

The ability to perform in specific (workplace) situations is certainly but not only rooted in the availability of elements of knowledge. It also needs approaches of how to tackle tasks and how to proceed through a sequence of steps. An early model illustrating this problem-solving concept is the TOTE unit defined by Miller, Galanter, and Pripram (1960). Based on a sequence of status explorations (*t*ests) and operations a person performs in a larger task, the overall task becomes decomposed into subtasks. A specific subtask is executed (*o*perated on) until it has been accomplished (*t*est and *e*xit). This includes the knowledge of when to test what against which standards. The result is to start working on the next subtask. Such sequences of performance can become automated. The result is the buildup of schemata in the sense of Piaget, which can be used adaptively to varying situations. The development of schemata needs to be repeated in experiences within varying contexts. Simulations are one approach to provide the necessary repetition in the required variations. When schemata become applied to newly encountered needs, they provide a basis for domain-specific problem-solving activities.

Human problem-solving activities have a tendency for failure (Doerner, 1996). Among the reasons for potential failure are the tendencies for sequential, causal inferences as well as the neglecting of side effects and undesired long-term effects within decision making for complex, dynamic environments. Approaches for counteracting this tendency are given within system dynamics (Forrester, 1968) and within system thinking (Senge, 1990). Both highlight the specifics of complex, dynamic environments, which incorporate, among others, delays over time, nonlinear interrelations between variables and feedback processes within systems and thus are likely to confront problem solvers with counterintuitive system behavior. System thinking highlights the notion of systemic, not just systematic, structures of complex processes. System dynamics adds the aspect of modeling to these structures for the purpose of simulating the corresponding dynamics. Both refer to the concept of mental models (Johnson-Laird, 1983, 1988) as a basis for action within solving complex, dynamic problems. In this respect, Senge pointed out that, "*Mental models* are deeply ingrained assumptions, generalizations, or even pictures or images that influence how we understand the world and how we take action (1990, p. 8)." Such mental models are highly resistant against changes. For modification, they need alternative, powerful models that may be provided by active modeling and simulation-based learning activities (Hillen, 2004).

The motivational effect of simulation-based learning activities is well recognized (Jonassen & Tennyson, 1997). This is one reason for their long-term use in education. The strength of such motivational effects becomes obvious from reports on flow experiences within simulation-based learning processes. Motivation is considered to contribute to problem-solving activity in a significant way (O'Neil, 1999). Processes of planning and of self-monitoring can be elicited within simulation-based learning activities. They can give room for self-reflection and for external feedback on such processes. This construct of motivation is beyond conventional objectives for teaching. Nevertheless, we consider motivation to constitute one specific potential of educational simulation use.

Web-based simulations can give access to problem-solving processes from different perspectives. For a single learner, this may be achieved by being assigned to different activities within a given simulation. In local networks, this can be extended to assigning activities to different learners who have to compete or to collaborate with respect to the objectives of the simulation. Web-based installations can extend this option for role taking into the distance. This can be accomplished both in an asynchronous as well as in a synchronous design. Role players can compete or collaborate in indirect or in direct electronic contact with their coagents. In this respect, technology can provide a significant contribution to this field.

Finally, a primary objective of educational simulations from its first roots shall not be omitted; that is, the exposure of learners to the dynamics of processes. Whether there is a market process, a chemical process, a physical process, or a technical process, in each case there is a development of a system over time that a learner can experience and into which she or he can intervene by means of given variables. Such dynamics in many cases can hardly be studied in real settings, due to their restricted accessibility. This can allow for learning processes at the skill level, it can allow for problem-solving activities, it can allow for processes of self-reflection, it can represent a subject matter in a mode that attracts attention and evokes motivation and/or interest. This can result in the development of specific skills in a playful as well as in a serious approach.

WEB-BASED APPROACHES TO SIMULATION DESIGN

In the early applications, simulations were used primarily within military, political, and economic scenarios for the purpose of decision-making support. That way, risky and costly strategies could be analyzed and evaluated with respect to probable consequences. The option of testing and evaluating the probable results of decisions without being faced with the outcomes from failure made simulations an interesting tool for education and training. For instructional purposes, the significant structures of a real-world environment can be depicted within a model. Learners can intervene into the model by means of decisions and can observe and evaluate the consequences of these decisions. The conclusions of each decision (or set of decisions) constitute the basis for follow-up decision making. The model used can be defined at both a qualitative and a quantitative level. For example, in an economic model, the effect of workers' wages are often more related to quality of the work environment (i.e., qualitative) than monetary variables (quantitative). In reference to Wilbers (2001), we address Web-based approaches of technical simulations, business simulations and games, modeling, role-playing exercises, case studies, microworlds, and animations.

Technical Simulations

Simulators represent a technical simulation system within a model. The learner can manipulate the variables of the model directly. For that, the model depicts the regulation and adaptation processes within the real system. That way, the learner can improve through training the handling (process control as well as maintenance) of the system. Specific procedures can be trained and automated. Errors in handling the system have no impact on the real system and thus do not cause negative consequences such as cost, damage, or loss. This allows for testing of new procedures as well as of risky or dangerous ones. CNC-simulators, which represent the functions of automated drilling, metal shaping or wood processing machines, can include the option for transferring debugged procedures of code to a real machine. This provides realistic feedback to the trainee. In virtual laboratories, the performance of the real equipment, based on the learner's commands, is represented by means of animations. This includes handling and measurement processes and can reduce the need for manipulative skills on the learner's side. Because these approaches are computer based to begin with, this makes it possible to represent the learner/system interaction in a Web-based approach, given the necessary IT-technology.

Business Simulations

Two defining features represent the *business simulations* approach. There are a model-based simulation component and a social component. The model based defines the task environment with its basic structures. This does not include the social aspects of the situation. Learners who have to perform with respect to the given knowledge base, the defined communication, and the decision-making processes control the social variables

(Capaul, 2001). The outcomes from these processes, the decisions, are entered into the simulation model. Decision results are calculated and represent the environmental conditions for the follow-up period of social interaction. This may comprise only one or more social parties competing against each other on a virtual market in a sequence of several periods. As there are a huge variety of such simulations and games, reflecting all kinds of markets, industries, strategies, and highlighting the two sides of the approach, there is the distinction between *tactical-decision simulations* and *social process simulations* (Gredler, 1992). The first highlights the systematic approach to information retrieval and uses within decision making. This approach is included in many business games. The category of social process simulations stresses the interaction between learners and their references to attitudes and values. Learners have to act on a defined role within a social framework and are requested to solve a given problem by means of specific interaction processes (Haritz & Breuer, 1995). Technological support can be given to this approach by means of Web-based discussion groups and by video conferencing. However, there may be restrictions to personal interaction processes especially with respect to nonverbal communication. High flying technology-based approaches in military systems and in corporate settings are referring to this approach as an electronic war-room.

Modeling

The *modeling* approach refers to the active development or elaboration of models to represent a given system. Within this approach, the previously addressed approaches of system thinking and especially of system dynamics come into play (Sterman, 2000). Following the modeling of a system is the study of its dynamics in simulation runs. A simulation construction process includes the analysis of the system behavior, which may provide reason for redefining or enhancing the model to achieve the representation of a certain aspect. Alessi (2000) referred to these two activities by applying the labels, building and using models. Both activities are considered to contribute to the development of refined mental models for acting within the respective system (Hillen, 2004). Of special relevance here is the aspect that both technical and business simulations are based on models of the underlying system. The construction of the model is a necessary prerequisite for the simulation of the system. What makes a difference, however, is the degree of transparency that is associated with the modeling approach. Most technical and business simulations are based on black-box models, which are defined by their programming language code. Such code in addition becomes compiled and is stored in binary format. There is no readability of it for any user. The alternative is to make use of a system dynamics-based modeling tool. This allows for the development of glass-box models or at least opaque ones, which the user may access for elaboration of her or his mental model on the simulated system (Berendes & Breuer, 1999). That way, in addition to the process of building and refining models, the system itself can be of educational relevance. Open, glass-box models can also support participants using technical and business simulations to develop valid mental models for their decision-making process in running such simulations.

Role-Playing Exercises

As stated regarding business simulations, the social aspects of decision-making processes can be considered in simulations (Haritz & Breuer 1995). For example, a learner takes over a role, with which he or she is not yet familiar, and experiences a situation from an unknown perspective. This is meant to improve the ability for empathy (Capaul, 2001). A significant aspect of *role-playing exercises* is the option for a repeated experience of social situations and their analysis with respect to alternative interpretation and perception. Role-playing exercises do not necessarily depend on a technical platform. The Web comes into play when there is support from discussion groups (Wilbers, 2001) or when interactions become based on video clips offering options to the learner for tactical decisions in social processes. This, for example, is used for the training of sales strategies or for counseling processes (Schwarzer & Buchwald, 2001).

Case Studies

The fifth approach, *case studies*, originates from law studies and is based on the casuistic methodology. At the Harvard Business School, the approach has been adopted to business administration studies. From that basis there is transfer into additional subjects, especially for fostering problem-solving abilities (Frey, 1995). Cases represent authentic, that is from specific professional demands, derived problems. Students are to solve these by defining respective measures. Here too the decision-making situation is handled as a simulation. Also, there is no direct need for technical support. There are, however, more and more approaches for support of the case study approach within the Internet by means of corresponding Web pages and by video clips.

Microworlds

The concept of computer-based *microworlds* has been introduced in education from at least two perspectives. One is from the context of the first revival of computer-based instructional and learning activities in the early

1980s based on the newly emerging microcomputer technology (Breuer, 1983). In this respect, the statements on simulators and on business simulations and games given earlier can be applied without essential differences. The technical platform has been stand-alone microcomputers. The options for graphical representation were low level but were emerging. The major educational advantage can be considered in the better accessibility of the technology within educational settings, which could provide an interactive access to simulation-based learning activities. This has been one of the lines of developments already addressed in the introductory statements.

The second perspective is from psychological research on complex problem solving as initiated by the work group of Dietrich Doerner (1996) in Germany. For a brief orientation on these works, the reader can refer to O'Neil (1999) and Frensch and Funke (1995) respectively. The basic purpose of this approach concerns the performance of individuals or of small groups of people in complex, dynamic, and at least partly transparent environments, similar to many all-day situations people encounter. This approach too was based on the emerging microcomputer technology. It has made use of simulation programs in order to represent the problem-solving space with which research subjects have been confronted. In the beginning, subjects had no direct access to the respective computer-based model, but were monitored and advised by a mediator. This has been modified with the emerging user friendliness of technology and with the transfer of the approach into the field of management diagnostics (Frensch & Funke, 1995) and into the field of instructional/learning activities (Breuer, 1983, 1985; Breuer & Kummer, 1990).

Here too there is no basic difference to the characteristics given before with respect to business simulations. In fact, some of the simulations used for complex problem-solving research have been grounded in scenarios from business administration.

Animations

Computer-based *animations*, from a surface glance, can look similar to the interfaces (GUIs) of computer-based simulations. Looking at animations representing chaos systems for example, gives evidence that they are also based on simulation models. Additionally, there are options to vary parameters within the simulation model, which results in the modification of the dynamic pattern on a simulation's interface. With respect to virtual laboratories, we have already stated that the real equipment becomes represented by means of animations. Thus, there is no clear division between computer-based simulations and computer-based animations. We may make a distinction based on the stress that is given to the purpose of the underlying model. If it serves as a driver for an animation, we would not consider that to be a computer-based simulation. On the other hand, in cases where the animation represents features of the problem space with which a user has to cope, we would refer to that as a simulation. This, however, remains a weak point and is included in this line of argument for purposes of a more comprehensive view toward the field of simulations.

The six approaches to computer-based simulations have in common the following two features: They allow the learner to explore decision-making outcomes; and, second, the problem solving space is free of risks for the learner and her or his environment. The results of errors may be experienced, but they are not associated with real costs. That way, options for action as well as hypotheses on the outcomes of measures taken can be tested, and hypothesis-based approaches for solving complex, dynamic problems can be encountered. Errors experienced by a learner can become a driving source for additional learning activities (Kriz, 2001).

The distinctions given between the approaches to simulations only highlight the variability of the concept. A sharp differentiation cannot be achieved. This becomes obvious with business simulations because they include elements of role playing and case studies (Capaul, 2001). Learners become assigned to a specific task as part of the role of a decision maker or a problem solver. Within a market simulation, for example, this may be the role of a marketing manager. This role of a manager has to be performed within a given scenario. Such a scenario can be considered to be the case of the simulation. In consequence, there has to be a close correspondence between the paper-based scenario and the model that is driving the simulation for the calculation of the future system statuses. Each new system status represents a variation of the starting scenario and gives cause for new learning activities to define new measures of action in order to modify a given, less desirable system status into a more desirable one. This constitutes the dynamics of the simulation environment. The description given closely matches the concept of microworlds. These are learning environments, which aspects of a segment of reality are represented within a simulation model and that allow students to explore the environment including the model it is based on (Edwards, 1995).

Due to the tradition of the case approach within the concept of simulations and games, we use this label within our follow-up thesis. We stress the tactical decision-making approach because this is in large part based on a computer-based model of the represented environment. We focus on the functions that simulations and games should have as part of learning environments and on which specifics can be enhanced by means of Web-based approaches. Again, we assume that the reader can transfer to the field of technical simulations and to related approaches.

PROBLEM-ORIENTED SIMULATION ENVIRONMENTS

Approaches to instructional design differ. They have developed over time and have stressed different perceptions of the learning process. Major effects on the discussions have come from the paradigmatic orientation within learning theories. Differences are due in large part to the cognitive shift in learning theories and, following that, to the constructivist view (Reimann-Rothmeier & Mandl 1996). This is not the place to elaborate on this development. Instead we follow two orientations. The first is to base our Web-based simulations approach in an up-to-date orientation. The second is to refer to an orientation that is in accordance with the underlying assumptions, which have at least partly been addressed already with respect to learning activities, grounded in computer-based simulations.

We refer to the pragmatic approach published by the working group around Heinz Mandl at Munich that takes up a mediating position between the constructivist and the preceding cognitive approach (Reinmann-Rothmeier & Mandl, 1999). This pragmatic approach provides room for teaching activities that support individual processes of knowledge construction.

One basic orientation for Web-based simulations is that of a problem-oriented approach (Tennyson, in press). Learning activities should be based on problems that are either authentic or at least refer to authentic problems situations relevant to the learner, based on present general or individual significance, and that evoke personal involvement. This orientation is based on the assumption that such problems result in four main effects:

- Lead to an active enquiry of the issue by the learner
- Result in self-regulated learning activities
- Evoke situated cognitions in that inferences, solutions, points of view, and interpretations are related to the problem situation
- Allow for developing solutions by means of social interaction

Behind these expectations, there is the concept of a learner that is predominantly active out of her or his own efforts and is receptive only for interim phases. The teaching environment in reverse should be able to switch between a mostly supportive and to a limited degree active performance. This position clearly objects to teaching approaches that favor unguided discovery activities on the one hand and externally directed learning activities on the other hand to avoid overstrain, which can cause a decrease in motivation and hence lower learning outcomes.

Problem-oriented learning activities are centered on five instructional design principles and corresponding objectives (Table 18.1).

TABLE 18.1

Principles and Objectives of Problem-Oriented Learning Activities

Principle of Learning	Objective
Authentic problems in a situated orientation	Applicability of new knowledge
Multiple contexts	Usability of knowledge; reduced adherence of knowledge to specific situations
Multiple perspectives	Extended flexibility of knowledge
Social context	Reduced idiosyncrasies, social entrenchment, and knowledge
Instructional support	Reduced risk of failure, efficiency, and effectiveness

The interpretation of this orientation with respect to learning with computer-based simulations is biased in favor of the simulation approach. There are, however, some rather obvious features to relate to at first glance. Simulation environments are set up for active explorations and interventions into the simulation model. They share the notion of active learners, who regulate their processes of orientation, learning, decision making and problem solving.

Simulations represent a problem space in which the learner can engage. So, by definition, this is a problem-oriented approach. The degree of authenticity of the problem space will vary across context; this can be considered and planned for during the development of the simulation environment. This should be done with the case(s) in which a simulation is grounded and with respect to the features of the model(s) that drive the simulation. Given the multimedia features of contemporary computer systems, authenticity may also be supported by the inclusion of realistic and authentic images and video clips. Taking this approach would mean that there should be no simulations that merely represent a subject matter per se without providing for the opportunity to embed it into an authentic problem. This can also be considered as another claim for open designs, which allow for multiple uses of a simulation model. Realism also can be used in designing the GUI for a simulation. Students may look at features and information in a simulation as these can be seen in reality. A simple example may be the presentation of a gains and loss calculation on the financial status of a company. For that information, there is a professional format in business administration. Thinking for example of trainees in business administration to be a target group for a simulation, the information can be presented in the professional format. This is not only an issue of authenticity but can be considered also from the perspective of the ecological validity of the simulation system.

Multiple contexts can be offered by a variation of cases (scenarios) in which simulations can be embedded. There is also the chance to have students actively relate from a simulation to their real (vocational or business) environment with respect to the structures and processes simulated.

Multiple perspectives are for the most part a defining feature of simulations based on their dynamics. For example, over time, systems achieve different statuses of variables and thus have to be interpreted differently. This holds true for a single status representation. The level of a variable can or has to be read differently from different perspectives.

There is also a social context approach to this principle by having students' assigned to different activities in a simulation. In a single-user approach, this can be accomplished by default parameter settings to a set of variables while the student is in charge of one specific variable. This provides a certain perspective on the system to the student, which will become different when she or he becomes in charge of another variable. In a multi-user approach, this can be accomplished by assigning students to different activities and then having them rotate on these assignments in a sequence of simulation runs. Each change in assignments provides a different perspective toward the system and to the actions taken by the coparticipants.

The fifth principle, instructional support, is effective within simulation environments at a basic level as they are responsive to the decision-making processes of students. An input into the system generates an output. Students can figure out whether this output is reasonable and conclude from that on the appropriateness of their perception of the system. For such support, a simulation system would need a diagnostic component, which is not yet available. On that we elaborate in the next section, taking into account the potentials of a Web-based approach.

DIAGNOSTIC WEB-BASED BUSINESS SIMULATIONS

The thesis presented thus far can be condensed into on overview toward what simulations can contribute to the problem-oriented learning and instructional approach. Table 18.2 represents essentials from the authors' view, but does not claim to be comprehensive. With respect to most specifics of the Web-based enhancements we cannot elaborate on all these within this chapter. We propose to make cross-references within this chapter for that. Instead, the thesis turns to the specific issue of online diagnostic support for Web-based simulations based on assumptions with respect to the computer infrastructure within educational environments. The Web-based approach targets at providing computer-based simulations to a wider audience within the educational system or within training organizations. This orientation

TABLE 18.2

Problem-Oriented Learning Activities and Online Simulations

Principle of Learning	Simulations & Games	Web-Based Enhancements
Authentic problems in a situated orientation	• Starting case(s), • Multimedia representation(s) • Glass-box (opaque) models	• Downloads for starting cases • Downloads for multimedia features • Model-based GUIs • Pop-ups • Flash animations
Multiple contexts	• Multiple scenarios • Variations of models	• Access to multiple scenarios • Access to varying models
Multiple perspectives	• F eedback on dynamics • Role taking within different activities of a simulation	• Online feedback to dynamics • GUI-based representation of different activities • Role taking within different activities • (Asynchronous; synchronous)
Social context	• Collaborative problem solving	• Distributed collaboration (Asynchronous, synchronous)
Instructional support	• Interactivity (feedback on system-statuses) • Diagnostic features	• Online feedback to dynamics • Dedicated Web pages • Web-based discussion groups (asynchronous, synchronous) • Web-tutoring • Online diagnostics

has to take into account the average infrastructure, which today is, and in the near future supposedly will be, given within such settings.

Schools, training institutes, and training departments today have computer laboratories giving students and teachers access to computing resources. Such computer labs are linked to the Web. Work stations are equipped with standard software products. Among these is a standard browser for navigating the Web. For installation of additional, specific software, there are restrictions for administrative privileges and financial resources. Access to the Internet is via technology, which is shared for all the work stations within a lab. This causes a bottleneck for data exchange. In addition, there are firewalls or software installations for security against the hazards within the Internet. That way the user side of Web-based simulations is considered a constrained environment with little options only for the use of sophisticated technology. This side should be served in a lean approach.

On the side of the provider, however, there are options for scaling the computer recourse needs. Computing power and speed for a server center can become available today with almost no restrictions. Different from the situation for the side of the many users, this is a single need only. Restrictions on the server side concern security issues. The server needs control of access and defense against pirates in the Internet at the server side too. The conclusion from the technical perspective is that requirements for the educational settings should be limited to the standard features available and that the process of data exchange should be designed for a lean and secure approach. Options for scaling the needs are on the side of the provider for Web-based simulations. We refer to this background as it applies to three aspects of the design of Web-based simulations:

- Design of a glass-box access to simulations.
- Implementation of a basis for online diagnostics for simulation runs.
- Introduction of a process perspective to the use of simulations.

The rational of a glass-box view on the model driving a simulation has been previously presented. In short, it is a method to provide the basis for the exploration of the complexity and the structural dynamics of the model. This can support the development of a holistic, systemic view toward the simulation, can help with elaborations of the knowledge base, and can support processes of metacognitive control. We approach that objective by means of the design of the GUI for a simulation game.

The approach is grounded in the use of a system dynamics-based simulation model. Such models can be designed in a graphical format on the computer screen. A necessary requirement is the use of system dynamics-based modeling software. The model can be developed in a graphical representation and can drive the corresponding simulation directly due to the underlying mathematical integration procedures (Berendes, 2002). We discussed this in the preceding section on Web-based approaches to simulation within the paragraph on modeling. Recent research has come up with the finding that such models can be read by students and can foster the development of higher level cognitive processes that cover a systemic view toward the simulation model (Hillen, 2004). On that basis, Molkenthin (2003) has developed a GUI-based approach for using the model within the Internet. There is a prototype system running now at the Johannes-Gutenberg-University Mainz, which can be accessed, on request. Factually, the GUI is made up from a set of corresponding pages that become presented to the user with a standard browser after a login at the simulation server.

The basis for online diagnostics in simulation runs is defined in the set up of the simulation server. Between the simulation driver and the user, there is a data bank server. All communication from the simulation model to the user and vice versa becomes channeled through the data bank. This allows for keeping track of all exploratory actions a learner takes when working with the GUI. All decisions a learner enters into the system become recorded before they are entered into the simulation model. Likewise, all information on the status of the simulation model becomes stored in the database. This covers essential information available on the use of a simulation, which can be collected within a run of the system.

The content of the data bank can be accessed in parallel to the simulation run and processed by a diagnostic routine with respect to structural information. This can refer to the patterns within the exploratory activities of a learner as a basis for her or his decision-making process. An approach for the retrieval of such pattern is given within the works of Streufert and coauthors (Breuer & Streufert, 1995; Streufert & Satish, 1997). The moves of the user within her or his exploratory activities can be displayed and mirrored back to the user. This provides information for fostering self-reflection on the individual decision-making processes. In addition, a set of parameters can be calculated that represent qualities within the processes. Examples here may be given by the breadth of the information search, which is applied, by the level of initiative a user takes or by the follow through within the individual decision-making processes. Streufert and coauthors have defined such measures. They will have to be revalidated within the given context. Such process-related information can become available in addition to the standard system status-related information, which has always been given to the user since the early days of educational simulation uses. The interrelation between the two sets of information will be a focus for our future research efforts. The approach is considered to be an implementation of 4th generation measurement as defined by Bunderson, Inouye, and Olsen (1993).

In a medium perspective, the diagnostic information may become useful for instructional support to the learner. Feedback and feed forward on decisions could be accomplished as the adaptation of simulation runs to the level of abilities at which individual learners can perform. This however is an issue of research and development activities still to come.

CONCLUSION

Web-based simulations and games have been implemented in a variety of examples. They make use of features provided by technology. The application of principles of instructional design up to now does not seem to be a key issue in the field. This may in part result from the technical problems that have to be solved in the set up of Web-based simulations. The solution of such problems is essential. Beyond that, there is the need for substantial foundation of the Web-based approach in teaching and learning theory. The mere use of technical options can have an exploratory meaning. This however cannot be the level of professional developmental activities, which have to be grounded in principles of instructional systems design. We have outlined such an approach. Further, we have tried to elaborate on the potentials that can be derived from that with respect to the implementation of diagnostic procedures, which can provide online information on significant objectives of learning to the user.

The learning principle underlining our thesis is that thinking strategies are acquired in reference to employment of the learner's own knowledge base and that they are not independent thinking skills (Tennyson & Breuer, 2002). Our instructional principle is that, because cognitive complexity is ability, it can be developed and improved with instructional intervention. As this chapter indicates, problem-oriented simulations focus on the improvement and development of higher order thinking strategies (i.e., problem solving within the context of employing the knowledge base).

Following this line of argument, we can look at two major perspectives. The first refers to research on learning processes that make use of computer-based simulations. Diagnostic procedures can be used to collect information on such learning processes. Unlike blind tracing procedures from information technology, the approach defined has a direct link to information on the content within a simulation. Working with controlled groups under experimentally controlled conditions can provide new insights into learning and teaching processes. Such research can take place in the field, given the accessibility of core elements of the learning environment via the Web. This can include additional data collection in a Web-based approach. Our second perspective is defined within a large-scale assessment of learning outcomes. Given the use of simulations in the diagnostics of managerial competencies and for the measurement of problem-solving skills, this could be extended to the diagnosis of competencies in the vocational or business administration field.

REFERENCES

Alessi, S. (2000). Building versus using simulations. In J. M. Spector & T. M. Andersen (Eds.), *Integrated and holistic perspectives on learning, instruction and technology: Improving understanding in complex domains* (pp. 175–196). Dordrecht, Netherlands: Kluwer.

Berendes, K. (2002). *Lenkungskompetenz in komplexen ökonomischen Systemen* [Masterminding-competency within complex economic systems]. Wiesbaden, Germany: Gabler.

Berendes, K., & Breuer, K. (1999) Potentiale von systemdynamisch basierten Mikrowelten [Potentials of system dynamics based microworlds]. In G. Hohmann (Ed.), *Simulationstechnik* (pp. 113–116). Erlangen/Ghent: SCS Publishing House.

Breuer, K. (1983). Lernen mit computersimulierten komplexen dynamischen Systemen [Learning in computer-simulated complex dynamic systems]. In E. Lechner & J. Zielinski (Eds.), *Wirkungssysteme und Reformansätze in der Pädagogik* (pp. 341–351). Frankfurt, Germany: Lang.

Breuer, K. (1985). Computer simulations and cognitive development. In K. A. Duncan & D. Harris (Eds.), *The proceedings of the world-conference on computers in education 1985 WCCE/85* (pp. 239–244). Amsterdam: North Holland.

Breuer, K., & Kummer, R. (1990). Cognitive effects from process learning with computer-based simulations. *Computers in Human Behavior, 6,* 69–81.

Breuer, K., & Streufert, S. (1995). Strategic management simulations in the German case. In M. Mulder, W. J. Nijhoff, & R. O. Brinkerhoff (Eds.), *Corporate training for effective performance* (pp. 195–208). Dordrecht, Netherlands: Kluwer.

Bunderson, C. V., Inouye, D. K., & Olsen, J. B. (1993). The four generations of computerized educational measurement. In R. L. Linn (Ed.), *Educational measurement* (pp. 367–407). Phoenix, AZ: Oryx Press.

Capaul, R. (2001). Didaktische und methodische Analyse der Planspielmethode [Analysis of business gaming from the educational perspective]. *Erziehungswissenschaft und Beruf, 1,* 3–14.

de Jong, T. (1991). Learning and instruction with computer simulations. *Education & Computing, 6,* 217–229.

Doerner, D. (1996). *The logic of failure: Why things go wrong and what we can do to make them right.* New York: Metropolitan Books.

Edwards, L. D. (1995). Microworlds as representations. In A. A. DiSessa, C. Hoyles, & R. Noss (Eds.), *Computers and exploratory learning, computer and systems sciences* (pp. 127–154). Berlin: Springer.

Forrester, J. W. (1968). *Principles of systems.* Cambridge, MA: MIT Press.

Frensch, P. A., & Funke, J. (1995). *Complex problem solving: The European perspective.* Hillsdale, NJ: Lawrence Erlbaum Associates.

Frey, K. (1995). *Die Projektmethode* [The project-method] (6th ed.). Weinheim, Germany: Beltz.

Gredler, M. E. (1992). *Designing and evaluating games and simulations: A process approach.* London: Kogan Page.

Haritz, J., & Breuer, K. (1995). Computersimulierte und dynamische Entscheidungssituationen als Element der multikulturellen Personalentwicklung [Computer simulated and dynamic decision-making situations as part of multicultural personal development]. In J. M. Scholz (Ed.), *Internationales change-mangement* (pp. 109–120). Stuttgart: Schäffer-Poeschel.

Hillen, S. (2004). *Systemdynamische Modellbildung und Simulation im kaufmännischen Unterricht* [System dynamics based modeling and simulation within business administration education]. Frankfurt: Peter Lang.

Johnson-Laird, P. N. (1983). *Mental models. Towards a cognitive science of language. Inferences and consciousness.* Cambridge, MA: University Press.

Johnson-Laird, P. N. (1988). *The computer and the mind. An introduction to cognitive science.* Cambridge, MA: University Press.

Jonassen, D., & Tennyson, R. D. (Eds.). (1997). *Handbook of research on educational communications and technology.* Washington, DC: Association for Educational Communications and Technology.

Kass, A., Burke, R., & Fitzgerald, W. (1996). How to support learning from interactions with simulated characters. In B. Gorayska & J. L. Mey (Eds.), *Cognitive technology: In search of a human interface* (pp. 84–111). Amsterdam: Elsevier.

Kriz, W. C. (2001). Die Planspielmethode als Lernumgebung [The business gaming approach used as learning environment]. In H. Mandl, C. Keller, M. Reiserer, & B. Geier (Eds.), *Planspiele im Internet: Konzepte und Praxisbeispiele für den Einsatz in Aus- und Weiterbildung* (pp. 41–64). Bielefeld, Germany: Bertelsmann.

Lierman, B. C. (1993). Training simulations. In G. M. Piskurich (Ed.), *The ASTD handbook of instructional technology* (pp. 24.1–24.12). New York: McGraw-Hill.

Merrill, M. D. (1997). Instructional transaction theory: An instructional design model based on knowledge objects. In R. D. Tennyson, F. Schott, N. Seel, & S. Dijkstra (Eds.), *Instructional design: International perspectives. Vol. 1: Theory and research* (pp. 381–394). Hillsdale, NJ: Lawrence Erlbaum Associates.

Miller, G. A., Galanter, E., & Pripram, K. H. (1960). *Plans and the structure of behaviour*. London: Holt, Rinehart & Winston.

Molkenthin, R. (2003). *Zur Entwicklung einer systemdynamischen Unternehmenssimulation als Komponente von e-Learning* [The development of a system dynamics based business simulation as a component of e-learning]. Unpublished master's thesis, Johannes Gutenberg-University, Mainz, Germany.

O'Neil, H. F. (1999). Perspectives on computer-based performance assessment of problem solving. *Computers in Human Behavior, 15*, 269–282.

Reimann-Rothmeier, G., & Mandl, H. (1996). Lernen auf der Basis des Konstruktivismus. Wie Lernen aktiver und anwendungsorientierter wird [Learning based on Constructivism. How learning becomes more active and applied]. *Computer und Unterricht, 23*, 41–44.

Reimann-Rothmeier, G., & Mandl, H. (1999). *Unterrichten und Lernumgebungen gestalten* [Teaching and designing learning environments]. Göttingen, Germany: Hogrefe.

Renkl, A., Gruber, H., Mandl, H., & Hinkhofer, L. (1994). Hilft Wissen bei der Identifikation und Steuerung eines komplexen ökonomischen Systems? [Does knowledge support the exploration and control of a complex economic system?] *Unterrichtswissenschaft, 22*, 195–202.

Schwarzer, C., & Buchwald, P. (2001). Beratung [Counseling]. In A. Krapp & B. Weidenmann (Eds.), *Pädagogische Psychologie* (4th ed., pp. 565–600). Weinheim, Germany: Beltz Psychologie.

Senge, P. (1990). *The fifth discipline*. New York: Doubleday.

Sterman, J. D. (2000). *Business dynamics: System thinking and modeling for a complex world*. Boston: McGraw-Hill.

Streufert, S., & Satish, U. (1997). Graphic representations of processing structure: The time-event matrix. *Journal of Applied Social Psychology, 27*, 2122–2131.

Tennyson, R. D. (in press). Learning theories and instructional design: An historical perspective of the linking model. In J. M. Spector, C. Ohrazda, & A. Van Schaak (Eds.), *Innovations in instructional technology: Essays in honor of M. David Merrill*. Mahwah, NJ: Lawrence Erlbaum Associates.

Tennyson, R. D. (2002). Linking learning theories to instructional design, *Educational Technology, 42*(3), 51–55.

Tennyson, R. D., & Breuer, K. (2002). Improving problem solving and creativity through use of complex-dynamic simulations. *Computers in Human Behavior, 18*, 650–668.

Tennyson, R. D., & Foshay, W. R. (1998). Instructional systems development. In P. J. Dean & D. E. Ripley (Eds.), *Performance improvement interventions: Methods for organizational learning* (Vol. 2, pp. 64–106). Washington, DC: The International Society for Performance Improvement.

van der Boom, G., Paas, F., van Morriënboer, J., & van Gog, T. (2004). Reflection prompts and tutor feedback in a web-based learning environment: Effects on students' self-regulated learning competence. *Computers in Human Behavior, 20*, 551–568.

Wilbers, K. (2001). E-Learning didaktisch gestalten [Educational design for e-learning]. In A. Hohenstein & K. Wilbers (Eds.), *Handbuch E-Learning: Expertenwissen aus Wissenschaft und Praxis* (pp. 102–135). Köln: Fachverlag Deutscher Wirtschaftsdienst.

Chapter 19

The Use of Technology in Education

Lisa Neal
eLearn Magazine

Diane Miller
Aptima, Inc.

Technology is becoming pervasive in all areas of life, and the greatest impact is arguably in education. This is not only because of the myriad of ways technology can be used to enhance or fundamentally change education, but because of the impact of the introduction and use of technology on future generations and their ability to function in an increasingly technology-driven society. "Conceptions of the skills and knowledge children will need to become successful adults and the relevant educational experiences they should encounter while attending school" have changed as a result of the "technological revolution," leading to technology becoming a major current focus of education policy and reform (NCES, 2000, p. 2).

Technology can be used to fundamentally alter aspects of education that have been static for decades, including where students are located, the type of work students are doing, how educational materials are developed, class size, and the role of the teacher as well as that of the student(s). This chapter looks at the current state of technology in education; how education and learning are changing as a result of technology; and the implications for the future, in particular, for Web-based learning, also known as e-learning and online learning. The chapter focuses primarily on how technology is used in elementary, secondary, and higher education in the United States; the observations here, especially in the discussion of how education and learning are changing as a result of technology, are applicable to other countries and other types of education, such as professional development and continuing education.

THE CURRENT STATE OF TECHNOLOGY IN EDUCATION

Education accounts for $700 billion in annual expenditures in the United States, according to the U.S. Department of Commerce (IDC, 2000, p. 7). Traditional educational expenditures include little that is technological. Funding is typically allocated to buildings, furniture, books, and salaries. As technology's role has become more prominent in education, there has been a huge drive to bring computers to the classroom and to provide high bandwidth connections to the Internet. In addition to using technology to augment traditional classroom learning, technology is being used to serve populations for whom traditional education is not available or is not possible; this includes homeschoolers, hospitalized or incarcerated children, children who don't have local access to needed courses, and people who are working and need courses for a degree or for professional development and continuing education.

Technology, and bandwidth in particular, can limit what is possible educationally, such as how media-rich content is and the opportunities for communication and collaboration (Downes, 1998). With the current state of technology and its infiltration into schools, "technology, the art of teaching, and the needs of learners are converging" (Bonk, 2004, p. 2); as technology is more pervasive, the stumbling block is generally not technology access but how to develop and select educational materials and how to use them effectively to ensure educational outcomes that are as good as or better than classroom instruction alone. Efforts to train teachers in the use of technology and to determine the most effective ways to integrate technology into the curriculum lag behind the presence of technology in schools. "Simply having technology doesn't mean that schools are revolutionizing teaching and learning, introducing project-based learning and making other departures from the traditional factory model for schools. A number of recent studies have shown that computer use remains primitive in many schools" with teachers using computers to keep track of attendance and grades (Seal, 2003, p. 1).

Many students use computers in school for drill-and-practice or word processing. In spite of these basic tasks, students often possess more advanced technological skills than their teachers. "The Market Data Retrieval survey (which contacted 25,585 k–12 public schools during the 2001–2002 school year) found that only 11% report that the majority of their teachers 'are at an advanced skill level,' meaning that they are innovative technology leaders, or can integrate technology into the curriculum" (Seal, 2003, p. 1).

A National Center for Education Statistics survey of public school teachers in 1999 found that approximately one-third of teachers reported feeling well or very well prepared to use computers and the Internet for classroom instruction. Teachers who reported feeling better prepared to use technology were generally more likely to use instructional activities on the computer than teachers who indicated that they felt unprepared. Additionally, 93% of teachers cited independent learning as preparing them for technology use, followed by 88% who said professional development activities. Eighty-seven percent said their colleagues prepared them for technology use (NCES, 2000).

The same survey found a correlation between the teachers who were more likely to integrate computers into the classroom and technology access, specifically, that "teachers were generally more likely to use computers and the Internet when located in their classrooms than elsewhere in the school." Additionally, "teachers and students with more computers or computers connected to the Internet in their classrooms generally used these technologies more often than teachers with fewer computers or Internet connections" (NCES, 2000, p. 5). Teachers may do a considerable amount of work from home, where they may not have Internet access or their access is at a lower bandwidth, impacting their ability to prepare for their courses.

There are other factors blocking progress, including school culture and organization; "strong, visionary leaders are needed to achieve the school-wide transformation that technology often entails" (Seal, 2003, p.3). In addition to training, teachers need guidance, support, time, and incentives to make the investment of time and effort seem worthwhile, while gaining an understanding of the benefits of technology use for themselves as educators and for their students. Even when training and support are in place, it must be ongoing because technology is a moving target: "There has been such a proliferation of technology during the past decade that it is difficult to fault instructors and students for any reservations or hesitancy in their use" (Bonk, 2004, p. 4). As technologies continue to change and new ones to emerge, they can overwhelm any teacher who is trying to determine how to best utilize technology in the classroom.

K–12 EDUCATION

In the United States, in kindergarten through high school (k–12), there has been considerable expenditure on hardware and software. Such funding may be more readily available than funding to, say, reduce classroom size or provide more professional development for teachers. Although it is difficult to have technology integrated into education without adequate hardware, software, and bandwidth, these are not sufficient; teachers must be trained in the use of computers and in the effective integration of technology into the classroom. The all too common computer in the back of the room or weekly visit to the computer lab do not constitute integration.

Some of the major changes in k–12 education have occurred because of the emphasis at the state level on standards-based testing and because of federal funding priorities. "The No Child Left Behind Act of 2001 provided $700.5 million for teacher education in technology for 2002. In addition, the federal Preparing Tomorrow's Teachers to Use Technology (PT3) initiative allocated $125 million in fiscal year 2001 and $62.5 million in 2002" (Seal, 2003, p. 4).

As the Internet's prominence has increased, the focus has shifted from computers in the classroom and schools to connected computers, ideally at high bandwidths. Ninety-eight percent of all public schools in the United States had access to the Internet in 2000, in contrast to 35% in 1994. By 2000, there were virtually no differences in access to the Internet by school characteristics, such as poverty level and urban or rural status (Cattagni & Westat, 2001, p. 4). Those differences may have diminished in just a few years, however.

> The Clinton-era legislation aimed at connecting American schools to the Internet succeeded. According to the market research firm Market Data Retrieval, 94% of public schools today have Internet access, and more than three-quarters have high-speed lines rather than dial-up connections. The ratio of students to computers is 3.8 to 1. (Seal, 2003, p. 1)

Although a standalone computer can be used for activities using installed software, such as word processors, or educational software available on a CD-ROM, new models of learning are possible with increased connectivity in schools and the home. "The Internet is no longer viewed by the education community as a 'nice-to-have' tool but rather as a requirement for enhancing teaching and learning," with the potential to revolutionize education through research, collaborative projects, and electronic field trips (IDC, 2001, p. 6). Connectivity to the Internet allows students to use educational Web sites and to search for information online. Connectivity also allows for participation in online courses, although the popularity of Web-based learning is much higher for adult education and training, in particular for professional development and continuing education, than it is for k–12 education. A National Center for Education Statistics study (NCES, 2002, Table 425) looks at the use of the Internet by persons 3 years old and over in September 2001, and shows that although the percentage of students, prekindergarten through college, using the Internet is 66.1%, only 3.5% use the Internet for online courses (0.9% of all prekindergarten–12 students and 9.3% of all college students).

In addition to what is available in the classroom and in schools, many states, cities, and school districts, such as the state of Maine, have instituted programs to provide laptops to children in certain grades. The laptops are used in the classroom and are taken home. Many homes have computers that are used, in part, for educational purposes, and many homes have high-speed Internet access. Whereas 90.9% of all elementary and secondary students use home computers to play games, only 68.4% use computers for school assignments, according to a September 2001 study of student home computer users study (NCES, 2002, Table 427). Even when schools integrate technology into the curriculum, they may not provide seamless ways for students to work from locations other than school; this further integration may encourage and promote the use of home computers for schoolwork.

Laptops offer portability and also provide continuity for a student who may be in multiple locations; different classrooms, the library, at home, at friend's houses, or traveling. Computers are becoming smaller, available as handhelds and PDAs or embedded in other devices such as cell phones, offering more portability than laptops. As these trends continue, with technology becoming increasing pervasive and ubiquitous, the impact on k–12 education can be enormous.

What is even more interesting than how technology is used is the impact of technology on student achievement. A study (U.S. Department of Education, 2001) looked at average scores by time spent using the computer to write reports in grades 8 and 12. Eighth grade scores went from 253, for students not using the computer, to 270, for students using the computer to a large extent. An even larger difference was shown for 12th graders, who went from an average score of 270 when not using the computer at all, to 300, when using the computer to a large extent. One would expect these results to be even more dramatic when the computer is integrated directly into the course of study. This data is for public schools and comes from only one study; data may differ for private schools, where there are different budgets and constraints, and for other measures of student achievement.

Overall, achievement is difficult to measure and the many factors influencing achievement are hard to separate. Despite the increased prevalence of technology in schools, American high school students in 2004 are no better prepared for college or the workforce than they were a decade earlier, based on an ACT study (formerly American College Testing) of 1.2 million students who took college entrance examinations in 2004 (Arenson, 2004). One could hypothesize that the increased use of technology could lead to a shift in how teachers use their classroom time, an increase in time students spend on learning activities outside of the classroom, more personalized instruction, or other outcomes, all with a potential impact on college entrance exam scores. Although the lack of an increase in scores does not mean technology has shown no benefits, it does make one ponder which benefits have been realized and what further changes need to be made for benefits to be reaped. Current findings (or lack thereof) also indicate the need for further measurement and analysis with, perhaps, a different focus. Whereas entrance exam scores may not show dramatic increases in traditional subject matter knowledge, an increased familiarity with and use of technology tools (i.e., experience using word processing tools, spreadsheets, communication tools such as e-mail and chat, Internet-based research, creating Web pages, etc.) might significantly impact preparedness for the workforce.

Besides schools, technology is playing a pivotal role in other institutions, such as libraries and museums, and in providing educational materials to homeschoolers and hospitalized and incarcerated children, advanced courses to gifted students in remote regions, remedial courses to students who need them, and so on. Although the list is extensive, there are strong commonalities: high-quality educational materials need to be created and shared, their quality and relevance must stand out from the masses of material available, and the materials should be usable either stand alone or integrated into a curriculum.

PLIMOTH PLANTATION'S ONLINE LEARNING CENTER

One example of a museum that developed online curriculum is Plimoth Plantation, whose online learning center (OLC) is designed to teach third and fifth graders about the 1621 harvest celebration that later became known as the First Thanksgiving. The OLC is available for free at www.plimoth.org/olc, and challenges children to become historians and to conduct their own investigation. A teacher's guide is provided online and addresses the standards met by the OLC as well as how a teacher can use the OLC in the computer lab or classroom. A print teacher's guide, encompassing the online version and adding additional textual and visual information, is available from Plimoth Plantation. These documents greatly assist in the integration of the OLC into the curriculum.

In developing the OLC, one challenge faced was how to bring the powerful, personal experience of physical visitors to the online experience to reflect the unique characteristics of Plimoth Plantation. Another challenge was to produce a site that was appealing, engaging, fun, and educational for children (Neal & Van Wormer, 2004). Although the resulting OLC can supplement a physical visit to the museum, the heaviest use is among teachers and students who would never have the opportunity to visit the museum, yet benefit from the wealth of expertise that the museum has on a topic that is of interest to children and that meets the educational needs of children and teachers while addressing social studies standards. Many museums and other institutions with an educational charter are increasing their online presence, and this, when done well, can provide highly effective educational experiences that are far beyond what is available within the confines of the traditional classroom. These experiences can be enriching for children in multiple ways; for example, although Plimoth Plantation's OLC is focused on the events of 1621, it is also providing a wealth of information about two cultures, the Wampanoag and the early Colonists, and how they lived. The OLC also challenges children to become a historian and conduct their own investigation; teaching children that history is more than a set of facts is a lesson that serves them well in other educational situations.

VIRTUAL HIGH SCHOOL

The Virtual High School (VHS) collaborative offers a variety of online courses to high school students worldwide. The program began with some grant funding and has evolved over the past several years into a not-for-profit international program. VHS does not award high school diplomas—it is intended to supplement existing high school programs by offering online courses to high school students, taught by high school teachers at participating high schools around the world. The organization offers professional development for prospective teachers, as well as the opportunity to network with other participating educators to share best practices and lessons learned. In exchange for a teacher's participation in the program, his or her school can register up to 25 students per semester in any online course offered through the VHS program. The VHS collaborative enables schools to offer courses to students that otherwise might be unavailable due to small student enrollment, limited resources, lack of teaching expertise in a specialized topic area, or other factors.

According to the Virtual High School 2003 Annual Report,

> from the 28 schools, 30 courses and 710 students participating in VHS during our first year, back in 1997–1998, VHS has grown to 200 high schools as members of the collaborative and over 5,000 students enrolled in nearly 150 NetCourses. This is very impressive growth in a short period of time. However, the most significant achievement is that VHS is now self-sustaining and no longer dependent on grant funds. The fact that schools have chosen to invest their resources at a time when most school districts are challenged by the economic downturn demonstrates the value VHS offers to its members. (VHS, 2003a, p. 4)

VHS surveys participants (e.g., superintendents, site coordinators, teachers, etc.) from member schools about their satisfaction with the program as well as the benefits derived from it. According to survey items related to the quality and perceived challenge/rigor of VHS courses,

> data suggests that 85% of VHS students spend about the same or more time studying for their VHS course as compared to their schools' face-to-face

courses. Over 90% of the students enrolled in a VHS course complete their course, far exceeding industry completion rates. An overwhelming 98% of VHS members suggest that VHS provides an opportunity to take courses not otherwise offered in their school. Site coordinators commented that 15% of students took fewer courses taught by teachers trained outside of their areas of expertise, suggesting that VHS is an asset that can help schools address their accreditation requirements for highly qualified teachers. (VHS, 2003b, p. 7)

COLLEGE AND UNIVERSITY EDUCATION

Technology is more pervasive in colleges and universities due to larger budgets and better trained teachers. Many colleges and universities similarly require laptops or PDAs for all students, and many use technology in the classroom, ranging from computers to handheld devices to record answers or to indicate questions. Classroom education is changing because of technology, in particular, when technology is creatively used. For instance, handhelds can allow a teacher to get more feedback from students about their level of understanding in a large lecture hall, as well as gauge their attentiveness by the speed of their response (Neal, 2003b). While some believe that a teacher's "role evolve(s) from 'sage on the stage' to 'guide on the side'" (Sonwalkar, 2001, p. 11) with technology, that is only desirable in situations where the students have sufficient maturity and discipline to learn more independently, which is much more likely in postsecondary programs.

Colleges and universities, motivated by classrooms shortages, are encouraging or requiring teachers to offer fully or partially online courses to better serve the needs of campus-based students when expansion is not feasible. At the same time, many traditional higher education institutions are expanding their reach to students who are remote. Nontraditional institutions are providing only Web-based instruction, many, like the British Open University, with stellar reputations. Unfortunately, at the same time, nonaccredited institutions are competing for students, many of whom do not know the difference or who are attracted by advertising (Neal, 2003a). Other new models are emerging, such as university–industry partnerships, in which joint programs are offered or university courses are provided to companies for internal education.

Most colleges and universities are offering at least a single course or degree program via the Internet; a 2003 report by the Sloan Foundation and Babson College suggests that 81% of all higher education institutions in the United States offer at least one online course (Gallagher, 2004, p. 9). International Data Corporation (IDC) estimates that the number of students taking distance learning courses will grow at a 1999–2004 compound annual growth rate (CAGR) of 33%, with enrollment expected to top 2.23 million in 2004 (IDC, 2000, p. 7). IDC estimated that 47% of higher education institutions currently offer courses that make use of distance learning, and 87% will do so in 2004, with increasing numbers of public and private higher education institutions devoting resources to developing online courses as solutions become less expensive and less complicated (IDC, 2000, p. 7). Enrollment in fully online distance education programs, such as Title IV-eligible, degree-granting institutions taking for-credit courses delivered over the Internet, will grow 30% in 2004 from 703,570 unique students in 2003 to reach an estimated 915,641 students by the end of 2004, and is projected to exceed one million students by the end of 2005. With the numbers of enrollments expected at the end of 2004, fully online distance education will account for approximately 6% of total postsecondary enrollment in 2004 (Gallagher, 2004, p. 3).

Web-based learning's growth is attributed to the changing needs of students as well as institutions' needs. Online learners include both traditional and nontraditional students; the latter, who are not traditionally matriculated full-time college students, are lifelong learners (continuing education); adults seeking to finish degrees through part-time course work; workers seeking additional skills or training to advance in their careers; and teachers who need skill updating to comply with state certification requirements (IDC, 2000, p. 25). New categories may emerge, and the numbers of people in these aforementioned categories will likely grow as work becomes increasingly knowledge based and as people work for more companies and have more jobs within their careers. "Likewise, interest in online learning will increase as advanced high-speed Internet access reaches more households" (IDC, 2000, p. 25) because it increases a student's ability to take a course as well as the likelihood of identifying the need and opportunity.

Drivers for higher educational institutions include the desire to increase enrollment; accommodate a more diverse student body; improve access to education where it might not otherwise be available; achieve learning improvements; catalyze institutional transformation; and reduce institutional per-student costs (IDC 2000, p. 26). Each of these is complex, especially achieving learning improvements, because the introduction and use of technology in and of itself does not improve learning, and in far too many instances, institutions do not know which technologies to use and how to use them effectively. This is exemplified by high dropout rates and by the notable failures of a number of online programs in the United States. New opportunities exist for institutions, however, such as providing better opportunities for alumni to become lifelong learners (IDC, 2000, p. 26).

The prevailing view of university lectures was as an imparting of knowledge through lecture; this resulted in a "passive reception of given knowledge" (Laurillard, 2002, p. 13). This approach evolved into a focus on making student learning possible through active engagement of the learner. The increased responsibility of the learner to construct knowledge requires different approaches to teaching that place much more responsibility on the teacher than lecturing; however, university faculty, unlike k–12 teachers, often have no profession training requirements (Laurillard, 2002, p. 12). Laurillard provided "the perspective that it is better to identify the unique qualities of a technology and exploit those so that one is doing what could not otherwise be done rather than seeking to replicate existing practices" (Neal & Miller, 2005, p. 458), offering students opportunities to think, explore, create, and collaborate to have an educational experience that is different, but potentially deeper, than is typical in the classroom. LeBaron and Miller (2004) described the successful infusion of various instructional techniques, implemented within an online graduate-level course, to provide for the social construction of peer knowledge, facilitate an overall sense of course community, and accommodate individual learning styles and preferences. They described several strategies designed to meet these instructional objectives including a graded "icebreaker" assignment, weekly e-mail updates, and audio-video greetings from the course instructor, and a role play—all carried out using simple Web-based tools such as threaded discussion and chat. Feedback from students and results observed by the instructors indicated that the technologically simple techniques used to promote community and to advance student knowledge construction enabled learning in ways that traditional classroom techniques might easily have missed. As one student put it, "This course, with the use of all the technical and innovative instructional tools was very rewarding for me personally and professionally" (LeBaron & Miller, 2004, p. 123).

HOW EDUCATION AND LEARNING ARE CHANGING AS A RESULT OF TECHNOLOGY

Traditional methods of education and learning are changing as a result of the integration of technology into the classroom, work place, and home. It is not just that new possibilities exist for access to online materials, references, and courses, but that new approaches are being used to design and deliver education. Initially, educational software presented a stream of information or was used a drill-and-practice approach, resulting in a passive learner experience and barely capitalizing upon what technology can provide. Passivity was cited as a common reason for an experience that was not fun: When a learner has no control of his or her learning and is just reading—or skimming—page after page of materials (Neal, Miller, & Perez, 2004). Although presentation of materials can have an impact, what is more effective is encouraging learners to be active, be it through exploration and creation, challenges, or collaborations.

Common approaches to the design of Web-based learning are goal- and scenario-based, where the learner is given a problem to solve, and where he or she can learn from a successful solution and can potentially learn even more by recovering from failure (Schank, 1997, p. 35), or where the learner is placed in an environment where the information needed for success will be actively sought and mastered (Downes, 1998). Engagement theory refers to when students are "meaningfully engaged in learning activities through interaction with others" on relevant and authentic tasks requiring cognitive processes such as creating, problem solving, reasoning, decision making, and evaluation. "While in principle, such engagement could occur without the use of technology, we believe that technology can facilitate engagement in ways which are difficult to achieve otherwise" (Kearsley & Shneiderman, 1999). In these scenarios, students are intrinsically motivated to learn due to the meaningful nature of their activities.

Innovative approaches and learning from other disciplines can aid in improving Web-based learning. Tom Malone and Mark Lepper in the 1980s characterized video games as highly motivating because they encouraged engagement in repetitive practice, learning through exploration, and striving for mastery through more difficult goals (Neal et al., 2004), yet all of these techniques motivate learners in educational settings. "The underlying strategies of games can be applied, such as the use of challenge levels and rewards, using stories or scenarios to place the learner in a particular context, and using 'what-if' scenarios to encourage the learner to think about cause and effect" (Neal et al., 2004, p. 2). Games provide countless opportunities to fail, and a

> player learns through trial and error and especially from mistakes, trying a different approach to accomplish the task at hand. Games often provide multiple opportunities and methods for a player to succeed. If a player fails using one approach, there are other ways to solve the problem. e-learning can leverage this gaming approach, offering multiple means of solving problems to encourage exploration and learning from failure. (Neal et al., 2004, p. 2)

To create motivating and fun online courses,

> it helps to take into account what people want to learn about, to make it as relevant as possible, and to bring creativity and innovation to course design and delivery. Fun can motivate, but learning will occur only when the fun is purposeful; a game can be highly motivating but may not promote a deeper understanding of the topic. A balance between fun and learning is important but difficult to achieve. (Neal et al., 2004, p. 2)

Web-based learning too often minimizes the role of or entirely removes the teacher as well as peers. Collaboration, expressed as a key component of engagement theory, can make projects more rewarding and fun, as well as enhancing learning. "Learners learn more and are more likely to enjoy a learning experience involving a good instructor. Learners often learn more from each other than from an instructor, but opportunities for meaningful peer interaction have to be designed into a course" (Neal et al., 2004, p. 2). A better understanding is emerging of how to translate or massage classroom techniques to be effective online. An example is storytelling, with a long history of educational use, which is now being incorporated into Web-based learning to provide rich learning experiences (Neal, 2001). Storytelling is a useful technique for encouraging learning, reflection, and active participation in a course because stories can be more entertaining to read than expository text, more engaging to listen to than a lecture, can add an element of realism to otherwise dry course materials, and require more creativity and reflection to write.

Finally, Web-based learning can be customized to match an individual learner's needs and interests. Although a teacher may continue to define course content, courses can be designed to enable students to explore content collaboratively and to pursue their own interests. When students are expected to join course discussions and be active participants and contributors, they can be more motivated and become more self-directed learners. LeBaron and Miller (2004, p. 123) reported the perceived benefits articulated by students when a constructivist philosophy is applied to course design and delivery: "This course would have had very little purpose without the many opportunities afforded to apply learning to my individual experiences. This made the learning meaningful and gave much greater depth to my understanding."

However, innovation and creativity in the design, development, and deployment of Web-based learning does not necessarily lead to successful education. Existing and possibly new measures for effectiveness are needed, as well as an understanding of the impact of any changes. Many "studies focus on grades and ignore questions such as what factors account for success and to what degree is competency actually demonstrated" in an online course, with a "paucity of credible research by which to support a claim that digital learning is at least as effective as traditional classroom training in areas such as retention, relevance, satisfaction and performance" (Moyer, 2003, p. 1).

THE IMPLICATIONS FOR THE FUTURE FOR WEB-BASED LEARNING

The role of technology in education will always be twofold; to enhance education and to increase the technological adeptness of students so they can function in the workforce. A National Center for Education Statistics study

(NCES, 2002, Table 424) showed that 54.2% of workers, 18 years old and over, are using computers on the job in 2001, a number that is likely much higher today. As technology becomes more pervasive in all avenues of life, schools bear a responsibility to provide those technological skills that help people succeed. Whereas some skills are obvious, such as the adept use of computers and software for routine activities and the ability to learn to use new hardware and software, other essential skills include an understanding of the quality and reliability of information available online and the ability to locate reference materials. And, most importantly, if children have become accustomed to Web-based learning and are comfortable learning online, then that skill remains with them throughout their entire education and work lives and the Internet becomes a resource that is turned to when a need arises.

Of course, technology may change dramatically, and there are many visions that exist. Although cheaper, smaller, and faster are obvious trends in technology, the increased embedding of computers in other devices may have an enormous impact on education in ways that are difficult to foresee. One change that is easy to predict is that teachers will be increasingly comfortable and conversant with technology, as they are introduced to it themselves at younger ages, and will likely be able to use it adeptly and integrate it better into their teaching as a result. Another change that is likely is that enhanced communication and collaboration will impact how teachers and students work together, with more sharing of resources and learning from each other than is currently possible. This will break down the walls of the classroom somewhat; however, the classroom is unlikely to ever go away, because the classroom provides a place for people to congregate and a vehicle for social and other development, which is important not only for children but for adults who want networking opportunities. Another area where innovation is taking place is in understanding student reactions and emotions. As an example, a classroom teacher can gauge when students are attentive through facial expression, eye contact, and body language, all of which are absent at a distance. New approaches, including sensors and biometric devices, show promise, although still perhaps too invasively, at helping a teacher more accurately assess the attention level and response of distant students (Neal & Feldstein, 2004).

As more is known about the use of technology in learning, what will evolve is a better understanding of when to use it and how to use it to provide more effective educational experiences. "Institutions are beginning to shift their focus from proving online education's viability to improving the quality of online education programs and boosting student retention" (Gallagher, 2004, p. 10). What is needed is better designed and higher quality educational software and online courses that provide challenging and engaging learning experiences. But to get to that point, what is needed is a deeper understanding of what is meant by quality in Web-based learning, as well as better tools to make the design and development of online materials and online courses easier for teachers, not just instructional designers, and better measures for when Web-based learning has been successful. Ideally, the goal of any educator working with technology will be to provide educational experiences that surpass what is possible in the classroom and enrich and engage learners to help them meet their personal learning goals as well as the goals of the institutions in which they are enrolled.

REFERENCES

Arenson, K. W. (2004, October 14). Study of college readiness finds no progress in decade. *NY Times*, p. A26.

Bonk, C. (2004). *The perfect e-storm: Emerging technology, enormous learner demand, enhanced pedagogy, and erased budgets*. London, UK: The Observatory on Borderless Higher Education.

Cattagni, A., & Westat, E. F. (2001). *Internet access in U.S. public schools and classrooms: 1994–2000*. National Center for Education Statistics. Retrieved October 15, 2004, from http://nces.ed.gov/pubsearch/pubsinfo.asp?pubid=2001071

Downes, S. (1998). The future of on-line learning. *On-line Journal of Distance Learning Administration*, 1(3). Retrieved October 15, 2004, from http://www.westga.edu/~distance/downes13.html

Gallagher, S. (2004). *Online distance education market update: A nascent market begins to mature*. Boston, MA: Eduventures.

International Data Corporation (IDC). (2000). *Distance learning in higher education: Market forecast and analysis, 1999–2004*.

International Data Corporation (IDC). (2001). *The state of technology usage in K–12 education: Highlights from the 2000 K–12 district technology survey*.

Kearsley, G., & Shneiderman, B. (1999). *Engagement theory: A framework for technology-based teaching and learning*. Retrieved October 15, 2004, from http://home.sprynet.com/~gkearsley/engage.htm

Laurillard, D. (2002). *Rethinking university teaching: A framework for the effective use of learning technologies*. London and New York: Routledge Falmer.

LeBaron, J., & Miller D. (2004). The teacher as agent provocateur: Strategies to promote community in online course settings. In T. Latomaa, J. Pohjonen, J. Pulkkinen, & M. Ruotsalainen (Eds.), *eReflections—Ten years of educational technology studies at the University of Oulu. Essays contributed by the network builders* (pp. 109–125). Retrieved January 19, 2005, from http://herkules.oulu.fi/isbn9514276329/

Moyer, L. G. (2003). Is digital learning effective in the workplace? *eLearn Magazine*. Retrieved October 14, 2004, from http://www.elearnmag.org/subpage/sub_page.cfm?section=7&list_item=2&page=1

National Center for Education Statistics. (NCES). (2000). *Teachers' tools for the 21st century: A report on teachers' use of technology*. Retrieved October 14, 2004, from http://nces.ed.gov/surveys/frss/publications/2000102/2.asp

National Center for Education Statistics. (NCES). (2002). *Digest of education statistics, 2002*. Retrieved October 14, 2004, from http://nces.ed.gov/programs/digest/d02/

Neal, L. (2001). Storytelling at a distance. In H.-J. Bullinger & J. Ziegler (Eds.), *Human-interaction: Communication, cooperation, and application design*. Lawrence Erlbaum Associates. Retrieved October 15, 2004, from http://www.elearnmag.org/subpage/sub_page.cfm?section=7&list_item=1&page=1

Neal, L. (2003a). Degrees by mail: Look what you can buy for only $499!!! *eLearn Magazine*. Retrieved October 15, 2004, from http://www.elearnmag.org/subpage/sub_page.cfm?article_pk=10201&page_number_nb=1&title=COLUMN

Neal, L. (2003b). Expectations of privacy: Data collected in class should not be misused. *eLearn Magazine*. Retrieved October 15, 2004, from http://www.elearnmag.org/subpage/sub_page.cfm?article_pk=9344&page_number_nb=1&title=COLUMN

Neal, L., & Feldstein, M. (2004). Paying attention to attention. *eLearn Magazine*. Retrieved October 15, 2004, from http://www.elearnmag.org/index.cfm

Neal, L., & Miller, D. (2005). Distance education. In R. Proctor & K. Vu (Eds.), *The handbook of human factors in Web design* (pp. 454–470). Mahwah, NJ: Lawrence Erlbaum Associates.

Neal, L., Miller, D., & Perez, R. (2004). Online learning and fun. *eLearn Magazine*. Retrieved October 15, 2004, from http://www.elearnmag.org/subpage/sub_page.cfm?article_pk=12265&page_number_nb=1&title=FEATURE%20STORY

Neal, L., & Van Wormer, K. (2004). Making learning fun: Plimoth Plantation's on-line learning center. In D. Bearman & J. Trant (Eds.), *Museums and the Web 2004: Proceedings*. Toronto, Canada: Archives & Museum Informatics. Retrieved October 14, 2004, from http://www.archimuse.com/mw2004/papers/neal/neal.html

Schank, R. (1997). *Virtual learning: A revolutionary approach to building a highly skilled workforce*. New York: McGraw-Hill.

Seal, K. (2003). Transforming teaching and learning through technology. *Carnegie Reporter*, 2(2). Retrieved October 14, 2004, from http://www.carnegie.org/reporter/06/learning/

Sonwalkar, N. (2001). Changing the interface of education with revolutionary learning technologies. *Syllabus, 15*(4), 10–13.

U.S. Department of Education. (USDoE). (2001). *U.S. Department of Education, National Center for Education Statistics, National Assessment of Educational Progress (NAEP), 2001 U.S. History Assessment*. Retrieved October 14, 2004, from http://nces.ed.gov/quicktables/Detail.asp?Key=736

VHS. (2003a). *Virtual high school 2003 annual report*. Retrieved January 19, 2005, from http://www.govhs.org/

VHS. (2003b). *Virtual high school program evaluation 2001–2003*. Retrieved January 19, 2005, from http://www.govhs.org/

Chapter 20

Five Critical Issues for Web-Based Instructional Design Research and Practice

Richard E. Clark
David F. Feldon
Keith Howard
Sunhee Choi
University of Southern California

The goal of this chapter is to discuss five Web-based instructional design opportunities and problems and to briefly summarize the results of current research on each issue. The chapter is intended to encourage discussion about the instructional design models and methods used to plan and evaluate distance education courses. The choice of topics was influenced by perceived benefits and difficulties with the models and assumptions that underlie the design of current Web-based courses.

WHAT IS INSTRUCTIONAL "DESIGN"

In this chapter, "design" is used to focus attention on all instructional strategies that aid the learning of the information content reflected in the learning goals of a Web-based course. A design is a plan or a "blueprint" for a module or course of Web-based instruction. It answers the questions "What do these learners need to know to achieve the learning and performance goals of this course?" and "What pedagogical support do they need to achieve learning and performance goals effectively and efficiently?" Development answers the questions "What media and representational format will be used to structure and present the information and pedagogical support needed by learners?" For example, a design plan might call for and describe the parameters of a simulation for a complex process that students need to experience in order to learn how something works. During development, the instructional team would produce a specific multimedia-based simulation that would implement the design blueprint.

In the best distance learning organizations, designs for instruction are completed and approved by stakeholders before instructional materials and media are developed. It is our impression that most Web-based instruction suffers from the failure to separate design and development. This impression is shard by many educators who specialize in the development and testing of instructional design theories (e.g., Dick & Carey, 1990; Merrill, 2002; Reigeluth, 1983, 1987; van Merriënboer, 1997). When new courses are planned and their content is specified, many educators start immediately to plan the production of media-based lessons for a finished course. It is our experience that media production issues impose such a heavy cognitive load on educators that design issues are largely ignored or handled in a very shallow fashion. As a result, course developers are often skilled in media production but not grounded in or focused on the results of current research on instruction and learning. One result of this problem is that Web-based courses are often excellent examples of media production but poor examples of pedagogical support (e.g., Clark, 2001). The five issues chosen for this chapter represent some of the areas often ignored when Web-based course teams invest very little mental effort on design and jump prematurely to media development. The discussion begins with new models for the design of Web courses that attempt to teach highly complex knowledge.

INSTRUCTIONAL DESIGN MODELS FOR WEB-BASED PRESENTATIONS OF COMPLEX KNOWLEDGE AND SKILLS

The role of structure in training applications has been seriously questioned in recent years. Advocates of unguided constructivist and discovery learning models maintain that the optimal way to facilitate learning is to present the learner with authentic problems to be solved in the target domain and allow them to pursue a solution unguided until a successful technique is discovered. This approach seems to have considerable intuitive appeal to Web-based instructional developers in part because it seems compatible with the distance context and with North American cultural values. Unguided approaches seem to assume that a learner should benefit most from situations where they are challenged to achieve with minimal resources or "use the help menu if you wish" support through nothing more than self-reliant determination.

Unfortunately, decades of research on the effectiveness of instructional methods has failed to provide any evidence that supports this perspective. Instead, it has been consistently demonstrated that learning goals are best realized when research-based instructional principles are used to guide the learning process and are implemented on the basis of careful design analysis (Mayer, 2004). This finding has been replicated across a number of different lenses for viewing learning. For example, Clark (1982) found in a review of aptitude-treatment interaction (ATI) studies that learners often selected the instructional formats that were least helpful for their achievement. Among the reasons that he postulates to explain this phenomenon is the fact that less structured environments provide less accountability to specific instructional goals. As a result, lower prior knowledge learners (i.e., those who are least knowledgeable and so have the most to gain from instruction) will select strategies that allow them to "fly under the radar" and avoid demonstrating the weaknesses in their skills by avoiding problematic tasks. In another approach, John Sweller and his colleagues have identified the instructional benefits of carefully regulating the type and complexity of learning tasks that are presented to students. By preventing the overload of learners' attentional capacities, cognitive load theory (Sweller, 1988, 1989) holds that students will be more successful as appropriate scaffolds are matched to a learner's level of skill and slowly removed from problem solving processes over time (Atkinson, Derry, Renkl, & Wortham, 2000; Sweller, Chandler, Tierney, & Cooper, 1990).

First Principles of Design

The identification of these "first principles" for instructional design is currently the focus of several major research efforts. David Merrill (2002), for example, has reviewed many successful design models used for distance education and summarized the design principles they seem to share in common. His review emphasized five core design principles:

- Learners should engage in solving "real-world" problems.
- Learners' existing knowledge should be activated as a foundation for new knowledge.
- New knowledge should be demonstrated for the learner.
- Learners should practice the application of the knowledge during the training.
- Learners benefit from encouragement and opportunities to use their newly acquired knowledge in their activities after training.

Using the metaphor of ripples in a pond, Merrill has identified common elements in a number of major instructional design systems. In each system, the design process begins with an authentic problem that learners must be trained to solve and serves as the impetus (i.e., the pebble thrown into the pond) for the emanating ripples of the process. The next phase is to identify the progressively more difficult series of tasks that will, when mastered, represent the full range of competencies required for the domain. Once this has been accomplished, it is then necessary to analyze these tasks to determine the relevant skills and concepts that will enable them to be performed. The nature of these knowledge elements in turn provides a rationale for the selection of appropriate instructional strategies to most efficiently train the learner. Finally, in the last "ripple," a delivery method (e.g., computer-based training, seminar, etc.) is selected or developed on the basis of its cost efficiency or logistical demands of the organization (see Clark, 2001 for a comprehensive discussion of the evidence that the media used to deliver instruction, in and of itself, cannot impact learning).

The critical element of the pebble-in-a-pond model is the temporal ordering of the instructional design decisions. Each ripple relies exclusively on the one previous to determine the selection of its necessary components, which carries with it two distinct advantages: First, no resources, for example time and money, are invested in training development that are not strictly necessary to the specific instructional requirements of the required skill set, which maximizes the organizational benefits in relation to the cost of development. Second, it helps to avoid the inclusion of unnecessary or distracting information that can slow down or limit the effectiveness of the training for the targeted learners.

In order to implement this model effectively after the identification of the authentic problem, the series of tasks and their requisite knowledge must also be systematically identified. Traditionally, experts are called on to explain the necessary skills and knowledge associated with their domains of expertise in either the format of a lecture/workshop or in written instructional materials. However, this approach has proven remarkably unreliable due to the implicit nature of many expert skills (see the following section on automaticity and expertise). It has prompted a need for knowledge elicitation experts to develop highly specified techniques for identifying all of the component skills necessary to complete a complex task.

Cognitive Task Analysis

Recent research by Clark and his colleagues (Lee, 2004; Velmahos et al., 2004) has demonstrated the value and powerful instructional effects of these cognitive task analysis techniques for instruction in complex knowledge areas such as surgery. For example, Velmahos, et al. (2004) conducted a study in which medical students were taught a foundational medical procedure through either a traditional instructional approach involving explanatory lecture and demonstration by an expert followed by learner practice, or an instructional approach that relied on a cognitive task analysis of the skill to structure the information presented. The students in each condition were followed during their subsequent hospital work performing the procedure on multiple live subjects, and the performance difference between the two groups was striking. Students taught through the method that was not grounded in cognitive task analysis were significantly more likely to commit a procedural error as evaluated by a 14-item checklist ($M = 12.6$, $SD = 1.1$ vs. $M = 7.5$, SD 2.2, $p = 0.001$) and often took considerably longer to complete the procedure ($M = 15.4$, $SD = 9.5$ vs. $M = 20.6$, $SD = 9.1$ min, $p = 0.149$).

Complex Knowledge Design Models and Methods

Once the tasks and knowledge have been identified, the instructional strategies must be determined. Four key principles that govern the effective selection of strategies have emerged from the literature and warrant discussion as a promising new direction for instructional design. Jeroen van Merriënboer's 4C/ID model (1997; van Merriënboer, Clark, & de Croock, 2002) argued that when learning complex tasks, it is necessary to do more than master the simpler component tasks and try to execute them in a prescribed order to achieve successful performance. On this basis, it is necessary to strategically provide integrated and comprehensive learning activities with the following characteristics:

- Concrete learning tasks must be provided that capture the authentic complexity of the problems to be solved as a result of the training.
- Supportive information must be provided that helps to bridge learners' prior knowledge with the new skills that they are acquiring in task-relevant ways.
- Information must be provided at the time when it is needed and in a directly usable format. As such, procedural knowledge must be formulated as production rules that specify both the technique and the desired outcome.
- Practice opportunities must be provided that facilitate not only the automatic performance of subtasks, but also require learners to automate the sequencing and connections between subtasks necessary to the authentic whole-task performance.

The approaches described previously represent powerful and actionable progress toward a comprehensive understanding of the principles for effective distance learning and where possible, they should be implemented in the design of distance courses. Of course there is still much empirical work to be done. With numerous approaches that utilize many but not all of these guidelines, one important future research agenda is to carefully evaluate the relative effectiveness of these methods through carefully designed and executed head-to-head design theory comparison studies. Clark and Estes (1999, 2000) have described one approach to this kind of research and development work they call "authentic technology".

Much of the focus in contemporary Web-based instruction tends to reside in the dissemination of concepts and facts, rather than in developing complex, integrated skills that are directly applicable to the completion of authentic tasks. Even instruction that is explicitly designed to teach procedures most often requires learners to simply memorize a list of steps or instructions without any opportunity for sustained practice or performance- based assessment. Although prevalent, the drawbacks to this approach are self-evident: No one would want to be a passenger on an airplane whose pilot had memorized the flight manual but had not practiced using the controls. Although all of the necessary steps are clearly listed in the book, and the pilot could recall any of them at need, the fact remains that without extensive practice, our faith in his ability to transport us safely from point A to point B is justifiably lacking. Whereas part of the solution to this problem is in the selection of design models that accommodate complex knowledge, another consideration is to attempt to apply principles drawn from research on the development of advanced expertise. We turn next to a consideration of the goals of adult distance education courses— the development of advanced expertise.

THE DEVELOPMENT OF ADVANCED EXPERTISE IN DISTANCE LEARNING COURSES

The functional and physical distinctions between conceptual and procedural knowledge have been well established in the neuropsychological and cognitive science literatures (Squire, Knowlton & Musen, 1993). Although both are necessary for the acquisition of expertise at complex cognitive skills (Anderson, Fincham, & Douglas, 1997; Rittle-Johnson, Siegler, & Alibali, 2001), it is only through extensive practice that the fluidity of action associated with competent performance develops (Binder, 2003).

STAGES IN EXPERTISE DEVELOPMENT

Anderson and colleagues (Anderson, 1982; VanLehn, 1996) have provided evidence for three identifiable stages in the development of the accurate, effective procedural knowledge that characterizes advanced experts. These stages represent successive improvement in performance and an accompanying reduction of the mental effort necessary to execute the skill. In the initial cognitive stage, the learner is assembling new knowledge and drawing on relevant, previously learned declarative knowledge of prescribed steps to complete a predefined task. In the second (associative) stage, newly assembled proceduralized steps gradually automate as they are practiced and tuned. At the final (autonomous) stage, procedural knowledge is automated, such that task execution is fast, highly consistent, tends to be uninterruptible, and requires little to no mental effort during performance. At this stage, high levels of cognitive efficiency due to automaticity allow performers to multitask, by eliminating the need for conscious intermediate decision points (Blessing & Anderson, 1996).

A common illustration of this phenomenon is the process of learning to drive a car: As a new driver first learns, each step is a separate intentional thought ("Release the parking brake, press the brake and the clutch, start the ignition, move my foot from the brake to the gas, slowly begin to give the car gas while gradually letting up on the clutch ... "). The result is a very halting implementation with a lot of sudden starts and stops. Over time, the skills begin to integrate, such that the conscious thoughts of the driver are only at a higher level ("Start the car, pull onto the road, go to the store ... "). With more practice, not only do the component skills of driving become less consciously controlled through automation, but the resulting increase in cognitive capacity makes it significantly less dangerous for the driver to talk on a cellular phone or change the radio station as the act of driving requires fewer attentional resources.

Although automated procedures are often initiated through conscious decision making and goal setting, recent research has found that the setting of these behavioral goals can also occur automatically when triggered by familiar cues in the environment (Bargh & Ferguson, 2000). For example, many drivers who follow the same route every day experience arriving at their destination without recalling the trip that got them there (i.e., not making conscious decisions about what route to take). Other times, a driver may coincidentally be following a familiar route as part of his progress to an unfamiliar destination and unintentionally follow the familiar route too far, due to tendency for automated routines to be uninterruptible. Because planning and decision making are cognitive skills, they can become automated through practice in the much same way that psychomotor skills like driving do. Such occurrences provide both advantages and disadvantages. On one hand, the lighter cognitive load allows learners to consider a larger number of relevant cues to determine optimal responses (like an advanced driver can spare more attention to a phone conversation). On the other hand, an automatic evaluation may lead to inappropriate or nonoptimal responses on the basis of habit, rather than conscious deliberation (like accidentally following a familiar route instead of taking the newer one that had been intended).

When individuals endure extraneous cognitive load that hinders their access to an existing schema or their ability to learn a new one, it is possible that the overload will result in a cognitive default, by which a schema or procedure that is automated to a greater extent than the target representation will be accessed and utilized unintentionally (Sweller, 1989). That is, in response to the diminishing availability of attentional resources, the mind automatically and unconsciously disengages from effortful, nonautomated procedures and activates older, more automated routines. Specifically, Clark (1999, p. 11) argued that "when working memory [capacity] is exceeded, the more recently learned (and presumably more effective and less destructive) strategies will be inhibited in favor of the older and more automatic and destructive alternatives." The result is that despite the intention of the individual, older, less adaptive, or more frequently repeated procedures will manifest in both reasoning and behavior.

Reducing Extraneous Cognitive Load During Learning

It is for this reason that Web-based training must attempt to help learners learn and integrate both declarative and procedural knowledge while carefully controlling the amount of cognitive load endured by learners as they work to practice integrated knowledge and skills. In a number of experiments, John Sweller and his colleagues have provided compelling evidence that many learning and problem-solving activities unintentionally redirect cognitive resources from the primary objectives of a task to other, less relevant goals (Sweller, 1999; Sweller, van Merriënboer, & Paas, 1998). This reallocation of mental resources imposes "extraneous" cognitive load on the individual, inherently leaving less space in working memory dedicated to achieving the intended outcome (Chandler & Sweller, 1991; Sweller et al., 1990). Sweller (1999) distinguished three categories of endured cognitive load based on the properties of the tasks performed. Intrinsic cognitive load represents the burden to working memory required for the assessment and comprehension of some situation. That is, it includes the minimum amount of information both necessary and sufficient to process the details entailed in the attainment of a goal. In contrast, extraneous load refers to the sensory and cognitive content that occupies working memory but that is not relevant to the task at hand (i.e., an external or internal distraction).

What is Expertise?

When an individual has mastered the skills in his field, he is often referred to as an expert. Although this term is often used casually in situations where there is one person present whose skills are better suited to a given situation than others who happen to be available, there has emerged from several decades of research a more sophisticated understanding of the qualities that an expert exhibits. Classic work by Robert Glaser and Michelene Chi (1988) identified the following key characteristics that are evident in various configurations among experts within their own domains: They excel at their chosen tasks, perceive large meaningful patterns, are faster than novices, quickly solve problems with little error, have superior domain specific short-term and long-term term memory, see and represent problems at a deeper (more principled) level than novices, spend a great deal of time analyzing a problem qualitatively, and have strong self-monitoring skills.

In a review of more recent research, Ericsson and Lehmann (1996) have proposed two additional characteristics of expertise. First, they have noted that advanced expertise at the very highest levels of performance in a given domain (i.e., where new contributions are made to the field) typically requires a minimum of 10 years of deliberate practice to develop. Deliberate practice is considered to be highly effortful, intended to improve performance, not inherently motivating, and not intended to attain any goal beyond continued skill development. Second, he has described an expert process as one exhibiting a "maximal adaptation to task constraints." Such constraints include the physical limitations of the human body and the demands of the laws of physics, as well as the functional rules that are associated with the task (e.g., the rules of chess, established flight paths, etc.), and the limitations of short-term memory and other cognitive functions (Casner, 1994). It is the continuous development of performance toward the limits of these constraints, Ericsson argued, that allows experts to succeed where others fail. Due to their extensive practice and skill refinement, they have to a great extent shaped the development of their physiological and cognitive capacities to meet the demands required for performance in their areas of expertise.

Cognitive Efficiency

Ultimately, each aspect of expert performance improves the cognitive efficiency of the problem-solving process. This phenomenon not only emerges as a result of acquired expertise, but also further improves performance by freeing up cognitive resources to accommodate atypical features or other added cognitive demands that may arise within a task (Bereiter & Scardamalia, 1993; Sternberg & Horvath, 1998). However, as discussed earlier, automated procedures become more ingrained and difficult to change to the extent that both goals and processes can manifest without conscious activation. Thus, the question arises: How accurately can experts explain their reasoning processes?

Unconscious Expertise

Although experts' highly refined mental models and automated procedures are adaptive for problem solving, they may interfere with the accurate recall of problem-solving situations after the fact. In a number of recall studies, experts were found to be both less complete and less accurate in their recall of information than were intermediate level performers, because the automaticity with which they processed events prevented some information from being processed at a conscious level (Rikers, Schmidt, & Boshuizen, 2000). Williams (2000, p. 165) explained that "production units are not interpreted but are fired off automatically in sequences, which produce skilled performance. They are automatic to the extent that experts at a specific skill may not be able to recall why they perform the skill as they do." As a result, a retrospective account of the event may fall victim to the errors of generalizability and rationalization that Wilson and Nisbett (1978) described in their critique of self-report accuracy. "Such reports may well be based more on people's *a priori* causal theories about stimulus effects than on direct examination of their cognitive processes, and will be inaccurate whenever these theories are inaccurate" (p. 130).

Although we have come a long way toward understanding expert performance, a number of critical problems related to issues of training remain. It is not clear why expertise typically requires 10 years to develop. It is possible that with further advances in the effectiveness and efficiency of training, the importance of a decade's experience could diminish significantly. One step in pursuing this goal will most likely involve the accurate identification and representation of experts' mental models and problem-solving processes. In order to do this, better methods of eliciting knowledge from experts and verifying its validity in relation to their actual performances will need to be developed. The continuously improving technologies for the capture of process data, especially in neuropsychological techniques such as EEG, positron emission topography, and fMRI may contribute significantly to this effort.

In summary, Web-based instruction that employs research-based design models and focuses adult learning goals on content derived from research on the learning of advanced expertise will significantly improve the impact of current efforts. Research on advanced expertise also offers insight into another of the thorny problems facing designers of Web and classroom based courses—the evidence that not enough of what is learned transfers beyond narrow application contexts.

ACHIEVING TRANSFER OF LEARNING FROM DISTANCE COURSES TO AUTHENTIC CONTEXTS

The goal of instruction is not only that students learn but that they are also able to apply their knowledge after instruction and, if necessary, revise it to accommodate novel situations as well. Most reviews of transfer research (see for example, Barnett & Cecci, 2002; Clark & Blake, 1997; Detterman, 1993) conclude that studies most often demonstrate transfer failure. This depressing evidence suggests that learning from instruction is most typically "situated," that is, once learned, it is only applied in the narrow context or types of problems where it was learned. Thus, students who receive instruction in science and pass exams on science tend not to transfer their scientific knowledge outside of the classroom or a distance course and use it to generate novel solutions to problems.

Routine and Adaptive Expertise

Noting the transfer problem, Hatano and others (Hatano, 1982; Hatano & Inagaki, 1986, 2000) have distinguished between the development of "routine expertise" and "adaptive expertise." Routine expertise manifests as high proficiency within a stable environment that does not involve the changes and adaptations often necessary in more fluid contexts. Although typical tasks are completed with a high level of proficiency, when the task constraints change, these individuals are not able to maintain their high levels of performance.

For example, Frensch and Sternberg (1989) studied the impact of changes to features of the game of bridge on expert-level players and novices. Although both groups were impacted equivalently by surface-level changes (i.e., changing the assigned suits), changes to deeper levels of the game structure proved to be a relatively greater impediment to the experts than the novices, indicating that the experts had lower levels of adaptability than the novices. Such occurrences may be due to automated planning behaviors that can constrain the flexibility of approaches to a task (Aarts & Dijksterhuis, 2000). In response to the increasing levels of mental effort that may be required in novel situations, the mind may automatically disengage from effortful, nonautomated procedures and activate older, more automated routines that may not be as successful in different circumstances from those for which they were developed (Clark, 1999). Stellan Ohlsson's (1996) displacement model further suggests that older, more automated knowledge and procedures may not only resurface in times of overload, but may also actively inhibit the mastery of newer performance goals.

Besnard (2000; Besnard & Bastien-Toniazzo, 1999; Besnard & Cacitti, 2001) has studied the constraints of routine expertise in technical troubleshooting. After recording the time and sequence of troubleshooting steps taken by novices and experts, he found that experts tended to take longer to find faulty components with unusual errors, because they exhibited a frequency bias, spending more time examining components typically responsible for circuit faults (Besnard, 2000; Besnard & Bastien-Toniazzo, 1999). Similarly, Besnard and Cacitti (2001) observed expert mechanics troubleshoot a malfunctioning engine. While only 25% of the experts and none of the novices successfully identified the problem, experts checked potential sources of the malfunction as a function of the overall frequency with which they cause problems. In contrast, novices were not constrained by the heuristic approach to the task and were thus more likely to examine the relevant part sooner, but were ultimately less successful in identifying the nature of the problem once it was located.

In contrast, adaptive experts are highly successful even under novel conditions. Bereiter and Scardamalia (1993) observed that often when experts have automated procedures within their domain, their skills are highly adaptable to complex, ill-structured, and novel situations, because minimal space in working memory is occupied by the process, thereby allowing mental effort to be reinvested in attending to relevant new details. In one example, Gott, Hall, Pokorny, Dibble, and Glaser (1993) reported that highly successful air force technicians were able to adapt knowledge to novel situations despite high levels of consistent, effortless performance. This description is reminiscent of the differences described by supervisors between the experts and "super-experts" in a study of high performing computer programmers (Koubek & Salvendy, 1991). Although their analysis of the data suggested that there was no difference in the levels of automaticity between the two groups, it is likely that there were differences in the nature of the automated routines or the mental models on which they were based.

Teaching for Adaptive Expertise

Developing adaptive expertise requires a substantial level of self-regulatory skills. When assessing novel situations and monitoring the success of previously developed routines, the ability to notice which elements are effective and which are not and adjust accordingly is critical to success in the task. Bransford, Brown, and Cocking (1999, p. xiii), observed that "experts notice features and meaningful patterns of information that are not noticed by novices." Further, after an extensive review of the literature, Perkins and Grotzer (1997) argued that such skills can be taught to facilitate the solution of novel and challenging problems through restructuring their mental model of the situation presented to accommodate more flexible strategies.

De Corte (2003; Masui & De Corte, 1999) described the design of a learning environment that facilitates the development of the necessary characteristics for successful transfer of existing skills in which orienting (problem framing) and self-judging were taught according to the following guidelines:

- Skills and knowledge instruction must be taught in environments that are as authentic as possible to facilitate the successful development of accurate mental models that emphasize the importance of relevant cues.
- Metacognitive and self-regulatory skills must be linked to tangible and personally relevant outcomes.
- Instruction must be sequenced to allow for gradually increasing levels of necessary self-regulation (see also extensive research on the design of instruction using worked examples by, for example, Atkinson et al., 2000; Paas & van Merriënboer, 1993; Sweller, 1999).
- The characteristics of learning and performance tasks and practice must be varied over the course of instruction to maximize opportunities to develop flexibility.
- Students must be provided with opportunities to receive targeted feedback and consider alternatives for more effective approaches.

Such strategies provide promising opportunities for advanced instruction and research. In addition to attempting to identify which elements of these strategies should be considered first principles in the work by Merrill (2002a, 2002b) and others discussed earlier, understanding the role of motivation and goals in directing transfer learning tasks could provide greater insight into self-regulation and the willingness to exert high levels of mental effort while avoiding detrimental cognitive defaults. Remaining issues are more narrowly focused on the way that pedagogical support is given and on ways to determine how much and what type of support a learner needs to succeed in a distance context. Multimedia developers have an understandable need to make their presentations as motivating and engaging to learners as possible. One of the popular devices for giving learning help and motivating learners at the same time is the use of animated pedagogical agents. We turn next to a brief review of the research on the use of these agents including some counterintuitive findings from research and suggestions for future research (that is, what can and should be done).

THE USE OF PEDAGOGICAL AGENTS IN WEB-BASED COURSES: HELPFUL OR HURTFUL TO LEARNING?

Animated pedagogical agents are defined by Craig, Gholson, and Driscoll (2002) as " … a computerized character (either humanlike or otherwise) designed to facilitate learning" (p. 428). Atkinson (2002) suggested that these animated computerized instructional characters exploit communicative behaviors typically reserved for human–human interaction (i.e., gestures, motion, facial expression). Several pedagogical agents with names such as Herman, Steve, Adele, and SmartEgg have been developed recently to serve a variety of instructional goals in computer-based instruction, some of them in Web-based learning environment. The purpose of this section is to analyze the existing empirical studies on animated pedagogical agents (i.e., what and how research has been done) and to provide future directions for those who want to do research on this area as well as other technology-related topics (i.e., what can and should be done).

Confusion About the Source of Measured Benefits

Discussions about the uses of agents suggest that they may have three types of possible learning benefits: (1) They may have a positive impact on learners' motivation and perception of their experiences with the systems; (2) they may attract learners' attention to areas of the computer screen or to specific tasks through the use of motion, gesture, and facial expression; and (3) they may provide learners with context-specific learning help and advice. Despite the claimed effects, very little empirical research has been conducted and the results of published studies are mixed (Clark, 2003; Dehn & van Mulken, 2000), due largely to the way that they are designed.

Many agent studies fail to provide all of the learning and motivational support available in the agent condition to the control or nonagent condition. However, an adequate test requires that the nonagent or control condition has all of the learning and motivational support available from the agent condition; otherwise the comparison between agent and nonagent conditions will be confounded by the uncontrolled effects of the instructional methods the agent provides and the agent itself. Dehn and van Mulken (2000) also explained that without this type of design control, " ... differences between the two conditions cannot be attributed *exclusively* to ... the agent" (Italicized word added, p. 18).

For example, Andre and colleagues (1999) conducted a well-controlled agent study to find empirical support for the affective and cognitive benefits of their "PPP Persona" agent. Both experiment and control conditions provided the same treatments except that the control groups did not have the "PPP Persona" agent. They heard a voice conveying the same explanations as those provided to the experimental group and saw an arrow pointing to important information instead of the agent's pointing gestures. Following the presentations, affective and cognitive impacts of both conditions were measured. The results showed significant differences only in the affective measures whereas no significant differences were found between the experimental and control groups on cognitive measures. Another good design example can be found in Craig et al (2002).

Confounding in Agent Studies

On the other hand, Atkinson (2002) failed to control for instructional supports when comparing a "voice plus agent" group with "voice only" and "text only" groups (Experiment 2). In the voice plus agent group, participants listened to the agent's verbal explanations and simultaneously saw the agent highlighting relevant information on the screen by using pointing gestures. Alternatively, participants in the voice only and text only conditions only received the same explanations delivered either in voice or text, respectively, but they did not have the benefit of seeing important information being highlighted. The lack of visual indicator might have forced the nonagent participants to use their limited cognitive resources in matching aural information with corresponding elements on the computer screen instead of building necessary schema. Therefore, the voice plus agent group's better performance in far-transfer performance cannot be exclusively attributed to the agent itself.

Beyond Simple Learning Outcome Measures

In the existing agent studies, factual recall and the solving of simple problems are commonly used to measure students' cognitive learning outcomes (Lester, Converse, Stone, Kahler, & Barlow, 1997; Mitrovic & Suraweera, 2000; Moundridou & Virvou, 2002), together with self-report measures to assess learners' subjective reactions to the agent and agent-delivered instruction. In order to design effective computer and Web-based instruction, however, it is crucial to know if agents work better than other media formats for instruction. This can't be done by employing a variety of learning and motivational outcome measures including retention tests and problem-solving measures that provide both near and far transfer problems along with motivational measures that go beyond simple reaction questionnaires. In effect, only a few empirical studies show that agents might be beneficial more for solving of far-transfer problems than for other types of learning objectives.

In the first two of the Moreno and colleagues' (2001) studies, for instance, an agent who "personalized" instruction did not aid recall of facts or the transfer of simpler knowledge to solving problems. These treatments also failed to demonstrate a positive impact on student ratings of the "understandability and difficulty" of problems or their motivation to learn the material. However, their personalizing treatment using the agent was found to be superior for the solving of complex problems that required more cognitive effort. Atkinson (2002) also reported superior performance of the voice plus agent group in far-transfer problems, whereas no significant difference was found in near-transfer problems between the voice plus agent group and the voice only group. Atkinson's explanation for this finding is that the voice only group's lack of visual indicators that connect aural information with corresponding visual elements (e.g., the agent's pointing gestures) might have forced its participants to use their limited cognitive capacity in finding the links between aural and visual information, instead of achieving deeper understanding of the instructional material required by far-transfer problems.

Although we have doubts about the controls for instructional supports in nonagent conditions in both Atkinson (2002) and Moreno et al. (2001) studies, the far transfer learning benefits of agents are worth further research.

Testing the Use of Agents in Diverse Domains of Knowledge

In addition, the fact that only a small number of knowledge domains has been the focus of agent studies poses another challenge to be overcome by agent researchers. To date, most pedagogical agent studies have employed discovery-based learning environments and scientific materials for instruction even though there is evidence that agent effect is domain specific (van Mulken, Andre, & Muller, 1998). Due to the lack of the variety in subject matters tested in the field, we still do not know what knowledge domains could benefit most from animated pedagogical agents with what kinds of functionalities. The focus of future studies should be broadened both in the scope of domain knowledge and instructional functions conveyed by agents.

Cognitive Efficiency Studies

Another missing element in agent studies is the measurement of agents' effects on learning process. Media researchers now agree to a certain extent that questioning about the effect of one medium over another on cognitive products is a circular and fruitless argument, and it is time to move our focus on media impact on learners' cognitive process and on how to utilize media to improve the process (Clark, 1998; Mayer, 1997, 2001). One example of process-oriented approach is the "cognitive efficiency" idea proposed by Tom Cobb (1997). Cognitive efficiency refers to "one medium being more or less effortful than another, more or less likely to succeed with a particular learner, or interacting more or less usefully with a particular prior knowledge set" (p. 25), leading to faster learning, or requiring less conscious effort from the learner for processing learning material (Cobb,

1997). Learning process measures including cognitive efficiency can be incorporated in agent studies by measuring the amount of mental effort or cognitive load required for processing a unit of instruction while the learner is interacting with the agent. Another potential process measure is how much time the learner invested in processing agent-delivered material or whether the agent group participants persisted longer in the system to solve problems compared to those in the nonagent low technology condition.

The Entertaining Agent: Helpful or Harmful?

The underlying premise of including an animated agent in instructional presentation is that the agent itself and its human-like behaviors (i.e., gaze, eye contact, body language, emotional expression) cause learners to feel that the learning material is interesting and less difficult, and motivates them to work harder. This effect is also called "persona effect," which precisely refers to learners' positive perception of their learning experience triggered by the presence of the agent (Moreno et al., 2001). Persona effect is also the basis of the claim that the positive feeling and perception elicited by the agent foster interest in tasks and lead students to exert more efforts to make sense of instructional material (Lester et al., 1997; Moreno et al., 2001).

Salomon (1984), however, presented compelling evidence that when students perceive the material to be easy and entertaining because of its familiarity and life likeness, they tend to expend less mental effort in elaborating the material and to learn it less well. This might be the reason why several agent studies found no significant effect of the agent on learning outcome despite the fact that the agent group apparently enjoyed the system more than the nonagent group (i.e., Andre et al., 1999; Lester et al., 1997; Moreno et al., 2001). Therefore, future researchers in this field should adopt a more fine-grained approach to investigating the agent's effects on motivation and achievement instead of assuming a simple positive relationship among these three rather complex variables. In particular, we recommend the excellent discussion by Pintrich & Schunk (2002) about "motivational indexes" for assessing the agent's motivational effects. This approach suggests that the measurement of motivation should include at least three different types of motivational outcomes (not just surface level and immediate indices such as interest and future choice); active choice (moving from intention to action), persistence over time at learning in the face of distractions, and the amount of mental effort invested in learning.

The mental effort expended by the learner will not be representative of motivation, however, if it is not invested directly in the learning task. Another possible harm caused by including entertaining but conceptually irrelevant media in instruction is overloading learners' limited working memory. Working memory will, on the average, tolerate only 4 ± 2 chunks of information before learners become overloaded (Cowan, 2001). This estimate is more current and accurate than the 7 ± 2 estimate suggested in the 1950s. Mayer (2001) has documented the learning deficits experienced by learners who are overloaded by adding interesting but conceptually irrelevant material (i.e., animation, pictures, background music) to a computer-based lesson. Cognitive load theory (Kalyuga, Chandler, & Sweller, 1999) also predicts that the mere presence of an animated pedagogical agent can be detrimental to learning by dividing a learner's limited cognitive resources into different visual segments in a multimedia presentation. This appears to cause a condition where the learning strategies the agent is attempting to covey are never used by learners. Therefore, it seems important to avoid including a complex and noisy agent and to focus an agent on learning goals and provide both the simplest, least distracting and most conceptually relevant support for the achievement of learning objectives.

Future Research on Agents

The suggestions for future studies on animated pedagogical agents offered in this discussion could well be applied to all attempts to design studies that examine new electronic media based audio-visual formats for instructional methods. Historically, interest in new media and technology has been so intense that it has often overwhelmed our substantive prior learning about the instructional support for learning and the design of adequate experiments. This was true when movies and television were adopted for use in instruction and it continues to be an issue in the design of studies that attempt to benefit from the introduction of personal computers, multi-media, and virtual reality (Clark, 2001). In fact, the major source of learning deficits of animated pedagogical agents seems to be a lack of attention to past research. Research in this area has been largely driven by strong technology-based perspectives and a majority of the agent studies published to date have focused on technological capacity of agents without paying much attention to theory- and research-based principles (Bradshaw, 1997). Yet, enthusiasm and cautious design are not necessarily antagonistic. We believe that only through adequate design and a concern with theories of learning and instruction will we develop evidence for the benefits of new technologies similar to the tempting insight about the impact of agents on far transfer of knowledge that was found in the studies by Moreno et al. (2001) and Atkinson (2002). We will also discover counterintuitive and negative effects imposed by new instructional devices such as those identified by Mayer (2001) and so advise instructional designers about the pitfalls they should avoid when developing instructional programs.

In the next section we address another intuitively appealing belief—that instruction can be tailored for the learning styles of students.

TAILORING INSTRUCTION TO DIFFERENCES IN LEARNING STYLE, MOTIVATION, AND PRIOR KNOWLEDGE

The importance of individual differences in the design of instruction has long been the subject of debate (Cronbach and Snow, 1977; Stahl, 1999). This section focuses on three individual differences that have been considered in research on instruction; learning styles, motivation, and prior knowledge. The best evidence from current work on individual differences in learning suggest that learning styles do not work, that motivational differences are promising but not yet fully developed for routine use, and that the most effective instruction is tailored differently for students with more or less prior knowledge.

Learning Styles

The notion that learning may be optimized when instruction is tailored to learning-related individual learning style differences among students has taken many forms in past research. The hope that, because of different learning styles, some people learn the same information better through different modalities, or are somehow better able to grasp a difficult concept when it is presented in one format over another is apparently very intuitively appealing. For example, students can presumably be classified as "visual or verbal" learners. Once diagnosed with a style preference, the student is prescribed a teaching method intended to either strengthen the detected weakness (for example, by providing visual instruction to low visual ability students), or take advantage of the learner's strong underlying ability (for example, by providing visualization of information to be learned for students with higher visual ability scores), with the ultimate aim of increased learning (Arter & Jenkins, 1979).

Capitalize on Strengths or Compensate for Weaknesses? Unfortunately, the evidence in the search for positive effects of the learning styles model has not matched the enthusiasm of its proponents (for example, Irvine & York, 1995; Stahl, 1999). The presumption that students can be reliably classified and that once classified, will respond positively to different formats of instructional messages tailored to draw on their style "strengths" or compensate for "weaknesses" is dubious, because the instruments used to form these diagnoses seem not to pass reasonable tests of diagnostic reliability or validity (Arter & Jenkins, 1979; Henson & Hwang, 2002). Reliability problems with style instruments undermines the foundation of the expectations for their utility, making any instruction based on them suspect at best, and potentially harmful at worst. Kavale and Forness (1987) highlighted logical problems associated with style categorization, such as when one subject has a modality profile of high verbal versus low visual, and another has a profile of low verbal and even lower visual, and both are categorized as verbal learners. It is illogical to expect consistency in the learning patterns of students who are categorized as verbal learners using this or similar systems.

Questioning the Value of Research. It is unfortunate that a lack of research support for learning styles has caused some to question the value of the research that examines this issue for educational practice. For example, some contend that teachers are only interested in "how to better serve their students," whereas researchers simply look for "evidence beyond chance that a performance difference exists" (Ojure & Sherman, 2001). Although these two goals might appear to be compatible to educators trained as researchers or who understand research, there are those who appear to believe so strongly in learning styles that they question the merit of research that cannot provide positive evidence for learning styles.

Assuming that the reliability and validity issues can be resolved in the future, another area of debate has been the lack of a solid consensus on whether to capitalize on the basis of learners' presumed style strengths or attempt remediation of their style weaknesses. This "strength versus deficit" issue has resulted in varied approaches to prescriptive teaching based on learning style analysis. The deficit approach (remediation of the weakness) relies on the questionable assumption that the alleged deficit can be altered. The strength approach, or capitalizing on the learner's strength can result in a wider discrepancy between the learners' strengths and weaknesses than existed prior to the remediation, hindering sensory integration (Tarver & Dawson, 1978).

Mayer and his colleagues have recently begun a program of research that attempts to remedy some of the problems with the reliability and predictive validity of visual and verbal style measures. A report of work on a new visual and verbal style measure that seems to have solid reliability and construct validity was reported by Mayer and his colleagues (Mayer & Massa, 2003). Perhaps in the next few years, Mayer's work will be extended to instructional contexts. Until new work is reported with much more solid evidence to support learning styles, practitioners must exercise caution.

Learning Styles do not Work. The questionable diagnostic validity of the learning styles assessment instruments and the varied approaches to remediation have led to research results that should not be viewed as unexpected. Several studies have examined different aspects of prescriptive teaching based on diagnoses of differential learning styles. Stahl (1999) cited numerous research reviews that provide evidence for the claim that research has yet to document any effect of learning styles on learning when attempts are made to match instructional methods to styles. Five research reviews, examining over 80 studies that span 27 years, consistently lead to the same conclusion: Learning styles do not improve learning (see Arter & Jenkins, 1979; Kampwirth & Bates, 1980; Kavale & Forness, 1987; Snider, 1992; and Tarver & Dawson, 1978).

Motivational Differences in Goal Orientation

The fact that the research is not promising in the area of learning styles does not mean that instructional designers should ignore all individual differences. Research on student motivation is illustrative of how different individual achievement goal orientations are predictive of achievement behavior, and how the structure of the learning environment can influence the types of achievement goals that students adopt. Students with mastery goal orientations are those who tend to focus on understanding, as well as achieving mastery of new knowledge according to self-referenced standards of excellence (Pintrich & Schunk, 2002). This approach connotes learning for learning's sake, rather than performing to please others. Conversely, students with performance goal orientations define ability and self-worth based on their levels of success as measured against others. This orientation has been linked to preoccupation with external influences such as other's view of them. While there seems to be relative consensus on the positive benefits of mastery goal orientations, the effect of performance goal orientations appears to be more complex. Some of the previously assumed negative effects of performance goal orientations, such as challenge avoidance to protect perceived image, or poor learning strategy selection, have not consistently been confirmed in research studies (Harackiewicz, Barron, & Elliot, 1998).

Performance goals can result in positive achievement outcomes, depending on how they interact with other situational cues, and with other goals present in the educational environment. Mastery and performance goal orientations can positively coexist, as a learner can value both the opportunity to gain knowledge and the chance to demonstrate their abilities for others. Rather than encouraging learners to adopt one type of goal orientation over another, instructional designers would be better served by considering an environment that promotes multiple goals, and by seeking to understand the various research findings that delineate when the different goal orientations best complement one another to produce the most effective learning environment.

Prior Knowledge Differences

The most promising individual difference seems to be the amount of relevant prior knowledge already learned by students. In general, evidence from a great variety of studies extending over many types of learning tasks and contexts support the generalizations that students who have less prior knowledge need more pedagogical support than those who are more advanced.

The Expertise Reversal Effect. Kalyuga et al. (2003) reviewed studies where learners with advanced knowledge in a subject matter actually learned less when provided with pedagogical support that was very beneficial for lower prior knowledge students. Apparently, more advanced students have effective learning strategies for very familiar subject matter and so, imposing novel strategies on them imposes a heavy cognitive load and decreases their learning. This effect was described earlier by Clark (1982, 1989) who cautioned that advanced students seem to prefer the pedagogical support even though it is not helpful to them. He was concerned that when students can choose a more elaborate and pedagogically rich version of a course or one with less learning support, many advanced students select the version that leads to less learning and like it better. Other studies (for example Touvinen & Sweller, 1999) have found no differences in the benefits of instructional support in the form of worked examples between students with lower and higher prior knowledge. These results are consistent with comprehensive reviews of individual differences research dating back at least a quarter century (see for example, the comprehensive review by Cronbach & Snow, 1977). As a result of these studies and others, it seems reasonable to suggest that designers can increase the learning in Web-based courses by focusing more pedagogical support on learners with less experience or prior knowledge relevant to what is to be learned. Very advanced students do not require the support and may sometimes be harmed by it. Instructional designers who wish to measure the prior knowledge of students in Web-based courses in order to assign them to more and less supported versions of the same course should consult Kalyuga and Sweller (in press) for a very quick and reliable measurement method.

SUMMARY AND CONCLUSIONS

This chapter describes a number of research-based opportunities and cautions about the design of Web-based instruction for adults. At least five opportunities were noted in the areas of: 1) New instructional design models that specialize in the teaching of highly complex knowledge; 2) First principles of instructional methods and strategies that are drawn from very successful approaches to Web-based design; 3) Using cognitive task analysis to capture authentic knowledge that supports the development of advanced expertise; 4) Tailoring Web-instruction differently by offering more scaffolding support for students with less prior knowledge; and 5) Techniques for achieving adaptive expertise and farther transfer of learning through the solving of varied, increasingly novel authentic problems.

Further, about five problems and misconceptions that creep into Web-based design are described in the following areas: 1) Some observers have noted a pattern where Web-based course producers combine instructional design and media development. The point was made that this pattern tends to confuse the selection of powerful instructional methods with the development of state-of-the-art graphics and media production. The recommendation was made to separate these two stages and complete a design blueprint before developing mediated instructional materials; 2) It was suggested that many Web-based course designers develop visually and aurally complex screens to depict instructional information. This practice comes from a healthy intention to provide visually and aurally attractive and motivating instruction but in fact, the result is that noisy multimedia often overloads learner' working memory and sometimes defeats learning. It was recommended that screen designs be simplified and focused only on information necessary to achieve learning goals; 3) One example of cognitive overload, the increasing frequency of "animated pedagogical agents" was used as an example of devices that are intended to be helpful to learners but turn out to seductively distract and overload them and sometimes defeat leaning. Very little evidence was found for the benefits from animated pedagogical agents and significant evidence exists that they tend to distract the most vulnerable learners; 4) Despite the intuitive attraction many of us have for tailoring instruction to the learning styles of students in Web-courses, the evidence from 30 years of empirical research does not support their use. We recommend more research on motivational strategies that could be designed into Web-based courses and the use of prior knowledge differences to tailor Web-based courses; and finally, 5) We describe evidence that learning seldom transfers from Web-based courses (or classroom courses). We recommend the use of several techniques that have been found to support the development of adaptive expertise. Most of those techniques involve the use of varied authentic problems of increasing novelty during practice exercises.

REFERENCES

Aarts, H., & Dijksterhuis, A. (2000). Habits as knowledge structures: Automaticity in goal-directed behavior. *Journal of Personality and Social Psychology, 78*(1), 53–63.

Andre, E., Rist, T., & Muller, J. (1999). Employing AI methods to control the behavior of animated interface agents. *Applied Artificial Intelligence, 13*, 415–448.

Anderson, J. R. (1982). Acquisition of cognitive skill. *Psychological Review, 89*, 369–406.

Anderson, J. R., Fincham, J. M., & Douglas, S. (1997). The role of examples and rules in the acquisition of a cognitive skill. *Journal of Experimental Psychology: Learning, Memory, and Cognition, 23*(4), 932–945.

Arter, J. A., & Jenkins, J. R. (1979). Differential diagnosis—prescriptive teaching: A critical appraisal. *Review of Educational Research, 49*(4), 517–555.

Atkinson, R. K. (2002). Optimizing learning from examples using animated pedagogical agents *Journal of Educational Psychology, 94*(2), 416–427.

Atkinson, R. K., Derry, S. J., Renkl, A., & Wortham, D. (2000). Learning from examples: Instructional principles from the worked examples research. *Review of Educational Research, 70*(2), 181–214.

Bargh, J. A., & Ferguson, M. J. (2000). Beyond behaviorism: On the automaticity of higher mental processes. *Psychological Bulletin, 126*(6), 925–945.

Barnett, S. M., & Cecci, S. (2002). When and where do we apply what we learn? A taxonomy for far transfer. *Psychological Bulletin, 128*(4), 612–637.

Bereiter, C., & Scardamalia, M. (1993). *Surpassing ourselves: An inquiry into the nature and implications of expertise.* Chicago, IL: Open Court.

Besnard, D. (2000). Expert error. The case of trouble-shooting in electronics. *Proceedings of the 19th International Conference SafeComp2000* (pp. 74–85). Rotterdam, Netherlands.

Besnard, D., & Bastien-Toniazzo, M. (1999). Expert error in trouble-shooting: An exploratory study in electronics. *International Journal of Human-Computer Studies, 50*, 391–405.

Besnard, D., & Cacitti, L. (2001). Troubleshooting in mechanics: A heuristic matching process. *Cognition, Technology & Work, 3*, 150–160.

Binder, C. (2003). Doesn't everybody need fluency? *Performance Improvement, 42*(5), 14–20.

Blessing, S. B., & Anderson, J. R. (1996). How people learn to skip steps. *Journal of Experimental Psychology: Learning, Memory, and Cognition, 22*(3), 576–598.

Bradshaw, J. M. (1997). *Software agents.* Cambridge, MA: MIT Press.

Bransford, J. D., Brown, A. L., & Cocking, R. R. (1999). *How people learn: Brain, mind, experience, and school.* Washington, DC: National Academy Press.

Casner, S. M. (1994). Understanding the determinants of problem-solving behavior in a complex environment. *Human Factors, 36*(4), 580–596.

Chandler, P., & Sweller, J. (1991). Cognitive load theory and the format of instruction. *Cognition and Instruction, 8*, 293–332.

Clark, R. E. (1982). Antagonism between achievement and enjoyment in ATI studies. *Educational Psychologist, 17*(2), 92–101.

Clark, R. E. (1989). When teaching kills learning: Research on mathemathantics. In H. N. Mandl, N. Bennett, E. de Corte, & H. F. Freidrich (Eds.), *Learning and instruction. European research in an international context* (Vol. 2, pp. 1–26). London, England: Pergamon.

Clark, R. E. (1998). *Cognitive efficiency research on media: A rejoinder to Cobb.* Unpublished manuscript.

Clark, R. E. (1999). Yin and yang: Cognitive motivational processes operating in multimedia learning environments. In J. van Merriënboer (Ed.), *Cognition and multimedia design* (pp. 73–107). Herleen, Netherlands: Open University Press.

Clark, R. E. (2001). *Learning from media: Arguments, analysis and evidence*. Greenwich, CT: Information Age Publishers.

Clark, R. E. (2003). Research on web-based learning: A half-full glass. In R. Bruning, C. Horn, & L. PytlikZillig (Eds.), *Web-based learning: Where do we know? Where do we go?* (pp. 1–22). Greenwich, CT: Information Age Publishers.

Clark R. E., & Blake, S. (1997). Analyzing cognitive structures and processes to derive instructional methods for the transfer of problem solving expertise. In S. Dijkstra & N. M. Seel (Eds.), *Instructional design perspectives. Vol. II: Solving instructional design problems* (pp. 183–214). Oxford, England: Pergamon.

Clark, R. E., & Estes, F. (1999). The development of authentic educational technologies. *Educational Technology, 37*(2) 5–16.

Clark, R. E., & Estes, F. (2000). A proposal for the collaborative development of authentic performance technology. *Performance Improvement, 40*(4), 48–53.

Cobb, T. (1997). Cognitive efficiency: Toward a revised theory of media. *Educational Technology Research & Development, 45*(4), 21–35.

Cowan, N. (2001). The magical number 4 in short-term memory: A reconsideration of mental storage capacity. *Behavioral and Brain Sciences, 24*(1), 87–114.

Craig, S. D., Gholson, B., & Driscoll, D. M. (2002). Animated pedagogical agents in multimedia educational environments: Effects of agent properties, picture features and redundancy. *Journal of Educational Psychology, 94*(2), 428–434.

Cronbach, L. J., & Snow, R. E. (1977). *Aptitudes and instructional method*. Mahwah, NJ: Lawrence Erlbaum Associates.

De Corte, E. (2003). Transfer as the productive use of acquired knowledge, skills, and motivations. *Current Directions in Psychological Science, 12*(4), 143–146.

Dehn, D. M., & van Mulken, S. (2000). The impact of animated interface agents: A review of empirical research. *International Journal of Human-Computer Studies, 52*, 1–22.

Detterman, D. K. (1993). The case for the prosecution: Transfer as an epiphenomenon. In D. K. Detterman & R. J. Sternberg (Eds.), *Transfer on trial: Intelligence, cognition and instruction* (pp. 1–24). Norwood, NJ: Ablex.

Dick, W., & Carey, L. (1990). *The systematic design of instruction (3rd ed.)*. New York: Harper Collins.

Ericsson, K. A., & Lehmann, A. C. (1996). Expert and exceptional performance: Evidence of maximal adaptation to task constraints. *Annual Review of Psychology, 47*, 273–305.

Frensch, P. A., & Sternberg, R. J. (1989). Expertise and intelligent issues: When is it worse to know better? In R. J. Sternberg (Ed.), *Advances in the psychology of human intelligence* (Vol. 5, pp. 157–188). Hillsdale, NJ: Lawrence Erlbaum Associates.

Glaser, R., & Chi, M. T. H. (1988). Overview. In M. T. H. Chi, R. Glaser, & M. J. Farr (Eds.), *The nature of expertise* (pp. xv–xxviii). Mahwah, NJ: Lawrence Erlbaum Associates.

Gott, S. P., Hall, E. P., Pokorny, R. A., Dibble, E., & Glaser, R. (1993). A naturalistic study of transfer: Adaptive expertise in technical domains. In D. K. Detterman & R. J. Sternberg (Eds.), *Transfer on trial: Intelligence, cognition, and instruction* (pp. 258–288). Norwood, NJ: Ablex.

Harackiewicz, J. M., Barron, K. E., & Elliot, A. J. (1998). Rethinking achievement goals: When are they adaptive for college students and why? *Educational Psychologist, 33*(1), 1–21.

Hatano, G. (1982). Cognitive consequences of practice in culture specific procedural skills. *Quarterly Newsletter of the Laboratory of Comparative Human Cognition, 4*, 15–18.

Hatano, G., & Inagaki, K. (1986). Two courses of expertise. In H. Stevenson, H. Asuma, & K. Hakauta (Eds.), *Child development and education in Japan* (pp. 262–272). San Francisco, CA: Freeman.

Hatano, G., & Inagaki, K. (2000, April). *Practice makes a difference: Design principles for adaptive expertise*. Presented at the Annual Meeting of the American Education Research Association, New Orleans, LA.

Henson, R. K., & Hwang, D.-Y. (2002). Variability and prediction of measurement error in Kolb's Learning Style Inventory scores: A reliability generalization study. *Educational and Psychological Measurement, 62*(4), 712–727.

Irvine, J. J., & York, D. E. (1995). Learning styles and culturally diverse students: A literature review. In J. A. Banks & C. A. M. Banks (Eds.), *Handbook of research on multicultural education* (pp. 484–497). New York: Simon & Schuster.

Kalyuga, S., Chandler, P., & Sweller, J. (1999). Managing split-attention and redundancy in multimedia instruction. *Applied Cognitive Psychology, 13*, 351–371.

Kalyuga, S., & Sweller, J. (in press). Measuring knowledge to optimize cognitive load. *Journal of Educational Psychology*.

Kampwirth, T. J., & Bates, M. (1980). Modality preference and teaching method: A review of research. *Academic Therapy, 15*, 597–605.

Kavale, K. A., & Forness, S. R. (1987). Substance over style: Assessing the efficacy of modality testing and teaching. *Exceptional Children, 54*(3), 228–239.

Koubek, R. J., & Salvendy, G. (1991). Cognitive performance of super-experts on computer program modification tasks. *Ergonomics, 34*, 1095–1112.

Lee, R. L. (2004). *Cognitive task analysis: A meta-analysis of comparative studies*. Unpublished doctoral dissertation, University of Southern California.

Lester, J., Converse, S., Stone, B., Kahler, S., & Barlow, T. (1997). Animated pedagogical agents and problem solving effectiveness: A large scale empirical evaluation. *Proceedings of the Eighth World Conference on Artificial Intelligence in Education* (pp. 23–30), Kobe, Japan.

Masui, C., & De Corte, E. (1999). Enhancing learning and problem solving skills: Orienting and self-judging, two powerful and trainable learning tools. *Learning and Instruction, 9*, 517–542.

Mayer, R. E. (1997). Are we asking the right questions? *Educational Psychologist, 32*(1), 1–19.

Mayer, R. E. (2001). *Multi-media learning*. Cambridge, England: Cambridge University Press.

Mayer, R. E. (2004). Should there be a three-strikes rule against pure discovery learning? *American Psychologist, 59*(1), 14–19.

Mayer, R. E., & Massa, L. J. (2003). Three facets of visual and verbal learners: Cognitive ability, cognitive style and learning preference. *Journal of Educational Psychology, 95*(4), 833–846.

Merrill, M. D. (2002a). First principles of instruction. *Educational Technology Research and Development*.

Merrill, M. D. (2002b). A pebble-in-the-pond model for instructional design. *Performance Improvement, 41*(7), 39–44.

Mitrovic, A., & Suraweera, P. (2000). Evaluating an animated pedagogical agent. *Lecture notes in computer science* (No. 1839), 73–82.

Moreno, R., Mayer, R. E., Spires, H. A., & Lester, J. C. (2001). The case for social agency in computer-based teaching: Do students learn more deeply when they interact with animated pedagogical agents? *Cognition and Instruction, 19*(2), 177–213.

Moundridou, M., & Virvou, M. (2002). Evaluating the persona effect of an interface agent in a tutoring system. *Journal of Computer Assisted Learning, 18*(3), 253–261.

Ohlsson, S. (1996). Learning from performance errors. *Psychological Review, 103*(2), 241–262.

Ojure, L., & Sherman, T. (2001, November 28). Learning Styles. *Education Week,* 33–34.

Paas, F., & van Merriënboer, J. J. (1993). The efficiency of instructional conditions: An approach to combine mental effort and performance measures. *Human Factors, 35*(4), 737–743.

Perkins, D. N., & Grotzer, T. A. (1997). Teaching intelligence. *American Psychologist, 52*(10), 1125–1133.

Pintrich, P. R., & Schunk, D. H. (2002). *Motivation in education: Theory, research and practice* (2nd ed.). Englewood Cliffs, NJ: Prentice Hall.

Reigeluth, C. M. (Ed.). (1983). *Instructional design theories and models*. Mahwah, NJ: Lawrence Erlbaum Associates.

Reigeluth, C. M. (Ed.). (1987). *Instructional theories in action: Lessons illustrating selected theories and models*. Hillsdale, NJ: Lawrence Erlbaum Associates.

Rikers, R., Schmidt, H., & Boshuizen, H. (2000). Knowledge encapsulation and the intermediate effect. *Contemporary Educational Psychology, 25*(2), 150–166.

Rittle-Johnson, B., Siegler, R. S., & Alibali, M. W. (2001). Developing conceptual understanding and procedural skill in mathematics: An iterative process. *Journal of Educational Psychology, 93*(2), 346–362.

Salomon, G. (1984). Television is easy and print is tough: The differential investment of mental effort in learning as a function of perceptions and attributions. *Journal of Educational Psychology, 76*(4), 647–658.

Singley, M. K., & Anderson, J. R. (1989). *Transfer of cognitive skill*. Cambridge, MA: Harvard University Press.

Snider, V. E. (1992). Learning styles and learning to read: A critique. *Remedial and Special Education, 13*(1), 6–18.

Squire, L. R., Knowlton, B., & Musen, G. (1993). The structure and organization of memory. *Annual Review of Psychology, 44*, 453–495.

Stahl, S. A. (1999). Different strokes for different folks? A critique of learning styles. *American Educator, 23*(3), 27–31.

Sternberg, R. J., & Horvath, J. A. (1998). Cognitive conceptions of expertise and their relations to giftedness. In R. C. Friedman & K. B. Rogers (Eds.), *Talent in context* (pp. 177–191). Washington, DC: American Psychological Association.

Sweller, J. (1988). Cognitive load during problem solving: Effects on learning. *Cognitive Science, 12*, 257–285.

Sweller, J. (1989). Cognitive technology: Some procedures for facilitating learning and problem solving in mathematics and science. *Journal of Cognitive Psychology, 81*(4), 457–466.

Sweller, J. (1999). *Instruction design in technical areas*. Camberwell, Australia: ACER.

Sweller, J., Chandler, P., Tierney, P., & Cooper, M. (1990). Cognitive load as a factor in the structuring of technical material. *Journal of Experimental Psychology: General, 119*(2), 176–192.

Sweller, J., van Merriënboer, J. G., & Paas, F. G. (1998). Cognitive architecture and instructional design. *Educational Psychology Review, 10*, 251–296.

Tarver, S. G., & Dawson, M. M. (1978). Modality preference and the teaching of reading: A review. *Journal of Learning Disabilities, 11*(1), 17–29.

Touvinen, J. E., & Sweller, J. (1999). A comparison of cognitive load associated with discovery learning and worked examples. *Journal of Educational Psychology, 91*, 334–341.

VanLehn, K. (1996). Cognitive skill acquisition. *Annual Review of Psychology, 47*, 513–539.

van Merriënboer, J. J. G. (1997). *Training complex cognitive skills: A four-component instructional design model for technical training*. Englewood Cliffs, NJ: Educational Technology Publications.

van Merriënboer, J. J. G., Clark, R. E., & de Croock, B. M. (2002). Blueprints for complex learning: The 4C/ID-Model. *Educational Technology Research and Development, 50*(2), 39–64.

van Mulken, S., Andre, E., & Muller, J. (1998). The persona effect: How substantial is it? In H. Johnson, L. Nigay, & C. Roast (Eds.), *People and Computers XIII: Proceedings of HCI'98* (pp. 53–66). Berlin: Springer.

Velmahos, G. C., Toutouzas, K. G., Sillin, L. F., Chan, L., Clark, R. E. Theodorou, D., et al. (2004). Cognitive task analysis for teaching technical skills in an inanimate surgical skills laboratory. *The American Journal of Surgery, 187*, 114–119.

Williams, K. E. (2000). An automated aid for modeling human-computer interaction. In J. M. C. Schraagen, S. F. Chipman, & V. L. Shalin (Eds.), *Cognitive task analysis* (pp. 165–180). Mahwah, NJ: Lawrence Erlbaum Associates.

Wilson, T. D., & Nisbett, R. E. (1978). The accuracy of verbal reports about the effects of stimuli on evaluations and behavior. *Social Psychology, 41*(2), 118–131.

Chapter 21

Ten Research-Based Principles of Multimedia Learning

Richard E. Mayer
University of California, Santa Barbara

A multimedia instructional message is a presentation containing words and pictures that are intended to foster learning. Examples include narrated animations, annotated illustrations, interactive simulations, and educational games. Given the increasing role of graphics in Web-based learning systems (such as illustrations, photos, animation, and video), this chapter examines research that is needed to inform the design of multimedia instructional messages. For the past 15 years, my colleagues and I at the University of California, Santa Barbara have conducted dozens of studies on how to incorporate pictures and words into multimedia instructional messages (Mayer, 2001, 2002). For example, we have examined narrated animations and annotated illustrations aimed at explaining how the human respiratory system works, how lightning storms develop, how a car's braking system works, how a bicycle tire pump works, and how an airplane achieves lift; and we have examined simulations and games aimed at teaching how an electric motor works, how to identify geological formations on a planet's surface, how a plant's physical features are suited to a environmental conditions, and how to add and subtract signed numbers. In general, the learners were low knowledge students in their first year of college or in high school. In this chapter, after briefly describing my research rationale, example materials, and theory, I summarize 10 research-based principles for the design of multimedia instructional messages. For each principle, I provide examples, summarize the research evidence, and relate the principle to a cognitive science model of learning.

RATIONALE

For hundreds of years, words—including spoken and printed words—have been the main medium for instruction. Research on academic learning has also focused on verbal learning. However, my interest in multimedia learning is motivated by the idea that pictures—including illustrations, photos, animation, and video—offer a complementary medium that may be particularly well suited for helping people understand causal explanations of how things work. Recent advances in computer-based graphics—including stunning pictures and interactive simulations—further heighten my interest in the proposition that pictures can add value to words in helping people understand explanations. Research on how people learn from graphics and words is not as well developed as research on how people learn from words alone, but such research is needed in light of the potential power of graphics to foster understanding. This chapter provides an overview of one research program intended to understand how people learn from words and pictures.

Example

In our research, we have focused on multimedia instructional messages designed to explain how some mechanical, physical, biological, or mathematical system works. For example, suppose you received a 45-second narrated animation on human respiration that showed the steps in the processing with animation and described the steps in spoken words (see Mayer & Sims, 1994, Fig. 6). This is a multimedia message because it includes both words (i.e., spoken words, as indicated in the quotation marks) and pictures (i.e., an animation, as indicated in the selected frames). This is an instructional message because it is intended to help people learn (i.e., to help people understand how the human respiratory system works). To assess how well people learn, we ask transfer questions, such as, "Suppose you are a scientist trying to improve the human respiratory system. How could you get more oxygen into the bloodstream faster?" or "Not enough oxygen is getting to the brain and a person is about to faint. What could be wrong with the respiratory system?" Transfer questions assess how well the learner can apply the learned material to new situations. In this chapter, I focus on transfer test performance because I am mainly interested in how to use graphics to improve people's understanding of scientific explanations.

As another example, suppose you are sitting at a computer that is running an interactive simulation aimed at teaching how an electric motor works (see Mayer, Dow, & Mayer, 2003, Fig. 1). The screen shows a graphic representation of the inside of an electric motor, and you may click on any part—such as the battery, wires, commutator, wire loop, or magnet. Then, a list of questions appears, and you can click on any question. In response, an animated character named Dr. Phyz appears on the screen and provides an answer in words along with corresponding changes in the electric motor. You can click on any part and any question as many times as needed. Some transfer questions used to assess learning are, "What could you do to reverse the movement of the electric motor, that is, to make the wire loop rotate in the opposite direction?" or "Suppose you switch on an electric motor, but nothing happens. What could have gone wrong?"

Theory

I begin with three theoretical assumptions derived from cognitive science theories of learning—the dual channel assumption, the limited capacity assumption, and the active learning assumption. Drawing on Paivio's dual coding theory (1986; Sadoski & Paivio, 2001) and Baddeley's (1986, 1999) working memory theory, the dual channel assumption is that humans have separate information processing channels for verbal and pictorial material. As information impinges on the learner's sense receptors, the eyes and the ears constitute two separate input channels—visual and auditory. As information is processed in working memory, it may be represented verbally or pictorially and processed in separate verbal and pictorial processing channels. Good instructional design makes efficient use of both information-processing channels.

Drawing on Sweller's (1999) cognitive load theory and Baddeley's (1986, 1999) working memory theory, the limited capacity assumption is that learners are able to hold and process only a limited amount of material in each channel. Learning is hindered when the amount of required cognitive processing exceeds the available cognitive capacity. Good instructional design is sensitive to the need to not overload working memory, that is, to the idea that the required cognitive processing in an instructional episode should not exceed the learner's cognitive capacity.

Drawing on Wittrock's (1989) generative theory and Mayer's (1996, 2003) select-organize-integrate (SOI) model of learning, the active processing assumption is that learners must engage in relevant cognitive processing for meaningful learning to occur. These cognitive processes include selecting relevant information from what is presented for further processing, organizing the selected material into a coherent cognitive structure, and integrating the material with existing knowledge. Good instructional design is based on the idea that multimedia instructional messages must not only present information to learners, but must also guide their cognitive processing of the presented material.

Figure 21.1 shows a cognitive model of multimedia learning based on these three assumptions. A multimedia instructional message may consist of words (such as spoken text or printed text) and pictures (such as animation). The pictures impinge on the eyes; the spoken words impinge on the ears (or printed words impinge on the eyes). If the learner pays attention to the incoming visual information—pictures (and printed words) entering through the eyes—then some of the visual material will be represented in the visual/pictorial channel of working memory. This process is labeled *selecting images* in Fig. 21.1. If the learner pays attention to the incoming auditory information—spoken words entering through the ears—then some of the auditory material will be represented in the auditory/verbal channel of working memory. This process is labeled *selecting sounds*. Next, indicated by the organizing images arrow, the learner may mentally organize the pictorial images into a coherent mental representation that I call a pictorial model. Similarly, indicated by the organizing sounds arrow, the learner may mentally organize the words (i.e., either spoken words or converted from printed words) into a coherent mental representation that I call a *verbal model*. Finally, the learner builds connections between the pictorial and verbal models as well as between the models constructed in working memory and relevant prior knowledge imported from long-term memory. These processes are indicated by the arrows labeled *integrating* in Fig. 21.1. For meaningful learning to occur, all five cognitive processes must take place. I define meaningful learning as high performance on both retention and transfer tests.

In the following sections, I briefly describe 10 research-based principles for the design of multimedia instructional messages, along with supporting empirical evidence and relevant cognitive theory. In this review, I limit my focus to evidence from computer-based presentations, although book-based presentational also fit my definition of multimedia instructional messages. The 10 principles are listed in Table 21.1.

MULTIMEDIA PRINCIPLE

An important starting point for research on the design of multimedia instructional messages is to determine whether students learn more deeply when appropriate pictures are added to text. To examine this question, I compared the transfer test performance of students who received scientific explanations presented in words—such as spoken text—with that of students who received both words and pictures—such as spoken text with animation. I computed an effect size for each study by subtracting the mean transfer test score of the words-alone group from the mean transfer score of

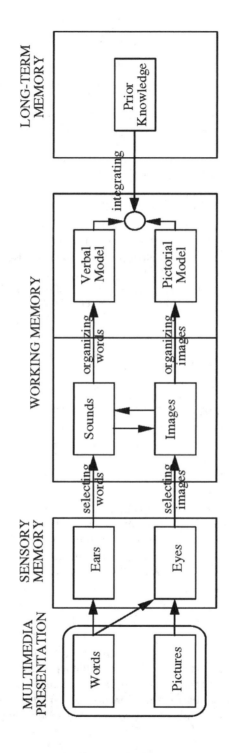

FIG. 21.1. A cognitive model of multimedia learning.

TABLE 21.1

Ten Research-Based Principles of Multimedia Learning

---

1. Multimedia Principle: People learn better from words and pictures than from words alone.

2. Contiguity Principle: People learn better when corresponding words and pictures are presented near rather than far from each other in time or on the screen.

3. Coherence Principle: People learn better when extraneous words, pictures, and sounds are excluded rather than included.

4. Modality Principle: People learn better from words and pictures when words are spoken rather than printed.

5. Redundancy Principle: People learn better from animation and narration than from animation, narration, and on-screen text.

6. Personalization Principle: People learn better when words are presented in conversational style rather than formal style.

7. Voice Principle: People learn better when words are spoken in a nonaccented human voice than in machine voice or accented voice.

8. Signaling Principle: People learn better when the voice signals important words rather than when there are no signals.

9. Interactivity Principle: People learn better when they can control the pace of presentation than when they receive a continuous presentation.

10. Pretraining Principle: People learn better when they receive pretraining on each component rather than no pretraining.

---

the words-and-pictures group and then dividing the result by the standard deviation of the words-alone group. Table 21.2 shows consistent results in favor of the words-and-picture group across five comparisons involving explanations of how a bicycle tire pump works, how a car's braking system works, how lightning storms develop, and how to add and subtract signed numbers. The median effect size was 1.67, indicating a strong effect. I refer to this finding as a *multimedia effect*: People learn better from words and pictures than from words alone.

Let's examine how this finding relates to the cognitive theory of multimedia learning summarized in Fig. 21.1. In the word-alone treatment, learners can engage in the cognitive processes of selecting sounds, organizing sounds, and integrating prior knowledge with a verbal model. The other processes require that the learner build a pictorial model based solely on the presented words, which may be a difficult task for low knowledge learners. In contrast, learners in the words-and-pictures treatment can engage more easily in all five cognitive processes, including building a picto-

TABLE 21.2

Evidence for the Multimedia Principle

Source	Medium	Content	Effect Size
Mayer & Anderson, 1991, Experiment 2a	Screen	Pumps	2.43
Mayer & Anderson, 1992, Experiment 1	Screen	Pumps	1.90
Mayer & Anderson, 1992, Experiment 2	Screen	Brakes	1.67
Moreno & Mayer, 2002b, Experiment 1	Screen	Lightning	0.50
Moreno & Mayer, 1999a, Experiment 1	Game	Arithmetic	0.47
	Median		1.67

rial model and integrating it with the verbal model. Thus, the words-and-pictures group is more likely to understand the explanation.

This research shows that pictures can provide some "value added" to words alone, in terms of improving learners' understanding. However, not all pictures are equally effective so the focus of our research shifts to the question of how to use pictures effectively to promote understanding.

Contiguity Principle

The second principle listed in Table 21.1 concerns the coordination of verbal and pictorial material. For example, in a multimedia lesson explaining how lightning storms develop, we could present corresponding words and pictures simultaneously. In this case, when the narration says, "the negatively charged particles fall to the bottom of the cloud," the animation shows minus signs moving to the bottom of the cloud. Alternatively, we could present corresponding words and pictures successively, such as first presenting the entire narration and then the entire animation (or vice versa).

Do people understand an explanation better when corresponding words and pictures are presented simultaneously or successively? In both cases, identical material is presented. However, according to the cognitive theory of multimedia learning, the simultaneous treatment should lead to deeper understanding than does the successive treatment. This is so because learners in the simultaneous treatment have a better chance to hold corresponding verbal and pictorial representations in their working memory at the same time, thus increasing the chance for integrating them.

My colleagues and I tested this prediction in a series of eight studies in which people learned from narration and animation designed to explain how bicycle tire pumps work, how a car's braking system works, how the human respiratory system works, and how lightning storms develop. As shown in Table 21.3, in all eight comparisons, simultaneous presentation of narration and animation led to better transfer test performance than did successive presentation. The median effect size was 1.30, which is a large effect.

Similarly, when the instructional material consists of on-screen text and animation, people learn better when each sentence is placed next to the action it describes than when it is placed at the bottom of screen (Moreno & Mayer, 1999b, Experiment 1). Thus, the contiguity effect appears to hold both for temporal contiguity (i.e., better learning when corresponding narration and animation are presented simultaneously rather than successively) and for spatial contiguity (i.e., better learning when printed words are placed near rather than far from corresponding portions of pictures on the screen). Overall, people perform substantially better on transfer tests when words and pictures are coordinated in a way that promotes meaningful cognitive processing, such as making connections between corresponding verbal and pictorial representations in working memory. We refer to this finding as the *contiguity principle*: People learn better when corresponding words and pictures are presented near rather than far from each other in time or on the screen.

TABLE 21.3

Evidence for the Contiguity Principle

Source	Medium	Content	Effect Size
Mayer & Anderson, 1991, Experiment 1	Screen	Pumps	1.00
Mayer & Anderson, 1991, Experiment 2	Screen	Pumps	1.05
Mayer & Anderson, 1992, Experiment 1	Screen	Pumps	1.61
Mayer & Anderson, 1992, Experiment 2	Screen	Brakes	1.33
Mayer & Sims, 1994, Experiment 1	Screen	Brakes	0.83
Mayer & Sims, 1994, Experiment 2	Screen	Lungs	1.60
Mayer, Moreno, Boire, & Vagge, 1999, Experiment 1	Screen	Lightning	1.96
Mayer, Moreno, Boire, & Vagge, 1999, Experiment 2	Screen	Brakes	1.27
	Median		1.30

Coherence Principle

The third principle listed in Table 21.1 is the coherence principle, which concerns the role of extraneous material in a multimedia presentation. For example, a narrated animation on lightning formation could be modified by adding interesting but irrelevant sentences and short video clips depicting lightning striking a golfer or spectacular lightning storms in the desert, or by adding background music and environmental sounds. These additional materials can be called *seductive details*—interesting but irrelevant materials intended to make the lesson more enjoyable (Garner, Gillingham, & White, 1989).

Do students learn more deeply when we add seductive details? According to interest theory, the seductive details should increase the learners' level of arousal and therefore result in better learning. Thus, interest theory predicts that adding seductive details will increase performance on the transfer test. According to the cognitive theory of multimedia learning, the seductive details can overload working memory and detract from the process of building a coherent cognitive representation. Thus, the cognitive theory of multimedia learning predicts that adding seductive details will result in lower performance on the transfer test.

To test these predictions, we asked students to view a narrated animation that either had or did not have seductive details—such as several interspersed narrated video clips or background music and environmental sounds. In three out of three studies involving computer-based narrated animation explaining how lightning storms develop and how a car's braking system works, adding interesting but irrelevant material resulted in decreases in transfer test performance as compared to not adding extraneous material. As shown in Table 21.4, the median effect size was .96, which is a large effect.

Similar results were obtained using paper-based presentations, in which adding interesting sentences and photos resulted in poorer transfer test

TABLE 21.4

Evidence for the Coherence Principle

Source	Medium	Content	Effect Size
Mayer, Heiser, & Lonn, 2001, Experiment 1	Screen	Lightning	0.55
Moreno & Mayer, 2000a, Experiment 1	Screen	Lightning	1.27
Moreno & Mayer, 2000a, Experiment 2	Screen	Brakes	0.96
	Median		0.96

performance (Harp & Mayer, 1997, Experiment 1; Harp & Mayer, 1998, Experiments 1, 2, 3, & 4; Mayer, Bove, Bryman, Mars, & Tapangco, 1996, Experiments 1, 2, & 3). In addition, researchers have found that adding interesting but irrelevant facts or stories to a text passage either hurts or does not help students' remembering of the main information in the passage (Garner et al., 1989; Renninger, Hidi, & Krapp, 1992).

Overall, people perform better on transfer tests when extraneous material is excluded from a multimedia instructional message. We refer to this finding as the *coherence principle*: People learn better from a multimedia instructional message when extraneous words, pictures, and sounds are excluded rather than included.

Modality Principle

So far, our three principles suggest that students learn best when concise words and pictures are presented in coordination. Does it matter whether the words are presented as on-screen text—which may be easier to implement on line—or as spoken text. This is the question underlying our examination of the modality principle, listed in the forth line of Table 21.1.

According to an information delivery view of multimedia learning, it should not matter whether words are printed or spoken. As long as people have access to the words, both presentations should result in similar levels of transfer test performance. According to the cognitive theory of multimedia learning, spoken words can result in better understanding—and hence better transfer test performance—than printed words. Printed words can overload the visual channel because the animation and the printed words must compete for attentional resources during learning. When words are presented as spoken text, this offloads some of the cognitive demand from the visual channel to the auditory channel.

In order to test these predictions, my colleagues and I conducted 15 tests of the modality principle in which we compared the transfer test performance of students who received animation with concurrent narration or animation with concurrent on-screen text explaining how lightning works or how brakes work; and we compared the transfer test performance of students who played an environmental science game about plant growth, a physics game about electric motors, or a simulation game about the fuel system of an aircraft in which explanations were presented as animation with concurrent narration or animation with concurrent on-line text. In some cases the game was presented on a desktop computer and in some cases the game was presented in virtual reality with a head-mounted display.

As you can see in Table 21.5, students who received spoken words performed better than students who received printed words in each of the 15 tests we conducted. The median effect size was 1.06, which is a large effect.

TABLE 21.5

Evidence for the Modality Principle

Source	Medium	Content	Effect Size
Mayer & Moreno, 1998, Experiment 1	Screen	Lightning	1.68
Mayer & Moreno, 1998, Experiment 2	Screen	Brakes	0.94
Moreno & Mayer, 1999b, Experiment 1	Screen	Lightning	1.06
Moreno & Mayer, 1999b, Experiment 2	Screen	Lightning	1.28
O'Neil et al., 2000, Experiment 1	VR Game	Aircraft	0.97
Moreno, Mayer, Spires, & Lester, 2001, Experiment 4a	Game	Plants	0.51
Moreno et al., 2001, Experiment 4b	Game	Plants	1.43
Moreno et al., 2001, Experiment 5a	Game	Plants	1.20
Moreno et al., 2001, Experiment 5b	Game	Plants	1.56
Moreno & Mayer, 2002a, Experiment 1a	Game	Plants	0.93
Moreno & Mayer, 2002a, Experiment 1b	VR Game	Plants	0.70
Moreno & Mayer, 2002a, Experiment 2a	Game	Plants	2.08
Moreno & Mayer, 2002a, Experiment 2b	VR Game	Plants	0.67
Moreno & Mayer, 2002a, Experiment 2c	VR Game	Plants	2.94
Mayer, Dow, & Mayer, 2003, Experiment 1	Game	Electric motor	0.86
	Median		1.06

These results provide consistent and strong support for the *modality principle*: People learn better from words and pictures when words are spoken rather than printed.

Redundancy Principle

Given the modality principle, a reasonable next question to ask is whether students learn better from animation, narration, and on-screen text than from animation and narration. On the one hand, giving students the option to focus on spoken or printed words could accommodate individual differences in learning style and thus result in better test performance. In contrast, according to the cognitive theory of multimedia learning, presenting printed text and animation could overload the visual channel and attempts to reconcile the printed and spoken text could waste precious processing capacity. To test these predictions, we conducted a series of related studies involving a narrated animation that explained lightning formation and an environmental science game that explained plant growth (in both desktop and virtual reality formats) in which some students received animation and narration whereas others received animation, narration, and on-screen text. As summarized in Table 21.6, we found evidence for a *redundancy principle*: People learn better from animation and spoken words than from animation, spoken words, and printed words. The median effect size was .69. These results complement the modality principle, and provide additional evidence that when the multimedia presentation is at a fast pace, it is best to minimize the amount of visual material on the screen.

Personalization Principle

The personalization principle, the sixth principle in Table 21.1, is concerned with the way that words are presented in a multimedia presentation. In particular, the personalization principle is concerned with whether it is better to present words in conversational style—using first and second person constructions—or in formal style—using only third person constructions. On the one hand, conversational style may act as another kind of seductive detail that distracts the learner. On the other hand, according to a version of the cognitive theory of multimedia learning, personalization can prime a conversational schema in learners in which they accept the computer as a social partner. When learners view the computer as a social partner, they are more likely to try to understand what the computer is saying to

TABLE 21.6

Evidence for the Redundancy Principle

Source	Medium	Content	Effect Size
Mayer, Heiser, & Lonn, 2001, Experiment 1	Screen	Lightning	0.84
Mayer, Heiser, & Lonn, 2001, Experiment 2	Screen	Lightning	1.65
Moreno & Mayer, 2002b, Experiment 2	Screen	Lightning	0.69
Moreno & Mayer, 2002a, Experiment 2a	Game	Plants	0.16
Moreno & Mayer, 2002a, Experiment 2b	VR Game	Plants	0.22
	Median		0.69

them, thereby engaging in the deeper cognitive processes of organizing and integrating.

In order to test these predictions, my colleagues and I conducted 10 comparisons of the transfer test performance of students who learned from personalized and nonpersonalized words, including narrated animations explaining how lightning works and how the human respiratory system works and an environmental science game (in desktop and virtual reality versions) in which plant growth was explained. For example, in three studies involving a narrated animation of the human respiratory system, the personalization treatment was quite modest—changing the word "the" to "your" in about a dozen places throughout the narration (e.g., saying "your lungs" rather than "the lungs"). As you can see in Table 21.7, in each of the 10 tests, the personalized group performed better on transfer than did the nonpersonalized group, yielding a median effect size of 1.29. There is consistent and strong support for the *personalization principle*: People learn better when words are presented in conversational style rather than in formal style.

TABLE 21.7
Evidence for the Personalization Principle

Source	Medium	Content	Effect Size
Moreno & Mayer, 2000b, Experiment 1	Screen	Lightning	0.96
Moreno & Mayer, 2000b, Experiment 2	Screen	Lightning	1.60
Moreno & Mayer, 2000b, Experiment 3	Game	Plants	1.55
Moreno & Mayer, 2000b, Experiment 4	Game	Plants	1.59
Moreno & Mayer, 2000b, Experiment 5	Game	Plants	0.88
Mayer, Fennell, Farmer, & Campbell, in press, Experiment 1	Screen	Lungs	0.61
Mayer et al., in press, Experiment 2	Screen	Lungs	1.10
Mayer, et al., in press, Experiment 3	Screen	Lungs	0.74
Moreno & Mayer, in press, Experiment 1a	Game	Plants	1.49
Moreno & Mayer, in press, Experiment 1b	VR Game	Plants	2.06
	Median		1.29

Voice Principle

If spoken text is an important element in multimedia presentations, it is useful to explore the role of the speaker's voice. The voice principle is the seventh principle listed in Table 21.1. In particular, we examined the transfer performance of students who received a narrated animation explaining lightning formation in which the words were spoken in a standard accent by a human versus in a Russian accent by a human or in a machine simulated voice. According to the version of the cognitive theory of multimedia learning described in the previous section, a standard accented human voice should be the most likely to prime the conversational schema in learners and thus most likely to lead to deep processing of the presented material.

Table 21.8 summarizes the results of two studies—the first comparing standard accented and Russian accented voices, and the second comparing human and machine voices. As you can see, the standard accented human voice resulted in better transfer test performance across both tests, yielding a median effect size of .78. Although additional research is needed, these results provide preliminary support for the *voice principle*: People learn better when words are spoken with in a nonaccented human voice than in machine voice or accented voice.

Signaling Principle

The eighth principle in Table 21.1 is the signaling principle, which is concerned with highlighting the important aspects of the narration through stress in speech. In particular, consider a narrated animation that explains how airplanes achieve flight. For some learners (i.e., signaled group), the key terms and major ideas were spoken with stronger stress, relational terms such as "as a result" were added, and the key ideas were repeated as headings to each section. For other learners (nonsignaled group), there was no signaling. According to the cognitive theory of multimedia learning, signaling should help guide learners so they select relevant material for further processing in working memory. They, then, could devote more

TABLE 21.8

Evidence for the Voice Principle

Source	Medium	Content	Effect Size
Mayer, Sobko, & Mautone, 2003, Experiment 1	Screen	Lightning	0.81
Mayer, Sobko, & Mautone, 2003, Experiment 2	Screen	Lightning	0.76
	Median		0.78

cognitive capacity to organizing and integrating the material, resulting in better transfer test performance.

Table 21.9 shows that in two tests of this prediction, students performed better on a transfer test when they received a narrated animation using signaled rather than nonsignaled narration. The median effect size is .60. Although more research is needed, these findings provide preliminary support for the *signaling principle*: People learn better when the voice signals important words rather than when there are no signals.

Interactivity Principle

Conventional wisdom is that students learn more deeply when they can interact with the computer rather than when they must passively listen to a multimedia presentation. We examined a straightforward aspect of interactivity by comparing situations in which learners could or could not control the pace of presentation of a narrated animation about lightning, plant growth, or how an electric motor works. For example, for the interactive group, the lightning lesson was broken into 16 segments with a "continue" bottom appearing on the screen after each segment. When the learner clicked on the continue button, the next segment was presented. For the noninteractive group, the narrated animation was presented as a single continuous lesson. According to the cognitive theory of multimedia learning, learner control of pacing could result in deeper understanding especially when the narrated animation is otherwise presented at a fast pace to novices. When students can pause at various points, they are able to engage in cognitive processes such as organizing and integrating a segment of the material before moving on.

Table 21.10 summarizes the transfer test performance of interactive and noninteractive learners across four different experiments. In each comparison, the interactive group performed better than the noninteractive group, yielding a median effect size of .86. Based on these findings, there is evidence for an *interactivity effect*: People learn better when they can control

TABLE 21.9

Evidence for the Signaling Principle

Source	Medium	Content	Effect Size
Mautone & Mayer, 2001, Experiment 3a	Screen	Airplane lift	0.58
Mautone & Mayer, 2001, Experiment 3b	Screen	Airplane lift	0.62
	Median		0.60

TABLE 21.10

Evidence for the Interactivity Principle

Source	Medium	Content	Effect Size
Mayer & Chandler, 2001, Experiment 2	Screen	Lightning	1.36
Moreno et al., 2001, Experiment 3	Game	Plants	0.70
Dow & Mayer, 2003, Experiment 2a	Game	Electric motor	0.70
Dow & Mayer, 2003, Experiment 2b	Game	Electric motor	1.03
	Median		0.86

the pace of presentation than when they receive a continuous presentation. Although learner control of pacing may be helpful, additional research is needed to determine if other forms of interactivity are equally beneficial.

Pretraining Principle

The learners in almost all of the studies reported so far were first-year college students or high-school students who lacked rich prior knowledge about the material in the multimedia lessons. Does providing pretraining in some of the background material help students understand causal explanations from subsequent multimedia presentations? This is the issue underlying the pretraining principle in the Table 21.3.

For example, suppose we present students with a narrated animation explaining how a car's braking system works. Before the presentation, we introduce the learner to each part of the system and its behavior—for example, the piston in the master cylinder can move forward or backward, the brake fluid can be compressed or uncompressed, the brake shoe can press or not press against the drum, and so on. The words and images in the pretraining are identical to those in the narrated animation.

According to the cognitive theory of multimedia learning, such pretraining can reduce the cognitive load in working memory, freeing cognitive capacity to be used for organizing and integrating the material. This deeper cognitive processing would result in better transfer test performance. To test this prediction, in five experiments, we compared a pretrained group that received brief descriptions of the parts of the system, with a nonpretrained group that did not. The content included brakes, pumps, and a geology game.

As you can see in Table 21.11, in each of five tests, the pretrained group outperformed the nonpretrained group on the transfer test, yielding a median effect size of .91. These consistent findings provide evidence for the *pretraining principle*: People learn better when they receive pretraining on each component rather than no pretraining.

CONCLUSION

The major goal of this chapter is to show that there is an emerging set of research-based principles that can be helpful in guiding the design of Web-based instruction. The 10 principles listed in Table 21.1 represent the fruits of a 15-year research program at the University of California, Santa Barbara. The consistency and strength of the current evidence supporting each principle encourage the prospect that continued research on the design of Web-based instruction will be fruitful. Importantly, the results are consistent with the cognitive theory of multimedia learning summarized in Fig. 21.1 (see also Mayer, in press).

Clearly, this review was confined to my research program, which focuses mainly on multimedia instructional messages that explain how things work. The research consisted mainly of short-term studies, often with college students in laboratory settings, testing short narrated animations as stand-along messages or within the context of computer games and simulations. We limited our focus to learning outcomes involving conceptual knowledge (i.e., the construction of mental models of how systems work) and relied mainly on tests of problem-solving transfer as our measures of learning. Thus, further research is needed to determine the applicability of the 10 principles in other contexts. For example, Sweller (1999) has provided evidence for some of the same principles—such as modality, contigu-

TABLE 21.11

Evidence for the Pretraining Principle

Source	Medium	Content	Effect Size
Mayer, Mathias, & Wetzell, 2002, Experiment 1	Screen	Brakes	0.91
Mayer, Mathias, & Wetzell, 2002, Experiment 2	Screen	Brakes	1.53
Mayer, Mathias, & Wetzell, 2002, Experiment 3	Screen	Pumps	1.03
Mayer, Mautone, & Prothero, 2002, Experiment 2	Game	Geology	0.59
Mayer, Mautone, & Prothero, 2002, Experiment 3	Game	Geology	0.75
	Median		0.91

ity, and coherence—in studies involving other contexts, including students in schools and workers in industrial training programs.

Advances in computer and communication technologies provide opportunities for the creation of Web-based learning environments. The major challenge facing instructional designers concerns the degree to which these emerging Web-based learning environments can be designed in ways that foster productive learning. In my opinion, educational psychology has something useful to offer in the struggle to create productive Web-based learning environments. Overall, this chapter demonstrates that the design of Web-based learning environments can be guided by reliable research evidence and a cognitive theory of how people learn.

ACKNOWLEDGMENTS

Preparation of this chapter was supported by a grant from the Office of Naval Research.

REFERENCES

Baddeley, A. (1986). *Working memory*. Oxford, England: Oxford University Press.

Baddeley, A. (1999). *Human memory*. Boston: Allyn & Bacon.

Garner, R., Gillingham, M., & White, C. (1989). Effects of seductive details on macroprocessing and microprocessing in adults and children. *Cognition and Instruction, 6*, 41–57.

Harp, S. F., & Mayer, R. E. (1997). The role of interest in learning from scientific text and illustrations: On the distinction between emotional interest and cognitive interest. *Journal of Educational Psychology, 89*, 92–102.

Harp, S. F., & Mayer, R. E. (1998). How seductive details do their damage: A theory of cognitive interest in science learning. *Journal of Educational Psychology, 90*, 414–434.

Mautone, P. D., & Mayer, R. E. (2001). Signaling as a cognitive guide in multimedia learning. *Journal of Educational Psychology, 93*, 377–389.

Mayer, R. E. (1996). Learning strategies for making sense of expository text: The SOI model for guiding three cognitive processes in knowledge construction. *Educational Psychology Review, 8*, 357–371.

Mayer, R. E. (2001). *Multimedia learning*. New York: Cambridge University Press.

Mayer, R. E. (2002). Multimedia learning. *Psychology of Learning and Motivation, 41*, 85–140.

Mayer, R. E. (2003). *Learning and instruction*. Upper Saddle River, NJ: Prentice Hall.

Mayer, R. E. (Ed.). (in press). *Cambridge handbook of multimedia learning*. New York: Cambridge University Press.

Mayer, R. E., & Anderson, R. B. (1991). Animations need narrations: An experimental test of a dual-coding hypothesis. *Journal of Educational Psychology, 83*, 484–490.

Mayer, R. E., & Anderson, R. B. (1992). The instructive animation: Helping students build connections between words and pictures in multimedia learning. *Journal of Educational Psychology, 84*, 444–452.

Mayer, R. E., Bove, W., Bryman, A., Mars, R., & Tapangco, L. (1996). When less is more: Meaningful learning from visual and verbal summaries of science textbooks. *Journal of Educational Psychology, 88*, 64–73.

Mayer, R. E., & Chandler, P. (2001). When learning is just a click away: Does simple user interaction foster deeper understanding of multimedia messages? *Journal of Educational Psychology, 93*, 390–397.

Mayer, R. E., Dow, G. T., & Mayer, S. (2003). Multimedia learning in an interactive self-explaining environment: What works in the design of agent-based microworlds? *Journal of Educational Psychology, 95*, 806–813.

Mayer, R. E., Fennell, S., Farmer, L., & Campbell, J. (in press). A personalization effect in multimedia learning: Students learn better when words are presented in conversational style rather than formal style. *Journal of Educational Psychology, 96*.

Mayer, R. E., Heiser, J., & Lonn, S. (2001). Cognitive constraints on multimedia learning: When presenting more material results in less understanding. *Journal of Educational Psychology, 93*, 187–198.

Mayer, R. E., Mathias, A., & Wetzell, K. (2002). Fostering understanding of multimedia messages through pre-training: Evidence for a two-stage theory of mental model construction. *Journal of Experimental Psychology: Applied, 8*, 147–154.

Mayer, R. E., Mautone, P., & Prothero, W. (2002). Pictorial aids for learning by doing in a multimedia geology simulation game. *Journal of Educational Psychology, 94*, 171–185.

Mayer, R. E., & Moreno, R. (1998). A split attention effect in multimedia learning: Evidence for dual processing systems in working memory. *Journal of Educational Psychology, 90*, 312–320.

Mayer, R. E., Moreno, R., Boire, M., & Vagge, S. (1999). Maximizing constructivist learning from multimedia communications by minimizing cognitive load. *Journal of Educational Psychology, 91*, 638–643.

Mayer, R. E., & Sims, V. K. (1994). For whom is a picture worth a thousand words? Extensions of a dual-coding theory of multimedia learning. *Journal of Educational Psychology, 84*, 389–401.

Mayer, R. E., Sobko, K., & Mautone, P. D. (2003). Social cues in multimedia learning: Role of speaker's voice. *Journal of Educational Psychology, 95*, 419–425.

Moreno, R., & Mayer, R. E. (1999a). Multimedia-supported metaphors for meaning making in mathematics. *Cognition and Instruction, 17*, 215–248.

Moreno, R., & Mayer, R. (1999b). Cognitive principles of multimedia learning: The role of modality and contiguity. *Journal of Educational Psychology, 91*, 358–368.

Moreno, R., & Mayer, R. E. (2000a). A coherence effect in multimedia learning: The case for minimizing irrelevant sounds in the design of multimedia instructional messages. *Journal of Educational Psychology, 92*, 117–125.

Moreno, R., & Mayer, R. E. (2000b). Engaging students in active learning: The case for personalized multimedia messages. *Journal of Educational Psychology, 92*, 724–733.

Moreno, R., & Mayer, R. E. (2002a). Learning science in virtual reality multimedia environments: Role of methods and media. *Journal of Educational Psychology, 94*, 598–610.

Moreno, R. E., & Mayer, R. E. (2002b). Verbal redundancy in multimedia learning: When reading helps listening. *Journal of Educational Psychology, 94*, 156–163.

Moreno, R., & Mayer, R. E. (in press). Personalized messages that promote science learning in virtual environments. *Journal of Educational Psychology, 96*.

Moreno, R., Mayer, R. E., Spires, H. A., & Lester, J. (2001). The case for social agency in computer-based teaching: Do students learn more deeply when they interact with animated pedagogical agents? *Cognition and Instruction, 19,* 177–213.

O'Neil, H. F., Mayer, R. E., Herl, H., Niemi, C., Olin, K., & Thurman, R. A. (2000). Instructional strategies for virtual environments. In H. F. O'Neil & D. H. Andrews (Eds.), *Aircraft training: Methods, technologies, and assessment* (pp. 105–130). Mahwah, NJ: Lawrence Erlbaum Associates.

Paivio, A. (1986). *Mental representations.* New York: Oxford University Press.

Renninger, K. A., Hidi, S., & Krapp, A. (Eds.). (1992). *The role of interest in learning and development.* Hillsdale, NJ: Lawrence Erlbaum Associates.

Sadoski, M., & Paivio, A. (2001). *Imagery and text.* Mahwah, NJ: Lawrence Erlbaum Associates.

Sweller, J. (1999). *Instructional design in technical areas.* Camberwell, Australia: ACER Press.

Wittrock, M. C. (1989). Generative processes of comprehension. *Educational Psychologist, 24,* 345–376.

SUMMARY AND CONCLUSIONS

Chapter 22

Summary and Conclusions

Ray S. Perez
Office of Naval Research

John Cherniavsky
National Science Foundation

Eric R. Hamilton
U.S. Air Force Academy

The purpose of this chapter is to summarize the preceding chapters, highlight important issues in each chapter, draw some general conclusions, and suggest some future research and development (R&D). The summaries follow the order of the chapters in this book. The book is divided into two major sections: Policy, practice, and implementation issues; and theory and research issues. Thus, the summaries of the chapters are also divided into two major sections. This chapter concludes with some research suggestions for Web-based learning.

POLICY, PRACTICE, AND IMPLEMENTATION ISSUES

Drs. Baker (a Professor of Education at UCLA/CRESST) and O'Neil (a Professor of Education at USC/CRESST) in their chapter describe Web-based evaluation, how it could work, and at what points of entry the process may begin. They first describe nine overlapping conceptions of Web-based learning. The conceptions ranged from more formal uses to environments where learning is incidental to achieving other goals. After the discussion of the overlapping terms, they then offer some clarification of terms used in the Web-based learning domain including summative evaluation, formative evaluation, developmental testing, performance, and assessment. Using these conceptions and terms, they offer goals for the evaluation of Web-based instruction that result in either systematic studies or post hoc evaluations. They suggest that a clear direction to start is that the evaluation should be able to authenticate claims that the provided interactions result in planned outcomes; that is, the allegations that students learned something are supported. With this in mind, when they consider different types of evaluation practice, they did so by linking them to the nine types of evaluation mentioned earlier. In addition, a few key precepts on avoiding studies that damage interventions and innovations and poison the well for new settings or users of technology of learning are also proposed. In the end, they suggest several kinds of evaluation design architectures.

Dr. Kenneth Lane and Mr. Steve Hull, California State University, San Bernardino, in their chapter addresses the state of infrastructure to support Web-based learning. Perhaps the most revealing aspect of their analysis of present Web-based learning systems is that there are no "turn key" systems commercially available. The consequence of this is that institutions have to purchase components, such as content management, portal systems, authoring tools, and back-end student record systems separately and then try to "glue" them together into an integrated and stable system. According to these authors, much time, effort, and variety of support are required to make these systems work and "talk" to other systems.

Dr. J. D. Fletcher, Senior Researcher, Institute for Defense Analyses, begins his chapter with a description of the goals and objectives of the Department of Defense's advanced distributive learning (ADL) initiative. ADL should enable education, training materials, and performance aiding to be readily accessible, anytime, anywhere. This is to be accomplished by developing all courseware to be compliant with the sharable content objective reference model (SCORM). SCORM is an evolving specification for creating instructional courseware units called instructional objects.

Fletcher lays out a vision of the future of Web-based learning as ADL evolves, which included the development and evolution of three technologies. For example, the development of the global information grid is seen as providing the infrastructure populated with a multitude of reusable instructional objects. Servers in this vision are the key component that will have the capability to facilitate searching (e.g., a semantic Web), locating, and assembling instructional objects into education and training materials to support interactions with learners. What would future instruction delivered by these technologies look like? To Fletcher, instruction over the Web would resemble an intelligent tutoring system that engages learners in a set of conversations. These conversations would draw on effective instructional strategies, accurate representations of the user, and comprehensive representations of relevant subject matter.

Dr. Ruimin Shen is the Director of the School of Network Education at Shanghai Jiao Tong University, China. He and his coauthors, Fan Yang and Peng Han also of Shanghai Jiao Tong University, describe an "Open Learning Model for Web-Based Learning Architecture." There are three general themes guiding the development of this system, "Everything is easy, everything is available, and everyone is different."

Everything is easy consists of tools to enable teachers to make the development and delivery of Web-based learning easy. The rationale is if you make the transition from traditional lectures to Web-based learning difficult, traditional teachers will not participate. Examples of tools designed to make Web-based courseware easy range from the use of compression programs to store data to tools for capturing audio and video content from a class session.

For everything is available, tools are made available to teachers and students to make instructional content accessible using search tools and content-based indexing and retrieval systems for audio and tutorial material. An example of an interest tool is a computer program that deals with the problem of providing real-time feedback to students' questions. The solution they developed is a key-word matching algorithm that matches a question to an answer, enabling the instructor to answer questions in real time.

For everyone is different, they created a data analysis center that uses a learning specification based on an analysis of learner attributes and learning behaviors. They introduce the notion of the assessment of a student's "knowledge point." A knowledge point is a measure of the keyword or concept being presented in the courseware and can be measured in two ways as an interest or mastery measure.

Dr. Ann Majchrzak is a Professor in the Department of Information and Operations Management, Marshall School of Business, University of Southern California, and Dr. Cynthia Mathis Beath is on the faculty in the Department of Management and Information Systems at the University of Texas. In their chapter, they outline a process for the development of information age software. They argue that today's software development focuses on developing cross-functional and cross-firm information systems for strategic and innovative uses. Thus, the software requires the involvement of a more diverse set of stakeholders than previously. However, the authors point out that there is a lack of theory-based advice on how to structure encounters between stakeholders and developers. The authors offer a framework for conducting research in this area, as well as to guide the development of software.

Drs. Hamilton (U.S. Air Force Academy) and Cherniavsky (National Science Foundation) in their chapter present a method for characterizing

Web-based learning platforms and communications. This method consists of a series of questions along several dimensions. These include control of the learning activities, who or what is in charge of the learning; communication bandwidth, how much information can be transmitted and/or retained and in what time frame; granularity of the information to be shared, what is the content level–symbols, information, knowledge–of the shared information; representation forms of the shared knowledge, such as text, graphics, animation, sound, video, and so forth; persistence of knowledge representations in the learning environments, are artifacts readily available to participants in the learning environments; pedagogical frameworks that characterize the learning environment, is it preassembled, constructed individually, and so forth. The authors applied these dimensions to distinguish between Web-based learning (WBL) and face-to-face (F2F) classrooms. One of the most interesting ideas is that one can use these dimensions to characterize the degree of proximity between F2F and WBL environments.

Dr. Ray S. Perez is a Program officer at the Office of Naval Research, Dr. Wayne Gray is on the faculty in the Department of Cognitive Psychology Rensselaer Polytechnic Institute, and Mr. Tom Reynolds is a Human Factors Engineer with Serco North America. The chapter by Perez, Gray, and Reynolds presents a review of the literature on virtual environments, or virtual reality (VR), and suggests how VR might be incorporated in Web-based learning. VR as a teaching and learning environment is seen as a promising but an emerging technology in that there is little empirical work as to its effectiveness. Although some research of the effectiveness of VR has been conducted in the military, much less has been conducted on educational VR systems and the empirical results are mixed. The minimal number of research studies on the impact of VR systems on learning is reflective of the current immaturity of this training technology. For example, immersion and presence are key design variables for VR developers. However, very little data have been collected to support the learning value of these concepts regarding learning. Given the limited bandwidth of current Web-based systems, the use of VR as a training and education technology in this environment is not considered likely in the near future. Recommendations for the future include more rigorous research to determine what, if any, variables account for VR learning.

The chapter by Clark (University of Southern California), Bewley (UCLA/CRESST), and O'Neil (USC/CRESST) describe a relatively simple but powerful procedure for making a cost-beneficial decision between the classroom and a distance delivery platform for any one course. In general, they discuss that most media selection models suggest appropriately that such selection of media should be delayed until the end of the design process and before the development of instructional materials. However, they note that this rarely occurs and often the media selection precedes the design process. The media selection process for selecting between Web-based learning (WBL) and traditional classroom instruction (F2F) consists of a series of questions—can both WBL and F2F simulate all of the necessary conditions in the job setting; provide immediate (synchronous) and delayed (asynchronous) information and corrective feedback needed to achieve the learning objectives; provide the necessary sensory mode of information (visual, aural, kinesthetic, olfactory, tactile) required to achieve all learning objectives? If both WBL and F2F can meet these criteria, then one should consider cost factors and conduct a cost-per-student and value-enhanced cost analysis. Procedures for conducting this cost analysis are also presented in the form of a job aid.

Dr. Susan Chipman is a Program Officer at the Office of Naval Research. Her chapter begins by questioning what is advanced in advanced distributive learning (ADL). She points out that the SCORM specification for creating instructional courseware constrains the development of Web-based intelligent tutors that she considers the most advanced form of individualized instruction. For example, the most recent version of SCORM (Version 1.2) has enabled the capability for branching of instruction in response to student performance, a type of individualization of instruction that has been available in computer-based instruction (CBT) since the late 1950s. Current commercial authoring tools originally developed for the creation of computer-based instruction have been simplified for use on the Web resulting in the elimination of much of the flexibility and capability to produce individualized instruction and instead have produced what she terms Web-based "page turners." For example, Chipman points out the CBT and SCORM have presented problems for the implementation of diagnosis of student errors and have prevented the implementation of sophisticated instructional approaches, such as intelligent tutors. Chipman, much like Fletcher, envisions Web-based instruction as having the potential to deliver intelligent tutor systems with such advanced features as interactive intelligent simulations and coaches, natural language dialogues, and speech recognition and generation.

Dr. Wayne Zachary is President of CHI Systems, Inc., and Christopher McCollum, Jennifer McNamara, and James Stokes are also of CHI Systems. Dr. Elizabeth Blickensderfer is on the faculty in the Human Factors and Systems Department at Embry-Riddle Aeronautical University, and Dr. Janet Schofield is a Senior Researcher at the Learning Research and Development Center, University of Pittsburgh. Their chapter on the employment of Web-based learning is interesting in that it is one of a few efforts that has attempted to study the implementation process per se of Web-based learning. They appropriately point out that if the technology cannot be successfully employed, the expected benefits (e.g., cost saving) are reduced or never realized and can result in wasted investment of time, money, and effort. Employment is defined as the process of successfully applying Web-based learning to training. Not only is there a lack of research in this area but there is even less information on what employability of Web-based learning entails. The chapter's overall goal is to present practical advice and procedures to support employment of Web-based training. It describes the results of a 3-year study, providing three examples to illustrate what can go wrong when employment issues are not handled effectively, identifying issues that are central to successful employment, and providing a description of employment guidelines and support tools to facilitate the effective use of a Web-based training system.

THEORY AND RESEARCH ISSUES

Dr. Myron H. Dembo and Ms. Linda Gubler Junge of the University of Southern California, and Dr. Richard Lynch of Woosong University, South Korea, begin their chapter by citing dropout rates as high as 70%–80% for some Web-based university courses (Martinez, 2003). They discuss three categories of factors that predict dropout rates in Web-based learning. These factors are student factors (e.g., educational preparation, motivation, and persistence attributes); situational factors (e.g., family support and changes in life circumstances); and educational system factors (e.g., quality and difficulty level of instructional materials, quality and availability of instructional feedback). They focus on student factors, or the skills of students who are successful Web-based learners. These skills revolve around the notion of self-regulation. Self-regulation consists of six components; motive (how learners self-motivate), method (how learners self-regulate), time (how learners manage study time), environment (where the learners study and the available instructional supports), social environment, and performance (how learners monitor their learning). These six components are all grounded in theory, have metrics, and are argued that they can be taught. For students to do well in Web-based environments, they must be independent learners, be motivated, have self-regulation and time-management skills, and be able to monitor their learning.

   Dr. Sigmund Tobias is a faculty member of the Institute for Urban and Minority Education Teachers College, Columbia University. In his chapter, the author addresses a much often neglected area of research: The relationship between cognitive and affective variables in Web-based learning environments. More specifically, Tobias focuses on the relationship between important variables such as metacognition, motivation, and help-seeking behaviors. He argues that one reason that there is a high attrition rate for WBL as compared to traditional instruction (F2F) is that the instructional supports that are generally found in traditional education are not found in WBL. Moreover, he argues that there is a need to re-search the relationship between cognitive (metacognition) and affective variables (motivation and help-seeking behavior), which is essential to the design of a help system for WBL (extra help, prompts, hot buttons, and links to instructional resources).

Metacognitive processes may be specifically important in the WBL environment where a great deal of new material must be acquired with relatively little support. Students who are able to evaluate their own progress, select appropriate learning strategies, and plan more efficiently are likely to be more successful in a WBL environment than students who do not have these processes. Students who accurately differentiate between the known and the unknown have an advantage because they can omit, or skim the familiar and concentrate on what they do not know. Lastly, the author provides a discussion of existing methods for assessing metacognitive skills. He suggests a more direct measure is the knowledge monitoring assessment (KMA) test that is more reliable and valid.

Dr. Adrienne Lee is an Associate Professor in the Department of Psychology at New Mexico State University, Las Cruces. In her chapter, she addresses several issues with respect to the development and delivery of Web-based learning. These experiments not only involve participation of individual subjects but also groups and teams. This research is interesting in that not much research exists in the use of WBL for training teams and groups.

The first series of studies were based on the theory that individual students could benefit from the use of WBL tutors to supplement learning outside the classroom. Rather than using multiple choice, fill-in-the-blank, and traditional true-and-false test items, they chose to use essay questions to measure student learning. They used a new machine learning technology to automate the evaluation of their students' essays; latent semantic analysis (LSA).

The results of a series of studies indicate that learning is increased when Web-based tutors are used and that the learning of individual students receiving essay questions was superior to that of students who received multiple choice questions. The second series of experiments involved training and groups, either face-to-face or WBL (learning at a distance) conditions. Results indicate that WBL teams learned more quickly (reached asymptote) than colocated teams even though all received the same amount of training regardless of whether they were in WBL or colocated teams.

Drs. Chuang and O'Neil, both of the University of California Los Angeles/ CRESST, in their chapter research the role of feedback on a computer-based collaborative problem solving task involving searching. They extend the R&D of Hsieh and O'Neil (2002). By teaching searching strategies and by providing different types of feedback, Chuang and O'Neil explore the effects of teamwork and problem-solving processes on knowledge mapping performance with two different types of feedback (adapted knowledge of response feedback and task-specific adapted knowledge of response feedback).

Results show that task-specific adapted knowledge of response feedback was significantly more beneficial to group outcome than adapted knowledge of response feedback. In addition, problem-solving process, information seeking including request of feedback, browsing, searching for information, and searching using Boolean operators were all significantly related to group outcome for both groups. The study suggests that computer-based performance assessment in collaborative problem solving was effective. In this study, collaboration was effectively measured, that is, administered, scored, and reported by computer.

Dr. Allen Munro, Mr. Surmon, and Mr. Pizzini (of Behavioral Technology Laboratories at the University of Southern California) discuss the role and importance of procedural knowledge in troubleshooting Web-based applications and provide information for instructional designers for those applications. They describe procedural learning within the context of maintenance training. They argue that there are cognitive components of procedural learning and that these components along with procedural knowledge can be taught in a practice environment that provides an opportunity for interactive practice in the context of a functionally realistic task environment, such as a graphical simulation. These graphical simulations are dynamic and mimic the behavior of real hardware systems. The authors argue that complex skills and knowledge required to perform complicated maintenance tasks can be taught through the use of distance learning technology, with the exception of certain types of procedures where specialized motor skills must be learned.

They describe several tools they have developed for building these online intelligent simulations. These intelligent simulations include in their design special instructional modes, special types of assessments, and microassessments. They introduce the notion of "instructional primitives of procedural learning," which are instructional interactions called "primitives" that are essential in providing instruction to the student through simulations. These eight "instructional primitives" are lower level tactics and strategies used to teach procedures and are presented to provide guidance to developers.

Dr. John Sweller is a Professor in the School of Education at the University of South Wales, Sydney, Australia. In his chapter, he explores an analogy between biological evolution and brain development to support guidance in the instructional design of Web-based learning systems. He suggests that the human cognitive architectures are universal and that they have been shaped by the same biological evolutionary forces such as natural selection. Drawing from the research on human memory and on the human genome and reasoning that these psychological structures and processes are analogous to biological structures, he then argues for the inclusion and importance of human memory limitations in the design of instructional materials. His "cognitive load theory" suggests that instructional materials that put a heavy burden on student's working memory will inhibit learning. Cognitive load theory describes how instruction should be organized in order to take into account the limitations of the human cognitive architecture, working memory. He presents nine examples of instructional design principles that are based on research on cognitive load theory and that have important implications for instructional design. For example, one principle is the problem completion effect—where a partially worked problem is presented the student is asked to complete.

David Wiley (Utah State University) provides an extensive discussion of a taxonomy of Web-based learning systems, particularly those systems that support online self-organization. His chapter discusses scalability and sociability in online learning environments. He points out that the achievement of higher order learning outcomes requires social interaction to be an integral part of the learning experience. As institutions seek to scale their educational offerings over great distances to large numbers of people, social interaction has traditionally been seen as too expensive to include. While the automation or dehumanization of online courses does improve their scalability, it also hampers their ability to facilitate these inherently social higher order learning outcomes. One method of keeping both the scalability and sociability is online self-organizing social systems. Such systems are considered an important key to scalable online programs that are capable of facilitating the mastery of learning outcomes across the entire range of learning outcomes. Dr. Wiley describes a pilot project in which such software is integrated with seven collections of course material from MIT's OpenCourseWare.

Dr. Klaus Breuer and Dr. Rene Molkenthin are on the faculty of the Johannes Gutenberg-Universität Mainz, Germany, and Dr. Robert D. Tennyson is a Professor of Educational Psychology, University of Minnesota. In this chapter, they propose a theoretical framework for the integration of Web-based simulations with learning theories. This framework maps principles of learning (e.g., authentic problems in a situated orientation) to objectives (e.g., applicability of new knowledge). This framework is refined by examples of WBL drawn from the use of simulations in their existing WBL environments. The authors' goal in this chapter is not to show how to design simulations for Web-based learning but rather to describe the use of simulators in their research to study human problem-solving abilities. The study of human problem-solving abilities was accomplished by exposing students to complex, dynamic environments that vary from simple role-playing exercises to microworlds and observing their behavior. They describe six approaches to computer-based simulations; technical simulations, business simulations, modeling, case studies, microworlds, and animations (role-playing exercises can be either computer based or not). These six approaches have two features in common: They allow the learner to explore decision-making outcomes; and second, the problem-solving space is free of risks for the learner (e.g., errors may be experienced without the associated costs). They discuss the characteristics of problem-oriented learning activities to be included in these simulations.

Dr. Lisa Neal is the Editor-in-Chief of eLearn Magazine, and Dr. Diane Miller is a research scientist at Aptima Inc. Their chapter surveys the spectrum of information technology applications in schools and universities including Web-based learning (WBL). For example, the usage in classrooms of computers has shifted from activities such as installing and using word processors, making spreadsheets, building overhead slides, and using educational software available on CD-ROM, to the use of Web browsers to search the Web for educational resources (e.g., Web sites), access information online, and take online courses. Perhaps the most influential impact of this connectivity is that it enables students to participate in online courses or e-learning, although such usage is currently minimal.

An interesting question raised by these authors is what is the impact of computer use on student achievement. They cite a U.S. Department of Education study (USDoE, 2001) that attempted to examine the impact of computer usage time on academic achievement on 8th and 12th graders. They compared students using a computer to write reports to those who did not and found significant differences favoring the computer group. However, it is hard to draw conclusions from this one study; many more carefully controlled studies have been done to demonstrate the influence of computers on achievement (see for a discussion of the evidence for the impact of technology, Fletcher, 2003; Kulik, 1994, meta-analysis).

Dr. Richard Clark, Dr. David Feldon, Mr. Keith Howard, and Ms. Sunhee Choi, all of the Rossier School of Education, University of Southern California, present a review of the recent research in cognitive-based learning and motivation that has implications for the design of Web-based learning. The topics reviewed include advances in teaching expertise in distance learning; a reflective expertise model approach to achieving transfer; evidence for the use of animated pedagogical agents to provide help in Web-based learning; and tailoring Web-based learning materials for different types of learners. One of the most interesting topics is the five recommended core design (first) principles to teach complex knowledge and skills. They conclude their chapter with suggestions for future research.

The instructional design model for teaching complex knowledge and skills they propose is Jeron van Merriënboer's 4C/ID model (van Merriënboer, Clark, & de Croock, 2002). This model suggests that in order to achieve successful performance, a student must not only be taught to perform simple component tasks but it is essential that students execute these tasks in a prescribed order. They also identify five core design (first) principles to be used in the design to teach complex knowledge and skills. Areas suggested for future research include cognitive task analysis to capture knowledge that supports the development of expertise and the development of techniques and methods to foster the acquisition of adaptive expertise.

Dr. Richard Mayer is a Professor in the Department of Psychology at the University of California, Santa Barbara. He provides in his chapter an elegant and extensive discussion of cognitive science principles that should inform the design of multimedia Web-based instructional systems. Each principle is described with examples of the research, and a summary of the research evidence supporting the principle with an effect size and relating the principle to a cognitive model of learning.

The author also describes three theoretical assumptions that form the basis of his cognitive model. These are Paivio's dual coding theory (Paivio, 1986; Sadoski & Paivio, 2001), Baddeley's (1986, 1999) working memory theory, and Sweller's (1999) cognitive load theory. Briefly, these theories' assumptions state that verbal and visual sensory channels do not interfere, that there is limited processing capability in each channel, and finally, that learners must engage in relevant cognitive processing for learning to occur.

R & D: NEXT STEPS

Although the authors of the chapters provide, in general, a comprehensive state-of-the-art presentation of the theories, research, and practice currently influencing the development of Web-based learning systems, much is yet to be done. Among the topics that require further research is the basic cognitive research on how people learn, remember, and perform with implications for Web-based education/training. This is reflected in many of the specific research topics later.

These topics include research in technical innovations such as exploration and development of prototypes of new technologies (e.g., automated knowledge representation tools, the automatic generation of objectives, the automatic generation of answers to student questions in real time); object-based design and development tools; tools for supporting collaboration for distributed learning; and assessment and diagnostic tools for continuous assessment of student/user interactions.

Additionally, system tools that are needed include security tools for identification and authentication of learners; Web-based server services; authoring tools for delivery and assessment; tools for assembling objects tailored to dynamic representations of learner needs and abilities; and methods for "hardening" of prototypes that are open source.

Instructional design models are needed to teach complex cognitive tasks and skills at a distance and to support the retention of these perishable skills, and Web-based evaluation research is needed that focuses on Kilpatrick's levels III & IV evaluations and that focuses on in-school studies. New models of learning based on technology (e.g., virtual collaboration, asynchronous communications) are also needed to inform pedagogy in instruction using Web-based learning systems.

Lastly, and perhaps more importantly, research is needed on human resource development; training for teachers, technical support, and a new breed of researchers. We currently lack the human resources to do the required research and development.

REFERENCES

Baddeley, A. (1986). *Working memory*. Oxford, England: Oxford University Press.

Baddeley, A. (1999). *Human memory*. Boston: Allyn & Bacon.

Fletcher, J. D. (2003). Evidence for learning from technology-assisted instruction. In H. F. O'Neil Jr. & R. S. Perez (Eds.), *Technology applications in education: A learning view* (pp. 79–99). Mahwah, NJ: Lawrence Erlbaum Associates.

Hsieh, I. G., & O'Neil, H. F. (2002). Types of feedback in a computer-based collaborative problem-solving task. *Computers in Human Behavior, 18*, 699–715.

Kirkpatrick, D. L. (1994). Evaluation of training programs. *The four levels*. San Francisco, CA: Berrett-Koehler.

Kulik, J. A. (1994). Meta-analytic studies of findings on computer-based instruction. In E. L. Baker & H. F. O'Neil, Jr. (Eds.), *Technology assessment in education and training* (pp. 9–33). Hillsdale, NJ: Lawrence Erlbaum Associates.

Martinez, M. (2003). High attrition rates in e-learning: Challenges, predictors, and solutions. *The E-Learning Developers' Journal*. Retrieved August 30, 2004, from www.elearningguild.com

Paivio, A. (1986). *Mental representations*. New York: Oxford University Press.

Sadoski, M., & Paivio, A. (2001). *Imagery and text*. Mahwah, NJ: Lawrence Erlbaum Associates.

Sweller, J. (1999). *Instructional design in technical areas*. Camberwell, Australia: ACER Press.

USDoE. (2001). *U.S. Department of Education, National Center for Education Statistics, National Assessment of Educational Progress (NAEP), 2001 U.S. History Assessment.* Retrieved October 14, 2004, from http://nces.ed.gov/quicktables/Detail.asp?Key=736

van Merriënboer, J. J. G., Clark, R. E., & de Croock, B., M. (2002). Blueprints for complex learning: The 4C/ID-Model. *Educational Technology Research and Development, 50*(2), 39–64.

Author Index

Subject Index

via face-to-face contact, 339
vs. testing, 6
Associative learning, 256, 349
Astronomy training applications, 116–117, 127
Asynchronous Computer Conferencing, 221
Asynchronous instruction, *see* Synchronicity
ATI (aptitude–treatment interaction) studies, 345
Attention
  divided, 286
  measures of, 10
Attrition, *see* Dropout rates
Auditory presentations, 380–381, 384–385
  speech systems in, 150–154
Augmented reality, 115
Authentic technology, 348
Automaticity
  development of, 348–349
  unconscious nature of, 352
Autonomy, learner, *see* Control of learning activities
Avatars
  gestures used by, 155–156
  as tutors, 268–269
  in virtual reality systems, 124
Aviation training applications
  aircraft maintenance, 121–122, 267
  air traffic control, 154
  flight training, 148–149, 154, 231–234, 266

B

Bandwidth
  availability of, 26
  limitations to, 144–145
Bandwidth analogies
  communication bandwidth, 87–88
  interactional bandwidth, 103
  teacher–student ratio, 298
Barrier to CBT development, Internet as, 143–145
Bayesian inference networks, 42, 144, 147
Behavioral psychology, 36
Binocular omni-oriented monitor (BOOM) displays, 113
Blackboard, 55

Blended courses, 4
Blended synchronicity, 89
Books, 144
Boolean search strategies, training in, 239
BOOM (binocular omni-oriented monitor) displays, 113
BUGGY program, 146
Building security, training in, 115
Business settings
  assessment defined in, 7
  training in, 308, 313–314

C

Capella University, 89
Cardiac physiology, training in, 151
Case-based reasoning, 60–61
Case study approach to simulation, 315
CATAALYST (Classroom Aggregation Technology for Activating and Assessing Learning and Your Students' Thinking), 93
CAVES, 113
Central executive functions, 281
Change, designing for, 74–75
Chemistry education
  behavior of gas molecules, 92
  molecular structures and chemical bonding, 118
CIP (Common Indexing Protocol), 46
CIRCSIM-Tutor, 151
Classroom Aggregation Technology for Activating and Assessing Learning and Your Students' Thinking (CATAALYST), 93
Classtalk, 93
CMS (Content Management System), 26–28
CNC technologies, *see* Computer Numerically Controlled technologies
Coaching, interactive, 148–149
Cognitive architecture
  creativity and, 290–291
  elements of, 279–283
  instructional implications, 283–290
Cognitive learning, 256, 349
Cognitive load, 283–286
  effects of, 286–289
  expertise and, 350–351
  instructional design and, 345
  limited capacity assumption, 373